B. Mitch...

OXFORD EN...

General Editor: M...

Associate General Editors: MARTI...

FIVE ROMANTIC 1 ...~, 1768–1821

DURING the period of European revolutions the British Romantic theatre found itself re-examining the whole cast of social and sexual relations. The five plays grouped here represent some of the most radical and unusual examples of Romantic drama: Horace Walpole invented Gothic melodrama with his incest tragedy, *The Mysterious Mother* (1768), and Robert Southey imagined the theatre as a site of revolutionary protest in *Wat Tyler* (1794). Joanna Baillie's psychological case study in aristocratic hatred, *De Monfort* (1798), was thought too alarming to have been written by a woman, while Elizabeth Inchbald's hugely successful *Lovers' Vows* (1798) was sufficiently subversive for Jane Austen to analyse some of its illicit potential in *Mansfield Park* (1814). Byron's strenuous tragedy *The Two Foscari* (1821) explores an inescapable conflict between parental love and political authority. The stage imagined by these writers is an arena of tense and embattled desires, with sexual and political claims mapped onto the same conflicts of power.

PAUL BAINES is Lecturer in the Department of English Language and Literature, University of Liverpool. He has published many articles on Walpole, Pope, Johnson and writers of the 'long eighteenth century', and he is the author of *The House of Forgery in Eighteenth-Century Britain* (1999).

EDWARD BURNS is Senior Lecturer in the Department of English Language and Literature, University of Liverpool. His books include *Restoration Comedy: Crises of Desire and Identity* (1987) and *Character: Acting and Being on the Pre-Modern Stage* (1989). He has published a modern performing edition of the Chester Mystery Cycle, which is performed in Chester Cathedral every five years. He has recently edited *Henry VI Part One* for the Arden Shakespeare.

MICHAEL CORDNER is Reader in the Department of English and Related Literature at the University of York. He has edited George Farquhar's *The Beaux' Stratagem*, the *Complete Plays* of Sir George Etherege, *Four Comedies* of Sir John Vanbrugh, and, for Oxford English Drama, *Four Restoration Marriage Plays* and Sheridan's *The School for Scandal and Other Plays*. He is writing books on *The Comedy of Marriage* and *Shakespeare and the Actor*.

PETER HOLLAND is Professor of Shakespeare Studies and Director of the Shakespeare Institute, University of Birmingham.

MARTIN WIGGINS is a Fellow of the Shakespeare Institute and Lecturer in English at the University of Birmingham.

OXFORD ENGLISH DRAMA

J. M. Barrie
Peter Pan and Other Plays

Aphra Behn
The Rover and Other Plays

George Farquhar
The Recruiting Officer and Other Plays

John Ford
'Tis Pity She's a Whore and Other Plays

Ben Jonson
The Alchemist and Other Plays

Christopher Marlowe
Doctor Faustus and Other Plays

John Marston
The Malcontent and Other Plays

Thomas Middleton
*A Mad World, My Masters and
Other Plays*

Richard Brinsley Sheridan
*The School for Scandal and
Other Plays*

J. M. Synge
*The Playboy of the Western World and
Other Plays*

John Webster
*The Duchess of Malfi and
Other Plays*

Oscar Wilde
*The Importance of Being Earnest and
Other Plays*

William Wycherley
The Country Wife and Other Plays

Court Masques
ed. David Lindley

Four Jacobean Sex Tragedies
ed. Martin Wiggins

Four Restoration Marriage Plays
ed. Michael Cordner

Four Revenge Tragedies
ed. Katharine Maus

*The New Woman and
Other Emancipated Woman Plays*
ed. Jean Chothia

OXFORD WORLD'S CLASSICS

Five Romantic Plays, 1768–1821

HORACE WALPOLE
The Mysterious Mother

ROBERT SOUTHEY
Wat Tyler

JOANNA BAILLIE
De Monfort

ELIZABETH INCHBALD
Lovers' Vows

LORD BYRON
The Two Foscari

Edited by
PAUL BAINES   **EDWARD BURNS**
General Editor
MICHAEL CORDNER
Associate General Editors
PETER HOLLAND   **MARTIN WIGGINS**

OXFORD
UNIVERSITY PRESS

OXFORD
UNIVERSITY PRESS

Great Clarendon Street, Oxford OX2 6DP

Oxford University Press is a department of the University of Oxford.
It furthers the University's objective of excellence in research, scholarship,
and education by publishing worldwide in

Oxford New York

Athens Auckland Bangkok Bogotá Buenos Aires Calcutta
Cape Town Chennai Dar es Salaam Delhi Florence Hong Kong Istanbul
Karachi Kuala Lumpur Madrid Melbourne Mexico City Mumbai
Nairobi Paris São Paulo Singapore Taipei Tokyo Toronto Warsaw

with associated companies in Berlin Ibadan

Oxford is a registered trade mark of Oxford University Press
in the UK and in certain other countries

Published in the United States
by Oxford University Press Inc., New York

© Paul Baines and Edward Burns 2000

British Library Cataloguing in Publication Data

Data available

Library of Congress Cataloging in Publication Data

Data available

ISBN 0–19–283316–2

1 3 5 7 9 10 8 6 4 2

Typeset in Ehrhardt
by RefineCatch Limited, Bungay, Suffolk
Printed in Great Britain by
Cox & Wyman Ltd., Reading, Berkshire

CONTENTS

ACKNOWLEDGEMENTS

We wish to thank the following colleagues and friends for their generous encouragement and scholarly help: Anne Barton, Bernard Beatty, Peter Cochran, Brian Nellist, Jill Rudd, and Niall Rudd. We are grateful for periods of study leave granted by our Department to enable us to prepare this edition, and for the assistance of Lisa Leslie in proofreading the text. We also wish to thank Richard Williams and Anna Malicka of the Lewis Walpole Library, and Katy Hooper and Maureen Watry of the Special Collections and Archives Department of the Sydney Jones Library, University of Liverpool. Versions of material from the Introduction have been presented at the International Byron Conference, University of Prague (1998), the 28th Annual Meeting of the American Society for Eighteenth-Century Studies, Nashville (1997), the Staff–Student Seminar in the Department of English Language and Literature, University of Liverpool (1997), and the British Society for Eighteenth-Century Studies Annual Conference, Oxford (1997); we would like to thank those who contributed to discussion on these occasions. Finally we would like to thank the general editor of the series, Michael Cordner, for his close attention to our work on this edition, and others who have helped to see the text into print: Martin Wiggins, Jane Kingsley-Smith, Roberta Barker, and Alison Kelly.

INTRODUCTION

Of the plays we present in this volume, only one, Elizabeth Inchbald's *Lovers' Vows*, was a commercial success in its own time. Only one other, Joanna Baillie's *De Monfort*, was even performed in its author's lifetime. Unlike the other writers represented here, Inchbald belonged to the world of the commercial theatre, but if *Lovers' Vows* is remembered above her other work it is because of Jane Austen's *Mansfield Park* (1814). When Edmund, objecting in the course of the novel to the prospect of an amateur performance of the play by the young people of his family and their neighbours, contrasts his pleasure in 'real hardened acting' to the embarrassing performances of 'a set of gentlemen and ladies, who have all the disadvantages of education and decorum to struggle through', his terms expose the gap between the world of the novel, and so implicitly that of its writer and readers, and the more rough-and-ready environment to which theatre—and so Inchbald herself—can be seen to belong.[1] When the situations and characters of *Lovers' Vows* cross this divide, they become a dangerous intrusion into the entangled if superficially ordered life of the Bertram family.

In what one can loosely call Romantic culture—taking us in this volume from the late eighteenth-century Gothic of Walpole through to Byron's post-Napoleonic meditations on history—theatre plays an important but highly compromised part. Romantic anti-theatricalism is typified in Charles Lamb's essay 'On the Tragedies of Shakespeare, considered with reference to their Fitness for Stage Representation' (1812). Lamb privileges the private imagination, or domestic reading aloud, over public performance, with all its (to him) distracting material and social contingencies. Almost all Romantic writers enjoy theatre, but write from a position where its value cannot be taken for granted; on the one hand, as for Hazlitt and for Keats, London theatre is a vivid arena for charismatic individual performance, and for the public reflection of political conflict in times of censorship and oppression; on the other, Wordsworth, Byron, Coleridge, and Austen see the theatre, however diverting, as a crudely limited medium. This

---

[1] Jane Austen, *Mansfield Park*, ed. R. W. Chapman, 3rd edn. (Oxford, 1934), 124 (Ch. XIII).

does not involve a contempt for dramatic form as such; all these writers found some outlet for their concerns in writing plays, and texts originally written for the theatre, especially those of Shakespeare, acquired a new kind of life in solitary fantasy or the domestic reading of Dorothy and William Wordsworth at Grasmere, at Mansfield Park, or in the (surely risky) attempt of Byron and Shelley in 1822 to act in their own private staging of Shakespeare's *Othello*.[2]

It would of course have been possible to present a volume of plays which, like *Lovers' Vows*, belong to the 'hardened' world of 'real' theatre. But much of the interest of British Romantic theatre—as opposed to its much more culturally central counterpart in Germany or France—lies in the contradictory and only partially achieved nature of its project. Only two British plays from this period have remained in anything like theatrical currency. Though scarcely repertory pieces, Byron's *Cain* and Shelley's *The Cenci* have a twentieth-century performance history in this country and in Europe stretching from the great avant-garde practitioners of the early twentieth century— Stanislavsky in *Cain*'s case, Artaud in *The Cenci*'s—to relatively regular performance in the 1990s. *The Cenci* in particular, a Renaissance tale of father–daughter rape and parricidal revenge, combines the two dominant themes of 'experimental' Romantic drama, the family against itself and the struggle towards revolutionary change, and finds for them a compelling dramatic form in which each theme is expressive of the other: the family is a microcosm of the patriarchal structures of a Catholic world-view and of the Renaissance state, but the historical context acts as an externalization of unfathomable psychological states conditioning the individual's experiments on his or her own capacities of good or evil.

Shelley's play is the best-known presentation of themes central to the dramatic experiments of the period. Of the less familiar pieces chosen for this anthology, even *Lovers' Vows*, though notionally a comedy, finds its way into this territory. Patriarchal order is subverted by the son who threatens his (unknown) father, and by the daughter who woos her tutor; the progress of the beggar-woman of the first scene who becomes the lady of the manor in the last is an overriding of social distinctions in the name of natural justice. *Lovers' Vows* places its almost fairy-tale story in a roughly contemporary, that is, post-revolutionary, setting. The other plays in this volume are all set in the

---

[2] Byron was to act Iago. See Jane Stabler, 'Pisan Theatricals: Byron and Othello in 1822', *Byron Journal*, 26 (1998), 38–49.

past, but differ widely in the quality of their attention to historical period. *The Mysterious Mother* is a dream of the Reformation, focusing on an historical turning-point at which guilt and superstition, precisely by becoming open to redefinition, acquire a kind of autonomous and unpredictable power. Though the name *De Monfort* suggests a medieval Anglo-French figure, the play is set in a Germany of unspecified date, suddenly regressing from pseudo-contemporary social scenes to an atavistic world of Gothic horror. Even more than Walpole, Baillie has her post-Enlightenment cake and eats it; she presents a Gothic paraphernalia of nuns and thunderstorms in order to raise the theatrical profile of her play, while eschewing the supernatural in the name of psychological analysis. The nuns are, with the exception of the rather highly strung 'lay sister', sensible and coping. Until their appearance the social manners of the piece seem much of Baillie's own time, with only the names creating an atmosphere of historical masquerade. The play is set in an historical no-man's-land, a social landscape of abbeys, inns, and lonely paths that remains a staple of British Gothic until the films of the Hammer horror series. This provides a decorative frame for Baillie's exploration of suppressed emotion; incestuous attraction, the impulse to gratuitous violence, and irrational fascination with a *doppelgänger*/rival of the same sex are all recurrent themes in Gothic and Romantic writing, and Baillie's treatment of them is subtle and detailed, grounding them in the emotional life of individually plausible figures, and using the ersatz historical setting to isolate her psychological concerns and so focus audience attention on the characters' interiority.

In contrast, the plays by Byron and Southey shift the balance between the psychic economy of the family and the confrontation with social change towards an attention to historical story-telling, which links careful interpretation of their sources to a concern with the historical conditions at the time of writing. But in both plays a sense of the family is crucial. In its agitprop style, *Wat Tyler* mines a vein of clichés still current, though perhaps now more likely to be encountered in nationalist than in left-wing propaganda. Mel Gibson's Scottish nationalist film *Braveheart*, for example, revives the opposition of an effete aristocracy, there representing Englishness, to a virtuous native people whose worth is defined by their domesticity. It is part of this essentially conservative pattern of cliché that women only enter the story in order to be sexually abused, and so to provide a motive for male political action. Southey's vision of the domestic paradise that Wat and his family inhabit at the beginning of the play is coloured by the plans that he and Coleridge were evolving at the time of writing to establish a community in America (or, when funds turned out to be more limited, in Wales), where they would live without an idea of property in a simple self-regulating community of couples (the women would cook, launder, and bear children). They called this 'pantisocracy', and it was, after its collapse and their increasing identification with establishment views, a source of satirical attacks on them.

Byron invokes a religious pattern—the father sacrificing his only son—to present a patriarchal figure whose power is hollow, in that the Venetian state placed so many checks upon the doge that he became a highly charged but ultimately impotent symbol. This, the latest of the plays we present, takes the history play to an impasse. Where Southey can draw on the energy and traditional 'Englishness' of a Shakespearean model to give a kind of centrality to his revolutionary tale, Byron sets out to invent a new kind of play, given less to optimistic energy than to a kind of elegiac paralysis. The writing of a history play must have seemed a very different thing in the wake of Napoleon's career and defeat. In realizing that the genre cannot work simply through the imitation of models from the past, Byron succeeds in writing the only really serious historical drama by a British writer before that generation of mid-twentieth-century writers influenced by Bertolt Brecht. Most post-Romantic plays on 'historical' themes belong to the tellingly labelled subgenre of 'costume drama', exploited by Baillie and Walpole as a distanced, decorative frame for their psychological concerns.

A degree of ambivalence towards the stage on the authors' part presents different problems to the editors from those created by, for example, the fully professional but time-obscured practice of Elizabethan texts. We discuss some of these in our notes on the text of each play. But all the plays we present are conceived in terms of the stage, and are, in terms of the demands they make on actors and directors, eminently stageworthy. If we are to label 'private' plays like Walpole's and Byron's 'closet drama', we should distinguish two senses of the term. Plays like Byron's *Manfred* and Shelley's *Prometheus Unbound* are designed for solitary reading, and use dramatic form as a way of pushing the reader towards trying to imagine the unimaginable; Byron's other plays, like Walpole's *The Mysterious Mother*, are practicable stage plays withheld by their author from the theatre of their own time.

Horace Walpole, The Mysterious Mother *(1768)*

In many ways Walpole was ideally placed to initiate new trends in the theatre. A wealthy aristocrat with a private press, and an antiquarian conspicuously at the head of the 'Gothic revival', Walpole at once desired and feared public performance of his play. *The Mysterious Mother* (1768) has long been recognized as a foundational text of Gothic tragedy, in the same way as Walpole's *The Castle of Otranto* (1764) substantially invented the Gothic novel.[3] The scandalous nature of the action amply indicates the reason why the play (unlike the novel) remained a secret for most of Walpole's life: the 'mother' of the title is the widowed Countess of Narbonne (she has no personal name), who has banished her son Edmund for a sexual misdemeanour, while she herself resides in a decaying castle performing mysterious rituals of grief; sixteen years later he has returned, with a fellow soldier named Florian, to recover his inheritance, and marries an orphan, Adeliza. Through a villainous priest, Benedict, it is discovered that Adeliza is actually the offspring of Edmund's original transgression, which took place not with Beatrice the maid (as he assumed) but with his own mother: he has thus unwittingly married his own sister-daughter. The Countess, who has borne the knowledge of this secret since the fatal night, stabs herself.

Known only to Walpole's private circle during his life, the play was very influential on that strand of Romantic examination of sexuality and power which culminated in *The Cenci* (1819). Byron, for example, praised the play as 'a tragedy of the highest order, and not a puling love play'; Coleridge called it 'the most disgusting, detestable, vile composition that ever came from the hand of man. No one with a spark of true manliness, of which Horace Walpole had none, could have written it'.[4] More recently, critics have developed Coleridge's hint and associated the play with unresolved personal crises over sexuality and desire; in particular, psychoanalytic criticism has seen the play in terms of a Freudian 'punishment dream' in which Walpole unconsciously entreats the pardon of his dead father (the super-powerful prime minister Sir Robert Walpole) for compassing the death

[3] See for example Bertrand Evans, *Gothic Drama from Walpole to Shelley* (Berkeley and Los Angeles, 1947).

[4] See *Horace Walpole: The Critical Heritage*, ed. Peter Sabor (London, 1987), 147–8 for these and other early comments on the play.

of the father and union with the mother both in the play and in *The Castle of Otranto*.[5]

The well-defined tradition of incest dramas derives principally from the *Oedipus Tyrannus* of Sophocles (496–406 BC), in which Oedipus, king of Thebes, discovers that he has unwittingly murdered his own father and married his own mother, and the *Hippolytus* of Euripides (480–406 BC), in which Phaedra, stepmother of Hippolytus, falsely accuses her stepson of attempting to rape her, to divert attention from her own incestuous desire; the death of both results. Walpole partly validates his own drama by comparison with the extreme situations portrayed by unimpeachably classic authors. But while he adopts something closer to the *Hippolytus* model of the guilty mother, he does not limit his attention to her wayward sexuality. The sexual economy of incest is worked out to an unusually full extent: Adeliza loves Edmund (her father) precisely because of his 'parental' address to her, and the marriage takes place just after a notional mother figure, the Abbess, has died. Male sexuality, meanwhile, seems more aberrant and questionable in the play than female: the dead count, we learn, behaved much as the lax Edmund, who makes his attempt on his mother's maid on the night his father dies (a gesture which provokes surprise from Florian, himself 'of morals loose enough': 2.1.24). Even Peter the porter, notionally the guardian of the domestic space, admits to having desired the maid. There are several hints of Edmund's Hamlet-like interest in his mother's sexual life, and in the final act Edmund guesses his mother's revelation before she can speak it: one senses that it is less of a surprise than he thinks it is. Incest and inbreeding emerge from a domestic economy which cannot conceive another model of the family: outside the crippled Narbonne genealogy, there are only orphans and celibates.

The play, though unusually frank, does not display this apparent assault on family values without compromise; Walpole sets the action on the eve of the Reformation, contrasting superstitious Gothic mastery (Benedict) with the enlightened psychology of conscience (Countess, Florian). Yet this superficially Whig evolution, which is perfectly in line with Walpole's political position, is divided by the Countess's conflicting desires to disclose and to conceal the secret: the play moves *into* the recesses of the castle, *away* from the 'platform' where the action begins. Spatially the play is ambivalent, with fre-

---

[5] See in particular Betsy Perteit Harfst, *Horace Walpole and the Unconscious: An Experiment in Freudian Analysis* (New York, 1980).

quent use of zones of 'retirement' which are neither fully on stage nor off it; Peter, keeper of the gate, is made to 'retire' (5.1.233, S.D.) but never formally exits or returns.

No doubt some of this attention to the dynamics of theatrical display derives from Walpole's own sense of having written a drama both powerful and (by the standards of the contemporary stage) quite illegitimate. He began writing it on Christmas Day 1766 and completed it in March 1768; in his initial excitement, he confessed to George Montagu, 'I am not yet intoxicated enough with it, to think it would do for the stage, though I wish to see it acted'; but he refused to consider letting David Garrick, the most powerful actor-manager of the day, see the play for fear that his text would be meddled with.[6] Instead, he printed fifty copies of the play on his private press at Strawberry Hill, and distributed them among close friends who could be trusted with the secret. The Strawberry Hill edition of 1768 also contains an elaborately defensive postscript (reprinted here) in which he stated the ambivalent position on the play he was to maintain for the rest of his life: that the subject was repellent but that the dramatic possibilities could be exploited in the same exemplary way a Greek dramatist might have ventured. He also contrived aristocratic 'closet' readings of the play within his immediate circle, a practice taken up independently by groups of his friends and, on one disastrous occasion, by the novelist Fanny Burney with a group at Windsor Castle— perhaps the nearest thing to a public performance the play has ever received, and one which traumatized all those present into a cordial dislike for the author. Various attempts were made to publish the play in extract form or complete, and in 1791 Walpole finally allowed an edition to be published at Dublin, which was immediately reprinted in London. Walpole included the play among those writings which he wished to be preserved in his complete, posthumous *Works* of 1798. Thus the reception history of the play oddly mirrors the play's internal dynamic, with an instinct to publish or reveal a secret powerfully curtailed by a sense of possible scandal. Several friends attempted to assist Walpole in his dilemma; William Mason, a clergyman and dramatist, suggested altering the story to make the Countess's incestuous act unwitting rather than fully conscious, evidently feeling that this would make the play performable. But Walpole's most stable solution to the problem of his illicit drama came from Lady

---

[6] Letter to Montagu, 15 April 1768, *Horace Walpole's Correspondence*, ed. W. S. Lewis, 48 vols. (New Haven, Oxford, and London, 1937–83), x. 259–60.

Diana Beauclerk, who in 1775 began to produce a series of seven illustrations of scenes from the play. To house these drawings Walpole added one final room to his Gothic mansion. The 'Beauclerk Tower' was a conspicuous feature of the north-west end of the house; but the 'Beauclerk Closet' inside it was reserved for 'his most particular friends', as one favoured visitor put it. Here one could see, purified from the sexual crime itself, the emotionalism of the play frozen in sentimental postures: as the same visitor remarked, 'the story is the most horrible to be conceived, but these drawings, though they recall to mind the horrid subject, are most affectingly interesting'.[7] Walpole put in a drawer of the writing table in the room a copy of the play bound 'in blue leather and gilt', to explain the drawings.[8] It was one way of keeping theatre in the—literal—closet.

Robert Southey, Wat Tyler (1794)

By the time *Wat Tyler* appeared publicly in an unauthorized edition in 1817, its writer was Poet Laureate, and deeply embarrassed by the appearance in print of a revolutionary play from his Jacobin youth. Embarrassment had clearly been the intention of its publishers. The preface to the edition printed a few months later by the radical Hone puts it thus:

Since the year 1794, when Mr ROBERT SOUTHEY entered his Majesty's gaol of Newgate, with his late *dear departed bookseller and friend* hanging on his arm, and presented unto the Rev. Mr. WINTERBOTHAM the manuscript of 'WAT TYLER,' as *an offering on the altar of freedom*—since then, amongst the *things* that have changed, may be numbered Mr ROBERT SOUTHEY ... the first paragraph of his last article against Reform in the last *Quarterly Review*, ... thus beginneth—'*If the opinions of profligate and mistaken men may be thought to reflect disgrace upon the nation, of which they constitute a part, it might verily be said, that England was never so much disgraced as at this time*'. This passage, inscribed beneath a portrait of the Laureate, weeping for his principles, 'because they are not,' wearing a cap and bells, and writing a receipt for his next quarter's salary on the back of 'WAT TYLER,' ... would most appropriately illustrate the title-page to his works.[9]

This is inaccurate as narrative. Southey had in fact presented *Wat Tyler* to the then imprisoned printer Ridgeway, with a view to its

---

[7] Mary Hamilton's 'Journal' for 5 July 1783 and 21 June 1784, repr. Lewis *et al.* (eds.) *Correspondence*, xxxi. 206 and 216.

[8] See Walpole's *A Description of the Villa of Mr. Horace Walpole* (1784), 79–80.

[9] Preface to *Wat Tyler; A Dramatic Poem* (London, 1817), pp. v–vi.

cheap dissemination as 'a 2 shilling pamphlet', a plan that never came off.[10] But Hone's invective gives an accurate flavour of the pamphlet-and-essay war stirred up around the Laureate in the aftermath of Sherwood Neely and Jones's printing of the manuscript in February 1817. They published it anonymously, in the context not simply of Southey's ostentatious conservatism but of public meetings of radicals 'culminating in the Spa-fields meeting at which Henry Hunt addressed a huge crowd and a breakaway group tried to capture the Tower of London'.[11] The leaders of these demonstrations invoked the historical figure of Wat Tyler, whose story had been retold by Thomas Paine in a footnote to *The Rights of Man* (1791).[12] Printing of the play both revived the Tyler story as the precedent of an English popular revolution, and undercut the position of an increasingly anti-democratic voice of the establishment. Paine's narrative is reprinted as an appendix to the play in this volume (pp. 100–1), as it seems to have been Southey's source. Paine uses the same (not wholly accurate) version of events as David Hume in his much-reprinted *History of England*, the standard historical reference work of the time, but tells the story in Tyler's favour. Hume's account is angled towards praise of 'an extraordinary presence of mind which Richard discovered on the occasion. He ordered his company to stop; he advanced alone towards the enraged multitude . . . The populace overawed by his presence, implicitly followed him: he led them into the fields to prevent any disorder'. Hone printed an extract from Hume's narrative, ironically perhaps. The passage as quoted ends with a moral observation closer to Southey's position in 1817 than in 1794: 'of all the evils incident to human society, the insurrections of the populace, where not raised and supported by persons of higher quality, are the least to be dreaded; the mischiefs consequent to an abolition of all rank and distinction become so great, that they are immediately felt, and soon bring affairs back to their former order and arrangement'.[13]

It is not at all clear how Sherwood and company got hold of the manuscript. Southey's attempt to have it suppressed was thwarted by the Lord Chancellor's decision that as the piece was seditious it was not protected by copyright. And so, by a kind of Gilbert-and-Sullivan

[10] Mark Storey, *Robert Southey: A Life* (Oxford, 1997), 67.

[11] Ibid. 254.

[12] Paine, *Rights of Man, Common Sense, and Other Political Writings*, ed. Mark Philp (Oxford, 1998), 284.

[13] These extracts from Hume are reprinted in Hone's edition of *Wat Tyler: A Dramatic Poem* (1817), pp. xxi–xxiii.

logic, this left the field free for a proliferation of cheap editions that found a popular radical market. Sherwood's and Hone's, for example, retailed at 3s. 6d., Fairburn's at 2s.; according to Southey's son 60,000 or so copies were sold, which Southey could neither suppress nor profit from.[14]

It is in this controversy that Southey's identity becomes fixed as the 'Apostate Laureate', a byword for bad faith and lost principles. Byron, who had initially satirized Southey as part of a general attack on the Lake poets, started to single him out, alluding to the *Wat Tyler* affair in the appendix to the 1821 printing of *The Two Foscari*, and pillorying Southey's royalist *A Vision of Judgment* in his own *The Vision of Judgment* of the following year. Fairburn's printing of *Wat Tyler* (1817) has as an appendix an anonymous essay entitled 'THE STRIPLING BARD; OR THE *Apostate Laureate*', which quotes at length from William Hazlitt's piece on the play in the *Examiner* for 9 March 1817: 'He can comprehend but one idea at a time, and that is always an extreme one, because he will neither listen to, nor tolerate any thing that can disturb or moderate the petulance of his self-opinion.' In the *Courier* of 18 March 1817, Coleridge defended Southey:

we *do* affirm . . . that though his boyish *leaning* (far more to the honour of his heart than to the impeachment of his understanding) was in favour of the rebels, as more under intolerable oppressions, yet that the greater part of the speeches were even then designed to be read by imagined oppressors, not by the oppressed; that they were written as the natural sentiments of such men in such circumstances, at the utmost as *exaggerated* truths, characteristic of heated minds; and not as his own convictions, much less as his wish or will.

Fairburn's anonymous essayist quotes this only to ridicule it.

By 1837, when Southey published ten volumes of his collected works, he felt able to assimilate *Wat Tyler* to a fiction of development, and he uses the paraphernalia of epigraph, preface, and so on, of the kind that Hone had parodied, to present this. Hone's title-page epigraph on his 1817 printing of the play is excitedly satirical:

> Come, listen to a TALE OF TIMES OF OLD!—
> Come, for ye know me—I am he who sung
> The 'MAID OF ARC', and I am he who fram'd
> Of 'THALABA' the wild and wondrous song.
> SOUTHEY!

---

[14] Storey, *Southey*, 257.

And I was once like this! . . . .
. . . . Twenty years
Have wrought strange alteration.
SOUTHEY!!![15]

For Southey himself, 'the arrangement was the first thing to be considered. In this the order wherein the respective poems were written has been observed, so far as was compatible with a convenient classification. Such order is useful to those who read critically, and desire to trace the progress of an author's mind in his writings'.[16] The title-page quotation from George Wither, the seventeenth-century Protestant writer, emphasizes that 'What I WAS is passed by'.

As a kind of diagram of the motives of revolution, the play has considerable force in the radical context into which its unauthorized printing liberated it. The leading male characters—Tyler, the decent artisan and family man, pushed into revolt by an offence to his family pride and sense of decency, John Ball, the priest who rejects the church establishment and provides the revolt with a theory in continuity with Christian teaching, and Piers, the well-meaning but uneducated young activist—come together to provide a force which can give the actions of 'the mob' direction and meaning. Jack Straw represents revolutionary violence, of a kind that Southey's principled rebels endorse when it can be deployed strategically, as in the plan to kidnap the king, but which they must disavow when it becomes uncontrollable and anarchic. The court is similarly schematic in presentation, with the aristocratic or feudal reference downplayed in favour of figures of more modern authority, empty but potent symbols almost in the style of Jean Genet's *Le Balcon*—a mayor, a justice, a bishop.

Southey's play is direct in its aim and finds a style apt to its purpose—that of identifying a precursor in English history for the revolutionary activity labelled 'Jacobin' (after the example of the early French insurgents), which was growing in England at the time of writing. Southey uses the genre of the post-Shakespearean chronicle play to present the story in a vivid and accessible way. He can have had no hope of large-scale performance at the time of writing, but some kind of performance, at least at the level of group reading, seems to

[15] In *Joan of Arc* (1796) Southey celebrated the medieval heroine as 'a great democrat' (Storey, *Southey*, 32); in *Thalaba the Destroyer* (1801) he narrated the destruction of an autocratic kingdom by a lone hero.
[16] Southey, Preface to *The Poetical Works of Robert Southey, Esq. LL.D.*, vol. i (1837), pp. v–vi.

inform the dynamic rhetorical style of the piece; if it was not so recited in Jacobin circles, it may well have acquired such currency later; further cheap printings in the 1830s suggest a revival of interest in the play that coincides with the rise of the popular democratic movement of the time, Chartism.

Wat Tyler has a vigour, a sense of purpose, and a rhetorical panache that sets it apart from most post-Elizabethan historical drama in English. Attention to it also serves to reopen the case of Robert Southey. It is wrong to see him as simply taking the government's penny. His contradictions and awkwardnesses were spontaneous and his own. Perhaps the move from apparent radicalism to obvious reaction was less a U-turn than an exposure of a tangle of ideas common to many English writers not only of Southey's own time but in the twentieth century as well, where the radical and the reactionary cannot be clearly separated out from each other, even—or perhaps especially—by the writer him- or herself.

Joanna Baillie, De Monfort *(1798)*

Byron expressed his admiration of Joanna Baillie's ability to write tragedy thus: 'When Voltaire was asked why no woman has ever written even a tolerable tragedy? "Ah (said the Patriarch) the composition of a tragedy requires *testicles*".—If this be true Lord knows what Joanna Baillie does—I suppose she borrows them.'[17] Despite the Amazonian characterization which Baillie's foray into the masculine world of tragedy incurred, her work was never less than a critical success, winning respect not only from Byron, who attempted to have *De Monfort* restaged at Drury Lane in 1815, but also from Wordsworth, Rogers, Southey, and (especially) Sir Walter Scott. When the first volume of *A Series of Plays: In Which it is Attempted to Delineate the Stronger Passions of the Mind* was published anonymously in 1798, it was immediately assumed to be by a male author, perhaps because of the air of critical authority which the 'Introductory Discourse' presents and the absence of the apologetic stance which most female writers felt obliged to adopt. Mary Berry, Horace Walpole's friend and editor, guessed however that no man 'could or *would* draw such noble and dignified representations of the female mind as . . . Jane de Monfort. They often make us clever, captivating, heroic, but never ration-

---

[17] *Byron's Letters and Journals*, ed. Leslie A. Marchand, 12 vols. (London, 1973–82), v. 203. For Byron's attempt to revive *De Monfort* at Drury Lane, see ibid. iv. 336–7.

ally superior'.[18] The *Quarterly Review* described the 'astonishment' of the literary world when this collection of powerful, passionate dramas was acknowledged 'by a gentle, quiet and retiring young woman'.[19] The sister of an eminent doctor and daughter of a Presbyterian divine, Baillie moved with her family from Scotland to London and thence (in 1791) to Hampstead, where with her mother and sister she became the focus of a small circle of literary men and women; Wordsworth described her as the 'model of an English Gentlewoman' (she was of course Scottish).[20]

Baillie remained adamant that her plays were not for the closet but the stage: public performance was what she craved for her work, and she watched her own plays (on occasion in the company of Byron or Scott) with pleasure.[21] *De Monfort*, or at least John Philip Kemble's heavily cut and reworked version of it, received its first performance on Tuesday, 29 April 1800 at the Theatre Royal, Drury Lane. It was performed eight times in all during the season: a respectable if not exactly successful run. At least thirty singers were employed in additional musical material, and much effort went into publicizing the prodigious all-new 'Scenery, Musick, Dresses and Decorations'; the Gothic scenery in particular was massively spectacular and clearly this was a heartfelt effort to persuade an audience of the theatrical virtues of the play.[22] Kemble's performance in the title role was by all accounts an 'amazingly powerful' *tour de force*; Hazlitt says 'there is in the chief character . . . a nerve, a continued unity of interest, a setness of purpose and precision of outline which John Kemble alone was capable of giving'.[23] Sarah Siddons, Kemble's sister, was similarly magnificent in the role of Jane, which many thought designed for her. None the less, 'the excitement was great, and the disappointment commensurate . . . The audience yawned in spite of themselves and in spite of the exquisite poetry, the vigorous passion, and the transcendent acting'.[24] *De Monfort* became known as a play to read rather than act: Thomas

[18] Quoted in Margaret S. Carhart, *The Life and Work of Joanna Baillie* (New Haven, 1923), 15.

[19] Quoted in ibid. 17.

[20] Quoted in ibid. 3.

[21] See ibid. 153.

[22] Information on the stage history is derived from Carhart, *Baillie*, and *The London Stage 1660–1800, Part 5: 1776–1800*, ed. Charles Beecher Hogan (Carbondale, Ill., 1968), 2267–71.

[23] William Hazlitt, *Lectures on the English Poets/The Spirit of the Age*, ed. Catharine Macdonald Maclean (London, 1910), 147.

[24] See Carhart, *Baillie*, 17–18.

Campbell, paraphrasing the actor Edmund Kean, declared, 'though a fine poem, it would never be an acting play'; Elizabeth Inchbald thought it a 'fine play' but at the same time 'its very charm in the reading militates against its power in the acting'.[25] Like Baillie herself, she feared it was too subtle to make an impression in the large-scale and 'sometimes riotous' auditorium of the modern theatre. Actors and managers none the less continued to believe in the stageworthiness of the play. It was afterwards performed in New York (1801, 1809), in Edinburgh (1810), in Philadelphia (1811), in New York again (1820), with Edmund Kean as De Monfort, in a production which he brought back to Drury Lane for five nights in 1821, in Philadelphia and Bath (1822), and finally in New York (1826), with Kean again in the title role.

De Monfort has remained Baillie's best-known play, and it is the play which best exemplifies her stated concern to delineate the operations and growth of the 'passions' in an individual personality. The 'Introductory Discourse', which prefigures many of the concerns with simple diction and emotionally heightened situations which Wordsworth discusses in the famous 'Preface' to *Lyrical Ballads* (1800), advocates the display of individual consciousness under stress as a means to the enlargement of human sympathy. Baillie's comments on the essential privacy of the psyche, and her description of soliloquy as 'those over-flowings of the perturbed soul, in which it unburdens itself of those thoughts which it cannot communicate to others' (see the extract below, pp. 105–6) are echoed when De Monfort complains that his servant Manuel has been eavesdropping: 'dost thou watch, and pin thine ear to holes, | To catch those exclamations of the soul, | Which heaven alone should hear?' (3.3.25–8). De Monfort has already denied that any man's 'secret soul' can ever be 'opened to another's scan' (1.2.99); yet the play is precisely an attempt to 'catch' those 'exclamations' in public, to convert the scene of the closet into the public sphere of action, and to perform the morally unspeakable in a sympathetic and understandable way. Inevitably, the flagrantly wounded, malign figure, 'a sullen wand'rer on the earth, | Avoiding all men, cursing and accursed' (2.2.91–2) is privileged, and this was doubtless one reason for the play's appeal to star actors such as Kemble and Kean (not to mention to Byron).

It is important to realize that the play is more than a psychodrama of obsessive monomania; the design of the series was to treat the passions in pairs of plays, so that a tragic treatment would always be

---

[25] Both phrases quoted in Catherine B. Burroughs, *Closet Stages: Joanna Baillie and the Theater Theory of British Romantic Women Writers* (Philadelphia, 1997), 103.

complemented by a comic one. *The Election*, the comedy paired with
De Monfort, appeared in volume 2 of the series, in 1802. The 'Introductory Discourse' characterizes the passions as a sort of externalized
pathology, an 'enemy' to be resisted; these remarks are heard in ghostly
echo when Jane urges De Monfort to 'strive' with the 'sprite accursed'
which 'within thy bosom mates | To work thy ruin' (2.2.100–1). De
Monfort is not the stable, self-contained villain of Gothic type but a
contradictory being, lurching from mood to mood, from self-control to
wildness and back to restraint, unpredictably. Moreover, De Monfort
is never merely an individual, he is the representative of a moribund
baronial class, in retreat from the newly ennobled and enriched
Rezenvelt whose growing power so oppresses him. Locked into ter-
minal opposition, he hardly exists except in relation to this demonized
'other', the 'man most adverse to my nature' (3.1.20). After the murder,
the monks Bernard and Thomas speak at cross purposes; one has seen
the corpse of Rezenvelt, the other the murderer De Monfort, but each
monk is preoccupied with his own ghastly encounter, and murderer
and victim are momentarily confused (4.2.77–8), as they are again
when laid out as corpses (5.4.35).

Some critics have detected homoerotic overtones in De Monfort's
passionate characterizations of Rezenvelt; it is at least true that he
seems to conjure or invent him as much as discover him. One of the
moments which most struck Byron was when De Monfort preter-
naturally hears and identifies Rezenvelt's footstep (3.1.143), but again
this is a repeated motif across the play. De Monfort is always hearing
things before they happen, guessing the presence of someone who
is trying to remain secret (1.1.99, 3.3.1), or finding his actions pre-
empted by knocking, owl-hoots, or other warning signs. His curses
(2.2.175) turn into prophecies which are materially fulfilled; even
Jane's comments about the sisterly devotion which would sympathize
with De Monfort 'e'en with murder stained' (2.2.13) prefigure events.

One of the signs of the aristocracy's decline in the play, apart
from the childlessness of the Frebergs, is the premature orphaning
of De Monfort and his sister, leaving them in the situation of
parents to their younger siblings; the hint of incest would have been
one of the major emotional drives when the play was performed
by Kemble and Siddons, real-life sibling performers, and one
must remember that Jane too is a star part ('make me some more
Jane DeMonforts', Siddons is alleged to have requested Baillie).[26]

[26] *The Dramatic and Poetical Works of Joanna Baillie* (London, 1851), p. xi.

Rezenvelt and De Monfort virtually come to blows over the unveiling of Jane (2.1.249), a scene of disguise which resembles Shakespearean romance plots and allows De Monfort to eulogize his sister's beauty and faithfulness as 'the virgin mother of an orphan race', resisting 'the blandishments of love' (2.1.237–40); it is the rumour that Jane is engaged to Rezenvelt which drives De Monfort to murder. De Monfort's last living action in the play is to escort Jane from the stage (5.2.156), in glorying achievement of a gesture which Rezenvelt had offered and which Jane had denied at 3.1.232; it is the high point of romance in a play which envisions no possible future attachments: the only question throughout is whether Jane will stay with De Monfort or not, and she stays. Explicitly the emotional centre of the final scene, the men crowd round her and hang on her, but none of them is a suitor. Though less all-encompassing a disaster than that which concludes *The Mysterious Mother*, the denouement can only envisage a statuesque self-containment as its final posture.

Elizabeth Inchbald, Lovers' Vows *(1798)*

Of the authors presented here, Elizabeth Inchbald had the most purely theatrical career. In 1772, at the age of 19 she ran away from her Suffolk home to go on the stage and quickly married an actor twice her age, apparently for protection. After touring the provinces (playing, for example, Cordelia to her husband's Lear) she made her London acting début in 1780, and four years later began writing plays on her own account. She wrote a play a year for the next twenty years, retiring from acting in 1789. Most of her plays were comedies; *The Massacre*, a tragedy on the theme of the French Revolution, was not performed in her lifetime. Though latterly more famous as a novelist, it was in the theatre that she built her career; she was friendly with Kemble and Siddons, and edited anthologies of contemporary drama with strong prefatory criticisms.

Inchbald rewrote seven continental plays for the English stage, and was known as a skilful adapter. She was commissioned to adapt for the stage *Das Kind der Liebe*, a play by the German writer August Friedrich Ferdinand von Kotzebue, then greatly in vogue. As she indicates in her preface, she made many kinds of alteration. Several speeches of explanation and clarification were cut in the interests of dramatic economy, and Inchbald's play is at least one-fifth shorter than her model. Names have been made more accessible or more morally suggestive to an English audience: Wilhemina Boettcher becomes

Agatha Friburg, with a hint of 'free citizen' about it; Parson Ehrmann is renamed Anhalt, suggesting 'support'. Inchbald's play is funnier: Verdun, the comic rhyming butler, carves a space for self-expression which is both loyal to his master and family and yet subverts their commanding desire for more lucid, non-poetical explanation. Inchbald's play is also less sentimental: in the first scene, Kotzebue has five characters enact the parable of the Good Samaritan (three fail in charitable duty, and a Jew is the only one to give Wilhemina money); Inchbald cuts this to a more naturalistic three. In *Das Kind der Liebe*, 3.1, Kotzebue has Frederick indict humanity for its poor response to his begging, telling us that his greatest benefactor was another beggar; Inchbald cuts this, though without removing the spirit of the complaint. The two cottagers who take Wilhemina/Agatha in are made somewhat less saccharine at the end of 5.1: in Kotzebue both peasants staunchly refuse the parson's offer of a purse of gold in reward for their exemplary behaviour, but in Inchbald, after the man's refusal, the parson tells his wife to take the money and she complies with the words 'I always obey my pastor'—a welcome note of comic relief, economically suggesting that her obedience to patriarchy (against her husband's example) is tinged with a realistic sense of personal advantage.

Some of the alterations are designed to tone down the apparent ratification of the two heroines' immoral behaviour: Kotzebue's Wilhemina has contemplated suicide, for example. Kotzebue's Amalie is initially both more innocent and more direct in her affections than Amelia, more submissive to her father's commands, less able to confound his (and her tutor's) patriarchal position with cross-purpose wit than Inchbald makes Amelia. The contrasting scene where Amalie woos her tutor is the more disturbing for its basis in a kind of childish game; she tells the parson she loves him and means to marry him with a directness which Inchbald felt compelled to divert into a more bashful, coquettish humour which also has the effect of rendering the character more consistent. Other alterations have been made with the clear intention of softening the Jacobin aspects of the play. Graf von der Mulde (Inchbald's Count Cassel) has had a narrow escape from the Bastille mob during his last trip to Paris (he is disgusted at their poor taste in costume), but Cassel makes no mention of it. Kotzebue's Frederick is already explicitly contemplating robbery in 2.1; Inchbald's character swallows the thought. In 4.1, where Frederick discusses his case with Anhalt, Kotzebue allows him to state with complete confidence the rectitude of his Wat Tylerish position:

If we look round us and see how prodigally nature every where pours out her horn of plenty, bestowing riches and abundance on every place, and a son, at the same time, turns his eyes on a dying mother, whose parching tongue asks a drop of wine, and the wealthy man passes by that son, in the moment of despair, and refuses him a trifle to buy it—because, forsooth, a hare would escape, if he should deign to stop!—in such a moment, Sir, a sense of the equality of all men is roused, and the wretch, slighted by fortune,—for nature disregards none of her children—stands up for his right, and stretches out his arm, not to rob, but to take his due from the gifts bestowed on all;—and doing so—is right.[27]

The parson, who has educated Amalie/Amelia in Rousseauistic doctrines according to which nature supersedes social divisions of rank and heredity, does not seriously attempt to dissuade Frederick from his position; but Inchbald cuts the whole passage. Moreover, the parson comes to Frederick to tell him that Wildenhain (as he is in Kotzebue) has already forgiven him and ordered his release, and we are made to witness Wildenhain admitting that he had been wrong not to give more money to Frederick, and wishing he had let him escape (*Das Kind der Liebe*, 3.2). Inchbald, mindful of social antagonism towards the representation of banditry, makes much more of the likelihood of exemplary punishment; the release seems much more hard-won and Frederick somewhat less secure in his politics.

This is not to say that Inchbald has surgically removed all trace of Jacobin sentiment from her text. Sentimentalism itself could easily be recruited for political display, and though *Lovers' Vows* is less weepy than *Das Kind der Liebe*, the final renucleation of the family in resolved tableau is a display of emotion which offers a certain kind of theatrical satisfaction but also valorizes the Baron's decision to marry the servant-woman he seduced. The broad outline of the play remains the same: Anhalt can marry above his 'station' because his innate nobility ranks him equal with his social superiors, as the Baron announces in the final scene; Amelia can woo her tutor on the principle of a natural affection which supersedes economic arrangements; the Baron can and must marry Agatha the servant/beggar and legitimize his natural son as heir not only because lovers' vows must be upheld but because she is a *better* partner than his dead wife, who (like Cassel) represented class and nothing else.

---

[27] *Lovers' Vows, Or, The Child of Love . . . Translated . . . By Stephen Porter* (1798), 68. Another translation, by Anna Plumptre, was also published as *The Natural Son* late in 1798.

Lovers' Vows was first performed at Covent Garden on Thursday 11 October 1798, and was an immediate hit; altogether it ran for forty-two nights in the season, making it by some distance Covent Garden's most successful venture that season. The royal family went to see it on 24 October. Within six months it had been played at Bristol, Newcastle, Salisbury, Bath, and Daventry; during the time the Austen family lived in Bath, the play was performed there six times. It ran through several printings quickly and extracts were published in periodicals. The question of its politics was much debated, given the reputation for 'levelling' Kotzebue enjoyed; the *Morning Herald* of 12 October 1798 was shocked at the forgiveness shown to Frederick's criminal tendency and the privileging of the desires of 'a thoughtless young Miss' (Amelia), but the *Morning Chronicle* for 29 November 1798 remarked that the 'zealous moralists' of the government 'take great offence at the immorality of *Lovers' Vows*, the morality of which, from beginning to end, is wholly unexceptionable, and seems as well calculated to deter from licentiousness and vice as any Drama that was ever written'. Several other reviews defended the power of sentimental spectacle to awake sympathetic and humane response: 'the mind is roused from the most torpid indifference, and compelled to sympathise in the melting effusions of sorrow, or to exult with fervent joy in the vindication of distressed innocence . . . The grand principle of the play, exemplified on various occasions, is founded upon the successful opposition of the moral faculties to interested views and selfish desire'.[28]

None the less, the drama continued to arouse suspicion in some anti-theatrical quarters; one (fictional) father is made to complain in 1807 that the play has 'done nothing but prepare my boy for the highway, and my girls for a bagnio'.[29] The portrayal of Amelia gave particular concern: 'The artless and innocent *Amelia* appears to have suffered essentially in the alteration. She is depicted as the child of nature, but is now made to assume the boldness and pert manners of a country hoyden', commented *The Times*. The actress's performance opened the way for dangerous kinds of seduction: 'Mrs H. Johnston is so fascinating in her air and smile—her coquetry is so playful that even her errors please us. . . . She . . . plays the hoyden with so much grace, that we almost wish her to continue to trespass on truth, and please us

---

[28] *The Times*, 12 October 1798. This and several other reviews are discussed by Colin Pedley, '"Terrific and Unprincipled Compositions": The Reception of *Lovers' Vows* and *Mansfield Park*', *Philological Quarterly*, 74/3 (Summer 1995), 297–316.
[29] *Director* 1/15 (2 May 1807), 70–2.

by being wrong'.[30] It was, in other words, a gift part for Mary Crawford, in the *Mansfield Park* theatricals, to exploit. While Edmund the clergy-man has a true child of nature to tutor in Fanny, her truth can only be displayed by her refusal to 'perform'; the consummate artist Mary, on the other hand, can slip easily into role and flirt outrageously at the casting, asking 'Who is to be Anhalt? What gentleman among you am I to have the pleasure of making love to?'[31] Austen's novel wittily demon-strates that these situations, when liberated from Inchbald's astute and entertaining packaging into the raw atmosphere of a group of sexually hyperaware young people enjoying their father's absence, *become* dan-gerous and challenging; they might as well perform *The Cenci*.

Lord Byron, The Two Foscari (1821)

On 28 January 1821, Byron, having already published a Venetian tra-gedy, *Marino Faliero*, sketched in his journals the schedule for a sequence of tragic dramas: 'Sardanapalus, already begun, Cain, a metaphysical subject . . . Francesca of Rimini, in five acts; and I am not sure that I would not try Tiberius'.[32] Of these he completed the first two, but dropped the second pair to write another play on medieval Venetian history, *The Two Foscari* ('the third tragedy in twelve months').[33] That this extraordinary burst of dramatic creativity coincided with an introspective phase of journal-keeping and private writing may seem odd if we conceive of drama as essentially a public medium, but it is precisely individual privacy in conflict with larger, impersonal and inscrutable systems of statecraft, history, and divine law which provides these plays with their subject. The meaning of individual will and subjective freedom imperilled by time and memory—both personal time and memory, as in ageing and remin-iscence, and public, as in the relation of writing to history, in reputa-tion and the judgement of posterity—is the informing concern of Byron's writing at this point in his career, whatever the genre he works in.

This concern with the disclosure of the private into an at best uncaring, most probably hostile, world, carries over into Byron's atti-tude to the plays themselves. When a performance of a cut version of

[30] Quoted in Pedley, 'Reception', 307.
[31] Austen, *Mansfield Park*, 143 (Ch. XV).
[32] Marchand (ed.), *Byron's Letters and Journals*, viii. 36–7.
[33] Ibid. 147.

Marino Faliero was given at Drury Lane Byron tried unsuccessfully to suppress it: 'what damned fools these speculating buffoons must be not to see that it is unfit for their Fair or their Booth'.[34] Though the language of this suggests an aristocratic snobbery towards theatre, Byron's worries did not stem from ignorance—rather the opposite. He had been, at his friend the playwright Sheridan's prompting, appointed to the management committee of Drury Lane, and rather enjoyed the experience. But the aesthetic ambition of his own plays did not belong to the chaotic drink-fuelled *métier* he and Sheridan had amused themselves in, and he sensed, probably rightly, that either success or failure would be driven by, and read in terms of, his own personal notoriety. Conflicting accounts of the play's reception do none the less awake in him a wish for the play to succeed.

Byron deliberately eschewed the example of what he called 'the mad old dramatists' of the English tradition, including Shakespeare, and aimed for a tauter, more disciplined dramatic form, a more direct, less metaphorical verbal style, and a stringent respect for the letter of his historical and scriptural sources as he found them. This suggests a self-imposed discipline, as does the sometimes perversely undramatic placing of his protagonists: Sardanapalus refuses to commit himself to meaningful action; Cain spends most of the time wondering what kind of story he is in, to the extent that the action, when it eventually happens, seems like a rather puzzling accident. The central figures of the Venetian plays are extremely old, not only in a degree of physical immobility but in the political immobility of an entrappedness in their own accumulated careers and reputations.

The discipline involves a fierce interest in theatrical form, which is worked out as a kind of intellectual problem. Byron was pleased with the result: 'The simplicity of plot is intentional—and the avoidance of *rant* also—as also the compression of the Speeches in the more severe situations.—What I seek to show in "the Foscari's" is the *suppressed* passions—rather than the rant of the present day.'[35] Dramatic form involves Byron in imagining voices other than his own. In this context, Jonathan Wordsworth's comment that *The Two Foscari* fails because none of the characters speak with a 'Byronic voice' seems uncomprehending.[36] Byronic concerns like exile (and indeed a love of

---

[34] Ibid. 67.

[35] Ibid. 218.

[36] Preface to the facsimile reprint of *Three Plays: Sardanapalus, The Two Foscari, Cain* (1821; Oxford, 1990).

swimming) are approached through personalities and in an historical situation very different from his own. To want a Byronic voice from the plays is to push them back into that voyeuristic relation to his public character, to that uncontrollable appropriation of the self by a kind of theatre of gossip, from which, at the point of that accelerated mid-life crisis which produced the plays and the journals, Byron seemed particularly anxious to escape.

The long history of the Venetian republic was of especial interest to Byron's generation, as they had seen it end. In 1797 Bonaparte, on behalf of the French revolutionary government, had occupied Venice and received the resignation of its last doge. The influence and wealth of the city-state had by that time long been in decline, as other routes to the East than those through the eastern Mediterranean which Venice controlled, and the exploitation of the Americas, had taken away its pre-eminent position as a trading nation. Byron's Venetian plays focus on periods of late-medieval expansion, and have as their protagonists men who, though having been instrumental in this, are in their old age rendered powerless by their very acceptance, by becoming doge, of the nominally highest place in the state. The Venetian state was organized around an increasingly elaborate set of checks on personal power, which made it a byword for labyrinthine secrecy. Byron's sources— reprinted by his publisher Murray as an appendix to the 1821 edition, and quoted where relevant in the notes to this edition—are largely French. They reflect a bias by which, to justify French occupation, the role of torture and the extent of corruption and secrecy in the Venetian state was greatly exaggerated. Venice comes to be represented as a kind of prison, opened up by enlightened intervention. Byron—who was probably not conscious of bias in echoing this—heightens its emphasis by suppressing the complications of the Foscaris' relation to the Turks, the national enemy to whom they seem to have been in a complex and potentially treacherous diplomatic relation at the crucial point of the Ottoman capture of Constantinople. Byron is more interested in presenting them as innocent and paradoxically powerless victims.

The challenge of animating a story dominated by two entrapped male figures, both physically weak, one through age and the other as a result of torture, is met by Byron largely in the creation of a dynamic female figure, Marina, the wife of Jacopo Foscari. She questions the loyalty to the state shown by her husband and father-in-law, a loyalty which, under her questioning, comes to seem more and more like a perverse internalization of an incomprehensible oppressive force—a 'mystery', to use one of the key words of both the plays and the journals. Marina is rhetorically, conceptually, and physically 'free' in a way neither of the men can be, but by the same token she is much less 'of' Venice than they are. Though scrupulously attentive to history as a matter of record and reconstruction, with an awareness too of all the gaps and ambiguities this involves, Byron can be anachronistic to the extent that in his imagination the chronology of Venice, particularly in terms of its extant buildings, collapses in on itself; the city is both in endless slow decline *and* eternal, its existence both diachronic and synchronic. It is in Marina's speeches that the play veers most freely in and out of its time-scheme, suggesting that she is herself a kind of transhistorical, almost allegorical character, the voice of that which is not Venice; the sea, as her name suggests, against which it must define itself, the female, as opposed to a rigidly militaristic and legalistic male history, and reason, as that which must remain uncomprehending of Venice's sense of self, and so signal its eventual disestablishment.

Though designed in terms of, if not aimed at, the stage, *The Two Foscari* has achieved what little stage currency it can muster through Giuseppe Verdi's opera of 1844, *I due Foscari*. Verdi responds powerfully to the relationship between 'Marina' (given in the opera her historical name, Lucrezia) and Francesco, one of a series of father–daughter relationships (as in *Rigoletto*) or, more aptly to this play, relationships that start in apparent conflict, but become surrogate father–daughter relationships more emotionally intense than the real thing (as in *La traviata*), all of which shadow his never-realized project to set *King Lear* as an opera. He responds intensely too to the political thrust of the work, but diverts it to a more 'democratic' moral: the chorus, representing the Forty, point out, on their way into the trial of Jacopo, that no one is above the law. Marina/Lucrezia becomes in this context a very Catholic figure, operating a Christian, Marian, sense of mercy, interceding between the patriarchal Doge and Jacopo, who, Christ-like, suffers innocently, as if to redeem a communal guilt. These meanings are latent in Byron's text, but it is the history that takes us from Bonaparte's humiliation of Venice to Verdi's part in founding an independent unified Italy which unfolds them.

NOTE ON THE TEXTS

Copy-text for each play is the first authorized printed edition. The five plays were printed over a period of more than half a century and show a wide range of printing conventions and page layouts. These have been redesigned to accord with Oxford English Drama conventions. Stage directions, speech prefixes, and scene locations have been laid out in consistent fashion. A number of standardizations have been employed without specific notice: terms denoting stage areas have been regularized; 'without' and 'within' have normally been replaced by 'offstage'; Latin stage directions have been silently translated, with the exception of '*Exit*' and '*Exeunt*'; where '*Exit*' has been used in the original for a multiple departure and '*Exeunt*' for a solitary one, the forms have been silently corrected; 'aside' is used in preference to 'apart'. Names of characters have been made consistent within the plays; for example, the character Countess Freberg in *De Monfort* is sometimes referred to in the original stage directions and speech prefixes as 'Lady', 'Countess', or 'Countess Freberg'; in our edition she is 'Countess Freberg' throughout. Her waiting-woman, Theresa, is sometimes referred to as 'waiting-woman' or just 'woman' in the original; here she is 'Theresa' throughout. Character names have been preferred to pronouns such as 'she' or 'he' in stage directions without specific notice. Wholly editorial stage directions, or other major editorial interventions to existing stage directions, have been enclosed in square brackets. Spelling has been modernized and variant spellings of words (Ay/Aye, Oh/O, etc.) normalized to one form only. Punctuation has been modernized, but where original punctuation will not confuse readers it has been largely retained on the grounds that it may suggest a contemporary manner of phrasing. The printers of the plays used long dashes and short dashes without much apparent discrimination, and they have normally been standardized to a short dash, except where long dashes appear to have a specific function, in which case they have been retained.

Horace Walpole, The Mysterious Mother

Copy-text for the play and the postscript is the edition printed by Walpole at his private press at Strawberry Hill in 1768. A few misprints have been silently corrected on the authority of Walpole's own errata note and his own subsequent printings of the play: in 1770, for an abortive edition of his works which was not published; in 1781, to forestall a piracy which did not in the event appear; and in 1798, in the posthumous edition of his *Works* (5 vols.), edited by Mary Berry from Walpole's instructions and papers. The preface to the 1781 edition is here printed from that text. The prologue and epilogue do not appear in any edition before the 1798 *Works* and are here printed from that edition. In the twentieth century the play has been edited by Montague Summers (1924) and by Janet Dolan as a doctoral thesis (University of Arizona, 1970). No substantive emendations have been made to the text. Walpole's on-page notes to the 1768 printing and to subsequent printings have been incorporated in our own Explanatory Notes, clearly marked. Walpole begins a new scene at the entrance of each major character, and lists the characters present at the start of each scene, in accordance with a fashion which was beginning to go out of use as he was writing; but as the actual scene locations do not change there is only one true scene in each act, and in our edition the numbering has been adjusted accordingly. This makes clear the accuracy of Walpole's casual claim to have observed unity of place. It also necessitates the insertion of many otherwise unmarked entrances.

Robert Southey, Wat Tyler

In the case of *Wat Tyler* the very idea of a first authorized edition is a contradiction, given that its author did not wish it to appear at all. The version Southey prepared for volume 2 of *The Poetical Works of Robert Southey, Collected by Himself* (10 vols., 1837–8) is his nearest, perhaps half-hearted, approach to authorization, and it has been taken as the copy-text of this edition. Though Southey claimed he had not altered his original text, the 1837 text shows a number of differences from the pirated printings of *Wat Tyler; A Dramatic Poem* (1817). These earlier texts are all identical with each other, and can be taken as careful presentations of Southey's now lost manuscript. All verbal differences between the 1817 versions and the 1837 'official' version, and all changes in punctuation that can be seen to affect meaning, are recorded in the Explanatory Notes. Variant readings from the 1817 texts have been incorporated when they make more sense for a modern reader, or when the 1837 text seems to contain errors or mistranscriptions. Southey makes some changes when the 'original' seems silly; so 'primrose lifts' is the 1837 alteration of 1817's 'primrose rears'

(1.1.4). Misprints seem detectable in both texts. 'Good' (2.3.67) is 'food' in 1817; and 'cool deliberate' (3.1.42, from 1817, seems like the correct reading, where the 1837 text has 'calm deliberate'—the presence of 'calmer' in the next line here suggests that this is a mistranscription rather than a revision. The only substantial rewriting is at 3.1.146–7, where 'And let me have the hope to sweeten death | That thou at least hast 'scaped' (the 1817 reading, retained in this edition) becomes in 1837, 'Fain would I die in peace to hope thee safe. | I shall soon join thee, Tyler!' The shift—between Piers's hope that Ball and the rebellion have a future, and the later more fatalistic version in which he accepts his death and the end of rebellion—is small but significant.

Joanna Baillie, De Monfort

Copy-text for the play and the sections of the 'Introductory Discourse' is the first edition of volume 1 of *A Series of Plays: In Which it is Attempted to Delineate the Stronger Passions of the Mind* (1798). A second edition of this volume appeared in 1799, a third in 1800, a fourth in 1802, and a 'new edition' in 1821; *The Dramatic and Poetical Works of Joanna Baillie* (1851) contained her final version of the play. A number of obvious misprints have been silently corrected on the authority of the second, third, and fourth editions, and two small substantive emendations have been made on similar authority. Both are signalled in the Explanatory Notes. The play was issued separately and with no apparent authority in 1807, 1808, and 1809. Each time Baillie reissued the *Series of Plays* she made some alterations or corrections; the most significant are referred to in the Explanatory Notes, and a later version of one scene is reprinted here as a sample of her revisions. An eclectic text based on the 1798 printing and two manuscripts related to the stage adaptation of the play was produced by Jeffrey N. Cox in *Seven Gothic Dramas 1789–1825* (Athens, Oh., 1992).

Elizabeth Inchbald, Lovers' Vows

Lovers' Vows was published in 1798 after the play had opened at Covent Garden and was reprinted several times in that year, and again in 1799. A 'fourth edition' was reached in 1804, a fifth in 1805, and a sixth in 1806. The play appeared in several drama anthology series (*The British Theatre*, 1808; *Cumberland's British Theatre*, 1829; *The Acting Drama*, 1834; *The British Drama*, 1864). The text remained essentially the same in all editions, though a few misprints in the copy-text edition of 1798 have been corrected on the authority of subsequent printings.

Lord Byron, The Two Foscari

Byron was always careful and deliberate in his use of punctuation and layout; it is perhaps in his case that most is lost by regularization and modernization. But few changes have been made here; the printing of 1821 (*Sardanapalus, A Tragedy. The Two Foscari, A Tragedy. Cain, A Mystery. By Lord Byron*) provides a clear and elegant copy-text. This edition has preserved the distinction Byron makes between long dashes, which mark a breakdown of communication, an inability to find the right words, and short dashes, which create connection. Although Byron claimed that he was not writing for the stage, he imagines the action precisely in terms of the stage spaces that would have been available to him, had he changed his mind. As with Southey and Baillie, however, he is vague about the movements of subsidiary characters, and tends to resort to '*etc.*' a little too often for an editor's comfort. The movements of 'familiars', for example, are clearly significant but are not fully resolved by Byron; editorial intervention—as at 3.1.248—is most evident at moments of this kind.

Note: obscure and archaic words are explained in the Glossary (pp. 367–72). Words which have changed meaning significantly since the plays were written, and might mislead readers, are glossed or reviewed in the Explanatory Notes; words of this sort which occur more than once are also defined in the Glossary.

Although only one of these plays—*Lovers' Vows*—was directly written for the commercial theatre of the time, all observe staging conventions of the period, and so it has been relatively easy to adjust the sometimes casual stage directions of dramatists who were (with the exception of Elizabeth Inchbald) strictly speaking amateurs into something both idiomatic and self-explanatory. London theatre was dominated in this period by the so-called 'Patent Theatres' or Theatres Royal at Covent Garden and Drury Lane, established by the Licensing Act of 1737 as the only London theatres permitted to present spoken drama. The restrictions, introduced by a parliament hostile to the theatre as a platform for opposition and dissent, lasted until 1843; the censorship whereby all new plays had to be submitted to the lord chamberlain for approval lasted until 1968. In practice the theatre was not quite so limited, since the Haymarket was from 1766 permitted to perform plays out of season when the other theatres were shut, and smaller theatres did find ways of evading the law. But the plays in this volume were all more or less conditioned by the stages, auditoria, and acting conventions of the two main theatres. Walpole toyed for a moment with the idea of offering *The Mysterious Mother* to David Garrick's company at Drury Lane; Inchbald had a long association with Covent Garden, and *Lovers' Vows* opened there in 1798; Baillie's *De Monfort* opened at Drury Lane and was revived there; Byron tried to get Baillie's play performed there in 1815 when he was on the management committee. Southey would have known both the London theatres and the slightly scaled-down version of them represented by the Theatre Royal in Bristol, his early home.

The seating capacity of these theatres rose during various rebuildings from under 2,000 at the start of the period to over 3,000 by the end. In the 'pit', continuous backless benches ran straight across the auditorium; tiers of boxes rose vertically in a horseshoe shape, to be surmounted by a gallery. The auditorium was lit by large candelabras which remained alight throughout the performance. Performances normally consisted of a mainpiece or five-act play (such as *Lovers' Vows* or *De Monfort*), followed by lighter fare in the form of a two-act farce or musical entertainment. *Lovers' Vows*, for example, was first played with Charles Smith's *A Day at Rome*; *De Monfort* was followed at its première by John Cartwright Cross's one-act musical drama *The Purse*. Audiences were often rowdy and very demanding; there were riots over price rises at the rebuilt Covent Garden in 1809. A star actress such as Sarah Siddons might command packed houses, but could also be hissed off the stage for her alleged greed.

The two stages were basically modelled on the Restoration plan, with a large forestage allowing direct address to the audience, especially those in the pit and the boxes, and a large space behind the proscenium arch equipped with a system of shutters, wings, and drops, to allow the production of spectacular scenic effects. Actors entered the forestage, or left it, through doors on either side, next to (or under) stage boxes: Walpole makes use of a number of processions which appear to go straight across the forestage from one door to the other, though a diagonal route from a door in one of the painted buildings is imaginable. The space behind the proscenium arch allowed more subtle and inventive visual effects: the forestage is for Walpole a 'platform before the castle'; the castle and surrounding landscape could have been created by a sequence of carefully lit and meticulously painted two-dimensional pieces. The space behind the proscenium arch formed an area into which characters could 'retire' or 'withdraw' to eavesdrop or observe; they could also be 'discovered' at the start of a scene by the raising of a curtain or parting of shutters.

Walpole was writing at a time when the vogue for antiquarian or historical accuracy of scene-painting was just beginning. Later in the eighteenth century London theatre developed a more complex and original language of spectacle, inaugurated particularly by the collaboration between the painter and scene-designer Philippe Jacques de Louterbourg and the actor-manager in control of Drury Lane, David Garrick, from 1771. Garrick was primarily interested in realism, and encouraged Louterbourg to produce illusionistic sets aiming at 'the Sublime', the neo-Romantic aesthetic of awe which combined the beautiful with a sense of terror. Louterbourg's major innovation was in using coloured transparencies, gauzes, and moving 'cloud' and 'water' effects, of painted linen moved on cylinders, to create a careful illusion of the natural world. This style influenced Byron: though *The Two Foscari* makes modest demands, with only the lighting of Jacopo's prison making any technically demanding play of visual effect, the apparently impossible staging demands of others of his plays, such as *Manfred*, *Cain*, or *Heaven and Earth*, come out of the Louterbourg tradition. *Manfred*—complete with abysses, waterfalls, pandemonium, and an added avalanche—was successfully staged at Covent Garden in 1834 by Loutherbourg's successors, the Grieve brothers.

Both theatres were rebuilt on more than one occasion during the period, each time on a grander scale with yet more opportunity for spectacle. The competitive development of such spectacular displays hindered rather than helped Baillie's *De Monfort*: the ambitious scenic design for the version of the play 'adapted' by John Philip Kemble for Drury Lane made theatrical history but neither helped the play towards success nor answered Baillie's concern for psychological realism and a close focus on the characters. Kemble, and his scene-designer William Capon, both of whom professed antiquarian interests, provided 'a very unusual pile of scenery, representing a church of the fourteenth century church with its nave, choir and side aisles, magnificently decorated . . . It was positively a building'.[1] A writer who styled himself 'An Artist and Antiquary' commented: 'The Artist, at great pains and labour, followed the style of building of the fifteenth century among us, and, by an ingenious contrivance, gave practicable side ailes [*sic*], and an entrance into a choir, &c., whereby, the spectator, for a short space, might indulge his imagination to believe he was in some religious pile.'[2] Baillie's own theory of stage presentation depended on more intimate valencies of space, apt to the psychological chamber drama she saw as central to her work: almost all the action of the play takes place in confined spaces (closet or cell, most intensely), and a number of pieces of action require characters to see into or be visible inside small spaces behind the scenery: effects which were all but unperformable in the massive space of Drury Lane. After its rebuilding in 1794, Sarah Siddons, the Jane De Monfort of the play, called it 'a wilderness of a place', and the magnification of voice and gesture made necessary by the larger auditorium came at the expense of subtlety. John Byng lamented that performances by actresses as careful as Siddons were 'lost and sent to waste in this wild wide theatre, where close observation cannot be maintain'd. . . . Restore me . . . to the warm close, observant, seats of Old Drury . . . The nice [subtle] discriminations, of the actor's face, and the actor's feelings, are now all lost in the vast void of the new theatre'.[3] The huge expense of the new theatres led to the necessity of attracting packed houses,

[1] James Boaden, *Memoirs of John Philip Kemble*, quoted in Sybil Rosenfeld, *Georgian Scene Painters and Scene Painting* (Cambridge, 1981), 45–6.

[2] Quoted from the *Gentleman's Magazine* of May 1801 (408–9) in Sybil Rosenfeld, *A Short History of Scene Design in Great Britain* (Oxford, 1973), 98–9.

[3] *The Torrington Diaries*, ed. C. B. Andrews, 4 vols. (London, 1935–8), iv. 18.

xxxvi

and a new vogue for sensation and melodrama began (alongside other kinds of star attraction such as the boy actor 'Master Betty' or Carlo the performing dog of Drury Lane).

Capon's set for *De Monfort* was fated to end up recycled into a generalized 'Gothic hall', and this reliance on stock scenery, prevalent in British theatre from the Restoration onwards, informs the scenic conception of *Wat Tyler* and *Lovers' Vows*. Southey's scenic demands are generalized in a way that could be answered from the stock of a company touring provincial theatres. The first scene is idyllically rural, with a freestanding cottage/shop of a kind that would also come in handy for *Lovers' Vows*; the other sets—heath, market-place, Gothic palace—are all, despite their historical specificity, as simple to supply from stock as the roads, gardens, and fashionable rooms of Inchbald's carefully calculated commercial success.

The Two Foscari is tightly worked out for the conventional stage layout of the period. It could be done from stock, but given its intense historical specificity it would ideally require accurate scenery to evoke Venice. Visually, it is carefully imagined. Byron was well acquainted with all the locations presented (though the prison he would have seen was the eighteenth-century one, spacious and hygienically progressive by the standards of the time). The first act takes place in an ante-room to the room of the Council of Ten, probably the *Sala della Bussola*, where prisoners waited for their appointment with the Ten. If this is the case, the councillors pass from stage right (where Marina also enters) to a door immediately opposite, stage left, the entrance to the council room. Jacopo Foscari is brought in from downstage left, from the *Inquisitori*, possibly through a trap door to represent the secret staircase up from his cell. The 'lattice' from which he looks out over the Grand Canal, towards the Adriatic, would in this configuration be placed centrally, at the back of the stage. The prison of 3.1 would have a single entrance back centre, with a staircase visible behind it. Here, the dim watery light, later relieved by a single torch, provides a challenge to the scene-designer of a kind relished, as we have seen, in early nineteenth-century London theatres.

Good general introductions to various aspects of theatre in the period can be found in Cecil Price, *Theatre in the Age of Garrick* (Oxford, 1973) and Michael R. Booth, Richard Southern, Frederick and Lise-Lone Marker, *The Revels History of Drama in English*, vi. *1759–1880* (London, 1975). Valuable specialist essays can be found in Kenneth Richards and Peter Thomson (eds.), *The Eighteenth-Century Stage*

(London, 1972). The layout and design of theatres of the period can be studied in immense detail in Richard Leacroft, *The Development of the English Playhouse* (London, 1973). For scenery of the period, consult Sybil Rosenfeld, *A Short History of Scene Design in Great Britain* (Oxford, 1973); for more detail, the same author's *Georgian Scene Painters and Scene Painting* (Cambridge, 1981) is very useful. For music in the theatre see Roger Fiske, *English Theatre Music in the Eighteenth Century* (London, 1973). Costume is discussed in Diana de Marly, *Costume on the Stage 1600–1940* (London, 1982). Calendar details of the plays actually staged in London from the Restoration up to 1800 are to be found in William Van Lennep *et al.* (eds.), *The London Stage 1660–1800*, 11 vols. (Carbondale, Ill., 1965–8). Extensive biographical notices of performers such as John Philip Kemble are given in Philip H. Highfill, Jr., Kalman A. Burnim, and Edward A. Langhans (eds.), *A Biographical Dictionary of Actors, Actresses, Musicians, Dancers, Managers and Other Stage Personnel in London, 1660–1800*, 16 vols. (Carbondale and Edwardsville, Ill., 1973–93). For the audience, see Leo Hughes, *The Drama's Patrons: A Study of the Eighteenth Century London Audience* (Austin, Tex., and London, 1971) and Allardyce Nicoll, *The Garrick Stage: Theatres and Audience in the Eighteenth Century* (Manchester, 1980). For other aspects of the social and political placing of the theatre in the London world see James J. Lynch, *Box, Pit and Gallery: Stage and Society in Johnson's London* (Berkeley and Los Angeles, 1953); George Winchester Stone, Jr. (ed.), *The Stage and the Page: London's 'Whole Show' in the Eighteenth-Century Theatre* (Berkeley and Los Angeles, 1981); Marc Baer, *Theatre and Disorder in Late Georgian London* (Oxford, 1992); and Gillian Russell, *The Theatres of War: Performance, Politics, and Society, 1793–1815* (Oxford, 1995). For the theatre at Bristol see Kathleen Barker, *The Theatre Royal, Bristol, 1766–1966: Two Centuries of Stage History* (London, 1974). For the tradition of private theatricals perhaps implicit in some of Walpole's readings of *The Mysterious Mother*, and fictionalized in Austen's *Mansfield Park*, see Sybil Rosenfeld, *Temples of Thespis: Some Private Theatres and Theatricals in England and Wales, 1700–1820* (London, 1978).

SELECT BIBLIOGRAPHY

(For reading on the theatre of the period, see the books listed in the previous section, pp. xxxvii–xxxviii.)

General

A pioneering account of the dramatic genre to which two of the plays included here might be said to belong is Bertrand Evans, *Gothic Drama from Walpole to Shelley* (Berkeley and Los Angeles, 1947); a later account is Paul Ranger, *'Terror and Pity reign in every Breast': Gothic Drama in the London Patent Theatres, 1750–1820* (London, 1991). For a brief introduction to Romantic views of the stage see Edward Burns, '"The Babel din": Theatre and European Romanticism' in Geoff Ward (ed.), *Bloomsbury Guides to English Literature: Romantic Literature (A Guide to Romantic Literature: 1780–1830)* (London, 1993), 51–67; other general accounts of the theory and practice of the stage in this period are Jeffrey N. Cox, *In the Shadows of Romance: Romantic Tragic Drama in Germany, England, and France* (Athens, Oh., 1989), Frederick Burwick, *Illusion and the Drama: Critical Theory of the Enlightenment and Romantic Era* (Penn State, Pa., 1991), and Daniel P. Watkins, *A Materialist Critique of English Romantic Drama* (Gainesville, Fla., 1993). For an account of the participation of women writers in the drama of the period see Ellen Donkin, *Getting into the Act: Women Playwrights in London 1776–1829* (London, 1995). Modern texts of Gothic plays from the period (including *De Monfort*) can be found in Jeffrey N. Cox (ed.), *Seven Gothic Dramas 1789–1825* (Athens, Oh., 1992).

Walpole and The Mysterious Mother

The standard biographical account is R. W. Ketton-Cremer, *Horace Walpole: A Biography* (London, 1940); Martin Kallich, *Horace Walpole* (New York, 1971) is a useful overall guide with an accessible Freudian account of *The Mysterious Mother*. A summary of Walpole's relation to contemporary theatre can be found in Charles Beecher Hogan, 'The "Theatre of Geo. 3"' in Warren Hunting Smith (ed.), *Horace Walpole: Writer, Politician, and Connoisseur* (New Haven and London, 1967), 227–40. Betsy Perteit Harfst, *Horace Walpole and the*

Unconscious: An Experiment in Criticism (New York, 1980) has two chapters on the psychoanalytic aspects of *The Mysterious Mother*. Peter Sabor (ed.), *Horace Walpole: The Critical Heritage*, (London, 1987) contains a store of early responses to Walpole's work, including *The Mysterious Mother*; Peter Sabor, '"An old tragedy on a disgusting subject": Horace Walpole and *The Mysterious Mother*' in Paul Hyland and Neil Sammells (eds.), *Writing and Censorship in Britain* (London, 1992), 91–106, considers the publication and reception history of the play. Paul Baines's essay, '"This Theatre of Monstrous Guilt": Horace Walpole and the Drama of Incest', is published in *Studies in Eighteenth-Century Culture*, 28 (1999), 287–309.

Southey *and* Wat Tyler

Geoffrey Carnall, *Robert Southey and His Age: The Development of a Conservative Mind* (Oxford, 1960) considers Southey's changing political position; for more recent accounts of Southey's biography and literary career see Christopher Smith, *Quest for Home: Reading Robert Southey* (Liverpool, 1996) and Mark Storey, *Robert Southey: A Life* (Oxford, 1997). Lionel Madden (ed.), *Robert Southey: The Critical Heritage* (London, 1972) contains contemporary accounts of the reception of *Wat Tyler*. See also Ralph A. Manogue, 'Robert Southey's *Wat Tyler*', *Theatre Notebook*, 37/1 (1983), 22–4.

Baillie *and* De Monfort

The standard monograph is Margaret S. Carhart, *The Life and Works of Joanna Baillie* (New Haven, 1923; repr. Hamden, Conn. 1970). More recently, Catherine B. Burroughs, *Closet Stages: Joanna Baillie and the Theater Theory of British Romantic Women Writers* (Philadelphia, 1997) has considered Baillie's drama in relation to theatrical theory and practice, with a special emphasis on gender issues. Daniel P. Watkins, 'Class and Gender in *De Monfort*', *Wordsworth Circle*, 13/1 (Winter 1982), 17–20, is excellent on the internal politics of the play; for aspects of the culture which produced it see also Anne K. Mellor, 'Joanna Baillie and the Counter-Public Sphere', *Studies in Romanticism*, 33/4 (Winter 1994), 559–67. William D. Brewer, 'Joanna Baillie and Lord Byron', *Keats-Shelley Journal*, 44 (1995), 165–81, gives a useful account of the relation between Baillie and Byron.

Inchbald and Lovers' Vows

There is no adequate modern biography; some material can be found in James Boaden, *Memoirs of Mrs. Inchbald*, 2 vols. (London, 1833) and S. R. Littlewood, *Elizabeth Inchbald and her Circle* (London, 1921). On *Lovers' Vows* and its relation to Austen's *Mansfield Park* see in particular Dvora Zelicovici, 'The Inefficacy of *Lovers' Vows*', *ELH: A Journal of English Literary History*, 50/3 (1983), 531–40; Joseph Litvak, 'The Infection of Acting: Theatricals and Theatricality in *Mansfield Park*', *ELH: A Journal of English Literary History* 52/3 (1986), 331–55; Syndy McMillen Conger, 'Reading *Lovers' Vows*: Jane Austen's Reflections on English Sense and German Sensibility', *Studies in Philology*, 85/1 (Winter 1988), 92–113; and Colin Pedley, '"Terrific and Unprincipled Compositions": The Reception of *Lovers' Vows* and *Mansfield Park*', *Philological Quarterly* 74/3 (Summer 1995), 297–316.

Byron and The Two Foscari

Andrew Rutherford (ed.), *Byron: The Critical Heritage* (London, 1970) reproduces some early responses to the play. Bonamy Dobrée, *Byron's Dramas* (Nottingham, 1962) was one of the first attempts to appraise the dramatic part of Byron's career. Several subsequent articles on the political and historical aspects of the plays are worth citing: William Ruddick, 'Lord Byron's Historical Tragedies' in Kenneth Richards and Peter Thomson (eds.), *Nineteenth-Century British Theatre* (London, 1971), 83–94; Anne Barton, '"A Light to Lesson Ages": Byron's Political Plays' in John Jump (ed.), *Byron: A Symposium* (London, 1975); John Ehrstine, *The Metaphysics of Byron: A Reading of the Plays* (The Hague, 1976); Daniel P. Watkins, 'Violence, Class Consciousness, and Ideology in Byron's Historical Plays', *ELH: A Journal of English Literary History*, 48/4 (Winter 1981), 799–816; Giorgio Melchiori, 'The Dramas of Byron' in Richard Allen Cave (ed.), *The Romantic Theatre: An International Symposium* (Totowa, NJ, 1986); John Spalding Gatton, '"Pretensions to Accuracy": Byron's Manipulation of History in the Venetian Dramas' in Giulio Marra *et al.* (eds.), *Byron e la cultura veneziana* (Mira, 1989), 57–67. Martin Corbett, *Byron and Tragedy* (New York, 1988) and Richard Lansdowne, *Byron's Historical Dramas* (Oxford, 1992) are the fullest monographs on the subject. John Spalding Gatton, '"Put into Scenery": Theatrical Space in Byron's Closet Dramas' in James

Redmond (ed.), *The Theatrical Space* (Cambridge, 1987) is more directly theatrical in scope. Robert Gleckner and Bernard Beatty (eds.), *The Plays of Lord Byron: Critical Essays* (Liverpool, 1997) reprints several classic articles on Byron's drama, including some on *The Two Foscari*.

CHRONOLOGY

1717   Horace Walpole born (24 Sept.).

1732   Covent Garden Theatre founded.

1737   Licensing Act confirms Covent Garden and Drury Lane as the two 'Patent Theatres'; Walpole's mother dies.

1739   Walpole on Grand Tour (until 1741).

1742   Walpole's father resigns as First Lord of the Treasury; becomes Earl of Orford.

1745   Jacobite rising in favour of Young Pretender; Walpole's father dies.

1747   Walpole leases Strawberry Hill; writes *Aedes Walpolianae*.

1747   David Garrick (with John Lacy) takes over management of Drury Lane.

1748   Garrick poaches Hannah Pritchard for Drury Lane.

1749   Walpole buys Strawberry Hill.

1749   Pritchard stars in Samuel Johnson's *Irene*.

1753   Elizabeth Inchbald (Simpson) born (15 Oct.).

1756   England at war with France (Seven Years' War).

1757   Walpole institutes private press at Strawberry Hill; William Blake born.

1758   Walpole, *Catalogue of Royal and Noble Authors*.

1760   Accession of George III.

1762   Joanna Baillie born (11 Sept.).

1763   Seven Years' War ends; the radical John Wilkes arrested under general warrant.

1764   England's quarrel with American colonies begins; Walpole, *The Castle of Otranto*.

1765   Walpole meets Madame du Deffand in Paris.

1766   Walpole begins *Mysterious Mother*.

1768   Walpole completes *Mysterious Mother*; Pritchard retires, dying months later; Walpole resigns his seat in parliament.

1770   William Wordsworth born.

1772   Samuel Taylor Coleridge born.

1774   American Declaration of Rights; Thomas Harris assumes sole proprietorship of Covent Garden; Robert Southey born (12 Aug.).

1775   War of American Independence begins; Drury Lane interior remodelled by Robert Adam; Sarah Siddons makes unsuccessful début there; Jane Austen born.

1776 Garrick retires from Drury Lane; Richard Brinsley Sheridan assumes control.

1780 Drury Lane damaged in (anti-Catholic) Gordon Riots.

1781 Robert Jephson's dramatization of *The Castle of Otranto* is performed under the title *The Count of Narbonne*.

1782 Covent Garden gutted by fire; Sarah Siddons makes triumphant return to Drury Lane.

1783 Treaty of Versailles ends American war; John Philip Kemble makes début at Drury Lane.

1784 Walpole publishes revised *Description of the Villa of Horace Walpole* (orig. pub. 1774).

1788 Kemble becomes manager of Drury Lane; George Gordon, later Lord Byron born (22 Jan.).

1789 French Revolution begins with storming of the Bastille and inauguration of National Assembly.

1790 Baillie, *Fugitive Verses*; Wordsworth travels in France and Italy.

1791 Drury Lane closes. Walpole becomes 4th Earl of Orford; Byron's father dies; Inchbald, *A Simple Story.*

1792 Covent Garden reconstructed and enlarged; Percy Bysshe Shelley born.

1793 Execution of Louis XVI; England at war with France.

1794 Rebuilt Drury Lane opens; Southey writes *Wat Tyler.*

1795 England at war with Holland; suspension of habeas corpus; press freedom suppressed; Inchbald, *I'll Tell You What* produced; Wordsworth and Coleridge meet; John Keats born.

1796 Southey writes *Joan of Arc*; Inchbald, *Nature and Art.*

1797 Walpole dies (2 Mar.); Coleridge writes *Remorse.*

1798 Nelson defeats Napoleon in Battle of the Nile; rebellion in Ireland crushed; Baillie, *Series of Plays*, vol. 1, published; *Lovers' Vows* opens at Covent Garden and is published; Byron inherits aristocratic title; first volume of Wordsworth and Coleridge, *Lyrical Ballads*; Wordsworth begins *The Prelude.*

1800 *De Monfort* opens at Drury Lane; *Lyrical Ballads*, vol. 2, with Preface.

1802 Peace with France; Baillie, *Series of Plays*, vol. 2 published.

1803 Kemble and Siddons defect to Covent Garden.

1804 Baillie, *Miscellaneous Plays* published.

1805 Nelson defeats Napoleon at Trafalgar but is mortally wounded in battle; Byron declaims passages from *King Lear* and Young's *The Revenge* at Harrow Speech Day.

1806–9   Inchbald selects and writes prefaces for anthology series, *The British Theatre*.

1807   Southey receives government pension.

1808   Peninsular War with France; Covent Garden burns down; Harris gives up management of the theatre.

1809   Covent Garden reopens; audiences riot over increased prices; Drury Lane burns down; Byron takes seat in House of Lords and tours Portugal and Greece.

1810   Baillie, *The Family Legend* produced successfully.

1811   Byron makes speeches in House of Lords; Shelley expelled from Oxford; Austen, *Mansfield Park* begun (published 1814).

1812   Siddons retires; Byron writes Prologue for reopening of Drury Lane.

1813   Southey becomes Poet Laureate and writes *Life of Nelson*; Coleridge, *Remorse* produced at Drury Lane; Wordsworth becomes Stamp Distributor for Westmoreland; Shelley, *Queen Mab*.

1814   Edmund Kean makes début at Drury Lane; Byron's half-sister Augusta gives birth to a daughter rumoured to be Byron's.

1815   Wellington defeats Napoleon at Waterloo; Byron begins first play, the Gothic *Werner* (not completed; pub. 1822); marries Annabella Milbanke; daughter (Ada) born; separates from wife.

1816   Food riots and industrial discontent; Byron leaves England in disgrace and travels to Geneva in company with Shelley.

1817   Further rioting; Kemble retires; Southey's *Wat Tyler* published by radicals; Byron's daughter by Claire Claremont (Allegra) born; Byron moves to Venice and writes *Beppo*; Coleridge, *Biographia Literaria*.

1818   Peterloo massacre defended by Southey; Byron begins *Don Juan*; Shelley, *The Revolt of Islam*.

1819   Byron lives with Countess Guiccioli in Venice and Ravenna; Shelley, *The Cenci* and *The Mask of Anarchy*; Keats (with Charles Brown), *Otho the Great*.

1820   Accession of George IV; Kean ceases to act at Drury Lane; Byron writes *Marino Faliero* (pub. 1821 with a preface praising Walpole); Shelley, *Prometheus Unbound*.

1821   Baillie, *Metrical Legends* published; Southey attacks Byron in *A Vision of Judgment*; Byron writes *The Two Foscari*, *Sardanapalus*, *Cain*, *Heaven and Earth*, *The Deformed Transformed* at Pisa; Inchbald dies (1 Aug.).

1822　Byron and Shelley plan to perform *Othello*; Byron attacks Southey in *The Vision of Judgment*; Allegra dies; Byron travels to Leghorn and Genoa; Shelley dies.

1824　Byron travels to Missolonghi to fight for Greek independence against the Turks; dies of fever (19 Apr.).

1833　Kean retires.

1834　Coleridge dies.

1835　Southey receives pension from Sir Robert Peel.

1843　Southey dies (21 Mar.); Wordsworth becomes Poet Laureate.

1844　Monopoly of London 'Patent Theatres' ended.

1850　Wordsworth dies.

1851　Baillie dies (23 Feb.) shortly after final edition of her works is published.

THE MYSTERIOUS MOTHER

A TRAGEDY

by
HORACE WALPOLE

Sit mihi fas audita loqui!°
[Virgil]

[PREFACE to the 1781 edition]°

The author of the following tragedy is so far from thinking it worthy of being offered to the public, that he has done every thing in his power to suppress the publication—in vain. It is solely to avoid its being rendered still worse by a surreptitious edition, that he is reduced to give it from his own copy. He is sensible that the subject is disgust- 5 ing,° and by no means compensated by the execution. It was written several years ago; and to prevent the trouble of reading it, or having it transcribed, a few copies were printed and given away.° One or two have been circulated, and different editions have been advertised, which occasion the present publication.° All the favour the author 10 solicits or expects, is, to be believed how unwillingly he has submitted to its appearance: he cannot be more blamed than he blames himself for having undertaken so disagreeable a story, and for having hazarded the publicity by letting it go out of his own hands. He respects the judgment of the public too much to offer to them voluntarily what he 15 does not think deserves their approbation.

29 April 1781

THE CHARACTERS OF THE PLAY

Countess of Narbonne°
Count Edmund, *her son*
Florian, *his friend*
Adeliza,° *an orphan*
Benedict, *a friar*
Martin, *a friar*
Peter, *porter of the castle*
Maria and Elinor, *damsels attending the Countess*
[Orphan Girl]
[First Orphan]
[Second Orphan]
Chorus of Orphans
Chorus of Friars
[Servant]
[Attendants]

The scene lies at the castle of Narbonne; partly on a platform before the gate, partly in a garden within the walls.

PROLOGUE°

From no French model breathes the muse to-night;°
The scene she draws is horrid, not polite.°
She dips her pen in terror. Will ye shrink?
Shall foreign critics teach you how to think?
Had Shakespeare's magic dignified the stage,   5
If timid laws had schooled th'insipid age?
Had Hamlet's spectre trod the midnight round?°
Or Banquo's issue been in vision crowned?°
Free as your country, Britons, be your scene!°
Be Nature now, and now Invention, queen!   10
Be Vice alone corrected and restrained.
Can crimes be punished by a bard enchained?
Shall the bold censor back be sent to school,°
And told, 'This is not nice; That is not rule'?
The French no crimes of magnitude admit;   15
They seldom startle, just alarm the pit.°
At most, when dire necessity ordains
That death should sluice some king's or lover's veins,
A tedious confidant appears, to tell
What dismal woes behind the scenes befell.   20
Chilled with the drowsy tale, his audience fret,
While the starved piece concludes like a gazette.
The tragic Greeks with nobler licence wrote;
Nor veiled the eye, but plucked away the mote.°
Whatever passion prompted, was their game;   25
Not delicate, while chastisement their aim.
Electra now a parent's blood demands;°
Now parricide distains the Theban's hands,
And love incestuous knots his nuptial bands.°
Such is our scene; from real life it rose;   30
Tremendous picture of domestic woes.°
If terror shake you, or soft pity move,
If dreadful pangs o'ertake unbridled love;
Excuse the bard, who from your feeling draws
All the reward he aims at, your applause.   35

4

1.1

A platform before the castle

[*Enter Florian*]

FLORIAN What awful silence! How these antique towers°
And vacant courts chill the suspended soul,
Till expectation wears the cast of fear;
And fear, half-ready to become devotion,
Mumbles a kind of mental orison,   5
It knows not wherefore. What a kind of being
Is circumstance!°
I am a soldier; and were yonder battlements
Garnished with combatants, and cannon-mounted,
My daring breast would bound with exultation,   10
And glorious hopes enliven this drear scene.
Now dare not I scarce tread to my own hearing,
Lest echo borrow superstition's tongue,
And seem to answer me, like one departed.
I met a peasant, and enquired my way: 15
The carl, not rude of speech, but like the tenant°
Of some night-haunted ruin, bore an aspect°
Of horror, worn to habitude. He bade°
God bless me; and passed on. I urged him farther:
'Good master,' cried he, 'go not to the castle;   20
There sorrow ever dwells and moping misery.'
I pressed him yet.—'None there', said he, 'are welcome,
But now and then a mass-priest, and the poor;
To whom the pious Countess deals her alms,
On covenant, that each revolving night   25
They beg of heav'n the health of her son's soul
And of her own: but often as returns
The twentieth of September, they are bound°
Fast from the midnight watch to pray till morn.'—
More would he not disclose, or knew not more.   30
—What precious mummery! Her son in exile,
She wastes on monks and beggars his inheritance,
For his soul's health! I never knew a woman,
But loved our bodies or our souls too well.

5

Each master whim maintains its hour of empire,
And, obstinately faithful to its dictates,
With equal ardour, equal importunity,
They tease us to be damned or to be saved.
I hate to love or pray too long.
    [*Enter Peter*]

PETER   Methought
I heard a stranger's voice—What lack you, sir?   40
FLORIAN Good fellow, who inhabits here?
PETER   I do.
FLORIAN Belike this castle is not thine.
PETER   Belike so:
But be it whose it may, this is no haunt
For revellers and gallants—pass your way.
FLORIAN Thou churl! Is this your Gallic hospitality?   45
Thy lady, on my life, would not thus rudely
Chide from her presence a bewildered knight.°
PETER Thou know'st my lady then!—Thou know'st her not.
Canst thou in hair-cloths vex those dainty limbs?
Canst thou on reeking pavements and cold marble,   50
In meditation pass the livelong night?
Canst mortify that flesh, my rosy minion,
And bid thy rebel appetite refrain
From goblets foaming wine, and costly viands?
These are the deeds, my youngster, must draw down°   55
My lady's ever-heav'n-directed eye.
FLORIAN In sooth, good friend, my knighthood is not
    schooled
In voluntary rigours—I can fast,
March supperless, and make cold earth my pillow,
When my companions know no choicer fare;   60
But seldom roost in churches, or reject
The ready banquet, or a willing fair one.
PETER Angels defend us! what a reprobate!
Yon mould'ring porch for sixteen years and more
Has not been struck with such unhallowed sounds.   65
Hence to thy lewd companions!
FLORIAN   Father greybeard,
I cry you mercy; nor was't my intention°
To wound your reverence's saint-like organs.
But come, thou hast known other days—canst tell

6

Of banquetings and dancings—'twas not always thus.   70
PETER No, no—time was—my lord, the Count of Narbonne,
 A prosp'rous gentleman, were he alive,
 We should not know these moping melancholies.°
 Heav'n rest his soul! I marvel not my lady
 Cherishes his remembrance, for he was   75
 Comely to sight, and wondrous goodly built.
 They say, his son, Count Edmund's mainly like him.°
 Would these old arms, that served his grandfather,
 Could once enfold him! I should part in peace.
FLORIAN What, if I bring thee tidings of Count Edmund!   80
PETER Mercy befall me!—now my dream is out.
 Last night the raven croaked, and from the bars
 Of our lodge-fire flitted a messenger.—°
 I knew no good would follow—bring you ill tidings,
 Sir gentleman?
FLORIAN (aside)   This is a solemn fool,   85
 Or solemn knave. [To Peter] Shouldst thou indeed rejoice
 To see Count Edmund? Would thy noble mistress
 Spring with a mother's joy to clasp her son?
PETER Oh! no, no, no.—He must not here—alas!
 He must not here set foot—But tell me, stranger,   90
 I prithee say, does my old master's heir
 Still breathe this vital air! Is he in France?
 Is he within some ten, or twenty leagues,°
 Or fifty? I am hearty yet, have all my limbs,°
 And I would make a weary pilgrimage   95
 To kiss his gracious hand, and at his feet
 Lay my old bones—for here I ne'er must see him. (Weeps)
FLORIAN Thou good old man, forgive a soldier's mirth.
 But say, why Narbonne's heir from Narbonne's lands
 Is banished, driven by a ruthless mother?°   100
PETER Ah! sir, 'tis hard indeed—but spare his mother;
 Such virtue never dwelt in female form.
 Count Edmund—but he was indeed a stripling,
 A very lad—it was the trick of youth,
 And we have all our sins, or we have had;   105
 Yet still no pardon—Thinkst thou not my lord,
 My late kind master, ere he knew my lady,
 Wist not what woman was?—I warrant him—°
 But so—Count Edmund being not sixteen,

7

A lusty youth, his father's very image—   110
Oh! he has played me many a trick—good sir,
Does my young master ever name old Peter!
Well!—but I prate—you must forgive my age;
I come to th'point—Her name was Beatrice;
A roguish eye—she ne'er would look on me,   115
Or we had saved full many a woeful day!
Mark you me well?
FLORIAN   I do.
PETER   This Beatrice—
But hark! my lady comes—retire a while
Beyond those yews—anon I'll tell you more.
FLORIAN May I not greet her?
PETER   For my office, no: 120
'Twere forfeit of my badge to hold a parley
With one of near thy years.
          Florian withdraws. The Countess in weeds,° with a crucifix in
          her hand, issues from castle, accompanied by Maria and
          Elinor, and passes over the stage. When she is gone, Florian
          returns
                          'Tis ever thus.
At break of morn she hies to yonder abbey,
And prostrate o'er some monumental stone,
Seems more to wait her doom, than ask to shun it.   125
The day is passed in minist'ring to wants
Of health or means; the closing eve beholds°
New tears, new prayers, or haggard meditation.
But if cold moonshine, deep'ning ev'ry frown
Of these impending towers, invite her steps,°   130
She issues forth.—Beshrew me, but I tremble,
When my own keys discharge the drawbridge chains,
And rattle through the castle's farmost vaults.
Then have I seen this sad, this sober mourner,
With frantic gesture and disordered step—   135
But hush—who moves up yonder avenue?
It is—no—stay—i'faith! but it is he,
My lady's confessor, with friar Martin—°
Quick hie thee hence—should that same meddling monk
Observe our conf'rence, there were fine work toward.   140
FLORIAN You will not leave your tale unfinished?
PETER Mass! but I will—a tale will pay no stipend.°

These fifty winters have I borne this staff,
And will not lose my porridge for my prating.°
FLORIAN Well! but Count Edmund—wo't not hear of him?°   145
PETER Aye, bless his name! at any leisure hour.
This evening, ere the shutting of the gates,
Loiter about yon grange; I'll come to thee.
So now, begone—away.
          *Exeunt [Florian and Peter] severally.° [Enter Benedict and
          Martin]*
BENEDICT   Aye! sift her, sift her—
As if I had not probed her very soul,   150
And wound me round her heart—I tell thee, brother,
This woman was not cast in human mould:
Ten such would foil a council, would unbuild°
Our Roman church—In her, devotion's real:
Our beads, our hymns, our saints, amuse her not:°   155
Nay, not confession, not repeating o'er
Her darling sins, has any charms for her.
I have marked her praying: not one wand'ring thought
Seems to steal meaning from her words.—She prays
Because she feels, and feels, because a sinner.   160
MARTIN What is this secret sin, this untold tale,
That art cannot extract, nor penance cleanse?°
Loss of a husband, sixteen years enjoyed,
And dead as many, could not stamp such sorrow.
Nor could she be his death's artificer,°   165
And now affect to weep it.—I have heard,°
That chasing as he homeward rode, a stag,
Chafed by the hounds, with sudden onset slew
Th'adventurous Count.
BENEDICT   'Twas so; and yet, my brother,
My mind has more than once imputed blood   170
To this incessant mourner. Beatrice,
The damsel for whose sake she holds in exile
Her only son, has never, since the night
Of his incontinence, been seen or heard of.°
MARTIN 'Tis clear, 'tis clear; nor will her prudent tongue   175
Accuse its owner.
BENEDICT   Judge not rashly, brother.
I oft have shifted my discourse to murder:
She notes it not. Her muscles hold their place,

Nor discomposed, nor firmed to steadiness.
No sudden flushing, and no falt'ring lip: 180
Nor, though she pities, lifts she to her eyes
Her handkerchief, to palliate her disorder.
There the wound rankles not.—I fixed on love,
The failure of the sex, and aptest cause
Of each attendant crime—

MARTIN   Aye, brother, there   185
We master all their craft. Touch but that string—

BENEDICT Still, brother, do you err. She owned to me,°
That, though of nature warm, the passion love
Did ne'er anticipate her choice. The Count,
Her husband, so adored and so lamented,   190
Won not her fancy, till the nuptial rites
Had with the sting of pleasure taught her passion.
This, with such modest truth, and that truth heightened
By conscious sense, that holds deceit a weakness,°
She uttered, I would pawn my order's credit   195
On her veracity.

MARTIN   Then whither turn°
To worm her secret out?

BENEDICT   I know not that.
She will be silent, but she scorns a falsehood.
And thus while frank on all things, but her secret,
I know, I know it not.

MARTIN   Till she disclose it,   200
Deny her absolution.

BENEDICT   She will take none:
Offered, she scoffs it; and, withheld, demands not.°
Nay, vows she will not load her sinking soul
With incantations.

MARTIN   This is heresy;
Rank heresy; and holy church should note it.   205

BENEDICT Be patient, brother—Though of adamant°
Her reason, charity dissolves that rock—
And surely we have tasted of the stream.°
Nay, one unguarded moment may disclose
This mystic tale—then, brother, what a harvest,°   210
When masters of her bosom-guilt!—Age too
May numb her faculties.—Or soon, or late,°
A praying woman must become our spoil.°

MARTIN Her zeal may falter.
BENEDICT   Not in solitude.
    I nurse her in new horrors; form her tenants   215
    To fancy visions, phantoms; and report them.°
    She mocks their fond credulity—but trust me,°
    Her memory retains the colouring:
    Oft times it paints her dreams; and ebon night
    Is no logician. I have known her call   220
    For lights, ere she could combat its impressions.
    I too, though often scorned, relate my dreams,
    And wondrous voices heard; that she may think me
    At least an honest bigot; nor remember
    I tried to practise on her fears, and, foiled,   225
    Give o'er my purpose.
MARTIN   This is masterly.°
BENEDICT Poor mastery! when I am more in awe
    Of my own penitent, than she of me.
    My genius is command; art, but a tool
    My grovelling fortune forces me to use.   230
    Oh! were I seated high as my ambition,
    I'd place this naked foot on necks of monarchs,
    And make them bow to creeds myself would laugh at.°
MARTIN By humbler arts our mighty fabric rose.
    Win pow'r by craft; wear it with ostentation;   235
    For confidence is half-security.
    Deluded men think boldness, conscious strength;
    And grow the slaves of their own want of doubt.°
    Gain to the Holy See this fair domain;
    A crimson bonnet may reward your toils,°   240
    And the rich harvest prove at last your own.
BENEDICT Never, while Edmund lives. This steady woman
    Can ne'er be pious with so many virtues.
    Justice is interwoven in her frame;
    Nor will she wrong the son she will not see.   245
    She loves him not; yet, mistress of his fortunes,
    His ample exhibition speaks her bounty.°
    She destines him whate'er his father's love
    Gave blindly to her will. Her alms, her charities,
    Usurped from her own wants, she sets apart°   250
    A scanty portion only for her ward,°
    Young Adeliza.

11

MARTIN   Say her son were dead,
And Adeliza veiled—
BENEDICT   I press the latter°
With fruitless ardour. Often as I urge it,
She pleads the maiden's flushing cheek, and nature,   255
That speaks in characters of glowing rose
Its modest appetites and timid wishes.
Her sex, she says, when gratified, are frail;
When checked, a hurricane of boundless passions.
Then, with sweet irony and sad, she wills me   260
Ask my own breast, if cowls and scapularies°
Are charms all powerful to subdue desire?
MARTIN 'Twere wiser school the maiden: lead the train
Of young ideas to a fancied object.
A mental spouse may fill her hov'ring thoughts,°   265
And bar their fixing on some earthly lover.
BENEDICT This is already done—but Edmund's death
Were hopes more solid—
MARTIN   First report him dead:
His letters intercepted—
BENEDICT   Greatly thought!
Thou true son of the church!—and lo! where comes   270
Our patroness—leave me; I will not lose
An instant. I will sound her inmost soul,
And mould it to the moment of projection.°
          Exit Martin. Benedict retires within the castle. [*Enter Countess,*
          attended by Elinor and Maria]
COUNTESS Haste thee, Maria, to the western tower,
And learn if th'aged pilgrim dozes yet.   275
You, Elinor, attend my little orphans,
And when their task is done, prepare their breakfast.
But scant th'allowance of the red-haired urchin,
That maimed the poor man's cur—
          [*Exeunt Elinor and Maria*]
                              Ah! happy me!
If sentiment, untutored by affliction,   280
Had taught my temperate blood to feel for others,
Ere pity, perching on my mangled bosom,
Like flies on wounded flesh, had made me shrink
More with compunction than with sympathy!
Alas! must guilt then ground our very virtues!   285

Grow they on sin alone, and not on grace?
While Narbonne lived, my fully-sated soul
Thought none unhappy—for it did not think!
In pleasures rolled whole summer suns away;
And if a pensive visage crossed my path,   290
I deemed the wearer envious or ill-natured.
What anguish had I blessedly redressed,
But that I was too blessed!—Well! peace is fled,
Ne'er to return! nor dare I snap the thread°
Of life, while misery may want a friend.   295
Despair and Hell must wait, while pity needs
My ministry—Eternity has scope°
Enough to punish me, though I should borrow
A few short hours to sacrifice to charity.
        [*Benedict comes forward*]
BENEDICT I sought you, lady.
COUNTESS   Happily I'm found.   300
Who needs the widow's mite?
BENEDICT   None ask your aid.°
Your gracious foresight still prevents occasion:°
And your poor beadsman joys to meet your presence,
Uncumbered with a suit. It pains my soul,
Oft as I tax your bounty, lest I seem   305
A craving or immodest almoner.
COUNTESS No more of this, good father. I suspect not
One of your holy order of dissembling:°
Suspect not me of loving flattery.
Pass a few years, and I shall be a corpse—   310
Will flattery then new clothe my skeleton,
Fill out these hollow jaws? Will't give me virtues?°
Or at the solemn audit pass for truth,°
And varnish o'er my stains?
BENEDICT   The church could seal
Your pardon—but you scorn it. In your pride   315
Consists your danger. Yours are Pagan virtues:°
As such, I praise them—but as such, condemn them.
COUNTESS Father, my *crimes* are Pagan; my belief
Too orthodox to trust to erring man.
What! shall I, foul with guilt, and self-condemned,   320
Presume to kneel, where angels kneel appalled,
And plead a priest's certificate for pardon?

13

While he, perchance, before my blasted eyes°
Shall sink to woes, endless, unutterable,
For having fooled me into that presumption.   325
BENEDICT Is he to blame, trusting to what he grants?
COUNTESS Am I to blame, not trusting what he grants?
BENEDICT Yet faith—
COUNTESS   I have it not—why shakes my soul°
With nightly terrors? Courage such as mine
Would start at nought but guilt. 'Tis from within   330
I tremble. Death would be felicity,
Were there no retrospect. What joys have I?°
What pleasure softens, or what friendship soothes
My aching bosom?—I have lost my husband:
My own decree has banished my own son.   335
BENEDICT Last night I dreamt your son was with the blessed.
COUNTESS Would heav'n he were!
BENEDICT   Do you then wish his death?
COUNTESS Should I not wish him blessed?
BENEDICT   Belike he is:
I never knew my Friday's dreams erroneous.°
COUNTESS Nor I knew superstition in the right.   340
BENEDICT Madam, I must no longer hear this language.
You do abuse my patience. I have borne,
For your soul's health, and hoping your conversion,
Opinions most depraved. It ill beseems
My holy function to give countenance,   345
By lending ear, to such pernicious tenets.
The judgments hanging o'er your destined head°
May reach ev'n me—I see it! I am rapt
Beyond my bearing! My prophetic soul
Views the red falchion of eternal justice   350
Cut off your sentenced race—your son is dead!
COUNTESS Father, we no prophetic demon bear
Within our breast, but conscience. *That* has spoken
Words more tremendous than this acted zeal,
This poetry of fond enthusiasm   355
Can conjure up. It is the still small voice°
That breathes conviction. 'Tis that voice has told me,
'Twas my son's birth, not his mortality,°
Must drown my soul in woe.—Those tears are shed.
BENEDICT Unjust, uncharitable as your words,   360

I pardon them. Illy of me you deem; °
I know it, lady. 'Tis humiliation:
As such I bow to it—yet dear I tender
Your peace of mind. Dismiss your worthless servant:
His prayers shall still be yours.
COUNTESS   Forgive me, father: 365
  Discretion does not guide my words. I meant
  No insult on your holy character.°
BENEDICT No, lady; choose some other monitor,°
  Whose virtues may command your estimation.
  Your useless beadsman shall behold with joy   370
  A worthier man mediate your peace with heav'n.
COUNTESS Alas! till reconciled with my own breast,
  What peace is there for me!
BENEDICT   In th'neighb'ring district
  There lives a holy man, whose sanctity
  Is marked with wondrous gifts. Grace smiles upon him;   375
  Conversion tracks his footsteps: miracles
  Spring from his touch: his sacred casuistry°
  Pours balm into despair. Consult with him.
  Unfold th'impenetrable mystery,
  That sets your soul and you at endless discord.°   380
COUNTESS Consult a holy man! Inquire of him!
  —Good father, wherefore? What should I inquire?°
  Must I be taught of him, that guilt is woe?
  That innocence alone is happiness?
  That martyrdom itself shall leave the villain   385
  The villain that it found him? Must I learn
  That minutes stamped with crimes are past recall?
  That joys are momentary; and remorse
  Eternal? Shall he teach me charms and spells,
  To make my sense believe against my sense?   390
  Shall I think practices and penances
  Will, if he say so, give the health of virtue
  To gnawing self-reproach?—I know they cannot.
  Nor could one risen from the dead proclaim
  This truth in deeper sounds to my conviction.   395
  We want no preacher to distinguish vice
  From virtue. At our birth the god revealed
  All conscience needs to know. No codicil
  To duty's rubric here and there was placed

In some saint's casual custody. Weak minds°   400
Want their soul's fortune told by oracles
And holy jugglers. Me, nor oracles,°
Nor prophets, Death alone can certify,
Whether, when justice's full dues exacted,
Mercy shall grant one drop to slake my torment.°   405
—Here, father, break we off; you to your calling;
I to my tears and mournful occupation.
    Exeunt [*severally*]

2.1

[*Enter Edmund and Florian*]

EDMUND Doubt not, my friend; Time's pencil, hardships,
    war,
  Some taste of pleasure too, have chased the bloom
  Of ruddy comeliness, and stamped this face
  With harsher lineaments, that well may mock
  The prying of a mother's eye—a mother,   5
  Through whose firm nerves tumultuous instinct's flood
  Ne'er gushed with eager eloquence, to tell her,
  'This is your son! your heart's own voice proclaims him.'
FLORIAN If not her love, my lord, suspect her hatred.
  Those jarring passions spring from the same source: 10
  Hate is distempered love.
EDMUND   Why should she hate me?
  For that my opening passion's swelling ardour
  Prompted congenial necessary joy,°
  Was that a cause?—Nor was she then so rigid.
  No sanctified dissembler had possessed   15
  Her scared imagination, teaching her,
  That holiness begins, where nature ends.
  No, Florian, she herself was woman then;
  A sensual woman. Nor satiety,
  Sickness and age and virtue's frowardness,   20
  Had so obliterated pleasure's relish—
  She might have pardoned what she felt so well.
FLORIAN Forgive me, Edmund; nay, nor think I preach,
  If I, God wot, of morals loose enough,
  Seem to condemn you. You have often told me,   25
  The night, the very night that to your arms
  Gave pretty Beatrice's melting beauties,
  Was the same night on which your father died.
EDMUND 'Tis true—and thou, sage monitor, dost thou
  Hold love a crime so irremissible?   30
  Wouldst thou have turned thee from a willing girl,
  To sing a requiem to thy father's soul?

I thought my mother busied with her tears,
Her faintings, and her masses, while I stole
To Beatrice's chamber.—How my mother   35
Became apprised, I know not: but her heart,
Never too partial to me, grew estranged.
Estranged!—aversion in its fellest mood
Scowled from her eye, and drove me from her sight.
She called me impious: named my honest lewdness,   40
A profanation of my father's ashes.
I knelt and wept, and, like a puling boy,
For now my blood was cool, believed, confessed
My father's hov'ring spirit incensed against me.
This weak confession but inflamed her wrath;   45
And when I would have bathed her hand with tears,
She snatched it back with horror.
FLORIAN   'Twas the trick
Of over-acted sorrow. Grief fatigues;
And each collateral circumstance is seized°
To cheat th'uneasy feeling. Sable chambers,°   50
The winking lamp, and pomp of midnight woe,
Are but a specious theatre, on which
Th'inconstant mind with decency forgets
Its inward tribute. (*Ironically*) Who can doubt the love°
Which to a father's shade devotes the son?°   55
EDMUND Still must I doubt: still deem some mystery,
Beyond a widow's pious artifice,
Lies hid beneath aversion so relentless.
All my inheritance, my lordships, castles,°
My father's lavish love bequeathed my mother.   60
Chose she some second partner of her bed,
Or did she waste her wealth on begging saints
And rogues that act contrition, it were proof
Of her hypocrisy, or lust of fame
In monkish annals. But to me her hand   65
Is bounteous, as her heart is cold. I tell thee,
Bating enjoyment of my native soil,
Narbonne's revenues are as fully mine,
As if I held them by the strength of charters.
FLORIAN Why set them on the hazard then, when she,   70
Who deals them, may revoke? Your absence hence
The sole condition.

EDMUND   I am weary, Florian,
  Of such a vagrant life. Befits it me,
  Sprung from a race of heroes, Narbonne's prince,
  To lend my casual arm's approved valour°   75
  To quarrels, nor my country's nor my own?°
  To stain my sword with random blood!—I fought
  At Buda 'gainst the Turk—a holy war,°
  So it was deemed—I smote the turbaned race:
  Did zeal, or did ambition nerve my blow!   80
  Or mattered it to me, on Buda's domes
  Whether the crescent or the cross prevailed?°
  Meantime on alien climes I dissipated
  Wealth from my subjects wrung, the peasant's tribute,
  Earned by his toil. Meantime in ruin laid   85
  My mould'ring castles.—Yes, ye moss-grown walls!
  Ye tow'rs defenceless!—I revisit ye
  Shame-stricken.—Where are all your trophies now?
  Your thronged courts, the revelry, the tumult,
  That spoke the grandeur of my house, the homage   90
  Of neighb'ring barons? Thus did Thibalt, Raoul,
  Or Clodomir, my brave progenitors,°
  Creep like a spy, and watch to thrid your gates
  Unnoticed? No; with martial attributes,
  With waving banners and enlivening fifes,   95
  They bade your portal wide unfold its jaws,
  And welcome them and triumph.
FLORIAN   True, my lord:
  They reigned the monarchs of a score of miles;
  Imperial lords of ev'ry trembling cottage
  Within their cannon's mandate. Deadly feuds   100
  For obsolete offences, now arrayed°
  Their liveried banditti, prompt to deal
  On open valleys and unguarded herds,
  On helpless virgins and unweaponed boors,
  The vengeance of their tribe. Sometimes they dared   105
  To scowl defiance to the distant throne,
  Imprisoned, cantoned inaccessibly
  In their own rock-built dungeons—Are these glories
  My Edmund's soul ambitions to revive?
  Thus would he bless his vassals!
EDMUND   Thy reproof,   110

My friend, is just. But had I not a cause,
A tender cause, that prompted my return?
This cruel parent, whom I blame, and mourn,
Whose harshness I resent, whose woes I pity,
Has won my love, by winning my respect.   115
Her letters! Florian; such unstudied strains
Of virtuous eloquence! She bids me, yes,
This praying Magdalen enjoins my courage°
To emulate my great forefather's deeds.
Tells me, that shame and guilt alone are mortal;   120
That death but bars the possibility
Of frailty, and embalms untainted honour.
Then blots and tears efface some half-told woe
Lab'ring in her full bosom. I deciphered
In one her blessing granted, and erased.   125
And yet, what followed marked anxiety°
For my soul's welfare. I must know this riddle.
I must, will comfort her. She cannot, surely,
After such perils, wounds by her command
Encountered, after sixteen exiled years   130
Spurn me, when kneeling—Think'st thou, 'tis
    possible?
FLORIAN I would not think it; but a host of priests
    Surround her. They, good men, are seldom found
    To plead the cause of pity. Self-denial,
    Whose dissonance from nature's kindest laws,   135
    By contradicting wins on our perverseness,
    Is rank fanaticism's beloved machine.°
    Oh! 'twill be heroism, a sacrifice,
    To curb the torrent of maternal fondness!
    You shall be beggared, that the saint your mother   140
    May, by cowled sycophants and canting jugglers,
    Be hailed, be canonized a new Teresa.°
    Pray be not seen here: let's again to th'wars.
EDMUND No, Florian, my dulled soul is sick of riot:°
    Sick of the thoughtless jollity of camps,   145
    Where revelry subsists on desolation,°
    And shouts of joy contend with dying groans.
    Our sports are fleeting; snatched, perhaps, not granted.
    'Tis time to bid adieu to vagrant pleasure,
    And fix the wanderer love. Domestic bliss—   150

20

FLORIAN Yes, your fair pensioner, young Adeliza,°
    Has sobered your inconstancy. (*Ironically*) Her smiles
    Were exquisite—to rule a family!
    So matron-like an air—She must be fruitful.
EDMUND Pass we this levity—'Tis true, the maiden   155
    Is beauty's type renewed. Like blooming Eve°
    In nature's young simplicity, and blushing
    With wonder at creation's opening glow,
    She charms, unknowing what it is to charm.°
FLORIAN This is a lover's language—Is she kind?°   160
EDMUND Cold as the metal bars that part her from me;
    She listens, but replies not to my purpose.
FLORIAN How gained you then admittance?
EDMUND   This whole month,
    While waiting your arrival, I have haunted
    Her convent's parlour. 'Tis my mother's wish   165
    To match her nobly. Hence her guardian abbess°
    Admits such visitors as claim her notice
    By worthy bearing, and convenient splendour.°
    Oh Florian, union with that favoured maiden
    Might reconcile my mother—
        A chapel bell rings
                  hark! what sound—   170
FLORIAN A summons to some office of devotion.°
    My lord, weigh well what you project—
        Singing offstage
EDMUND   I hear
    Voices that seem approaching—hush! they sing.
    Listen!
FLORIAN   No; let us hence: you will be known.
EDMUND They cannot know me—see!   175
    A procession of Orphans of both sexes, neatly clothed in a white
    and blue uniform, issue from the castle, followed by Friar Martin,
    and advance towards the stage-door.° *They stop, and the*
    Orphans repeat the following hymn, part of which they
    should have sung within the castle.
ORPHANS [*sing*]
        Throne of justice! lo! we bend.
        Thither dare our hopes ascend,
        Where seraphs, rapt in lightning rays
        Dissolve in mercy's tender blaze?

Hear us! harmless orphans hear!   180
For her who dries our falling tear.
Hush her sorrows; calm her breast:
Give her, what she gives us, rest.

Guard our spotless souls from sin!
Grant us virtue's palm to win!°   185
Clothe the penitent with grace;
And guilt's foul spots efface! efface!

EDMUND   I'll speak to them.
  Sweet children—or thou sanctified conductor,°
  Give me to know what solemn pilgrimage,   190
  What expiation of offences past,
  Thus sadly ye perform? In whose behoof°
  To win a blessing, raise these little suppliants
  Their artless hands to heav'n? Pray pardon too
  A soldier's curiosity.
MARTIN   The dew   195
  Of grace and peace attend your steps. You seem
  A stranger, or you could but know, sir knight,
  That Narbonne's pious Countess dwells within:
  A lady most disconsolate. Her lord,
  Her best-beloved, by untimely fate   200
  Was snatched away in lusty life's full 'vantage—°
  But no account made up! no absolution!°
  Hence scant the distance of a mile he fell.°
  His weeping relict o'er his spot of doom
  A goodly cross erected. Thither we,   205
  At his year's mind, in sad and solemn guise,°
  Proceed to chant our holy dirge, and offer
  Due intercession for his soul's repose.
EDMUND 'Tis fitly done. And dared a voice profane
  Join in the chorus of your holy office,   210
  Myself would kneel for Narbonne's peace.
MARTIN   Young sir,
  It glads my soul to hear such pious breathings°
  From one, whose occupation rarely scans
  The distance 'twixt enjoyment and the tomb.°
  Say, didst thou know the Count?
EDMUND   I knew his son.   215

22

MARTIN Count Edmund? Where sojourns he?
EDMUND   In the grave.
MARTIN Is Edmund dead? Say, how?
EDMUND   He fell at Buda:
  And not to his dishonour.
MARTIN (*aside*)   Welcome sounds!
  I must know more of this—[*To Orphans*] Proceed, my children;
  Short of the cross I'll overtake your steps.   220
ORPHAN GIRL Oh! father, but I dare not pass without you
  By the church-porch. They say the Count sits there,
  With clotted locks, and eyes like burning stars.°
  Indeed I dare not go.
OTHER ORPHANS   Nor I. Nor I.
MARTIN My loves, he will not harm such innocents.   225
  But wait me at the bridge: I'll straight be with ye.°
     Orphans go out reluctantly
FLORIAN I marvel, father, gravity like yours
  Should yield assent to tales of such complexion;
  Permitting them in baby fantasy
  To strike their dangerous root.
MARTIN   I marvel not,   230
  That levity like yours, unhallowed boy,
  Should spend its idle shaft on serious things.
  Your comrade's bearing warrants no such licence.
FLORIAN Think'st thou, because my friend with humble fervour
  Kneels to Omnipotence, each gossip's dream,°   235
  Each village-fable domineers in turn
  His brain's distempered nerves? Think'st thou a soldier
  Must by his calling be an impious braggart?
  Or being not, a superstitious slave?
  True valour, owning no pre-eminence   240
  In equals, dares not wag presumption's tongue
  Against high heav'n.
MARTIN   In us, respect heav'n's servants.
FLORIAN Monks may reach heav'n, but never came from thence.
     Violent storm of thunder and lightning
MARTIN Will this convince thee! Where's the gossip's dream?
  The village-fable now? Hear heav'n's own voice   245
  Condemn impiety!
FLORIAN   Hear heav'n's own voice
  Condemn imposture!

23

EDMUND Here end your dispute.
   The storm comes on.
MARTIN   Yes, you do well to check
   Your comrade's profanation, lest swift justice
   O'ertake his guilt, and stamp his doom in thunder.   250
FLORIAN Father, art thou so read in languages
   Thou canst interpret th'inarticulate
   And quarrelling elements? What says the storm?
   Pronounces it for thee or me? Do none
   Dispute within the compass of its bolt   255
   But we? Is the same loud-voiced oracle
   Definitive for fifty various brawls?
   Or but a shock of clouds to all but us?
   What if two drunkards at this instant hour
   Contend for preference of taste, one ranking   260
   The vines of Burgundy before the juice
   That dances in a foam of brilliant bubbles
   From Champagne's berries, think'st thou thunder speaks
   In favour of the white or ruby grape?°
MARTIN What mockery!—I resign thee to thy fate. (*Going*)   265
     The Orphans run in terrified
FIRST ORPHAN Oh father, save us! save us, holy father!
MARTIN What means this panic?
FIRST ORPHAN   Oh! a storm so dreadful!
   Some demon rides in th'air.
MARTIN   Undoubtedly.
   Could ye distinguish aught?
FIRST ORPHAN   I fell to earth,
   And said the pray'r you taught me against spectres.   270
MARTIN 'Twas well—but none of you, had none the courage
   To face the fiend?
SECOND ORPHAN   I winked, and saw the lightning
   Burst on the monument. The shield of arms
   Shivered to splinters. Ere I could repeat
   An Ave-Mary, down with hideous crash   275
   The cross came tumbling—then I fled—
MARTIN   Retire;
   This is unholy ground. Acquaint the Countess.
   I will not tarry long.
     Exeunt Orphans
          (*To Florian*) Thou mouth accursed,

Repent, and tremble! Wherefore hast thou drawn
On Narbonne's plains, already visited   280
By long calamity, new storms of horror?
The seasons change their course; th'afflicted hind
Bewails his blasted harvest. Meteors ride
The troubled sky, and chase the darkened sun.
Heav'n vindicates its altars: tongues licentious   285
Have scoffed our holy rites, and hidden sins
Have forced th'offended elements to borrow
Tremendous organs! Sixteen fatal years
Has Narbonne's province groaned beneath the hand
Of desolation—for what crimes we know not!°   290
To edge suspended vengeance art thou come?°
EDMUND (*preventing Florian*) My friend, reply not—Father, I lament
This casual jarring—let us crave your pardon.
I feel your country's woes: I loved Count Edmund:
Revere his father's ashes. I will visit°   295
The ruined monument—and at your leisure
Could wish some conf'rence with you.
MARTIN (*aside*)   This is well:
I almost had forgotten—[*to Edmund*] be it so.
Where is your haunt?
EDMUND   A mile without the town;°
Hard by St Bridget's nunnery.
MARTIN   There expect me.°   300
   (*Aside*) I must to Benedict—[*to Edmund*] heav'n's peace be with
      you.
            Exeunt [*Martin, Edmund, and Florian. Enter Countess and
            Peter*]
PETER Return, my gracious lady. Though the storm
Abates its clamours, yonder angry clouds
Are big with spouting fires—do not go forth.
COUNTESS Wretches like me, good Peter, dread no storms.   305
'Tis delicate Felicity that shrinks,
When rocking winds are loud, and wraps itself
Insultingly in comfortable furs,
Thinking how many naked objects want
Like shelter and security. Do thou°   310
Return; I'll seek the monument alone.
PETER No, my good lady, never be it said
That faithful Peter his dear mistress left

Exposed to tempests. These thin-sprinkled hairs
Cannot hold long. If in your service shed,   315
'Twere a just debt—hark! sure I heard a groan!°
Pray let us in again—
COUNTESS   My honest servant,
Thy fear o'er-pow'rs thy love. I heard no groan;
Nor could it scape a sense so quick as mine
At catching misery's expressive note: 320
'Tis my soul's proper language.—Injured shade!
Shade of my Narbonne! if thy scornful spirit
Rode in yon whirlwind, and impelled its bolt—
Implacable! indignant!—'gainst the cross
Raised by thy wretched wife—behold she comes   325
A voluntary victim! Re-assemble
Thy lightnings, and accept her destined head.
PETER For pity, gracious dame! what words are these!
In any mouth less holy they would seem
A magic incantation. Goblins rise   330
At sounds less pow'rful. Last year's 'clipse fell out,°
Because your maidens crossed a gipsy's palm
To know what was become of Beatrice.
COUNTESS And didst thou dare inform them where she dwells?
PETER No, on my duty—true, they think I know;   335
And so thinks Benedict, your confessor.
He says, she could not pass the castle-gates
Without my privity—Well! I had a task
To say him nay. The honour of my keys,°
My office was at stake. No, father, said I,   340
None pass the drawbridge without Peter's knowledge.
How then to beat him from his point?—I had it—
Who knows, quoth I, but sudden malady
Took off the damsel? She might, or might not
Have sepulture within the castle-walls—   345
COUNTESS Peace, fool—and thus thy shrewd equivocation
Has stained my name with murder's foul suspicion!
—Oh peace of virtue! thy true votaries
Quail not with ev'ry blast! I cloak my guilt!
Things foreign rise and load me with their blackness.   350
Erroneous imputation must be borne;
Lest, while unravelling the knotty web,
I lend a clue may vibrate to my heart.

26

—But who comes here?—retire we and observe.
[Countess and Peter] withdraw. [Enter Florian]

FLORIAN 'Tis not far off the time the porter willed me 355
Expect him here. My friend, indulging grief,
Chose no companion of his pensive walk.
Yes, I must serve thee. May my prosp'rous care
Restore thee to thy state, and aid thy love
To make the blooming Adeliza thine! 360

COUNTESS *(aside to Peter)* Methought he spoke of love and Adeliza.
Who may it be?

PORTER   I never heard his name.

COUNTESS *(approaching)* Stranger, did chance or purpose guide thy
    steps
To this lone dwelling?
        Peter makes signs to Florian not to discover their former
        interview

FLORIAN   Pardon, gentle lady,
If curious to behold the pious matron 365
Whom Narbonne's plains obey, I sought this castle,
And deem my wish indulged in viewing thee.

COUNTESS Me, stranger! Is affliction then so rare
It occupies the babbler Fame?—Oh! no.
My sorrows are not new. Austerities 370
And rigid penance tempt no curious eyes.
Nor speaks your air desire of searching out
The house of mourning. Rather should you seek
Some unsunned beauty, some unpractised fair one,
Who thinks the first soft sounds she hears, are love. 375
There may be such at Narbonne: none dwell here,
But melancholy, sorrow, and contrition.

FLORIAN Pleasure has charms; but so has virtue too.
One skims the surface, like the swallow's wing,
And scuds away unnoticed. T'other nymph, 380
Like spotless swans in solemn majesty,
Breasts the full surge, and leaves long light behind.

COUNTESS Your courtly phrase, young knight, bespeaks a birth
Above the vulgar. May I ask, how old°
Your residence in Narbonne? Whence your race?° 385

FLORIAN In Brabant was I born: my father's name,°
The Baron of St Orme. I wait at Narbonne°
My letters of exchange, while passing homewards°

27

To gather my late sire's no mean succession.°
COUNTESS Dead is your father! and unwet your cheek!   390
   Trust me, young sir, a father's guardian arm
   Were well worth all the treasures it withheld.
   A mother might be spared.
FLORIAN   Mothers, like thee,
   Were blessings.
COUNTESS   Curses!
PETER   Lady, 'tis the hour
   Of pray'r. Shall I ring out the chapel-bell?   395
COUNTESS Stranger, I'm summoned hence. Within these walls
   I may not speak with thee: my solemn purpose
   Admits no converse with unsteady youth.
   But at St Bridget's nunnery, to-morrow,
   If you can spare some moments from your pastime,   400
   In presence of the abbess, I would talk with thee.
FLORIAN Madam, I shall not fail.
COUNTESS   Good angels guard thee!
      Exeunt Countess and Peter
FLORIAN (*alone*) So, this is well. My introduction made,
   It follows that I move her for her son.
   She seems of gentler mould than fame bespoke her.   405
   Nor wears her eye the saucy superiority°
   Of bigot pride. Who knows but she may wish
   To shake the trammels of enthusiasm off,°
   And reconcile herself to easier paths
   Of simple goodness? Women oft wear the mask   410
   Of piety to draw respect, or hide
   The loss of it. When age dispels the train
   That waits on beauty, then religion blows°
   Her trumpet, and invites another circle;
   Who, full as false as the preceding crew,   415
   Flatter her problematic mental charms:
   While snuffing incense, and devoutly wanton,
   The Pagan goddess grows a Christian saint,
   And keeps her patent of divinity.
   Well! Edmund, whatsoe'er thy mother be,   420
   I'll put her virtue or hypocrisy
   To the severest test.—Countess, expect me!
      Exit

3.1

*A small garden within the castle, terminated by a long cloister,
beyond which appear some towers*

[*Enter Countess*]
COUNTESS (*alone*) The monument destroyed!—Well! what of that!
Were ev'ry thunderbolt addressed to me,
Not one would miss me. Fate's unerring hand
Darts not at random. Nor, as fractious children
Are chid by proxy, does it deal its wrath°   5
On stocks and stones to frighten, not chastise us.
Omens and prodigies are but begotten
By guilt on pride. We know the doom we merit;°
And self-importance makes us think all nature
Busied to warn us when that doom approaches.   10
Fie! fie! I blush to recollect my weakness.
My Edmund may be dead: the house of Narbonne
May perish from this earth: poor Adeliza
May taste the cup of woe that I have drugged:
But lightnings play not to announce our fate: 15
No whirlwinds rise to prophesy to mites:
Nor, like inquisitors, does heav'n dress up°
In flames the victims it intends to punish,
Making a holiday for greater sinners.
—Greater! oh! impious! Were the faggots placed°   20
Around me, and the fatal torch applied,°
What wretch could view the dreadful apparatus,
And be a blacker criminal than I am?
—Perhaps my virtues but enhance my guilt.
Penance attracts respect, and not reproach.   25
How dare I be esteemed? Be known my crimes!
Let shame anticipate the woes to come!
—Ha! monster! wouldst disclose the frightful scene?
Wouldst teach the vicious world unheard-of sins,
And be a new apostle of perdition?   30
—My Edmund too! has not a mother's hand
Afflicted him enough? Shall this cursed tongue
Brand him with shame indelible, and sting

29

His honest bosom with his mother's scorpions?
Shall Adeliza hear the last of horrors,   35
Ere her pure breast, that sighs for sins it knows not,
Has learned the rudiments of human frailty?
No, hapless maid—
        Enter a Servant
SERVANT   Madam, young Adeliza
Entreats to speak with you. The lady Abbess
Sickens to death.
COUNTESS   Admit her.—
        Exit Servant
                                Now, my soul,   40
Recall thy calm; support alone thy torments;
And envy not the peace thou ne'er must know.
        [*Enter Adeliza*]
COUNTESS Approach, sweet maid. Thy melancholy mien
Speaks thy compassionate and feeling heart.
'Tis a grave lesson for thy blooming years,   45
A scene of dissolution! But when Death
Expands his pinions o'er a bed so holy,
Sure he's a welcome guest.
ADELIZA   Oh! do not doubt it.
The pious matron meets him like a friend
Expected long. And if a tender tear,   50
At leaving your poor ward, melts in her eye,
And downward sinks its fervent ecstasy;
Still does impatience to be gone, betray
Her inward satisfaction. Yesternight,
As weeping, praying, by her couch I knelt,   55
'Behold, my Adeliza, mark', she said,
'How happy the death-bed of innocence!'°
Oh! lady, how those sounds affected me!
I wished to die with her—and oh! forgive me,
If in that moment I forgot my patroness!   60
COUNTESS It was a wish devout. Can that want pardon?
But to confess it, speaks thy native candour.
Thy virtuous, thy ingenuous truth disdains
To hide a thought—
ADELIZA (*falling at her feet*)
                        Oh! can I hear this praise,
And not expire in blushes at thy feet?   65

        30

COUNTESS What means this passion?
ADELIZA   Ah! recall thy words:
    Thy Adeliza merits no encomium.
COUNTESS Thou art too modest. Praise is due to truth.
    Thou shouldst not seek it; nor should I withhold it.
ADELIZA For pity, spare me.—No, my honoured mistress,   70
    I merit not—oh! no, my guilty heart
    Deserves thy frowns—I cannot speak—
COUNTESS   Be calm:
    Thou know'st no guilt. Unfold thy lab'ring breast.
    Say, am not I thy friend? Me canst thou fear?
ADELIZA Can I fear aught beside? Fear aught but goodness?   75
    Has not thy lavish bounty clothed me, fed me?
    Hast thou not taught me virtue? Whom on earth,
    But such a benefactress, such a friend,
    Can Adeliza fear? Alas! she knows
    No other friend! and Christian fortitude   80
    Dreads not a foe. Methinks I would have said
    That Christian innocence—but shame restrained
    My conscious tongue—I am *not* innocent!°
COUNTESS Thou dearest orphan, to my bosom come,
    And vent thy little sorrows. Purity°   85
    Like thine affrights itself with fancied guilt.
    I'll be thy confessor; and trust me, love,
    Thy penance will be light.
ADELIZA   In vain you cheer me.
    Say, what is guilt, but to have known a thought
    I blushed to tell thee? To have lent mine ear,   90
    For three long weeks, to sounds I did not wish
    My patroness should hear! Ah! when till now
    Have I not hoped thy presence, thought it long,
    If two whole days detained thee from our mass?
    When have I wept, but when thou hast refused   95
    To let thy Adeliza call thee mother?
    I know I was not worthy of such honour,
    Too splendid for a child of charity.
    I am now most unworthy! I, undone,
    Have not desired thy presence; have not thought it   100
    Long, if two days thou hast declined our mass.
    Other discourse than thine has charmed mine ear;
    Nor dare I now presume to call thee mother!

COUNTESS My lovely innocence, restrain thy tears.
    I know thy secret; know, why beats and throbs   105
    Thy little heart with unaccustomed tumult.
ADELIZA Impossible—Oh! let me tell thee all—
COUNTESS No; I will tell it thee. Thou hast conversed
    With a young knight—
ADELIZA   Amazement! Who informed thee?
    Pent in her chamber, sickness has detained°   110
    Our Abbess from the parlour. There I saw him,
    Oft as he came, alone.
COUNTESS   He talked of love;
    And wooed thee for his bride.
ADELIZA   He did.
COUNTESS (*aside*)   'Tis well:
    This is the stranger I beheld this morning.
    [*To Adeliza*] His father dead, he hastes to take possession   115
    Of his paternal fortunes—is't not so?
ADELIZA He sorrows for a father—something too
    He uttered of a large inheritance
    That should be his—in truth I marked it not.
COUNTESS But when he spoke of love, thy very soul   120
    Hung on his lips. Say, canst thou not repeat
    Each word, each syllable? His accent too
    Thou noted'st: still it rings upon thine ear.
    And then his eyes—they looked such wondrous truth;
    Art thou not sure he cannot have deceived thee?   125
ADELIZA Alas! my noble mistress, thou dost mock
    Poor Adeliza—what can I reply!
COUNTESS The truth. Thy words have ever held its language.
    Say, dost thou love this stranger? Hast thou pledged
    Thy faith to him?   130
ADELIZA Angels forbid! What faith have I to give?
    Can I dispose of aught without thy leave?
COUNTESS Insinuating softness!—still thou turnest
    Aside my question. Thou dost love this stranger.
ADELIZA Yes, with such love as that I feel for thee.   135
    His virtues I revere: his earnest words
    Sound like the precepts of a tender parent:
    And, next to thee, methinks I could obey him.
COUNTESS Aye, as his wife.
ADELIZA   Oh! never. What, to lose him,

As thou thy Narbonne!
COUNTESS   Check not, Adeliza,   140
  Thy undeveloped passion. Should this stranger
  Prove what my wish has formed, and what his words
  Report him, it would bless my woeful days
  To see thee placed above the reach of want,
  And distant from this residence of sorrow.   145
ADELIZA What! wouldst thou send me from thee! oh! for pity!
  I cannot, will not leave thee. If thy goodness
  Withdraw its bounty, at thy castle-gate
  I'll wait and beg those alms thy gracious hand
  To none refuses. I shall see thee pass,   150
  And, passed, will kiss thy footsteps—wilt thou spurn me?
  Well then, I'll die and bless thee.—Oh! this stranger!
  'Tis he has done this; he has drawn thy anger
  On thy poor ward!—I'll never see him more.
COUNTESS Be calm, my lovely orphan; hush thy fears.   155
  Heav'n knows how fondly, anxiously I love thee!
  The stranger's not to blame. Myself will task him,°
  And know if he deserves thee. Now retire,
  Nor slack thy duty to th'expiring saint.
  A lover must not weigh against a friend.   160
    Exit Adeliza
  And lo! where comes the friar. 'Twere not fit
  He knew my purpose. Benedict, I fear,
  Has views on this side heav'n.
    [*Enter Benedict*]
BENEDICT   The dew of grace°
  Rest on this dwelling!
COUNTESS   Thanks, my ghostly friend.°
  But sure, or I mistake, in your sad eye   165
  I spell affliction's signature. What woes
  Call for the scanty balm this hand can pour?
BENEDICT You, lady, and you only need that balm.
COUNTESS To tutor my unapt and ill-schooled nature
  You come then—good my confessor, a truce   170
  With doctrines and authority. If aught
  Can medicate a soul unsound like mine,
  Good deeds must operate the healthful change,
  And penance cleanse it to receive the blessing.
  Shall I, for faith, shall I, for but believing   175

What 'tis my int'rest to believe, efface
The stains, which, though believing, I contracted?
BENEDICT Lady, your subtle wit, like daring infants,
Sports with a weight will crush it—but no more.
It is not mine to argue, but pronounce.   180
The church, on rock of adamant established,
Now inch by inch disputes not its domain.
Heav'n's law promulged, it rests, obedience follow.°
And when, supreme, it taxes that obedience,
Not at impracticable, vain perfection,   185
But rates its prodigality of blessings
At the slight credence of its pow'r to grant them,°
Shall man with stoic pride reject the boon,
And cry, 'We will do more, we will deserve it'?°
COUNTESS Deserve it!—oh! have all your sainted hosts,   190
Your choirs of martyrs, or your clouds of cherubim,
Deserved to feel the transport but of hope?
Away; nor tell me of this holy juggle
'Twixt faith and conscience. Shall the latter roam,
Wasting and spoiling with a ruffian hand,   195
While her accomplice faith, wrapped up at home
In proud security of self-existence,
Thinks that existence shall absolve them both?
BENEDICT 'Twas not to war with words, so heav'n's my judge,
That your poor-rated servant sought your presence.   200
I came with charitable friendly purpose
To soothe—but wherefore mitigate your griefs?
You mock my friendship, and miscall my zeal.
Since, then, to counsel, comfort, and reproof
Obdurate—learn the measure of your woes.   205
Learn, if the mother's fortitude can brave
The bolt the woman's arrogance defied.°
COUNTESS The mother! said'st thou?
BENEDICT   Yes, imperious dame:
Yes, 'twas no vision raised by dreams and fumes,
Begot 'twixt nightly fear and indigestion: 210
Nor was it artifice and pious fraud,
When but this morning I announced thy Edmund
Was numbered with the dead—
COUNTESS   Priest, mock me not!
Nor dally with a mother's apprehension.

34

Lives, or lives not, my son?
BENEDICT   Woman, heav'n mocks thee!   215
  On Buda's plain thy slaughtered Edmund lies.
  An unbeliever's weapon cleft his heart;
  But 'twas thy unbelief that poised the shaft,
  And sped its aim.
COUNTESS   To heav'n's high will I bow me.
  Oh! may its joys be open to his soul,   220
  Though closed to mine for ever!
BENEDICT   Then you loved him!
COUNTESS Loved him!—oh! nature, bleeding at my heart,
  Hearest thou this? Loved him!—ha! whither!—rage,
  Be dumb—Now listen, monk, nor dare reply
  Beyond my purpose. In the grave, thou say'st,   225
  My Edmund sleeps—how didst thou learn his fate?
BENEDICT No angel whispered it; no demon spoke it.
  Thou, by the self-same means I learned, may'st learn it.
COUNTESS Be brief.
BENEDICT   Then—but what boots his life or death°
  To a poor taunted friar—Benedict,   230
  Leave this proud mistress of the fleeting hour,
  Ere the destroying angel's kindling brand
  Smokes in the tow'rs of Narbonne—
COUNTESS   Hold! presumptuous!
  I am thy mistress yet: nor will I brook°
  Such insolent reproof. Produce thy warrant,°   235
  Assure my Edmund's death—or dread his vengeance!°
  Severely shall he question ev'ry throb
  His agonizing mother now endures.
BENEDICT My warrant is at hand—
     Benedict goes out and returns with Edmund
                This gentleman
  Beheld thy Edmund breathless on the ground.   240
COUNTESS Ha! is this sorcery? or is't my husband?
     [Countess] swoons
EDMUND Stand off, and let me clasp her in my arms!
  The flame of filial fondness shall revive
  The lamp of life, repay the breath she gave,
  And waken all the mother in her soul.   245
BENEDICT Ha! who art thou then?
EDMUND   Do not my fears tell thee!

35

[*To Countess*] Look up! Oh ever dear! behold thy son!
It is thy Edmund's voice; blessed, if thy eyes
Awake to bless him—soft! her pulse returns;
She breathes—oh! speak. Dear parent, mother, hear!   250
'Tis Edmund—[*To Benedict*] Friar, wherefore is this horror?
Am I then deadly to her eyes?—Dumb still!
Speak, though it be to curse me—I have killed her!
My brain grows hot—
BENEDICT   My lord, restrain your passion;
See! she revives—
EDMUND   Oh! if these lips, that quiver   255
With dread of thy disdain, have force to move thee
With nature's, duty's, or affection's voice,
Feel how I print thy hand with burning zeal,
Though tortured at this awful interval!
Art thou, or not, a mother?
COUNTESS   Ha! where am I?   260
Why do you hold me? Was it not my Narbonne?
I saw him—on my soul I did—
EDMUND   Alas!
She raves—recall thy wand'ring apprehension—°
It was no phantom: [*kneeling*] at thy feet behold—
COUNTESS Ha! whom! quick, answer—Narbonne, dost thou live?   265
Or comest to transport me to perdition?
BENEDICT Madam, behold your son: he kneels for pardon.
And I, I innocent, I ignorant
Of what he was, implore it too—
COUNTESS   Distraction!
What means this complicated scene of horrors?   270
Why thus assail my splitting brain?—be quick—
Art thou my husband winged from other orbs°
To taunt my soul? What is this dubious form,
Impressed with ev'ry feature I adore,
And ev'ry lineament I dread to look on?   275
Art thou my dead or living son?
EDMUND   I am
Thy living Edmund. Let these scalding tears
Attest th'existence of thy suff'ring son.
COUNTESS Ah! touch me not—
EDMUND   How!—in that cruel breast°
Revive then all sensations, but affection?   280

36

Why so adored the memory of the father,
And so abhorred the presence of the son?
But now, and to thy eyes I seemed my father—
At least for that resemblance-sake embrace me.

COUNTESS Horror on horror! Blasted be thy tongue!   285
 What sounds are those?

BENEDICT   Lady, though I excuse not
 This young lord's disobedience, his contrition
 Bespeaks no rebel principle. I doubt not,
 Your blessing first obtained and gracious pardon,
 But soon as morning streaks the ruddy East,   290
 He will obey your pleasure, and return
 To stranger climes—

EDMUND   'Tis false; I will not hence.
 I have been fooled too long, too long been patient.
 Nor are my years so green as to endure
 The manacles of priests and nurseries.   295
 Am I not Narbonne's prince? who shall rule here
 But Narbonne? Have I sapped my country's laws,°
 Or played the tyrant? Who shall banish me?
 Am I a recreant knight? has cowardice
 Disgraced the line of heroes I am sprung from?   300
 Shall I then skulk, hide my inglorious head?
 Or does it please your worship's gravity
 Dispatch me on some sleeveless pilgrimage,°
 Like other noble fools, to win you empires,
 While you at home mock our credulity,   305
 The masters of our wealth, our states, and wives?

COUNTESS (aside) Brave youth! there spoke his sire. How my soul
    yearns
 To own its genuine offspring!—[To Edmund] Edmund, hear me!
 Thou art my son, and I will prove a mother.
 But I'm thy sovereign too. This state is mine.   310
 Learn to command, by learning to obey.
 Though frail my sex, I have a soul as masculine
 As any of thy race. This very monk,°
 Lord as thou thinkest of my ductile conscience,
 Quails—look if 'tis not true—when I command.   315
 Retire thee to the village. 'Tis not ripe
 As yet my purpose—Benedict, attend me.°
 To-morrow, Edmund, shalt thou learn my pleasure.

Exeunt Countess and Benedict

EDMUND (*alone*) Why, this *is* majesty. Sounds of such accent
  Ne'er struck mine ear till now. Commanding sex!   320
  Strength, courage, all our boasted attributes,
  Want estimation; ev'n the pre-eminence
  We vaunt in wisdom, seems a borrowed ray,
  When virtue deigns to speak with female organs.
  Yes, Oh my mother, I *will* learn t'obey: 325
  I *will* believe, that, harsh as thy decrees,
  They wear the warrant of benign intention.
  Make but the blooming Adeliza mine,
  And bear, of me unquestioned, Narbonne's sceptre;
  Till life's expiring lamp by intervals   330
  Throws but a fainter and a fainter flash,
  And then relumes its wasted oil no more.
      Exit

4.1

[*The garden*]°

[*Enter Benedict and Martin*]

MARTIN I know thy spirit well; know how it labours,
When curbed, and driv'n to wear the mask of art.°
But till this hour I have not seen thy passions
Boil o'er the bounds of prudence. So impetuous,
And so reserved!

BENEDICT   Mistake me not, good brother: 5
I want no confidence: I know thy faith.°
But can I to thy naked eye unfold,
What I dare scarce reveal to my own bosom?
I would not know one half that I suspect,
Till I have acted as if not suspecting.   10

MARTIN How, brother! thou a casuist! and apply°
To thy own breast those damning subtleties,
Which cowards with half-winking consciences
Purchase of us, when they would sin secure,
And hope the penalty will all be ours!   15

BENEDICT Brother, this moment is too big with action
To waste on bootless curiosity.
When I try sins upon the touchstone conscience,
It is for others' use, not for my own.
'Tis time enough to make up our account,   20
When we confess and kneel for absolution.

MARTIN Still does thy genius soar above mankind!
How many fathers of our holy church
In Benedict I view!

BENEDICT   No flattery, brother.
'Tis true the church owes Benedict some thanks.   25
For her, I have forgot I am a man.°
For her, each virtue from my breast I banish.
No laws I know but her prosperity;
No country, but her boundless acquisitions.
Who dares be true to country, king, or friend,   30
If enemies to Rome, are Benedict's foes.

MARTIN Has it then gone so far? does she speak out?

Is Edmund too infected with like errors?
BENEDICT Both, brother, both are thinking heretics.
   I could forgive them, did some upstart sect   35
   With sharper rigours charm their headlong zeal.
   But they, in sooth, must *reason*—curses light
   On the proud talent! 'twill at last undo us.
   When men are gorged with each absurdity
   Their subtle wits can frame, or we adopt;   40
   For very novelty they will fly to sense,
   And we shall fall before that idol, fashion.
MARTIN Fear not a reign so transient. Statesmen too
   Will join to stem the torrent: or new follies
   Replace the old. Each chieftain that attacks us   45
   Must grow the pope of his own heresy.
   E'en stern philosophy, if once triumphant,
   Shall frame some jargon, and exact obedience
   To metaphysic nonsense worse than ours.°
   The church is but a specious name for empire,   50
   And will exist wherever fools have fears.
   Rome is no city; 'tis the human heart;
   And there suffice it if we plant our banners.
   Each priest cannot command—and thence comes sects.°
   Obdurate Zeno and our great Ignatius°   55
   Are of one faith, and differ but for power.
BENEDICT So be it—therefore interest bids us crush°
   This cockatrice and her egg: or we shall see
   The singing saints of Savoy's neighb'ring vale°
   Fly to the covert of her shadowy wings,   60
   And foil us at our own dexterity.
   Already to those vagrants she inclines;
   As if the rogues, that preach reform to others,
   Like idiots, minded to reform themselves.
MARTIN Be cautious, brother: you may lose the lady.   65
BENEDICT She is already lost—or ne'er was ours.
   I cannot dupe, and therefore must destroy her:
   Involve her house in ruin so prodigious,
   That neither she nor Edmund may survive it.
MARTIN How may this be accomplished?
BENEDICT   Ask me not.   70
   From hints long treasured up, from broken phrase
   In frenzy dropped, but vibrating from truth:

Nay, from her caution to explain away
What the late tempest of her soul had uttered,
I guess her fatal secret—or, no matter— 75
Say, I do not—by what she has forbidden,
I know what should be done—then haste thee, brother;
Facilitate Count Edmund's interview
With Adeliza; nourish their young passion—
Curse them—and if you can—why—join their hands. 80

MARTIN I tremble!

BENEDICT   Dastard, tremble, if we fail.°
What can we fear, when we have ruined them?
        A deep-toned voice is heard

VOICE Forbear!

BENEDICT   Ha! whence that sound?

VOICE (*again*)   Forbear!

BENEDICT   Again!
Comes it from heav'n or hell!

VOICE (*again*)   Forbear!

MARTIN   Good angels,
Protect me!—Benedict, thy unholy purpose— 85
        A procession of friars, chanting a funeral anthem, and followed
        by Adeliza, advances slowly from a cloister at the end of the
        stage

FRIARS [*chant*]

THE ANTHEM°

Forbear! forbear! forbear!
The pious are heav'n's care.
Lamentations ill become us,
When the good are ravished from us.
The pangs of death but smooth the way 90
To visions of eternal day.

BENEDICT (*aside to Martin*) Now, man of aspen conscience! lo! the gods,
That sentence Benedict's unholy purpose!
Art thou a priest? wast thou initiated
In each fond mummery that subdues the vulgar, 95
And standest thou appalled at our own thunders?

MARTIN Who trembled first? It was thy guilty conscience
That gave th'alarm to mine.

BENEDICT   Peace, dotard, peace!
   Nor when the lamb is nigh, must eagles wrangle.
   (*To Adeliza*) Fair saint, give us to know why flow these
     tears;   100
   Why sighs that gentle bosom? and why chant ye
   That heav'n-invoking soul-dissolving dirge?
ADELIZA Ah! holy father, art thou then to learn°
   The pious Abbess is at peace? We go
   To bear her parting blessing to the Countess.   105
BENEDICT It must not be. Occasions of much import
   Engross her faculties. By me she wills you
   Restrain your steps within the cloister's pale,°
   Nor grant access but to one stranger knight.
ADELIZA Is't possible? Can my dear mistress bar   110
   Her faithful handmaid from her gracious presence?
   Shall I not pour my sorrows in her bosom,
   And moisten it with grief and gratitude?
   Two friends were all poor Adeliza's wealth.
   Lo! one is gone to plead the orphan's cause.   115
   My patroness, like Tobit's guardian spirit,°
   Confirms my steps, and points to realms of glory.
   She will not quit me in this vale of bondage;
   She must be good, who teaches what is goodness.
BENEDICT (*aside*) Indeed! my pretty prattler!—then am I   120
   As sound a saint as e'er the rubric boasted.
      [*Enter Countess*]
   —Ha! 'tis the Countess—now for my obedience.
   (*To Adeliza*) Young lady, much I marvel at these murmurs.
   Just sense and sober piety still dictate
   The Countess's commands. With truth I say it,   125
   My sins diminish, as I copy her.
COUNTESS What voices heard I? Does my rebel son
   Attempt against my peace?—Ha! Adeliza!
   I charged thee guard thy convent—wherefore then
   This disobedience?
BENEDICT   Madam, I was urging   130
   The fitness of your orders; but vain youth
   Scoffed my importunate rebuke—
ADELIZA   Oh! no.
   I am the thing you made me. Crush me, spurn me,
   I will not murmur. Should you bid me die,
   I know 'twere meant in kindness.

COUNTESS   Bid *thee* die!   135
  My own detested life but lingers round thee!
  [*Aside*] Ha! what a glance was there! it spoke resemblance
  To all I hate, adore—[*To Adeliza*] My child, retire:
  I am much discomposed—the good old Abbess
  Claims thy attendance.
ADELIZA   Mercy crown her soul!   140
  She needs no duty we can pay her now!
COUNTESS How! art thou desolate! not a friend left°
  To guard thy innocence?—oh! wretched maid!
  Must thou be left to spoilers? or worse, worse,°
  To the fierce onset of thy own dire passions?   145
  Oh! is it come to this?
ADELIZA   My noble mistress,
  Can Adeliza want a minist'ring angel,
  When sheltered by thy wing?—yet Benedict
  Says, I must shun this hospitable roof.
  Indeed I thought it hard.
COUNTESS   Did Benedict,   150
  Did he, audacious, dare forbid my child,
  My little orphan to embrace her—curses
  Swell in my throat—hence—or they fall on thee.
ADELIZA Alas! for pity! how have I offended?°
BENEDICT Madam, it is the pupil of your care,   155
  Your favoured child—
COUNTESS   Who told thee so? Be dumb
  For ever!—What, art thou combined with Edmund,
  To dash me down the precipice? Churchman, I tell thee,
  I view it with impatience. I could leap
  And meet the furies—but must *she* fall with me!°   160
BENEDICT (*aside*) Yes, and thy Edmund too. [*To Countess*] Be
    patient, lady:
  This fair domain, thou know'st, acknowledges
  The sovereignty of the church. Thy rebel son
  Dares not attempt—
COUNTESS   Again I bid thee peace.
  There is no question of Lord Edmund. Leave us: 165
  I have to talk with her alone.
BENEDICT (*aside to Martin*)   Now tremble
  At voices supernatural; and forfeit
  The spoils the tempest throws into our lap.
    Exeunt Benedict and Martin

43

COUNTESS Now, Adeliza, summon all thy courage.
   Retrace my precepts past: nor let a tear   170
   Profane a moment that's worth martyrdom.
   Remember patience is the Christian's courage.
   Stoics have bled, and demigods have died.
   A Christian's task is harder—'tis to suffer.
ADELIZA Alas! have I not learnt the bitter lesson?   175
   Have I not borne *thy* woes? What is to come
   Can tax my patience with a ruder trial?°
COUNTESS Oh! yes, thou must do more. Adversity
   Has various arrows. When the soul is steeled
   By meditation to encounter sorrow,   180
   The foe of man shifts his artillery,
   And drowns in luxury and careless softness°
   The breast he could not storm. Canst thou bear wealth,
   And pleasure's melting couch? Thou hast known virtue
   But at a scanty board. She has awaked thee   185
   To chilling vapours in the midnight vault,
   And beckoned thee to hardships, tears, and penance.
   Wilt thou acknowledge the divine instructress,
   When siren pleasures lap thee in delights?°
ADELIZA If such the witchery that waits on guilt,   190
   Why should I seek th'enchantress and her wiles?
   The virgin veil shall guard my spotless hours,°
   Assure my peace, and saint me for hereafter.
COUNTESS It cannot be—
   To Narbonne thou must bid a last adieu!   195
   And with the stranger knight depart a bride.
ADELIZA Unhappy me! too sure I have o'erburdened
   Thy charity, if thou wouldst drive me from thee.
   Restrain thy alms, dear lady. I have learnt
   From our kind sister-hood the needle's art.   200
   My needle and thy smiles will life support.
   Pray let me bring my last embroidery;
   'Tis all by my own hand. Indeed I meant it
   For my kind lady's festival.
COUNTESS [*aside*]   Great justice!°
   Does this stroke pierce not deep enough? These tears,   205
   Wrung from my vital fondness, scald they not
   Worse than the living coal that sears the limbs?
ADELIZA Alas! thou hearest not! what grief o'erwhelms thee?

Why darts thy eye into my inmost soul?
Then vacant, motionless, arrests its course,   210
And seems not to perceive what it reads there?
My much-loved patroness!
COUNTESS   Oh Adeliza,
Thy words now slake, and now augment my fever!
But oh! ere reason quits this lab'ring frame,
While I dare weep these tears of anguish o'er thee—   215
Unutterable, petrifying anguish!—
Hear my last breath. Avoid the scorpion pleasure.
Death lurks beneath the velvet of his lip,
And but to think him over, is perdition!°
—Oh retrospect of horror!—to the altar!   220
Haste, Adeliza—vow thou wilt be wretched!
ADELIZA Dost thou then doom me to eternal sorrows?
Hast thou deceived me? is not virtue, happiness?
COUNTESS I know not that. I know that guilt is torture!
ADELIZA Sure pestilence has flapped his baleful wing,   225
And shed its poison o'er thy saintlike reason,
When thou so patient, holy, so resigned,
Doubtest of virtue's health, of virtue's peace!
—But 'tis to try me—[*produces an object*] look upon this relic:
'Twas the good Abbess's bequest. 'Twill chase   230
The fiend that walks at twilight.
COUNTESS [*aside*]   How she melts me!
What have I said—[*To Adeliza*] my lovely innocence,
Thou art my only thought—oh! wast thou formed
The child of sin?—and dare I not embrace thee?
Must I with eager ecstasy gaze on thee,   235
Yet curse the hour that stamped thee with a being!
ADELIZA Alas! was I then born the child of sin!
Who were my parents? I will pray for them.
COUNTESS Oh! if the bolt must come, here let it strike me!
        (*Flinging herself on the ground*)
Nature! these feelings were thy gift. Thou knowest   240
How ill I can resist thy forceful impulse.
If these emotions are imputed to me,
I have one sin I cannot yet repent of!
ADELIZA Oh! raise thee from the earth. Shall I behold thee
Prostrate, embracing an unfriended beggar?   245
Or dost thou mock me still? What is my lot?

45

Wilt thou yet cherish me? Or do the great
Exalt us but in sport, lend us a taste,
A vision of enjoyment, and then dash us
To poverty, more poignant by comparison?   250
Sure *I* could never wanton with affliction!

COUNTESS Ah! canst thou doubt this conflict of the soul!
Mock thee!—oh! yes, there are such savage natures,
That will deride thy woes—and thou must bear it—
With foul reproach will gall thy spotless soul,   255
And taunt thee with a crime past thy conceiving.
Oh! 'tis to shield thee from this world of sorrows,
That thou must fly, must wed, must never view
The tow'rs of Narbonne more; must never know
The doom reserved for thy sad patroness!   260

ADELIZA Who threatens thy dear life! Recall thy son.°
His valiant arm will stem a host of foes,
Replace thy lord, and woo thee to be happy.

COUNTESS Ha! little imp of darkness! dost thou wear°
That angel form to gird me with upbraidings!°   265
Fly, ere my rage forget distinction, nature,
And make a medley of unheard-of crimes.°
Fly, ere it be too late—

ADELIZA   For pity!
COUNTESS   Hence!
Pity would bid me stab thee, while the charm°
Of ignorance locks thee in its happy slumbers.   270

ADELIZA Alas! she raves—I will call help.
        Exit [Adeliza]

COUNTESS (*alone; after a long pause, in which she looks tenderly after
    Adeliza*)
                              She's gone.
—That pang, great God, was my last sacrifice!—
Now recollect thyself, my soul! Consummate
The pomp of horror with tremendous coolness.°
'Tis fit that reason punish passion's crime.   275
—Reason!—alas! 'tis one of my convulsions!
Now it empow'rs me past myself: now leaves me
Exhausted, spiritless, eyeing with despair
The heights I cannot reach. Then madness comes,
Imperial fool! and promises to waft me   280
Beyond the grin of scorn—but who sits there,

46

Supereminent?—'tis conscience!—frenzy, shield me!
I know the foe—see! see! he points his lance!
He plunges it all flaming in my soul,
And down I sink, lost in eternal anguish! 285
    [*Countess*] *runs out.* [*Enter Benedict and Adeliza*]
ADELIZA She is not here. Shall we not follow her?
Such agonies of passion! sure some demon
Assaults her. Thou shalt pray by her. Indeed
I tremble for her life.
BENEDICT   Thou know'st her not.
Her transport is fictitious. 'Tis the coinage° 290
Of avarice and caprice. Dost thou not see
Her bounty wearies? While thy babbling years
Wore the trick of novelty, thou wast her plaything.
The charity of the great must be amused.
Mere merit surfeits it; affliction kills it. 295
The sick must jest and gambol to attract
Their pity—come, I'll warrant, thou hast wept,
And told her heav'n would register each ducat
Her piety had spared to clothe and feed thee.
Go to; thou hast estranged her; and she means 300
To drive thee hence, lest thou upbraid her change.
ADELIZA Upbraid my patroness! I! I upbraid her,
Who see her now the angel that she will be!
How knew I virtue, goodness, but from her!
Her lessons taught me heav'n; her life revealed it. 305
The wings of gratitude must bear me thither,
Or I deserve not Paradise.
BENEDICT   Thou art young.
Thy novice ear imbibes each silver sound,
And deems the music warbled all by truth.
Grey hairs are not fooled thus. I know this Countess: 310
An errant heretic. She scoffs the church.°
When did her piety adorn our altars?
What holy garments glisten with her gifts?
The fabric of our convent threatens ruin—
Does she repair it?—no. On lazy lepers, 315
On soldiers maimed and swearing from the wars
She lavishes her wealth—but note it, young one;
Her days are numbered; and thou shalt do wisely
To quit her ere the measure is complete.

ADELIZA Alas! she bids me go. She bids me wed   320
   The stranger knight that wooed me at our parlour.
BENEDICT And thou shalt take her at her word. Myself
   Will join your hands—and lo! in happy hour
   Who comes to meet her boon.
     [*Enter Edmund*]
EDMUND   In tears!—that cowl
   Shall not protect th'injurious tongue, that dares   325
   Insult thy innocence—for sure, thou dear one,
   Thou hast no sins to weep.
BENEDICT   My gracious lord,
   Yourself and virgin coyness must be chidden,
   If my fair scholar wears the mien of sadness.
   'Tis but a blush that melts in modest showers.   330
EDMUND Unriddle, priest. My soul is too impatient,
   To wait th'impertinence of flow'ry dialect.
BENEDICT Then briefly thus. The Countess wills me join
   Your hand with this fair maiden's—now, my lord,
   Is my poor language nauseous?
EDMUND   Is it possible?   335
   Dost thou consent, sweet passion of my soul?
   May I then clasp thee to my heart?
ADELIZA   Forbear!°
   It must not be.—Thou shalt not wed a beggar.
EDMUND A beggar! Thou art riches, opulence.
   The flaming ruby and the dazzling di'mond,   340
   Set in the world's first diadem, could not add°
   A ray to thy least charm!—for pity, grant me
   To breathe my warmth into this marble hand.
ADELIZA Never!—this orphan, this abandoned wanderer,
   Taunted with poverty, with shameful origin,   345
   Dowered with no lot but scorn, shall ne'er bestow
   That, her sole portion, on a lordly husband.
BENEDICT My lord, the Countess is my gracious mistress:
   My duty bade me to report her words.
   It seems her charities circumscribe her wishes.°   350
   This goodly maiden has full long experienced
   Her amplest bounty. Other piteous objects
   Call for her largesse. Lovely Adeliza,
   Placed in your arms, can never feel affliction.
   This the good Countess knows—

EDMUND   By my sire's soul   355
   I will not thank her. Has she dared to scorn thee,
   Thou beauteous excellence?—then from this hour
   Thou art her equal. In her very presence
   I will espouse thee. Let us seek the proud one!
   —Nay, no resistance, love!
BENEDICT (*aside*)   By heav'n all's lost,   360
   Should they meet now—(*Aside to Edmund*) My lord, a word. The
     maiden
   Is tutored to such awe, she ne'er will yield
   Consent, should but a frown dart from the Countess.
   But now, and she enjoined your marriage. Better
   Profit of that behest—
EDMUND   I tell thee, monk,°   365
   My haughty soul will not—
BENEDICT (*in a low voice*)   Pray be advised.
   Heav'n knows how dear I tender your felicity.
   The chapel is few paces hence—nay, lead her
   With gentle wooing, nor alarm her fears:
   Arrived there, I will speedily pronounce   370
   The solemn words—
EDMUND   Well, be it so. [*To Adeliza*] My fair one,
   This holy man advises well. To heaven
   We will address our vows, and ask its pleasure.
   Come, come; I will not be refused—
ADELIZA   Yes, heav'n!
   To thee I fly; thou art my only refuge.   375
      Exeunt

5.1

[The garden]°

Enter Benedict

BENEDICT The business is dispatched. Their hands are joined.
    The puling moppet struggled with her wishes;
    Invoked each saint to witness her refusal:
    Nor heeded, though I swore their golden harps
    Were tuned to greet her hymeneal hour.   5
    Th'impetuous Count, fired with th'impure suggestion,°
    As if descending clouds had spread their pillows
    To meet the pressure of his eager transports,
    Would have forerun the rites. The maid, affrighted
    At such tumultuous unaccustomed onset,   10
    Sunk lifeless on the pavement. Hastily
    I mumbled o'er the spell that binds them fast,
    Like an envenomed robe, to scorch each other
    With mutual ruin—thus am I revenged.°
    Proud dame of Narbonne, lo! a bare-foot monk   15
    Thus pays thy scorn, thus vindicates his altars.
    Nor while this woollen frock shall wrap our order,°
    Shall e'en the lillied monarchs of our realm°
    Be placed so high, but a poor friar's knife°
    Shall fell their tow'ring grandeur to the earth,   20
    Oft as they scant obedience to the church.°
    [Enter Peter]

PETER Ah! woe of woes! good father, haste thee in,
  And speak sweet words of comfort to our mistress.
  Her brain is much disturbed—I fear some spell,
  Or naughty bev'rage—will you not in and pray by her?°   25
  In sooth she needs your pray'rs.

BENEDICT *(coldly)*   She scorns my pray'rs.

PETER Oh! no; but now she called for you. Pray seek
    her.°

BENEDICT I can administer no comfort to her.

PETER Yes, yes, you can. They say the foul fiend dreads
  A scholar—Tut, your holy wit can pose him,   30
  Or bind him to the red waves of the ocean.°

Oh! he afflicts her gentle spirit, and vomits
Strange menaces and terrible from her mouth!
Then he is sullen; gags her lab'ring lips,
And she replies not—

BENEDICT   Goodman exorcist,   35
Thy pains are unavailing. Her sins press her.
Guilt has unhinged her reason.

PETER   Beshrew thy heart,
Thou dost asperse her. I know those are paid
For being saints that—

BENEDICT   Stop that tongue profane!°
Thou art infected with her heresies.   40
Judgments already have o'erta'en thy mistress.°
Thou at thy peril leave her to her fate.

PETER Father, belike there is a different heaven
For learnèd clerks and such poor men as I am.°
Me it behoves to have such humble virtues   45
As suit my simple calling. To my masters
For raiment, food, for salary, and protection
My honest heart owes gratitude. They took me
From drudgery to guard their honoured persons.
Why am I called a man of worship? Why,°   50
As up the chancel I precede my lady,
Do th'vassals of the castle, ranged in rows,
Bow e'en to Peter—why? but, by the rood,
Because she placed this silver-garnished staff
In Peter's hand. Why, but because this robe,   55
Floating with seemly tufts, was her gift too.
For honours of such note owe I not thanks?
Were my life much to sacrifice for hers?

BENEDICT Peace with thy saucy lecture, or harangue
Thy maudlin fellows o'er the hall's dull embers   60
With this thy gossiping morality.—°
Now answer—mentions she her son?

PETER   Ah me!
I had forgotten—this old brain—'tis true,
'Tis very true—she raves upon her son,
And thinks he came in vision.

BENEDICT   'Twas no vision.   65

PETER How!—heav'nly fathers!

BENEDICT   He has spoken with her.

PETER And I not see him!—go to; it could not be.
   How did he pass the gate?
BENEDICT   I tell thee, Edmund,
   Thy quondam master's son, has seen his mother;
   Is but few paces hence.
PETER   Oh! joyous sounds!   70
   Where is my noble lord?
BENEDICT   Here—and undone.
     [*Enter Florian*]
FLORIAN Sure the foul fogs, that hang in lazy clouds
   O'er yonder moat, infect the moping air,°
   And steam with frenzy's melancholy fumes.
   But now and I met Edmund—with a voice   75
   Appalled and hollow like a parricide's,
   He told me he was wedded. When I asked
   To see his bride, he groaned, and said his joys
   Were blasted ere accomplished. As he urged
   His suit, the maiden's tears and shrieks had struck°   80
   On his sick fancy like his mother's cries!
   Th'idea writhing from his brain, had won
   His eye-balls, and he thought he saw his mother!
   —This ague of contagious bigotry
   Has gained almost on me. Methinks yon monk   85
   Might fell me with a chaplet.—Edmund left me°
   Abruptly—I must learn this mystery.
   (*To Benedict*) Health to your rev'rence—(*To Peter*) ha! my new
     acquaintance!
   In tears, my good old friend! What, has the cricket
   Chirped ominously?—come, away with sorrow:°   90
   Joy marks this day its own.
PETER   A joyful day!
   The twentieth of September!—note it, sir,
   Note it for th'ugliest of the calendar.
   'Twas on this day—aye, this day sixteen years°
   The noble Count came to his death!
FLORIAN   No matter.   95
   Th'arrival of a nobler, younger Count
   Shall mock prognostics past, and paint the year
   With smiling white, fair fortune's fav'rite livery.
   (*To Benedict*) But tell me, father, tell me, has the Countess
   Pardoned her son's return? has she received him   100

With th'overflowings of a mother's joy?
Smiles she upon his wishes?—as I entered
Methought I heard an hymeneal accent.
And yet, it seems, the favour of your countenance°
Wears not the benediction of rejoicing.   105
BENEDICT The Countess must unfold her book of fate.
I am not skilled to read so dark a volume.
FLORIAN Oracular as the Delphic god!—good Peter,°
Thy wit and mine are more upon a level.
Resolve me, has the Countess seen Lord Edmund?   110
Say, did she frown and chide? or bathe his cheek
With tears as warm as leaping blood?
PETER   Ah! master,
You seem too good to mock our misery.
A soldier causes woe, but seldom jeers it.
Or know'st thou not—and sure 'twill pity thee!°   115
The gracious Countess, our kind lady—indeed
I trust they will return—is strangely changed!
FLORIAN By my good sword, thou shalt unriddle, priest.
What means this tale? what mintage is at work°
To coin delusion, that this fair domain   120
May become holy patrimony? Thus
Teach you our matrons to defraud their issue
By artificial fits and acted ravings?
I have beheld your juggles, heard your dreams.
Th'imposture shall be known. These sixteen years   125
Has my friend Edmund pined in banishment:
While masses, mummings, goblins and processions
Usurped his heritage, and made of Narbonne
A theatre of holy interludes°
And sainted frauds. But day darts on your spells.   130
Th'enlightened age eschews your vile deceits,°
And truth shall do mankind and Edmund justice.
BENEDICT Unhallowed boy, I scorn thy contumely.
In camps and trenches vent thy lewd reproaches,
Blaspheming while ye tremble. Heav'n's true soldiers,   135
Endued with more than mortal courage, defy
Hosts numerous as the Pagan chivalry
Poured forth to crush the church's rising glories.°
—But this is an enlightened age!—behold
The triumphs of your sect! to yonder plains   140

53

Bend thy illumined eye! The Vaudois there,°
Writhing in flames, and quiv'ring at th'approach
Of Rome's impending knife, attest the blessings
Conferred on their instructed ignorance!
FLORIAN Monstrous! unparalleled! Are cries and groans   145
Of butchered conscientious men the hymns°
With which you chant the victories of the church?
Do you afflict and laugh? stab and huzza?
—But I am dallying with my own impatience—
Where is this mother? I will tent her soul;°   150
And warn thee, if I find suggestion's whisper
Has practised to the detriment of my friend,
Thy caitiff life shall answer to my sword,
Though shrined within the pillars of the Vatican.
BENEDICT Judge heaven betwixt us!   155
If, ere the dews of night shall fall, thou seest not
The cup of wrath poured out, and triple woes
O'ertake unheard-of crimes; call me false prophet,
Renounce my gods and join thee to the impious!
Thou in thy turn, if truth lives on my lips,   160
Tremble! repent!—behold! the hour approaches!
    [*Enter Countess*]
COUNTESS I dare not shoot the gulf—ha! Benedict!°
Thou art a priest, thy mission should be holy,
If thou beliest not heav'n—quick, do thy work!
If there is pow'r in pray'r, teach me some sounds   165
To charm my senses, lest my coward flesh
Recoil, and win the mastery o'er my will.
—'Tis not the wound; it is the consequence!
See! see! my Narbonne stands upon the brink,
And snatches from the readiest fury there   170
A blazing torch! he whirls it round my head,
And asks, 'where are my children'!
PETER   Split, my heart,
At this sad sight!
FLORIAN   Stand off! thou'rt an accomplice—
Madam, it was your morning's gracious pleasure
I should attend you. May I hope your pardon,   175
If I anticipate—
COUNTESS   Ha! Who art thou?°
FLORIAN Have you forgot me, lady?

COUNTESS   Memory
 Is full. A head distract as mine can hold°
 Two only objects, guilt and eternity!
FLORIAN No more of this. Time has abundant hours   180
 For holy meditation. Nor have years
 Traced such deep admonitions on your cheek,
 As call for sudden preparation—
COUNTESS (*wildly*)   Prayer
 Can do no more: its efficacy's lost—
 What must be, must be soon—He will return.   185
FLORIAN He is returned, your son—have you not seen him?
COUNTESS Would I had never!
FLORIAN   Come, this is too much.
 This villainous monk has stepped 'twixt you and nature;
 And misreported of the noblest gentleman
 That treads on Christian ground—are you a mother?   190
 Are legends dearer to you than your son?
 Think you 'tis piety to gorge these miscreants,
 And drive your child from your embrace—
COUNTESS   Ye saints!
 This was the demon prompted it—avaunt!
 He beckons me—I will not—lies my lord   195
 Not bleeding in the porch? I'll tear my hair
 And bathe his wounds—where's Beatrice!—monster! monster!
 She leads the demon—see! they spread the couch!
 No, I will perish with my Narbonne—oh!
 My strength, my reason faint—darkness surrounds me!   200
 Tomorrow!—never will tomorrow come!
 Let me die here!
   [*Countess*] *sinks on a bench*
FLORIAN   This is too much for art.°
 Chill damps sit on her brow: her pulse replies not.
BENEDICT No; 'tis fictitious all—'twas I inspired
 The horrors she has been so kind to utter   205
 At my suggestion.
FLORIAN   That insulting sneer
 Speaks more the devil than if thy words were serious.
 Be her distraction counterfeit or real,°
 Her sex demands compassion or assistance.
 But she revives!
COUNTESS   Is death then past! my brain   210

Beats not its wonted tempest—in the grave
There is peace then!
FLORIAN   Her agony abates.
Look up and view your friends.
COUNTESS   Alas! I fear me,
This is life still!—am I not in my castle?
Sure I should know this garden—good old Peter!   215
My honest servant, thou I see wilt never
Quit thy poor mistress!—
     [Peter weeps]
                              kind old man, he weeps!
PETER Indeed it is for joy—how fares my lady?
COUNTESS Exhausted, Peter, that I have not strength
To be distracted—ha! your looks betray°   220
Tremendous innuendoes!—gracious heaven!°
Have I said aught—has wildness—trust me, sirs,
In these sad fits my unhinged fancy wanders
Beyond the compass of things possible.
Sometimes an angel of excelling brightness°   225
I seem to whirl the orbs and launch the comet.°
Then hideous wings with forkèd points array me,°
And I suggest strange crimes to shuddering matrons—°
Sick fancy must be pardoned.
BENEDICT (*aside*)   Artful woman!
Thou subtle emblem of thy sex, composed   230
Of madness and deceit—but since thy brain
Has lost its poise, I will send those shall shake it
Beyond recovery of its reeling bias.°
     Exit Benedict. Countess makes a sign to Peter to retire, [which he
     obeys]°
COUNTESS [*aside*] This interval is well—'tis thy last boon,
Tremendous Providence! and I will use it   235
As 'twere th'elixir of descending mercy:
Not a drop shall be waste—accept my thanks!
Preserve my reason! and preserve my child!
(*To Florian*)—Stranger, thy years are green; perhaps may mock
A woman's words, a mother's woe!—but honour,   240
If I believe this garb, is thy profession.°
Hast thou not dealt in blood?—then thou hast heard
The dying groan, and sin's despairing accent.
Struck it not on thy soul? Recall it, sir!

What then was thy sensation, feel for me!   245
FLORIAN I shudder! listen, pity, and respect thee!
COUNTESS Resolve my anxious heart. Though vagrant pleasure,
    Th'ebriety of youth, and worse than passion,
    Example, lead thee to the strumpet vice;
    Say, if beneath the waves of dissipation,   250
    The germ of virtue blossoms in thy soul.
FLORIAN A soldier's honour is his virtue. Gownmen°
    Wear it for show, and barter it for gold,
    And have it still. A soldier and his honour
    Exist together, and together perish.   255
COUNTESS I do believe thee. Thus my Narbonne thought.
    Then hear me, child of honour! canst thou cherish
    Unblemished innocence? wilt thou protect it?
    Wilt thou observe its wand'rings? call it back,
    Confine it to the path that leads to happiness?   260
    Hast thou that genuine heroism of soul
    To hug the little fondling sufferer,
    When nestling in thy bosom, drowned in blushes,
    Nor cast her from thee, while a grinning world
    Reviles her with a mother's foul misdeeds?   265
FLORIAN My arm is sworn to innocence distressed:
    Point out the lovely mourner.
COUNTESS   'Tis enough.
    Nor suffer th'ebbing moments more inquiry.
    My orphan shall be thine—nay, start not, sir,
    Your loves are known to me. Wealth past th'ambition   270
    Of Gallia's proudest baron shall endow her.
        [*Countess produces a casket*]
    Within this casket is a monarch's ransom.°
    Ten thousand ducats more are lodged within.
    All this is thine with Adeliza's hand.
FLORIAN With Adeliza!
COUNTESS   Ha! dost thou recoil?   275
    Dost thou not love her?
FLORIAN   I, love Adeliza!
    Lady, recall thy wand'ring memory.
COUNTESS Dost thou reject her? and has hope beguiled me
    In this sad only moment? Hast thou dared
    With ruffian insolence gaze on her sweetness,   280
    And mark it for an hour of wanton dalliance?

57

Oh! I will guard my child, though gaping demons
Howl with impatience!

FLORIAN   Most revered of matrons,
    Though youth and rosy joy flush on my cheek,
    Though the licentious camp and rapine's holiday   285
    Have been my school; deem not so reprobate
    My morals, that my eye would note no distance
    Between the harlot's glance and my friend's bride.

COUNTESS Thy friend! what friend?

FLORIAN   Lord Edmund—

COUNTESS   What of him?

FLORIAN Is Adeliza's lord; her wedded bridegroom.   290

COUNTESS Confusion! frenzy! blast me, all ye furies!
    Edmund and Adeliza! when! where! how!
    Edmund wed Adeliza! quick, unsay
    The monst'rous tale—oh! prodigy of ruin!
    Does my own son then boil with fiercer fires   295
    Than scorched his impious mother's madding veins!
    Did reason reassume its shattered throne,
    But as spectatress of this last of horrors?
    Oh! let my dagger drink my heart's black blood,
    And then present my hell-born progeny   300
    With drops of kindred sin!—*that* were a torch
    Fit to light up such loves! and fit to quench them!

FLORIAN What means this agony? didst thou not grant
    The maiden to his wishes?

COUNTESS   Did I not couple
    Distinctions horrible? plan unnatural rites°   305
    To grace my funeral pile, and meet the furies
    More innocent than those I leave behind me!

FLORIAN Amazement!—I will hasten—grant, ye pow'rs!
    My speed be not too late!
            Exit [Florian]

COUNTESS   Globe of the world,
    If thy frame split not with such crimes as these,   310
    It is immortal!
            *Edmund and Adeliza enter at the opposite door from which
            Florian went out. They kneel to the Countess*

EDMUND Dear parent, look on us, and bless your children!

COUNTESS My children! horror! horror! yes, too sure
    Ye are my children!—Edmund, loose that hand;

'Tis poison to thy soul!—hell has no venom   315
Like a child's touch!—oh! agonizing thought!
—Who made this marriage? whose unhallowed breath
Pronounced the incestuous sounds?
EDMUND   Incest! good heavens!°
COUNTESS Yes, thou devoted victim! let thy blood°
Curdle to stone! perdition circumvents thee!   320
Lo! where this monster stands! thy mother! mistress!
The mother of thy daughter, sister, wife!
The pillar of accumulated horrors!
Hear! tremble!—and then marry, if thou darest!
EDMUND Yes, I do tremble, though thy words are frenzy.   325
So black must be the passions that inspired it,
I shudder for thee! pitying duty shudders!
COUNTESS For me!—Oh Edmund, I have burst the bond
Of every tie—when thou shalt know the crimes,
In which this fury did involve thy youth,   330
It will seem piety to curse me, Edmund!
Oh! impious night!—(*wildly*) ha! is not that my lord?
He shakes the curtains of the nuptial couch,
And starts to find a son there!
EDMUND   Gracious heaven!°
Grant that these shocking images *be* raving!   335
ADELIZA Sweet lady, be composed—indeed I thought
This marriage was thy will—but we will break it—
Benedict shall discharge us from our vows.
COUNTESS Thou gentle lamb, from a fell tiger sprung!
Unknowing half the miseries that await thee!   340
—Oh! they are innocent—Almighty pow'r!—
         [*Countess*] *kneels, but rises again hastily*
Ha! dare I pray! for others intercede!
I pray for them, the cause of all their woe!
—But for a moment give me leave, despair!
For a short interval lend me that reason   345
Thou gavest, heav'n, in vain!—it must be known,
The fullness of my crime; or innocent these
May plunge them in new horrors. Not a word
Can scape me, but will do the work of thunder,
And blast those moments I regain from madness!   350
[*After a pause*] Ye know how fondly my luxurious fancy°
Doted upon my lord. For eighteen months

An embassy detained him from my bed.
A harbinger announced his near return.
Love dressed his image to my longing thoughts   355
In all its warmest colours—but the morn,
In which impatience grew almost to sickness,
Presented him a bloody corpse before me.
I raved—the storm of disappointed passions
Assailed my reason, fevered all my blood—   360
Whether too warmly pressed, or too officious
To turn the torrent of my grief aside,
A damsel, that attended me, disclosed
Thy suit, unhappy boy!

EDMUND   What is to come?
Shield me, ye gracious pow'rs, from my own thoughts!   365
My dreadful apprehension!

COUNTESS   Give it scope!
Thou canst not harbour a foreboding thought
More dire, than I conceived, I executed.
Guilt rushed into my soul—my fancy saw thee
Thy father's image—

EDMUND   Swallow th'accursèd sound!   370
Nor dare to say—

COUNTESS   Yes, thou polluted son!
Grief, disappointment, opportunity,
Raised such a tumult in my madding blood,
I took the damsel's place; and while thy arms
Twined, to thy thinking, round another's waist,   375
Hear, hell, and tremble!—thou didst clasp thy mother!

EDMUND Oh! execrable!
        Adeliza faints

COUNTESS   Be that swoon eternal!
Nor let her know the rest—she is thy daughter,
Fruit of that monstrous night!

EDMUND (*drawing his dagger*)   Infernal woman!
My dagger must repay a tale like this!   380
Blood so distempered—no—I must not strike—°
I dare not punish what you dared commit.

COUNTESS (*seizing his dagger*) Give me the steel—my arm will not
    recoil.
Thus, Edmund, I revenge thee!
        [*Countess*] *stabs herself*

60

EDMUND   Help! hoa! help!
For both I tremble, dare not succour either!°   385
COUNTESS Peace! and conceal our shame—quick, frame some
     legend—°
They come!
       [*Enter Florian, Benedict, Attendants*]
            Assist the maid—an accident—
       [*Some of the Attendants*] *bear off Adeliza*°
By my own hand—ha! Benedict!—but no!
I must not turn accuser!
BENEDICT   Mercy, heaven!
Who did this deed?
COUNTESS   Myself.
BENEDICT   What was the cause?°   390
COUNTESS Follow me to yon gulf, and thou wilt know.°
I answer not to man.
BENEDICT   Bethink thee, lady—
COUNTESS Thought ebbs apace—Oh Edmund, could a blessing
Part from my lips, and not become a curse,
I would—poor Adeliza—'tis accomplished!°   395
       [*Countess*] *dies*
BENEDICT My lord, explain these horrors. Wherefore fell
Your mother? and why faints your wife?
EDMUND   My wife!
Thou damning priest! I have no wife—thou know'st it—°
Thou gavest me indeed—no—rot my tongue
Ere the dread sound escape it!—bear away   400
That hateful monk—
BENEDICT (*as he goes out, to Florian*) Who was the prophet now?
Remember me!
       [*Exit Benedict, guarded by Attendants*]
EDMUND   Oh Florian, we must haste°
To where fell war assumes its ugliest form:
I burn to rush on death!
FLORIAN   I dare not ask;°
But stiffened with amazement I deplore—   405
EDMUND Oh tender friend! I must not violate
Thy guiltless ear—(*wildly*) ha! 'tis my father calls!
I dare not see him!
FLORIAN   Be composed, my lord.
We are all your friends—

EDMUND   Have I no kindred here?
  They will confound all friendship! interweave   410
  Such monstrous union—
FLORIAN   Good my lord, resume
  Your wonted reason. Let us in and comfort
  Your gentle bride—
EDMUND   Forbid it, all ye pow'rs!
  Oh Florian, bear her to the holy sisters.
  Say, 'twas my mother's will she take the veil.   415
  I never must behold her!—never more
  Review this theatre of monstrous guilt!
  No; to th'embattled foe I will present
  This hated form—and welcome be the sabre
  That leaves no atom of it undefaced!   420
      [Curtain falls]°

Epilogue°

To be spoken by Mrs Clive°

Our bard, whose head is filled with Gothic fancies,°
And teems with ghosts and giants and romances,
Intended to have kept your passions up,
And sent you crying out your eyes, to sup.
Would you believe it—though *mine* all the vogue,   5
He meant his nun should speak the epilogue.°
His nun! so pious, pliant and demure—
Lord! you have had enough of her, I'm sure!
I stormed—for, when my honour is at stake,
I make the pillars of the green-room shake.°   10
Heroes half-dressed, and goddesses half-laced,°
Avoid my wrath, and from my thunders haste.
I vowed by all the gods of Rome and Greece,
'Twas I would finish his too doleful piece.
'I, flushed with comic roguery,'— said I,   15
'Will make 'em laugh, more than you make 'em cry.'
'Bless me!' said he—'among the Greeks, dear Kat'rine,
Of smutty epilogues I know no pattern.'
'Smutty!' said I—and then I stamped the stage
With all a turkey-cock's majestic rage—   20
'When did you know in public—or in private,
Doubles entendres my strict virtue drive at?
Your muses, sir, are not more free from ill
On mount Parnassus—or on Strawb'rry-hill.°
And though with her repentance you may hum one,°   25
I would not play your countess—to become one.
So *very* guilty, and so *very* good,
An angel, with such errant flesh and blood!
Such sinning, praying, preaching—I'll be kissed,°
If I don't think she was a methodist!'°   30
Saints are the produce of a vicious age:
Crimes must abound, ere sectaries can rage.
His mask no canting confessor assumes;
With acted zeal no flaming bigot fumes;
Till the rich harvest nods with swelling grain   35

And the sharp sickle can assure his gain.
But soon shall hypocrites their flights deplore,°
Nor grim enthusiasts vex Britannia more.
Virtue shall guard her daughters from their arts,
Shine in their eyes, and blossom in their hearts.   40
They need no lectures in fanatic tone:
Their lesson lives before them—on the throne.°

POSTSCRIPT

From the time that I first undertook the foregoing scenes, I never flattered myself that they would be proper to appear on the stage. The subject is so horrid, that I thought it would shock, rather than give satisfaction to an audience. Still I found it so truly tragic in the two essential springs of terror and pity,° that I could not resist the impulse   5
of adapting it to the scene,° though it should never be practicable to produce it there. I saw too that it would admit of great situations, of lofty characters, and of those sudden and unforeseen strokes, which have singular effect in operating a revolution° in the passions, and in interesting the spectator. It was capable of furnishing, not only a con-   10
trast of characters, but a contrast of vice and virtue in the same character: and by laying the scene in what age and country I pleased, pictures of ancient manners might be drawn, and many allusions to historic events introduced to bring the action nearer to the imagination of the spectator. The moral resulting from the calamities attend-   15
ant on unbounded passion, even to the destruction of the criminal person's race, was obviously suited to the purpose and object of tragedy.

The subject is more truly horrid than even that of Oedipus:° and yet I do not doubt but a Grecian poet would have made no scruple of   20
exhibiting it on the theatre. Revolting as it is, a son assassinating his mother, as Orestes° does, exceeds the guilt that appears in the foregoing scenes. As murder is the highest crime that man can commit against his fellow beings, parricide is the deepest degree of murder. No age but has suffered such guilt to be represented on the stage. And   25
yet I feel the disgust that must arise at the catastrophe° of this piece; so much is our delicacy more apt to be shocked than our good-nature. Nor will it be an excuse that I thought the story founded on an event in real life.

I had heard, when very young, that a gentlewoman, under uncom-   30
mon agonies of mind, had waited on Archbishop Tillotson,° and besought his counsel. A damsel that served her had, many years before, acquainted her that she was importuned by the gentlewoman's son to grant him a private meeting. The mother ordered the maiden to make the assignation, when, she said, she would discover herself, and   35
reprimand him for his criminal passion: but being hurried away by a much more criminal passion herself, she kept the assignation without

discovering herself. The fruit of this horrid artifice was a daughter, whom the gentlewoman caused to be educated very privately in the country: but proving very lovely, and being accidentally met by her 40 father-brother, who had never had the slightest suspicion of the truth, he had fallen in love with and actually married her. The wretched guilty mother, learning what had happened, and distracted with the consequence of her crime, had now resorted to the archbishop to know in what manner she should act. The prelate charged her never to let 45 her son and daughter know what had passed, as they were innocent of any criminal intention. For herself, he bade her almost despair.

Some time after I had finished the play on this ground-work, a gentleman to whom I had communicated it, accidentally discovered the origin of the tradition in the novels of the queen of Navarre,° vol. 1 50 nov. 30, and to my great surprise I found a strange concurrence of circumstances between the story as there related, and as I had adapted it to my piece: for though I believed it to have happened in the reign of King William,° I had, for a purpose mentioned below, thrown it back to the eve of the Reformation;° and the queen, it appears, dates the 55 event in the reign of Louis XII.° I had chosen Narbonne for the scene; the queen places it in Languedoc.° These rencounters are of little importance; and perhaps curious to nobody but the author.

In order to make use of a canvas° so shocking, it was necessary as much as possible to palliate the crime, and raise the character of the 60 criminal. To attain the former end, I imagined the moment in which she had lost a beloved husband, when grief, disappointment, and a conflict of passions might be supposed to have thrown her reason off its guard, and exposed her to the danger under which she fell. Strange as the moment may seem for vice to have seized her, still it makes her 65 less hateful, than if she had coolly meditated so foul a crime. I have endeavoured to make her very fondness for her husband in some measure the cause of her guilt.

But as that guilt could not be lessened without destroying the subject itself, I thought that her immediate horror and consequential 70 repentance were essential towards effectuating her being suffered on the stage.° Still more was necessary: the audience must be prejudiced in her favour; or an uniform sentiment of disgust would have been raised against the whole piece. For this reason I suppressed the story till the last scene; and bestowed every ornament of sense, unbigoted 75 piety, and interesting° contrition, on the character that was at last to raise universal indignation; in hopes that some degree of pity would linger in the breasts of the audience; and that a whole life of virtue and penance might in some measure atone for a moment, though a most odious moment, of a depraved imagination.° 80

Some of my friends have thought that I have pushed the sublimity of sense and reason, in the character of the Countess, to too great a height, considering the dark and superstitious age in which she lived. They are of opinion that the excess of her repentance would have been more likely to have thrown her into the arms of enthusiasm.° Perhaps 85 it might—but I was willing to insinuate that virtue could and ought to leave more lasting stings in a mind conscious of having fallen; and that weak minds alone believe or feel that conscience is to be lulled asleep by the incantations of bigotry. However, to reconcile even the seeming inconsistence objected to, I have placed my fable at the dawn of the 90 Reformation; consequently the strength of mind in the Countess may be supposed to have borrowed aid from other sources, besides those she found in her own understanding.

Her character is certainly new, and the cast of the whole play unlike any other that I am acquainted with. The incidents seem to me to flow 95 naturally from the situation; and with all the defects in the writing, of many of which I am conscious, and many more no doubt will be discovered, still I think, as a tragedy, its greatest fault is the horror which it must occasion in the audience; particularly in the fairer, more tender, and less criminal° part of it. 100

It will be observed that, after the discovery of her son, the Countess is for some moments in every scene disordered in her understanding by the violent impression of that interview, and from the guilt that is ever uppermost in her mind. Yet she is never quite mad—still less does she talk like Belvidera of 105

'Lutes, laurels, seas of milk, and ships of amber;'°

which is not being mad, but light-headed. When madness has taken possession of a person, such character ceases to be fit for the stage; or at least should appear there but for a short time; it being the business of the theatre to exhibit passions, not distempers.° The finest picture 110 ever drawn of a head discomposed by misfortune is that of King Lear. His thoughts dwell on the ingratitude of his daughters, and every sentence that falls from his wildness excites reflection and pity. Had frenzy entirely seized him, our compassion would abate: we should conclude that he no longer felt unhappiness. Shakespeare wrote as a 115 philosopher, Otway as a poet.

The villainy of Benedict was planned to divide the indignation of the audience, and to intercept some of it from the Countess. Nor will the blackness of his character appear extravagant, if we call to mind the crimes committed by Catholic churchmen, when the Reformation not only provoked their rage, but threatened them with total ruin.

I have said that terror and pity naturally arose from the subject, and that the moral is just. These are the merits of the story, not of the author. It is true also, that the rules laid down by the critics are strictly inherent in the piece—remark, I do not say, observed; for I had written above three acts before I had thought of, or set myself to observe those rules; and consequently it is no vanity to say that the three unities° reign throughout the whole play. The time necessary is not above two or three hours longer than that of the representation; and at most does not require half of the four-and-twenty hours granted to poets by those their masters. The unity of place is but once shifted, and that merely from the platform without the castle to the garden within it, so that a single wall is the sole infringement of the second law—and for the third, unity of action, it is so entire, that not the smallest episode intervenes. Every scene tends to bring on the catastrophe, and the story is never interrupted or diverted from its course. The return of Edmund and his marriage necessarily produce the denouement.

If the critics are pleased with this conformity to their laws, I shall be glad they have that satisfaction. For my own part, I set little value on such merit, which was accidental, and is at best mechanic, and of a subordinate kind; and more apt to produce improbable situations than to remove them.

I wish I had no more to answer for in the faults of the piece, than I have merit to boast in the mechanism. I was desirous of striking a little out of the common road, and to introduce some novelty on our stage. Our genius and cast of thinking are very different from the French; and yet our theatre, which should represent manners,° depends almost entirely at present on translations and copies from our neighbours. Enslaved as they are to rules and modes, still I do not doubt, but many both of their tragic and comic authors would be glad they dared to use the liberties that are secured to our stage. They are so cramped by the rigorous forms of composition, that they would think themselves greatly indemnified by an ampler latitude of thought. I have chalked out some paths that may be happily improved by better poets and men of more genius than I possess;° and which may be introduced in subjects better calculated for action than the story I have chosen.

The excellence of our dramatic writers is by no means equal in number to the great men that we have produced in other walks. The-

atric genius lay dormant after Shakespeare; waked with some bold and
glorious, but irregular, and often ridiculous flights in Dryden; revived   160
in Otway; maintained a placid pleasing kind of dignity in Rowe, and
even shone in his *Jane Shore*. It trod in sublime and classic fetters in
Cato, but void of nature, or the power of affecting the passions. In
Southerne it seemed a genuine ray of nature and Shakespeare; but
falling on an age still more Hottentot,° was stifled in those gross and   165
barbarous productions, tragicomedies.° It turned to tuneful nonsense
in *The Mourning Bride*; grew stark mad in Lee; whose cloak, a little the
worse for wear, fell on Young; yet in both was still a poet's cloak. It
recovered its senses in Hughes and Fenton,° who were afraid it should
relapse, and accordingly kept it down with a timid, but amiable hand—   170
and then it languished. We have not mounted again above the two last.

WAT TYLER°

by
ROBERT SOUTHEY

PREFACE°

Twenty years ago, upon the surreptitious publication of this notable drama, and the use which was made of it, I said what it then became me to say in a letter° to one of those gentlemen who thought proper to revile me, not for having entertained democratical opinions, but for having outgrown them, and learnt to appreciate and to defend the institutions of my country.

Had I written lewdly in my youth, like Beza°—like Beza, I would ask pardon of God and man; and no considerations should induce me to reprint what I could never think of without sorrow and shame. Had I at any time, like St Augustine,° taught doctrines which I afterwards perceived to be erroneous—and if, as in his case, my position in society, and the estimation in which I was held, gave weight to what I had advanced, and made those errors dangerous to others—like St Augustine, I would publish my retractions, and endeavour to counteract the evil which, though erringly, with no evil intention, I had caused.

Wherefore then, it may be asked, have I included *Wat Tyler* in this authentic collection of my poetical works? For these reasons—that it may not be supposed I think it any reproach to have written it, or that I am more ashamed of having been a republican, than of having been a boy. '*Quicunque ista lecturi sunt, non me imitentur errantem, sed in melius proficientum. Inveniet enim fortasse, quomodo scribendo profecerim, quisquis opuscula mea, ordine quo scripta sunt, legerit.*'°

I have endeavoured to correct in my other juvenile pieces such faults as were corrigible. But *Wat Tyler* appears just as it was written, in the course of three mornings, in 1794; the stolen copy, which was committed to the press twenty-three years afterwards, not having undergone the slightest correction of any kind.°

[THE CHARACTERS OF THE PLAY
(in order of speaking)°

Wat Tyler, *a blacksmith*°
Alice, *his daughter*
Piers, *Alice's suitor*
Hob Carter,° *Tyler's friend*
A collector of taxes
Tyler's wife
Tom Miller
Jack Straw°
John Ball,° *a poor priest*
King Richard, the second, of England°
Philpot, *a financier, previously Mayor of London*
Archbishop of Canterbury
Walworth, *Lord Mayor of London*°
Two messengers to the court
A herald, *sent from the court to the rebels*
Two soldiers
Two guards
Sir John Tresilian, *Chief Justice of the King's Bench*°
Tax-gatherers, Mob, the King's troops.]

1.1

A blacksmith's shop; Wat Tyler at work within; a may-pole°
before the door.

[Enter] Alice and Piers[, with other young people and Hob
Carter. The young people sing°]

> Cheerful on this holiday,
> Welcome we the merry May.
>
> On every sunny hillock spread
> The pale primrose lifts her head;°
> Rich with sweets, the western gale   5
> Sweeps along the cowslipped dale;
> Every bank, with violets gay,
> Smiles to welcome in the May.
>
> The linnet from the budding grove,
> Chirps her vernal song of love.   10
> The copse resounds the throstle's notes,
> On each wild gale sweet music floats;
> And melody from every spray,
> Welcomes in the merry May.
>
> Cheerful on this holiday,   15
> Welcome we the merry May.

A dance. During the dance, Tyler lays down his hammer, and sits
mournfully down before the door.°

HOB Why so sad, neighbour?—Do not these gay sports,
　　This revelry of youth, recall the days
　　When we too mingled in the revelry,
　　And lightly tripping in the morris dance,°   20
　　Welcomed the merry month?
TYLER   Aye, we were young,
　　No cares had quelled the heyday of the blood:°
　　We sported deftly in the April morning,
　　Nor marked the black clouds gathering o'er our noon,
　　Nor feared the storm of night.

HOB   Beshrew me, Tyler,   25
  But my heart joys to see the imps so cheerful !
  Young, hale, and happy, why should they destroy
  These blessings by reflection?
TYLER   Look ye, neighbour—
  You have known me long.
HOB   Since we were boys together,
  And played at barley-brake, and danced the morris.°   30
  Some five-and-twenty years!
TYLER   Was not *I* young,
  And hale, and happy?
HOB   Cheerful as the best.
TYLER Have not I been a staid, hard-working man?
  Up with the lark at labour; sober, honest,°
  Of an unblemished character?
HOB   Who doubts it?   35
  There's never a man in Essex bears a better.
TYLER And shall not these, though young, and hale, and happy,
  Look on with sorrow to the future hour?
  Shall not reflection poison all their pleasures?
  When I—the honest, staid, hard-working Tyler—   40
  Toil through the long course of the summer's day,
  Still toiling, yet still poor! When with hard labour
  Scarce can I furnish out my daily food,
  And age comes on to steal away my strength,
  And leave me poor and wretched! Why should this be?   45
  My youth was regular—my labour constant—
  I married an industrious, virtuous woman;
  Nor while I toiled and sweated at the anvil,
  Sat she neglectful of her spinning-wheel.
  Hob! I have only six groats in the world,°   50
  And they must soon by law be taken from me.
HOB Curse on these taxes—one succeeds another—
  Our ministers, panders of a king's will,
  Drain all our wealth away, waste it in revels,
  And lure, or force away our boys, who should be   55
  The props of our old age, to fill their armies,
  And feed the crows of France. Year follows year,
  And still we madly prosecute the war;
  Draining our wealth, distressing our poor peasants,
  Slaughtering our youths—and all to crown our chiefs   60

75

With glory!—I detest the hell-sprung name.
TYLER What matters me who wears the crown of France?
Whether a Richard or a Charles possess it?°
They reap the glory—they enjoy the spoil—
We pay—we bleed! The sun would shine as cheerly,   65
The rains of heaven as seasonably fall,
Though neither of these royal pests existed.
HOB Nay, as for that we poor men should fare better;
No legal robbers then should force away
The hard-earned wages of our honest toil.   70
The Parliament for ever cries 'more money,
The service of the state demands more money';
Just heaven! Of what service is the state?
TYLER Oh, 'tis of vast importance! Who should pay for
The luxuries and riots of the court?   75
Who should support the flaunting courtier's pride,
Pay for their midnight revels, their rich garments,
Did not the state enforce?—Think ye, my friend,
That I, a humble blacksmith, here at Deptford,
Would part with these six groats—earned by hard toil,   80
All that I have!—to massacre the Frenchmen,
Murder as enemies men I never saw,
Did not the state compel me?
        Tax-gatherers pass by
                              There they go,
Privileged ruffians!°
        Piers and Alice advance to him
ALICE Did we not dance it well to-day, my father?   85
You know I always loved these village sports,
Even from my infancy, and yet methinks
I never tripped along the mead so gaily.
You know they chose me queen, and your friend Piers°
Wreathed me this cowslip garland for my head—   90
Is it not simple?—You are sad, my father!°
You should have rested from your work to-day,
And given a few hours up to merriment—
But you are so serious!
TYLER   Serious, my good girl!
I may well be so: when I look at thee   95
It makes me sad! Thou art too fair a flower
To bear the wintry wind of poverty.

PIERS Yet I have often heard you speak of riches
      Even with contempt; they cannot purchase peace,
      Or innocence, or virtue; sounder sleep   100
      Waits on the weary ploughman's lowly bed,
      Than on the downy couch of luxury
      Lulls the rich slave of pride and indolence.
      I never wish for wealth; my arm is strong,
      And I can purchase by it a coarse meal,   105
      And hunger savours it.
TYLER   Young man, thy mind
      Has yet to learn the hard lesson of experience.
      Thou art yet young: the blasting breath of want
      Has not yet froze the current of thy blood.
PIERS Fare not the birds well, as from spray to spray,   110
      Blithesome they bound, yet find their simple food
      Scattered abundantly?
TYLER No fancied boundaries of mine and thine
      Restrain their wanderings. Nature gives enough
      For all; but Man, with arrogant selfishness,   115
      Proud of his heaps, hoards up superfluous stores
      Robbed from his weaker fellows, starves the poor,
      Or gives to pity what he owes to justice!
PIERS So I have heard our good friend John Ball preach.
ALICE My father, wherefore was John Ball imprisoned?   120
      Was he not charitable, good, and pious?
      I have heard him say that all mankind are brethren,
      And that like brethren they should love each other;
      Was not that doctrine pious?
TYLER   Rank sedition—
      High treason, every syllable, my child!   125
      The priests cry out on him for heresy,
      The nobles all detest him as a rebel,
      And this good man, this minister of Christ,
      This man, the friend and brother of mankind,
      Lingers in the dark dungeon!—My dear Alice,   130
      Retire awhile.
          Exit Alice
                  Piers, I would speak to thee,
      Even with a father's love! You are much with me,
      And I believe do court my conversation;
      Thou couldst not choose thee forth a truer friend.

77

I would fain see thee happy, but I fear   135
Thy very virtues will destroy thy peace.
My daughter—she is young—not yet fifteen:
Piers, thou art generous, and thy youthful heart
Warm with affection; this close intimacy
Will ere long grow to love.

PIERS   Suppose it so;   140
Were that an evil, Walter? She is mild
And cheerful, and industrious:—now methinks
With such a partner life would be most happy!
Why would ye warn me then of wretchedness?
Is there an evil that can harm our lot?   145
I have been told the virtuous must be happy,
And have believed it true: tell me, my friend,
What shall disturb the virtuous?

TYLER   Poverty,
A bitter foe.

PIERS   Nay, you have often told me
That happiness does not consist in riches.   150

TYLER It is most true; but tell me, my dear boy,
Couldst thou be happy to behold thy wife
Pining with want? the children of your loves
Clad in the squalid rags of wretchedness?
And, when thy hard and unremitting toil   155
Had earned with pain a scanty recompense,
Couldst thou be patient when the law should rob thee
And leave thee without bread and penniless?

PIERS It is a dreadful picture.

TYLER   'Tis a true one.

PIERS But yet methinks our sober industry   160
Might drive away the danger! 'Tis but little
That I could wish; food for our frugal meals,
Raiment, however homely, and a bed
To shield us from the night.

TYLER   Thy honest reason
Could wish no more: but were it not most wretched   165
To want the coarse food for the frugal meal?
And by the orders of your merciless lord,
If you by chance were guilty of being poor,
To be turned out adrift to the bleak world,
Unhoused, unfriended?—Piers, I have not been idle,   170
I never ate thc bread of indolence;

Could Alice be more thrifty than her mother?
Yet with but one child—and that one how good,
Thou knowest—I scarcely can provide the wants
Of nature: look at these wolves of the law,   175
They come to drain me of my hard-earned wages.
I have already paid the heavy tax
Laid on the wool that clothes me, on my leather,
On all the needful articles of life!
And now three groats (and I worked hard to earn them)   180
The Parliament demands—and I must pay them,
Forsooth, for liberty to wear my head.
   Enter [the Collector, with other] Tax-gatherers
COLLECTOR Three groats a head for all your family.
PIERS Why is this money gathered? 'Tis a hard tax
 On the poor labourer! It can never be   185
 That government should thus distress the people.
 Go to the rich for money—honest labour
 Ought to enjoy its fruits.
COLLECTOR   The state wants money.
 War is expensive—'tis a glorious war,
 A war of honour, and must be supported.—   190
 Three groats a head.
TYLER   There, three for my own head,
 Three for my wife's; what will the state tax next?
COLLECTOR You have a daughter.
TYLER She is below the age—not yet fifteen.
COLLECTOR You would evade the tax.
TYLER   Sir officer,   195
 I have paid you fairly what the law demands.
   Alice and her mother enter the shop.° The Tax-gatherers go
   to her. One of them lays hold of her. She screams. Tyler
   goes in
COLLECTOR You say she's under age.
   Alice screams again. Tyler knocks out the Tax-gatherer's brains.
   His companions fly
PIERS   A just revenge.
TYLER Most just indeed; but in the eye of the law
 'Tis murder: and the murderer's lot is mine.
   Piers goes out. Tyler sits down mournfully.
ALICE Fly, my dear father! Let us leave this place   200
 Before they raise pursuit.
TYLER   Nay, nay, my child,

Flight would be useless—I have done my duty;
I have punished the brute insolence of lust,
And here will wait my doom.

WIFE   Oh, let us fly,
My husband, my dear husband!

ALICE   Quit but this place,   205
And we may yet be safe, and happy too.

TYLER It would be useless, Alice; 'twould but lengthen
A wretched life in fear.

     [*Mob*] *cry offstage;* Liberty, Liberty!
     Enter Mob, with Hob [*and Tom Miller*], *crying* Liberty!
     Liberty! No Poll-tax! No War!

HOB We have broke our chains, we will arise in anger,
The mighty multitude shall trample down   210
The handful that oppress them.

TYLER   Have ye heard
So soon then of my murder?

HOB   Of your vengeance.
Piers ran throughout the village—told the news—
Cried out, 'To arms! Arm, arm for Liberty;
For Liberty and Justice!'

TYLER   My good friends,   215
Heed well your danger, or be resolute!
Learn to laugh menaces and force to scorn,
Or leave me. I dare answer the bold deed—
Death must come once: return ye to your homes,
Protect my wife and child, and on my grave   220
Write why I died; perhaps the time may come,
When honest Justice shall applaud the deed.

HOB Nay, nay, we are oppressed, and have too long
Knelt at our proud lords' feet; we have too long
Obeyed their orders, bowed to their caprices,   225
Sweated for them the wearying summer's day,
Wasted for them the wages of our toil,
Fought for them, conquered for them, bled for them,
Still to be trampled on, and still despised!
But we have broke our chains.

TOM MILLER   Piers is gone on   230
Through all the neighbouring villages, to spread
The glorious tidings.

HOB   He is hurried on

80

To Maidstone, to deliver good John Ball,
Our friend, our shepherd.
    Mob increases
TYLER   Friends and countrymen,°
Will ye then rise to save an honest man   235
From the fierce clutches of the bloody law?
Oh, do not call to mind my private wrongs,
That the state drained my hard-earned pittance from me,
That, of his office proud, the foul collector
Durst with lewd hand seize on my darling child,°   240
Insult her maiden modesty, and force
A father's hand to vengeance; heed not this;
Think not, my countrymen, on private wrongs,
Remember what yourselves have long endured;
Think of the insults, wrongs, and contumelies,°   245
Ye bear from your proud lords—that your hard toil
Manures their fertile fields—you plough the earth,
You sow the corn, you reap the ripened harvest,—
They riot on the produce!—that, like beasts,
They sell you with their land, claim all the fruits   250
Which the kindly earth produces, as their own,
The privilege, forsooth of noble birth!
On, on to freedom; feel but your own strength,
Be but resolved, and these destructive tyrants
Shall shrink before your vengeance.
HOB   On to London,—   255
The tidings fly before us—the court trembles,—
Liberty!—Vengeance!—Justice!°
    [*Curtain falls*]

2.1

Blackheath.°

[Enter] Tyler, Hob[, Jack Straw, Tom Miller, and their
supporters. They sing°]

> *'When Adam delved and Eve span,*
> *Who was then the gentleman?'°*
>
> *Wretched is the infant's lot,*
> *Born within the straw-roofed cot;*
> *Be he generous, wise, or brave,*   5
> *He must only be a slave.*
> *Long, long labour, little rest,*
> *Still to toil to be oppressed;*
> *Drained by taxes of his store,*
> *Punished next for being poor:*   10
> *This is the poor wretch's lot,*
> *Born within the straw-roofed cot.*
>
> *While the peasant works—to sleep,*
> *What the peasant sows—to reap,*
> *On the couch of ease to lie,*   15
> *Rioting in revelry;*
> *Be he villain, be he fool,*
> *Still to hold despotic rule,*
> *Trampling on his slaves with scorn!*
> *This is to be nobly born.*   20
>
> *'When Adam delved and Eve span,*
> *Who was then the gentleman?'*

JACK STRAW The mob are up in London—the proud courtiers
  Begin to tremble.
TOM MILLER   Aye, aye, 'tis time to tremble:
  Who'll plough their fields, who'll do their drudgery now,   25
  And work like horses, to give them the harvest?
JACK STRAW I only wonder we lay quiet so long.

We had always the same strength; and we deserved
The ills we met with for not using it.
HOB Why do we fear those animals called lords?°   30
What is there in the name to frighten us?
Is not my arm as mighty as a baron's?
    Enter Piers and John Ball
PIERS (*to Tyler*) Have I done well, my father?—I remembered
This good man lay in prison.
TYLER   My dear child,
Most well; the people rise for liberty,   35
And their first deed should be to break the chains
That bind the virtuous:—oh, thou honest priest,
How much hast thou endured!
JOHN BALL   Why, aye, my friend!
These squalid rags bespeak what I have suffered.
I was reviled, insulted, left to languish   40
In a damp dungeon; but I bore it cheerily—
My heart was glad—for I had done my duty.
I pitied my oppressors, and I sorrowed
For the poor men of England.
TYLER   They have felt
Their strength: look round this heath; 'tis thronged with
    men   45
Ardent for freedom: mighty is the event
That waits their fortune.
JOHN BALL   I would fain address them.
TYLER Do so, my friend, and preach to them their duty.°
Remind them of their long-withholden rights.
What ho there! Silence!
PIERS   Silence, there, my friends,   50
This good man would address you.
HOB   Aye, aye, hear him;
He is no mealy-mouthed court-orator,°
To flatter vice, and pamper lordly pride.
JOHN BALL Friends, brethren! for ye are my brethren all;
Englishmen, met in arms to advocate   55
The cause of freedom, hear me; pause awhile
In the career of vengeance!—It is true°
I am a priest, but, as these rags may speak,
Not one who riots in the poor man's spoil,
Or trades with his religion. I am one   60

Who preach the law of Christ; and, in my life,
Would practise what he taught. The Son of God
Came not to you in power: humble in mien,
Lowly in heart, the man of Nazareth
Preached mercy, justice, love: 'Woe unto ye,   65
Ye that are rich: if that ye would be saved
Sell that ye have, and give unto the poor'.°
So taught the Saviour: oh, my honest friends,
Have ye not felt the strong indignant throb
Of justice in your bosoms, to behold   70
The lordly baron feasting on your spoils?
Have you not in your hearts arraigned the lot°
That gave him on the couch of luxury
To pillow his head, and pass the festive day
In sportive feasts, and ease, and revelry?   75
Have you not often in your conscience asked,
Why is the difference; wherefore should that man,
No worthier than myself, thus lord it over me,
And bid me labour, and enjoy the fruits?
The God within your breasts has argued thus: 80
The voice of truth has murmured. Came ye not°
As helpless to the world? Shines not the sun
With equal ray on both? Do ye not feel
The self-same winds of heaven as keenly parch ye?
Abundant is the earth—the Sire of all,   85
Saw and pronounced that it was very good.°
Look round: the vernal fields smile with new flowers,
The budding orchard perfumes the sweet breeze,°
And the green corn waves to the passing gale.
There is enough for all; but your proud baron   90
Stands up, and arrogant of strength, exclaims,
'I am a lord—by nature I am noble:
These fields are mine, for I was born to them,
I was born in the castle—you, poor wretches,
Whelped in the cottage, are by birth my slaves.'   95
Almighty God! such blasphemies are uttered:
Almighty God! such blasphemies believed!
TOM MILLER This is something like a sermon.°
JACK STRAW   Where's the bishop
Would tell you truths like these?
HOB There never was a bishop among all the apostles.   100

84

JOHN BALL My brethren——
PIERS   Silence; the good priest speaks.
JOHN BALL My brethren, these are truths, and weighty ones,
 Ye are all equal: nature made ye so,
 Equality is your birthright.—When I gaze
 On the proud palace, and behold one man   105
 In the blood-purpled robes of royalty,°
 Feasting at ease, and lording over millions,
 Then turn me to the hut of poverty,
 And see the wretched labourer, worn with toil,
 Divide his scanty morsel with his infants,   110
 I sicken, and indignant at the sight,
 Blush for the patience of humanity.°
JACK STRAW We will assert our rights.
TOM MILLER   We'll trample down
 These insolent oppressors.
JOHN BALL   In good truth,
 Ye have cause for anger: but, my honest friends,   115
 Is it revenge or justice that ye seek?
MOB Justice! Justice!
JOHN BALL   Oh, then remember mercy;
 And though your proud oppressors spared not you,°
 Show you excel them in humanity.
 They will use every art to disunite you;   120
 To conquer separately, by stratagem,
 Whom in a mass they fear;—but be ye firm;
 Boldly demand your long-forgotten rights,
 Your sacred, your inalienable freedom.
 Be bold—be resolute—be merciful:°   125
 And while you spurn the hated name of slaves,
 Show you are men.
MOB   Long live our honest priest.
JACK STRAW He shall be made archbishop.
JOHN BALL My brethren, I am plain John Ball, your
  friend,
 Your equal: by the law of Christ enjoined   130
 To serve you, not command.
JACK STRAW   March we for London.
TYLER Mark me, my friends—we rise for Liberty—
 Justice shall be our guide: let no man dare
 To plunder in the tumult.

85

MOB   Lead us on.
  Liberty! Justice!   135
    Exeunt, with cries of Liberty! No Poll-tax! No War!

2.2

The Tower

King Richard, Archbishop of Canterbury, Sir John Tresilian,
Walworth, Philpot

KING What must we do? The danger grows more imminent.
  The mob increases.
PHILPOT   Every moment brings
  Fresh tidings of our peril.
KING   It were well
  To grant them what they ask.
ARCHBISHOP   Aye, that my liege°
  Were politic. Go boldly forth to meet them,   5
  Grant all they ask—however wild and ruinous—
  Meantime, the troops you have already summoned
  Will gather round them. Then my Christian power
  Absolves you of your promise.
WALWORTH Were but their ringleaders cut off, the rabble   10
  Would soon disperse.
PHILPOT   United in a mass,
  There's nothing can resist them—once divide them
  And they will fall an easy sacrifice.
ARCHBISHOP Lull them by promises—bespeak them
    fair.
  Go forth, my liege—spare not, if need requires,°   15
  A solemn oath to ratify the treaty.
KING I dread their fury.
ARCHBISHOP   'Tis a needless dread,
  There is divinity about your person;°
  It is the sacred privilege of Kings,
  Howe'er they act, to render no account   20
  To man. The people have been taught this lesson,
  Nor can they soon forget it.
KING   I will go—

I will submit to everything they ask;
My day of triumph will arrive at last.
>   *Shouts offstage. Enter [First Messenger]*
FIRST MESSENGER The mob are at the city gates.
ARCHBISHOP   Haste! Haste!   25
Address them ere too late. I'll remain here,
For they detest me much.
>   *Shouts again. Enter Second Messenger*
SECOND MESSENGER The Londoners have opened the city gates;
The rebels are admitted.
KING Fear then must give me courage. My lord mayor,   30
Come you with me.
>   *Exeunt. Shouts offstage*

2.3

Smithfield°

Wat Tyler, John Ball, Piers and Mob
PIERS So far triumphant are we. How these nobles,
These petty tyrants, who so long oppressed us,
Shrink at the first resistance.
HOB   They were powerful
Only because we fondly thought them so.
Where is Jack Straw?
TYLER   Jack Straw is gone to the Tower   5
To seize the king, and so to end resistance.
JOHN BALL It was well judged; fain would I spare the shedding
Of human blood; gain we that royal puppet
And all will follow fairly; deprived of him,
The nobles lose their pretext, nor will dare   10
Rebel against the people's majesty.
>   *Enter Herald*
HERALD Richard the Second, by the grace of God,
Of England, Ireland, France, and Scotland, King,
And of the town of Berwick-upon-Tweed,°
Would parley with Wat Tyler.
TYLER   Let him know   15
Wat Tyler is in Smithfield.

Exit Herald
                              I will parley
With this young monarch: as he comes to me,
Trusting my honour, on your lives I charge you
Let none attempt to harm him.
JOHN BALL   The faith of courts
Is but a weak dependence. You are honest—   20
And better is it even to die the victim
Of credulous honesty, than live preserved
By the cold policy that still suspects.
        Enter King, Walworth, Philpot[, and their supporters]°
KING I would speak to thee, Wat Tyler: bid the mob
Retire awhile.   25
PIERS   Nay, do not go alone—
Let me attend you.
TYLER   Wherefore should I fear?
Am I not armed with a just cause? Retire,
And I will boldly plead the cause of Freedom.
        [Wat Tyler] advances
KING Tyler, why have you killed my officer,
And led my honest subjects from their homes,   30
Thus to rebel against the Lord's anointed?°
TYLER Because they were oppressed.
KING   Was this the way
To remedy the ill? You should have tried
By milder means—petitioned at the throne—
The throne will always listen to petitions.   35
TYLER King of England,
Petitioning for pity is most weak—
The sovereign people ought to demand justice.°
I killed your officer, for his lewd hand
Insulted a maid's modesty. Your subjects   40
I lead to rebel against the Lord's anointed,
Because his ministers have made him odious,
His yoke is heavy, and his burden grievous.°
Why do we carry on this fatal war,
To force upon the French a king they hate,   45
Tearing our young men from their peaceful homes,
Forcing his hard-earned fruits from the honest peasant,
Distressing us to desolate our neighbours?
Why is this ruinous poll-tax imposed,

But to support your court's extravagance,   50
And your mad title to the crown of France?
Shall we sit tamely down beneath these evils
Petitioning for pity? King of England,
Why are we sold like cattle in your markets—
Deprived of every privilege of man?   55
Must we lie tamely at our tyrant's feet,
And, like your spaniels, lick the hand that beats us?
You sit at ease in your gay palaces,
The costly banquet courts your appetite,
Sweet music soothes your slumbers: we the while,   60
Scarce by hard toil can earn a little food,
And sleep scarce sheltered from the cold night wind;
Whilst your wild projects wrest the little from us
Which might have cheered the wintry hour of age.
The parliament for ever asks more money;   65
We toil and sweat for money for your taxes:
Where is the benefit, what good reap we°
From all the counsels of your government?
Think you that we should quarrel with the French?
What boots to us your victories, your glory?   70
We pay, we fight, you profit at your ease.
Do you not claim the country as your own?
Do you not call the venison of the forest,
The birds of heaven your own?—prohibiting us,
Even though in want of food, to seize the prey   75
Which nature offers. King! is all this just?°
Think you we do not feel the wrongs we suffer?
The hour of retribution is at hand,
And tyrants tremble—mark me, King of England.
   Walworth comes behind Tyler and stabs him
WALWORTH Insolent rebel, threatening the King!   80
PIERS Vengeance! Vengeance!
HOB Seize the King.
KING I must be bold. (*Advancing*) My friends and loving subjects,
 I will grant you all you ask; you shall be free—°
 The tax shall be repealed—all, all you wish.   85
 Your leader menaced me, he deserved his fate.
 Quiet your angers: on my royal word
 Your grievances shall all be done away;
 Your vassalage abolished. A free pardon°

Allowed to all: so help me God, it shall be.   90
JOHN BALL Revenge, my brethren, beseems not Christians:
    Send us these terms, signed with your seal of state.
    We will await in peace. Deceive us not—
    Act justly, so to excuse your late foul deed.
KING The charter shall be drawn out: on mine honour   95
    All shall be justly done.
        [*Curtain falls*]°

3.1

Smithfield

Enter John Ball, Piers, and others°
PIERS (*to John Ball*) You look disturbed, my father.
JOHN BALL   Piers, I am so.°
   Jack Straw has forced the Tower: seized the Archbishop,
   And beheaded him.
PIERS   The curse of insurrection.
JOHN BALL Aye, Piers, our nobles level down their vassals,
   Keep them at endless labour, like their brutes,   5
   Degrading every faculty by servitude,
   Repressing all the energy of mind:
   We must not wonder then, that like wild beasts,
   When they have burst their chains, with brutal rage
   They revenge them on their tyrants.
PIERS   This Archbishop!   10
   He was oppressive to his humble vassals:
   Proud, haughty, avaricious——
JOHN BALL   A true high priest!
   Preaching humility with his mitre on!°
   Praising up alms and Christian charity,
   Even whilst his unforgiving hand distressed   15
   His honest tenants.
PIERS   He deserved his fate, then.
JOHN BALL Justice can never link with cruelty.
   Is there among the catalogue of crimes
   A sin so black that only Death can expiate?
   Will Reason never rouse her from her slumbers,   20
   And darting through the veil her eagle eye,
   See in the sable garments of the law°
   Revenge concealed? This high priest has been haughty,
   He has oppressed his vassals: tell me, Piers,
   Does his death remedy the ills he caused?   25
   Were it not better to repress his power
   Of doing wrong, that so his future life
   Might remedy the evils of the past,
   And benefit mankind?

PIERS   But must not vice
  Be punished?
JOHN BALL   Is not punishment revenge?   30
  The momentary violence of anger
  May be excused: the indignant heart will throb
  Against oppression, and the outstretched arm
  Resent its injured feelings. The collector
  Insulted Alice, and roused the keen emotions   35
  Of a fond father. Tyler murdered him.
PIERS Murdered!—A most harsh word.
JOHN BALL   Yes, murdered him:
  His mangled feelings prompted the bad act,°
  And Nature will almost commend the deed
  That Justice blames: but will the awakened feelings   40
  Plead with their heart-emoving eloquence
  For the cool deliberate murder of Revenge?°
  Would you, Piers, in your calmer hour of reason,
  Condemn an erring brother to be slain?
  Cut him at once from all the joys of life,   45
  All hopes of reformation—to revenge
  The deed his punishment cannot recall?
  My blood boiled in me at the fate of Tyler,
  Yet I revenged not.
PIERS   Oh, my Christian father,
  They would not argue thus humanely on us,   50
  Were we within their power.
JOHN BALL   I know they would not;
  But we must pity them that they are vicious,
  Not imitate their vice.
PIERS   Alas, poor Tyler!°
  I do repent me much that I stood back,
  When he advanced, fearless in rectitude,   55
  To meet these royal assassins.
JOHN BALL   Not for myself,
  Though I have lost an honest virtuous friend,
  Mourn I the death of Tyler: he was one
  Gifted with the strong energy of mind,
  Quick to perceive the right, and prompt to act   60
  When Justice needed: he would listen to me
  With due attention, yet not yielding lightly
  What had to him seemed good: severe in virtue,

He awed the ruder people, whom he led,
By his stern rectitude.
PIERS   Witness that day   65
When they destroyed the palace of the Gaunt;°
And hurled the wealth his avarice had amassed,
Amid the fire: the people, fierce in zeal,
Threw in the flames a wretch whose selfish hand
Purloined amid the tumult.

JOHN BALL   I lament   70
The death of Tyler for my country's sake.
I shudder lest posterity enslaved,
Should rue his murder. Who shall now control°
The giddy multitude, blind to their own good,
And listening with avidity to the tale   75
Of courtly falsehood?

PIERS   The King must perform
His plighted promise.
        [*Mob*] *cry offstage* 'The charter! The charter! *Enter Mob*[, *with
        Tom Miller, Hob*] *and Herald*

TOM MILLER Read it out—read it out.

HOB Aye, ayc, let's hear the charter.

HERALD 'Richard Plantagenet, by the grace of God, King of England,   80
    Ireland, France, Scotland, and the town of Berwick-upon-Tweed,
    to all whom it may concern, these presents:° Whereas our loving
    subjects have complained to us of the heavy burdens they endure,
    particularly from our late enacted poll-tax; and whereas they have
    risen in arms against our officers, and demanded the abolition of   85
    personal slavery, vassalage and manorial rights; we, ever ready in
    our sovereign mercy to listen to the petitions of our loving subjects,
    do annul all these grievances.'

MOB Huzza! Long live the King.

HERALD (*continues*) 'And do of our royal mercy grant a free pardon to   90
    all who may have been anyways concerned in the late insurrections.
    All this shall be faithfully performed on our royal word, so help us
    God.'—God save the King.
        Loud and repeated shouts

HERALD Now then depart in quiet to your homes.

JOHN BALL Nay, my good friend, the people will remain   95
    Embodied peaceably, till parliament°
    Confirm the royal charter: tell your King so:
    We will await the charter's confirmation,

Meanwhile comporting ourselves orderly,
As peaceful citizens, not risen in tumult,   100
But to redress their evils.
    Exit Herald
HOB   'Twas well ordered.°
I place but little trust in courtly faith.
JOHN BALL We must remain embodied; else the King
Will plunge again in royal luxury,
And when the storm of danger is past over,   105
Forget his promises.
HOB   Aye, like an aguish sinner,°
He'll promise to repent, when the fit's on him,
When well recovered, laugh at his own terrors.
PIERS Oh I am grieved that we must gain so little.
Why are not all these empty ranks abolished,   110
King, slave, and lord, ennobled into MAN.°
Are we not equal all?—Have you not told me
Equality is the sacred right of man,
Inalienable, though by force withheld?
JOHN BALL Even so; but, Piers, my frail and fallible judgement   115
Knows hardly to decide if it be right,
Peaceably to return, content with little,
With this half restitution of our rights,
Or boldly to proceed, through blood and slaughter,
Till we should all be equal and all happy.   120
I chose the milder way:—perhaps I erred!
PIERS I fear me! By the mass, the unsteady people
Are flocking homewards—how the multitude
Diminishes!
JOHN BALL   Go thou, my son, and stay them.
Carter, do you exert your influence,   125
All depends upon their stay: my mind is troubled,
And I would fain compose my thoughts for action.
    Exeunt Hob and Piers
Father of mercies! I do fear me much
That I have erred. Thou gavest my ardent mind
To pierce the mists of superstitious falsehood;—   130
Gavest me to know the truth. I should have urged it
Through every opposition; now, perhaps,
The seemly voice of pity has deceived me
And all this mighty movement ends in ruin.

I fear me I have been like the weak leech,°   135
Who, sparing to cut deep, with cruel mercy
Mangles his patient without curing him.
  Great tumult [offstage]
What means this tumult? Hark! the clang of arms.
God of eternal justice—the false monarch
Has broke his plighted vow.   140
  Enter Piers wounded
Fly, fly, my father—the perjured King—fly, fly.
JOHN BALL Nay, nay, my child; I dare abide my fate.
Let me bind up thy wounds.
PIERS   'Tis useless succour.
They seek thy life; fly, fly, my honoured father,
And let me have the hope to sweeten death   145
That thou at least hast 'scaped. They are murdering°
Our unsuspecting brethren: half unarmed,
Trusting too fondly to the tyrant's word,°
They were dispersing:—the streets swim with blood.
Oh, save thyself.   150
  Enter Soldiers
FIRST SOLDIER This is that old seditious heretic.
  [First Soldier] seizes John Ball°
SECOND SOLDIER And here the young spawn of rebellion;
My orders aren't to spare him.
  [Second Soldier] stabs Piers
Come, you old stirrer-up of insurrection,
You bell-wether of the mob—you aren't to die°   155
So easily (*leading him off*).°
  Mob° fly across the stage—the troops pursue them—tumult
  increases—loud cries and shouts

3.2

Westminster Hall°

Enter King, Walworth, Philpot, Sir John Tresilian, and others
WALWORTH My liege, 'twas wisely ordered, to destroy
The dunghill rabble, but take prisoner
That old seditious priest: his strange wild notions

Of this equality, when well exposed,
Will create ridicule, and shame the people   5
Of their late tumults.
SIR JOHN TRESILIAN   Aye, there's nothing like
A fair, free, open trial, where the King
Can choose his jury and appoint his judges.
KING Walworth, I must thank you for my deliverance,
'Twas a bold deed to stab him in the parley.   10
Kneel down, and rise a knight, Sir William Walworth.
       Enter Messenger
MESSENGER I left them hotly at it. Smithfield smoked
With the rebels' blood! Your troops fought loyally,
There's not a man of them will lend an ear
To pity.
WALWORTH Is John Ball secured?
MESSENGER   They have seized him.   15
       Enter Guards, with John Ball
FIRST GUARD We've brought the old villain.
SECOND GUARD   An old mischief maker—
Why there's fifteen hundred of the mob are killed,
All through his preaching.
SIR JOHN TRESILIAN Prisoner, are you the arch-rebel John Ball?
JOHN BALL I am John Ball; but I am not a rebel.   20
Take ye the name, who, arrogant in strength,
Rebel against the people's sovereignty.
SIR JOHN TRESILIAN John Ball, you are accused of stirring up
The poor deluded people to rebellion;
Not having the fear of God and of the King   25
Before your eyes; of preaching up strange notions,
Heretical and treasonous; such as saying
That kings have not a right from Heaven to govern;
That all mankind are equal; and that rank°
And the distinctions of society,   30
Aye, and the sacred rights of property,
Are evil and oppressive; plead you guilty°
To this most heavy charge?
JOHN BALL   If it be guilt,
To preach what you are pleased to call strange notions,
That all mankind as brethren must be equal;   35
That privileged orders of society
Are evil and oppressive; that the right

96

Of property is a juggle to deceive
The poor whom you oppress; I plead me guilty.
SIR JOHN TRESILIAN It is against the custom of this court   40
    That the prisoner should plead guilty.
JOHN BALL   Why then put you
    The needless question? Sir Judge, let me save
    The vain and empty insult of a trial.
    What I have done, that I dare justify.
SIR JOHN TRESILIAN Did you not tell the mob they were oppressed;   45
    And preach upon the equality of man;
    With evil intent thereby to stir them up
    To tumult and rebellion?
JOHN BALL   That I told them
    That all mankind are equal, is most true:
    Ye came as helpless infants to the world;   50
    Ye feel alike the infirmities of nature;
    And at last moulder into common clay.
    Why then these vain distinctions?—Bears not the earth
    Food in abundance?—Must your granaries
    O'erflow with plenty, while the poor man starves?   55
    Sir Judge, why sit you there, clad in your furs;
    Why are your cellars stored with choicest wines?
    Your larders hung with dainties, while your vassal,
    As virtuous, and as able too by nature,
    Though by your selfish tyranny deprived   60
    Of mind's improvement, shivers in his rags,
    And starves amid the plenty he creates.
    I have said this is wrong, and I repeat it—
    And there will be a time when this great truth
    Shall be confessed—be felt by all mankind.   65
    The electric truth shall run from man to man,°
    And the blood-cemented pyramid of greatness
    Shall fall before the flash.
SIR JOHN TRESILIAN   Audacious rebel;
    How darest thou insult this sacred court,
    Blaspheming all the dignities of rank?   70
    How could the government be carried on
    Without the sacred orders of the King
    And the nobility?
JOHN BALL   Tell me, Sir Judge,
    What does the government avail the peasant?

97

Would not he plough his field, and sow the corn,   75
Aye, and in peace enjoy the harvest too?
Would not the sun shine and the dews descend,
Though neither King nor Parliament existed?
Do your court politics aught matter him?°
Would he be warring even unto death   80
With his French neighbours? Charles and Richard contend,
The people fight and suffer:—think ye, Sirs,
If neither country had been cursed with a chief,
The peasants would have quarrelled?

KING   This is treason!
The patience of the court has been insulted—   85
Condemn the foul-mouthed, contumacious rebel.

SIR JOHN TRESILIAN John Ball, whereas you are accused before us,
Of stirring up the people to rebellion,
And preaching to them strange and dangerous doctrines;
And whereas your behaviour to the court   90
Has been most insolent and contumacious,
Insulting Majesty—and since you have pleaded
Guilty to all these charges; I condemn you
To death: you shall be hanged by the neck,
But not till you are dead—your bowels opened—   95
Your heart torn out, and burnt before your face—
Your traitorous head be severed from your body—
Your body quartered, and exposed upon
The city gates—a terrible example—°
And the Lord God have mercy on your soul.   100

JOHN BALL Why, be it so. I can smile at your vengeance,
For I am armed with rectitude of soul.
The truth, which all my life I have divulged,°
And am now doomed in torments to expire for,°
Shall still survive. The destined hour must come,   105
When it shall blaze with sun-surpassing splendour,
And the dark mists of prejudice and falsehood
Fade in its strong effulgence. Flattery's incense
No more shall shadow round the gore-dyed throne;
That altar of oppression, fed with rites,   110
More savage than the priests of Moloch taught,°
Shall be consumed amid the fire of Justice;
The rays of truth shall emanate around,
And the whole world be lighted.

KING Drag him hence:
　　Away with him to death; order the troops   115
　　Now to give quarter, and make prisoners—
　　Let the blood-reeking sword of war be sheathed,
　　That the law may take vengeance on the rebels.
　　　　[Curtain falls]

APPENDIX: Thomas Paine on *Wat Tyler*

Southey is likely to have found his immediate inspiration for *Wat Tyler* in the partisan account of the Peasant's Revolt which Paine included as a footnote to the second part of *The Rights of Man* (1792). Edmund Burke's *Reflections on the Revolution in France* (1790) constituted the major conservative statement on revolutionary agitation; Paine's two-part *Rights of Man* (1791–2) was the most forceful and popular of the radical rebuttals of Burke. The account of Wat Tyler comes in the middle of Paine's account of English taxation and expenditure on war; he can account for the extortionate rise in taxes 'on no other ground, than extravagance, corruption, and intrigue'. Tyler is the appropriate forebear for such radical truth-telling.

Several of the court newspapers have of late made frequent mention of Wat Tyler. That his memory should be traduced by court sycophants, and all those who live on the spoil of a public, is not to be wondered at. He was, however, the means of checking° the rage and injustice of taxation in his time, and the nation owed much to his valour. The history is concisely this:—In the time of   5
Richard the second, a poll-tax was levied, of one shilling per head, upon every person in the nation, of whatever estate or condition, on poor as well as rich, above the age of fifteen years. If any favour was shewn in the law, it was to the rich rather than to the poor; as no person could be charged more than twenty shillings for himself, family, and servants, though ever so numerous; while all   10
other families, under the number of twenty, were charged per head. Poll-taxes had always been odious; but this being also oppressive and unjust, it excited, as it naturally must, universal detestation among the poor and middle classes. The person known by the name of Wat Tyler, whose proper name was Walter, and a tyler by trade, lived at Deptford. The gatherer of the poll-tax, on   15
coming to his house, demanded tax for one of his daughters, whom Tyler declared was under the age of fifteen. The tax-gatherer insisted on satisfying himself, and began an indecent examination of the girl, which enraging the father, he struck him with a hammer, that brought him to the ground, and was the cause of his death.   20

This circumstance served to bring the discontents to an issue. The inhabitants of the neighbourhood espoused the cause of Tyler, who, in a few days was joined, according to some histories, by upwards of fifty thousand men, and chosen their chief. With this force he marched to London, to demand an abolition of the tax, and a redress of other grievances. The court, finding itself   25
in a forlorn condition, and unable to make resistance, agreed, with Richard at its head, to hold a conference with Tyler in Smithfield, making many fair professions, courtier like, of its dispositions to redress the oppressions. While Richard and Tyler were in conversation on these matters, each being on horseback, Walworth, then mayor of London, and one of the creatures of the   30

court,° watched an opportunity, and like a cowardly assassin, stabbed Tyler with a dagger; and two or three others falling upon him, he was instantly sacrificed.

Tyler appears to have been an intrepid disinterested man, with respect to himself. All his proposals made to Richard, were on a more just and public 35 ground, than those which had been made to John by the Barons; and notwithstanding the sycophancy of historians, and men like Mr Burke, who seek to gloss over a base action of the court by traducing Tyler, his fame will outlive their falsehood. If the Barons merited a monument to be erected in Runnymede,° Tyler merits one in Smithfield. 40

[Source: Thomas Paine, *Rights of Man, Common Sense, and Other Political Writings*, ed. Mark Philp (Oxford, 1998), 284.]

DE MONFORT

A TRAGEDY

by
JOANNA BAILLIE

From Baillie's 'Introductory Discourse' to
A Series of Plays (1798)°

[...] I have been led to believe, that an attempt to write a series of tragedies, of simpler construction, less embellished with poetical decorations, less constrained by that lofty seriousness which has so generally been considered as necessary for the support of tragic dignity, and in which the chief object should be to delineate the progress of the higher passions in the human breast, each play exhibiting a particular passion, might not be unacceptable to the public. And I have been the more readily induced to act upon this idea, because I am confident, that tragedy, written upon this plan, is fitted to produce stronger moral effect than upon any other. I have said that tragedy in representing to us great characters struggling with difficulties, and placed in situations of eminence and danger, in which few of us have any chance of being called upon to act, conveys its moral efficacy to our minds by the enlarged° views which it gives to us of human nature, by the admiration of virtue, and execration of vice which it excites, and not by the examples it holds up for our immediate application. But in opening to us the heart of man under the influence of those passions to which all are liable, this is not the case. Those strong passions that, with small assistance from outward circumstances, work their way in the heart, till they become the tyrannical masters of it, carry on a similar operation in the breast of the monarch, and the man of low degree.° It exhibits to us the mind of man in that state when we are most curious to look into it, and is equally interesting to all. Discrimination of character is a turn of mind, though more common than we are aware of, which everybody does not possess; but to the expressions of passion, particularly strong passion, the dullest mind is awake; and its true unsophisticated language the dullest understanding will not misinterpret. To hold up for our example those peculiarities in disposition, and modes of thinking which nature has fixed upon us, or which long and early habit has incorporated with our original selves, is almost desiring us to remove the everlasting mountains, to take away the native land-marks of the soul; but representing the passions brings before us the operation of a tempest that rages out its time and passes away. We cannot, it is true, amidst its wild uproar, listen to the voice of reason, and save ourselves from destruction; but we can foresee its coming, we can mark its rising signs, we can know the situations that will most expose us to its rage, and we can shelter our heads from the coming blast. To change a certain disposition of mind which makes us view objects in a particular light, and thereby, often-times, unknown to ourselves, influences our conduct and manners, is almost impossible; but in checking and subduing those visitations of the soul, whose causes and effects we are aware of, everyone may make considerable progress, if he proves not entirely successful. Above all, looking back to the first rise, and tracing the progress of passion, points out to us those stages in the approach of the enemy, when he might have been combated most successfully; and where the suffering him to pass may be considered as occasioning all the misery that ensues.

[. . .]

In plays of this nature the passions must be depicted not only with their bold and prominent features, but also with those minute and delicate traits which distinguish them in an infant, growing, and re-pressed state; which are the most difficult of all to counterfeit, and one of which falsely imagined, will destroy the effect of a whole scene. The characters over whom they are made to usurp dominion, must be powerful and interesting, exercising them with their full measure of opposition and struggle; for the chief antagonists they contend with must be the other passions and propensities of the heart, not outward circumstances and events. Though belonging to such characters, they must still be held to view in their most baleful and unseductive light; and those qualities in the impassioned which are necessary to interest us in their fate, must not be allowed, by any lustre borrowed from them, to diminish our abhorrence of guilt. The second and even the inferior persons of each play, as they must be kept perfectly distinct from the great impassioned one, should generally be represented in a calm unagitated state, and therefore more pains is necessary than in other dramatic works, to mark them by appropriate distinctions of character, lest they should appear altogether insipid and insignificant. As the great object here is to trace passion through all its varieties, and in every stage, many of which are marked by shades so delicate, that in much bustle of events they would be little attended to, or entirely overlooked, simplicity of plot is more necessary, than in those plays where only occasional bursts of passion are introduced, to distinguish a character, or animate a scene. But where simplicity of plot is neces-sary, there is very great danger of making a piece appear bare and unvaried, and nothing but great force and truth in the delineations of nature will prevent it from being tiresome. Soliloquy, or those over-flowings of the perturbed soul, in which it unburdens itself of those thoughts which it cannot communicate to others, and which in certain situations is the only mode that a dramatist can employ to open to us the mind he would display, must necessarily be often, and to consider- 80 able length, introduced. Here, indeed, as it naturally belongs to passion, it will not be so offensive as it generally is in other plays, when a calm unagitated person tells over to himself all that has befallen him, and all his future schemes of intrigue or advancement; yet to make speeches of this kind sufficiently natural and impressive, to excite no 85 degree of weariness nor distaste, will be found to be no easy task.

[. . .]

The last play [i.e., *De Monfort*], the subject of which is hatred, will more clearly discover the nature and intention of my design. The rise and progress of this passion I have been obliged to give in retrospect, instead of representing it all along in its actual operation, as I could 90 have wished to have done. But hatred is a passion of slow growth; and to have exhibited it from its beginnings would have included a longer period, than even those who are least scrupulous about the limitation of dramatic time,° would have thought allowable. I could not have introduced my chief characters upon the stage as boys, and then as 95 men. For this passion must be kept distinct from that dislike which we conceive for another when he has greatly offended us, and which is almost the constant companion of anger; and also from that eager desire to crush, and inflict suffering on him who has injured us, which constitutes revenge. This passion, as I have conceived it, is that rooted 100 and settled aversion, which from opposition of character, aided by circumstances of little importance, grows at last into such antipathy and personal disgust as makes him who entertains it, feel, in the presence of him who is the object of it, a degree of torment and restlessness which is insufferable. It is a passion, I believe less frequent than 105 any other of the stronger passions, but in the breast where it does exist, it creates, perhaps, more misery than any other. To endeavour to interest the mind for a man under the dominion of a passion so baleful, so unamiable, may seem, perhaps, reprehensible. I therefore beg it may be considered that it is the passion and not the man which is held up to 110 our execration; and that this and every other bad passion does more strongly evince its pernicious and dangerous nature, when we see it thus counteracting and destroying the good gifts of heaven, than when it is represented as the suitable associate in the breast of inmates as dark as itself. This remark will likewise be applicable to many of the 115 other plays belonging to my work, that are intended to follow. A decidedly wicked character can never be interesting; and to employ such for the display of any strong passion would very much injure instead of improving the moral effect. In the breast of a bad man passion has comparatively little to combat, how then can it show its strength? 120

[. . .]

How little credit soever, upon perusing these plays, the reader may think me entitled to in regard to the execution of the work, he will not, I flatter myself, deny me some credit in regard to the plan. I know of no series of plays, in any language, expressly descriptive of the differ- 125 ent passions; and I believe there are few plays existing in which the display of one strong passion is the chief business of the drama, so written that they could properly make part of such a series. [. . .]

THE CHARACTERS OF THE PLAY°

De Monfort°
Rezenvelt
Count Freberg, *friend to De Monfort and Rezenvelt*
Manuel, *servant to De Monfort*
Jerome, *De Monfort's old landlord°*
Grimbald,° *an artful knave*
Bernard, *a monk*
[Thomas, *a monk*]
[Count Waterlan]
[Jacques,° *a servant*]
[First Gentleman]
[First Monk]
[Second Monk]
[First Officer]
[Second Officer]
Page
Monks
Gentlemen
[Guests]
[Servants]
[Men]

Jane De Monfort, *sister to De Monfort*
Countess Freberg, *wife to Freberg*
Theresa, *servant to the countess*
Abbess
Lay Sister°
[First Nun]
[Second Nun]
Nuns
Ladies

SCENE: A TOWN IN GERMANY°

1.1

Jerome's house. A large old-fashioned chamber

JEROME (*speaking offstage*) This way good masters.
    Enter Jerome, bearing a light, and followed by Manuel, and
    Servants carrying luggage

                                   Rest your burdens here.
This spacious room will please the marquis best.
He takes me unawares; but ill prepared:
If he had sent, e'en though a hasty notice,
I had been glad.

MANUEL   Be not disturbed, good Jerome;   5
Thy house is in most admirable order;
And they who travel o'cold winter nights
Think homeliest quarters good.

JEROME He is not far behind?

MANUEL   A little way.
(*To the Servants*) Go you and wait below till he arrives.   10
    [*Exeunt Servants*]

JEROME (*shaking Manuel by the hand*) Indeed, my friend, I'm glad to
    see you here,
Yet marvel wherefore.

MANUEL I marvel wherefore too, my honest Jerome:
But here we are, prithee be kind to us.

JEROME Most heartily I will. I love your master: 15
He is a quiet and a lib'ral man:
A better inmate never crossed my door.°

MANUEL Ah! but he is not now the man he was.
Lib'ral he will, God grant he may be quiet.°

JEROME What has befallen him?

MANUEL   I cannot tell thee;   20
But faith, there is no living with him now.°

JEROME And yet, methinks, if I remember well,
You were about to quit his service, Manuel,
When last he left this house. You grumbled then.

MANUEL I've been upon the eve of leaving him   25
These ten long years; for many times is he
So difficult, capricious, and distrustful,
He galls my nature—yet, I know not how,

A secret kindness binds me to him still.

JEROME Some, who offend from a suspicious nature,   30
  Will afterwards such fair confession make
  As turns e'en the offence into a favour.

MANUEL Yes, some indeed do so: so will not he;
  He'd rather die than such confession make.

JEROME Aye, thou art right, for now I call to mind   35
  That once he wronged me with unjust suspicion,
  When first he came to lodge beneath my roof;
  And when it so fell out that I was proved
  Most guiltless of the fault, I truly thought
  He would have made profession of regret;   40
  But silent, haughty, and ungraciously
  He bore himself as one offended still.
  Yet shortly after, when unwittingly
  I did him some slight service, o'the sudden
  He overpowered me with his grateful thanks;   45
  And would not be restrained from pressing on me
  A noble recompense. I understood
  His o'erstrained gratitude and bounty well,
  And took it as he meant.

MANUEL   'Tis often thus.
  I would have left him many years ago,   50
  But that with all his faults there sometimes come
  Such bursts of natural goodness from his heart,
  As might engage a harder churl than I°
  To serve him still.—And then his sister too,
  A noble dame, who should have been a queen: 55
  The meanest of her hinds, at her command,
  Had fought like lions for her, and the poor,
  E'en o'er their bread of poverty had blessed her—
  She would have grieved if I had left my lord.

JEROME Comes she along with him?   60

MANUEL No, he departed all unknown to her,
  Meaning to keep concealed his secret route;
  But well I knew it would afflict her much,
  And therefore left a little nameless billet.
  Which after our departure, as I guess,   65
  Would fall into her hands, and tell her all.
  What could I do? Oh 'tis a noble lady!

JEROME All this is strange—something disturbs his mind—

Belike he is in love.
MANUEL   No, Jerome, no.
Once on a time I served a noble master,   70
Whose youth was blasted with untoward love,
And he with hope and fear and jealousy
For ever tossed, led an unquiet life:
Yet, when unruffled by the passing fit,
His pale wan face such gentle sadness wore   75
As moved a kindly heart to pity him;
But Monfort, even in his calmest hour,
Still bears that gloomy sternness in his eye
Which sullenly repels all sympathy.°
Oh no! good Jerome, no, it is not love.°   80
JEROME Hear I not horses trampling at the gate? (*Listening*)
He is arrived—stay thou—I had forgot—
A plague upon't! my head is so confused—
I will return i'the instant to receive him.
        Exit [Jerome] hastily. A great bustle offstage. Exit Manuel with
        lights, and returns again lighting in De Monfort, as if just
        alighted from his journey
MANUEL Your ancient host, my lord, receives you gladly,   85
And your apartment will be soon prepared.
DE MONFORT 'Tis well.
MANUEL Where shall I place the chest you gave in charge?
So please you, say, my lord.
DE MONFORT (*throwing himself into a chair*)
                        Where'er thou wilt.
MANUEL (*pointing to certain things*) I would not move that luggage till
    you came.   90
DE MONFORT Move what thou wilt, and trouble me no more.
        Manuel, with the assistance of other Servants, sets about putting
        the things in order, and De Monfort remains sitting in a
        thoughtful posture. Enter Jerome, bearing wine, &c. on a salver.
        As he approaches De Monfort, Manuel pulls him by the sleeve
MANUEL (*aside to Jerome*) No, do not now; he will not be disturbed.
JEROME What, not to bid him welcome to my house,
And offer some refreshment?
MANUEL   No, good Jerome.
Softly, a little while: I prithee do.   95
        Jerome walks softly on tip-toes, till he gets near De Monfort,
        behind backs,° then peeping on one side to see his face

JEROME (*aside to Manuel*) Ah, Manuel, what an altered man is
 here!
 His eyes are hollow, and his cheeks are pale—
 He left this house a comely gentleman.

DE MONFORT Who whispers there?

MANUEL   'Tis your old landlord, sir:

JEROME I joy to see you here—I crave your pardon—   100
 I fear I do intrude.—

DE MONFORT No, my kind host, I am obliged to thee.

JEROME How fares it with your honour?

DE MONFORT   Well enough.

JEROME Here is a little of the fav'rite wine
 That you were wont to praise. Pray honour me.   105
   [*Jerome*] *fills a glass*

DE MONFORT (*after drinking*) I thank you, Jerome, 'tis delicious.

JEROME Aye, my dear wife did ever make it so.

DE MONFORT And how does she?

JEROME   Alas, my lord! she's dead.

DE MONFORT Well, then she is at rest.

JEROME   How well, my lord?

DE MONFORT Is she not with the dead, the quiet dead,   110
 Where all is peace? Not e'en the impious wretch,
 Who tears the coffin from its earthy vault,
 And strews the mould'ring ashes to the wind
 Can break their rest.

JEROME Woe's me! I thought you would have grieved for her.   115
 She was a kindly soul! Before she died,
 When pining sickness bent her cheerless head,
 She set my house in order—
 And but the morning ere she breathed her last,
 Bade me preserve some flaskets of this wine,   120
 That should the Lord De Monfort come again
 His cup might sparkle still.
   De Monfort walks across the stage, and wipes his eyes
 Indeed I fear I have distressed you, sir:
 I surely thought you would be grieved for her.

DE MONFORT (*taking Jerome's hand*) I am, my friend. How long has
 she been dead?   125

JEROME Two sad long years.

DE MONFORT   Would she were living still!
 I was too troublesome, too heedless of her.

JEROME Oh no! she loved to serve you.
    Loud knocking offstage
DE MONFORT What fool comes here, at such untimely hours,
    To make this cursèd noise. (*To Manuel*) Go to the gate.   130
    Exit Manuel
    All sober citizens are gone to bed;
    It is some drunkards on their nightly rounds,
    Who mean it but in sport.
JEROME I hear unusual voices—here they come.
    Enter Manuel, showing in Freberg and Countess Freberg
FREBERG (*running to embrace De Monfort*) My dearest Monfort! most
    unlooked-for pleasure.   135
    Do I indeed embrace thee here again?
    I saw thy servant standing by the gate,
    His face recalled, and learnt the joyful tidings.
    Welcome, thrice welcome here!
DE MONFORT I thank thee, Freberg, for this friendly visit,   140
    And this fair lady too. (*Bowing to Countess Freberg*)
COUNTESS FREBERG   I fear, my lord,
    We do intrude at an untimely hour:
    But now returning from a midnight mask,°
    My husband did insist that we should enter.
FREBERG No, say not so; no hour untimely call,   145
    Which doth together bring long absent friends.
    Dear Monfort, wherefore hast thou played so sly,
    To come upon us thus all suddenly?
DE MONFORT Oh! many varied thoughts do cross our brain,
    Which touch the will, but leave the memory trackless;   150
    And yet a strange compounded motive make
    Wherefore a man should bend his evening walk
    To th'east or west, the forest or the field.
    Is it not often so?
FREBERG I ask no more, happy to see you here   155
    From any motive. There is one behind,
    Whose presence would have been a double bliss:
    Ah! how is she? The noble Jane De Monfort.
DE MONFORT (*confused*) She is—I have—I have left my sister well.
COUNTESS FREBERG (*to Freberg*) My Freberg, you are heedless of
    respect: 160
    You surely meant to say the Lady Jane.
FREBERG Respect! No, madam; princess, empress, queen,

Could not denote a creature so exalted
As this plain native appellation doth,
The noble Jane De Monfort.   165
COUNTESS FREBERG (*turning from him displeased to De Monfort*) You
    are fatigued, my lord; you want repose;
Say, should we not retire?
FREBERG   Ha! is it so?
My friend, your face is pale, have you been ill?
DE MONFORT No, Freberg, no; I think I have been well.
FREBERG (*shaking his head*) I fear thou hast not, Monfort—Let it pass.   170
We'll re-establish thee: we'll banish pain.
I will collect some rare, some cheerful friends,
And we shall spend together glorious hours,
That gods might envy. Little time so spent
Doth far outvalue all our life beside.   175
This is indeed our life, our waking life,
The rest dull breathing sleep.
DE MONFORT Thus, it is true, from the sad years of life
We sometimes do short hours, yea minutes strike,
Keen, blissful, bright, never to be forgotten;   180
Which through the dreary gloom of time o'erpast
Shine like fair sunny spots on a wild waste.°
But few they are, as few the heav'n-fired souls
Whose magic power creates them. Blessed art thou,
If in the ample circle of thy friends   185
Thou canst but boast a few.
FREBERG Judge for thyself: in truth I do not boast.
There is amongst my friends, my later friends,
A most accomplished stranger. New to Amberg,
But just arrived; and will ere long depart.   190
I met him in Franconia two years since.°
He is so full of pleasant anecdote,
So rich, so gay, so poignant is his wit,
Time vanishes before him as he speaks,
And ruddy morning through the lattice peeps   195
Ere night seems well begun.
DE MONFORT   How is he called?
FREBERG I will surprise thee with a welcome face:
I will not tell thee now.
COUNTESS FREBERG (*to De Monfort*) I have, my lord, a small request
    to make,

And must not be denied. I too may boast   200
Of some good friends, and beauteous countrywomen:
To-morrow night I open wide my doors
To all the fair and gay; beneath my roof
Music, and dance, and revelry shall reign.
I pray you come and grace it with your presence.   205

DE MONFORT You honour me too much to be denied.

COUNTESS FREBERG I thank you, sir; and in return for this,
  We shall withdraw, and leave you to repose.

FREBERG Must it be so? (*To De Monfort*) Good night—sweet sleep to
  thee.

DE MONFORT (*to Freberg*) Good night. (*To Countess Freberg*) Good-
  night, fair lady.

COUNTESS FREBERG   Farewell!   210
      Exeunt Freberg and Countess Freberg

DE MONFORT (*to Jerome*) I thought Count Freberg had been now in
  France.

JEROME He meant to go, as I have been informed.

DE MONFORT Well, well, prepare my bed; I will to rest.
      Exit Jerome
(*Alone*) I know not how it is, my heart stands back,
And meets not this man's love.—Friends! rarest friends!   215
Rather than share his undiscerning praise
With every table wit, and book-formed sage,°
And paltry poet puling to the moon,
I'd court from him proscription; yea abuse,
And think it proud distinction.
      Exit

1.2

*A small apartment in Jerome's house: a table and breakfast set
out*

*Enter De Monfort, followed by Manuel, and sets himself down
by the table, with a cheerful face*

DE MONFORT Manuel, this morning's sun shines pleasantly:
  These old apartments too are light and cheerful.
  Our landlord's kindness has revived me much;

He serves as though he loved me. This pure air
Braces the listless nerves, and warms the blood: 5
I feel in freedom here. (*Filling a cup of coffee, and drinking*)
MANUEL   Ah! sure, my lord,
    No air is purer than the air at home.
DE MONFORT Here can I wander with assurèd steps,
    Nor dread, at every winding of the path,
    Lest an abhorrèd serpent cross my way,   10
    And move—(*Stopping short*)
MANUEL What says your honour?
    There are no serpents in our pleasant fields.
DE MONFORT Think'st thou there are no serpents in the world
    But those who slide along the grassy sod,   15
    And sting the luckless foot that presses them?
    There are who in the path of social life
    Do bask their spotted skins in Fortune's sun,
    And sting the soul—Aye, till its healthful frame
    Is changed to secret, fest'ring, sore disease,   20
    So deadly is the wound.
MANUEL Heaven guard your honour from such horrid scathe:
    They are but rare, I hope?
DE MONFORT (*shaking his head*) We mark the hollow eye, the wasted
        frame,
    The gait disturbed of wealthy honoured men,   25
    But do not know the cause.
MANUEL 'Tis very true. God keep you well, my lord!
DE MONFORT I thank thee, Manuel, I am very well.
    I shall be gay too, by the setting sun.
    I go to revel it with sprightly dames,   30
    And drive the night away. (*Filling another cup, and drinking*)
MANUEL I should be glad to see your honour gay.
DE MONFORT And thou too shalt be gay. There, honest Manuel,
    Put these broad pieces in thy leathern purse,
    And take at night a cheerful jovial glass.   35
    Here is one too, for Bremer; he loves wine;
    And one for Jacques: be joyful all together.
        Enter Jacques
JACQUES My lord, I met e'en now, a short way off,
    Your countryman the Marquis Rezenvelt.
DE MONFORT (*starting from his seat, and letting the cup fall from his
    hand*) Who, say'st thou?

JACQUES   Marquis Rezenvelt, an please you.   40
DE MONFORT Thou liest—it is not so—it is impossible.
JACQUES I saw him with these eyes, plain as yourself.
DE MONFORT Fool! 'tis some passing stranger thou hast seen,
  And with a hideous likeness been deceived.
JACQUES No other stranger could deceive my sight.   45
DE MONFORT (*dashing his clenched hand violently upon the table, and
    overturning every thing*) Heaven blast thy sight! it lights on
    nothing good.
JACQUES I surely thought no harm to look upon him.
DE MONFORT What, dost thou still insist? Him must it be?
  Does it so please thee well?
       Jacques endeavours to speak
                   Hold thy damned tongue.
  By heaven I'll kill thee. (*Going furiously up to him*)   50
MANUEL (*in a soothing voice*) Nay harm him not, my lord; he speaks
  the truth;
  I've met his groom, who told me certainly
  His lord is here. I should have told you so,
  But thought, perhaps, it might displease your honour.
DE MONFORT (*becoming all at once calm, and turning sternly to
    Manuel*) And how dar'st thou to think it would displease me?   55
  What is't to me who leaves or enters Amberg?
  But it displeases me, yea ev'n to frenzy,
  That every idle fool must hither come
  To break my leisure with the paltry tidings
  Of all the cursèd things he stares upon.   60
     Jacques attempts to speak. De Monfort stamps with his foot
  Take thine ill-favoured visage from my sight,
  And speak of it no more.
     Exit Jacques
  And go thou too; I choose to be alone.
     *Exit Manuel. De Monfort goes to the door by which Jacques and
     Manuel went out; opens it, and looks*
  But is he gone indeed? Yes, he is gone.
     [*De Monfort*] *goes to the opposite door, opens it, and looks: then
     gives loose to all the fury of gesture, and walks up and down in
     great agitation*
  It is too much: by heaven it is too much!   65
  He haunts me—stings me—like a devil haunts—
  He'll make a raving maniac of me—Villain!

The air wherein thou draw'st thy fulsome breath°
Is poison to me—Oceans shall divide! (*Pauses*)
But no; thou think'st I fear thee, cursèd reptile!   70
And hast a pleasure in the damnèd thought.
Though my heart's blood should curdle at thy sight,
I'll stay and face thee still.
    Knocking at the chamber door
                Ha! Who knocks there?
FREBERG (*offstage*) It is thy friend, De Monfort.
DE MONFORT (*opening the door*) Enter, then.   75
    Enter Freberg
FREBERG (*taking his hand kindly*) How art thou now? How hast thou
    passed the night?
Has kindly sleep refreshed thee?
DE MONFORT Yes, I have lost an hour or two in sleep,
And so should be refreshed.
FREBERG   And art thou not?
Thy looks speak not of rest. Thou art disturbed.   80
DE MONFORT No, somewhat ruffled from a foolish cause,
Which soon will pass away.
FREBERG (*shaking his head*) Ah no, De Monfort! something in thy face
    Tells me another tale. Then wrong me not:
If any secret grief distracts thy soul,   85
Here am I all devoted to thy love;
Open thy heart to me. What troubles thee?
DE MONFORT I have no grief: distress me not, my friend.
FREBERG Nay, do not call me so. Wert thou my friend,
Wouldst thou not open all thine inmost soul,   90
And bid me share its every consciousness?
DE MONFORT Freberg, thou know'st not man; not nature's man,
But only him who, in smooth studied works
Of polished sages, shines deceitfully
In all the splendid foppery of virtue.°   95
That man was never born whose secret soul
With all its motley treasure of dark thoughts,
Foul fantasies, vain musings, and wild dreams,
Was ever opened to another's scan.
Away, away! it is delusion all.   100
FREBERG Well, be reservèd then: perhaps I'm wrong.
DE MONFORT How goes the hour?
FREBERG 'Tis early: a long day is still before us,

Let us enjoy it. Come along with me;
I'll introduce you to my pleasant friend.   105
DE MONFORT Your pleasant friend?
FREBERG   Yes, he of whom I spake.
  (*Taking his hand*) There is no good I would not share with thee,
  And this man's company, to minds like thine,
  Is the best banquet-feast I could bestow.
  But I will speak in mystery no more,   110
  It is thy townsman, noble Rezenvelt.
          De Monfort pulls his hand hastily from Freberg, and shrinks back
  Ha! What is this? Art thou pain-stricken, Monfort?
  Nay, on my life, thou rather seem'st offended:
  Does it displease thee that I call him friend?
DE MONFORT No, all men are thy friends.   115
FREBERG No, say not all men. But thou art offended.
  I see it well. I thought to do thee pleasure.
  But if his presence is not welcome here,
  He shall not join our company to-day.
DE MONFORT What dost thou mean to say? What is't to me   120
  Whether I meet with such a thing as Rezenvelt
  Today, tomorrow, every day, or never?
FREBERG In truth, I thought you had been well with him.
  He praised you much.
DE MONFORT I thank him for his praise—Come, let us move: 125
  This chamber is confined and airless grown.
  (*Starting*) I hear a stranger's voice!
FREBERG   'Tis Rezenvelt.
  Let him be told that we are gone abroad.
DE MONFORT (*proudly*) No; let him enter. Who waits there? Ho!
    Manuel!
          Enter Manuel
  What stranger speaks below?
MANUEL   The Marquis Rezenvelt.   130
  I have not told him that you are within.
DE MONFORT (*angrily*) And wherefore didst thou not? Let him
    ascend.
          *A long pause. De Monfort walking up and down with a quick
          pace. Enter Rezenvelt, and runs freely up to De Monfort*
REZENVELT (*to De Monfort*) My noble marquis, welcome.
DE MONFORT   Sir, I thank you.
REZENVELT (*to Freberg*) My gentle friend, well met. Abroad so early?

FREBERG It is indeed an early hour for me.   135
How sits thy last night's revel on thy spirits?
REZENVELT Oh, light as ever. On my way to you
E'en now I learnt De Monfort was arrived,
And turned my steps aside; so here I am. (*Bowing gaily to De Monfort*)
DE MONFORT (*proudly*) I thank you, sir; you do me too much honour.   140
REZENVELT Nay, say not so; not too much honour, marquis,
Unless, indeed, 'tis more than pleases you.
DE MONFORT (*confused*) Having no previous notice of your coming,
I looked not for it.
REZENVELT Aye, true indeed; when I approach you next,   145
I'll send a herald to proclaim my coming,
And make my bow to you by sound of trumpet.
DE MONFORT (*to Freberg, turning haughtily from Rezenvelt with affected indifference*) How does your cheerful friend, that good old man?
FREBERG My cheerful friend? I know not whom you mean.
DE MONFORT Count Waterlan.
FREBERG   I know not one so named.°   150
DE MONFORT (*very confused*) Oh pardon me—it was at Bâle I knew him.°
FREBERG You have not yet enquired for honest Reisdale.
I met him as I came, and mentioned you.
He seemed amazed; and fain he would have learnt
What cause procured us so much happiness.   155
He questioned hard, and hardly would believe
I could not satisfy his strong desire.
REZENVELT And know you not what brings De Monfort here?
FREBERG Truly, I do not.
REZENVELT   Oh! 'tis love of me.
I have but two short days in Amberg been,   160
And here with postman's speed he follows me,°
Finding his home so dull and tiresome grown.
FREBERG (*to De Monfort*) Is Rezenvelt so sadly missed with you?
Your town so changed?
DE MONFORT   Not altogether so:
Some witlings and jest-mongers still remain   165
For fools to laugh at.
REZENVELT But he laughs not, and therefore he is wise.
He ever frowns on them with sullen brow
Contemptuous; therefore he is very wise.

Nay, daily frets his most refinèd soul   170
With their poor folly, to its inmost core;
Therefore he is most eminently wise.
FREBERG Fie, Rezenvelt! You are too early gay;
Such spirits rise but with the ev'ning glass.°
They suit not placid morn.
     De Monfort, after walking impatiently up and down, comes close
     to Freberg's ear, and lays hold of his arm
                         What would you, Monfort?   175
DE MONFORT Nothing—Yet, what is't o'clock?
No, no—I had forgot—'tis early still.
     [De Monfort] turns away again
FREBERG (*to Rezenvelt*) Waltser informs me that you have agreed
To read his verses o'er, and tell the truth.
It is a dangerous task.
REZENVELT   Yet I'll be honest: 180
I can but lose his favour and a feast.
     Whilst Freberg and Rezenvelt speak, De Monfort walks up and
     down impatiently and irresolute; at last, pulls the bell° violently.
     Enter Jacques
DE MONFORT (*to Jacques*) What dost thou want?—
JACQUES   I thought your honour rung.
DE MONFORT I have forgot—Stay; are my horses saddled?
JACQUES I thought, my lord, you would not ride to-day,
After so long a journey.
DE MONFORT (*impatiently*)   Well—'tis good.   185
Begone!—I want thee not.
     Exit Jacques
REZENVELT (*smiling significantly*) I humbly crave your pardon, gentle
   marquis.
It grieves me that I cannot stay with you,
And make my visit of a friendly length.
I trust your goodness will excuse me now;   190
Another time I shall be less unkind.
(*To Freberg*) Will you not go with me?
FREBERG Excuse me, Monfort, I'll return again.
     Exeunt Rezenvelt and Freberg
DE MONFORT (*alone, tossing his arms distractedly*) Hell hath no greater
   torment for th'accursed
Than this man's presence gives—   195
Abhorrèd fiend! he hath a pleasure too,

A damnèd pleasure in the pain he gives!
Oh! the side glance of that detested eye!
That conscious smile! that full insulting lip!°
It touches every nerve: it makes me mad.   200
What, does it please thee? Dost thou woo my hate?
Hate shalt thou have! determined, deadly hate,°
Which shall awake no smile. Malignant villain!
The venom of thy mind is rank and devilish,
And thin the film that hides it.   205
Thy hateful visage ever spoke thy worth:
I loathed thee when a boy.
That men should be besotted with him thus!°
And Freberg likewise so bewitchèd is,
That like a hireling flatt'rer, at his heels   210
He meanly paces, off'ring brutish praise.
Oh! I could curse him too.
    Exit

2.1

A very splendid apartment in Freberg's house, fancifully decorated. A wide folding door opened, shows another magnificent room lighted up to receive company

Enter through the folding doors Freberg and Countess Freberg, richly dressed

FREBERG (*looking round*) In truth, I like those decorations well;
  They suit those lofty walls. And here, my love,
  The gay profusion of a woman's fancy
  Is well displayed. Noble simplicity
  Becomes us less on such a night as this   5
  Than gaudy show.
COUNTESS FREBERG Is it not noble, then?
     Freberg shakes his head
                                I thought it so,
  And as I know you love simplicity,
  I did intend it should be simple too.
FREBERG Be satisfied, I pray; we want tonight   10
  A cheerful banquet-house, and not a temple.
  How runs the hour?
COUNTESS FREBERG It is not late, but soon we shall be roused
  With the loud entry of our frolic guests.
     Enter a Page, richly dressed
PAGE Madam, there is a lady in your hall,   15
  Who begs to be admitted to your presence.
COUNTESS FREBERG Is it not one of our invited friends?
PAGE No, far unlike to them; it is a stranger.
COUNTESS FREBERG How looks her countenance?
PAGE So queenly, so commanding, and so noble,   20
  I shrunk at first in awe; but when she smiled,
  For so she did to see me thus abashed,
  Methought I could have compassed sea and land
  To do her bidding.
COUNTESS FREBERG Is she young or old?
PAGE Neither, if right I guess, but she is fair;   25
  For time hath laid his hand so gently on her,
  As he too had been awed.

COUNTESS FREBERG   The foolish stripling!
  She has bewitched thee. Is she large in stature?
PAGE So stately and so graceful is her form,
  I thought at first her stature was gigantic,   30
  But on a near approach I found, in truth,
  She scarcely does surpass the middle size.
COUNTESS FREBERG What is her garb?
PAGE I cannot well describe the fashion of it.
  She is not decked in any gallant trim,   35
  But seems to me clad in the usual weeds
  Of high habitual state; for as she moves°
  Wide flows her robe in many a waving fold,
  As I have seen unfurlèd banners play
  With the soft breeze.
COUNTESS FREBERG   Thine eyes deceive thee, boy,   40
  It is an apparition thou hast seen.
> *Freberg starts from his seat, where he has been sitting during the*
> *conversation between Countess Freberg and the Page*
FREBERG It is an apparition he has seen,
  Or it is Jane De Monfort.
> *Exit [Freberg] hastily*
COUNTESS FREBERG (*displeased*) No; such description surely suits not
  her.
  Did she enquire for me?   45
PAGE She asked to see the lady of Count Freberg.
COUNTESS FREBERG Perhaps it is not she—I fear it is—
  Ha! here they come. He has but guessed too well.
> *Enter Freberg, leading in Jane*
FREBERG (*presenting Jane to Countess Freberg*) Here, madam, welcome
  a most worthy guest.
COUNTESS FREBERG Madam, a thousand welcomes. Pardon me;   50
  I could not guess who honoured me so far;
  I should not else have waited coldly here.
JANE I thank you for this welcome, gentle countess,
  But take those kind excuses back again;
  I am a bold intruder on this hour,   55
  And am entitled to no ceremony.
  I came in quest of a dear truant friend,
  But Freberg has informed me—
  (*To Freberg*) And he is well you say?
FREBERG   Yes, well, but joyless.

JANE It is the usual temper of his mind:°   60
    It opens not, but with the thrilling touch
    Of some strong heart-string o'the sudden pressed.
FREBERG It may be so, I've known him otherwise.
    He is suspicious grown.
JANE Not so, Count Freberg, Monfort is too noble.   65
    Say rather, that he is a man in grief,
    Wearing at times a strange and scowling eye;
    And thou, less generous than beseems a friend,
    Hast thought too hardly of him.
FREBERG (*bowing with great respect*) So will I say;
    I'll own nor word, nor will, that can offend you.   70
COUNTESS FREBERG De Monfort is engaged to grace our feast,
    Ere long you'll see him here.
JANE I thank you truly, but this homely dress
    Suits not the splendour of such scenes as these.
FREBERG (*pointing to her dress*) Such artless and majestic
      elegance,   75
    So exquisitely just, so nobly simple,
    Will make the gorgeous blush.
JANE (*smiling*) Nay, nay, be more consistent, courteous knight,
    And do not praise a plain and simple guise°
    With such profusion of unsimple words.   80
    I cannot join your company tonight.
COUNTESS FREBERG Not stay to see your brother?
JANE Therefore it is I would not, gentle hostess.
    Here he will find all that can woo the heart
    To joy and sweet forgetfulness of pain;   85
    The sight of me would wake his feeling mind
    To other thoughts. I am no doting mistress,
    No fond distracted wife, who must forthwith
    Rush to his arms and weep. I am his sister:
    The eldest daughter of his father's house: 90
    Calm and unwearied is my love for him;
    And having found him, patiently I'll wait,
    Nor greet him in the hour of social joy,
    To dash his mirth with tears.—
    The night wears on; permit me to withdraw.   95
FREBERG Nay, do not, do not injure us so far!
    Disguise thyself, and join our friendly train.°
JANE You wear not masks tonight?

COUNTESS FREBERG We wear not masks, but you may be concealed
  Behind the double foldings of a veil.   100
JANE (*after pausing to consider*) In truth, I feel a little so inclined.
  Methinks unknown, I e'en might speak to him,
  And gently prove the temper of his mind:°
  (*To Countess Freberg*) But for the means I must become your
    debtor.
COUNTESS FREBERG [*calling offstage*] Who waits?
       Enter Theresa

                                     Attend this lady to my wardrobe,   105
  And do what she commands you.
       Exeunt Jane and Theresa
FREBERG (*looking after Jane, as she goes out, with admiration*) Oh! what
  a soul she bears! see how she steps!
  Nought but the native dignity of worth
  E'er taught the moving form such noble grace.
COUNTESS FREBERG Such lofty mien, and high assumèd gait   110
  I've seen ere now, and men have called it pride.
FREBERG No, faith! thou never didst, but oft indeed
  The paltry imitation thou hast seen.
  (*Looking at her*) How hang those trappings on thy motley gown?
  They seem like garlands on a May Day queen,°   115
  Which hinds have dressed in sport.
COUNTESS FREBERG I'll doff it, then, since it displeases you.
FREBERG (*softening*) No, no, thou art lovely still in every garb.
  But see the guests assemble.
       Enter groups of well dressed people, who pay their compliments to
       Freberg and Countess Freberg; and followed by her pass into the
       inner apartment, where more company appear assembling, as if
       by another entry. Freberg remains on the front of the stage, with
       a friend or two
FREBERG How loud the hum of this gay meeting crowd!   120
  'Tis like a bee-swarm in the noonday sun.
  Music will quell the sound. [*Calling offstage*] Who waits without?
  Music strike up.
       A grand piece of music is playing, and when it ceases, enter from
       the inner apartment Rezenvelt, with several Gentlemen, all
       richly dressed
FREBERG (*to those just entered*) What lively gallants quit the field so
  soon?
  Are there no beauties in that moving crowd   125

To fix your fancy?

REZENVELT Aye, marry, are there! men of ev'ry mind
　　May in that moving crowd some fair one find,
　　To suit their taste, though whimsical and strange,
　　As ever fancy owned.°　　　　　　　　　　　　130
　　Beauty of every cast and shade is there,
　　From the perfection of a faultless form,
　　Down to the common, brown, unnoted maid,°
　　Who looks but pretty in her Sunday gown.

FIRST GENTLEMAN There is, indeed, a gay variety.　　135

REZENVELT And if the liberality of nature
　　Suffices not, there's store of grafted charms
　　Blending in one the sweets of many plants
　　So obstinately, strangely opposite,
　　As would have well defied all other art　　　　140
　　But female cultivation. Agèd youth,
　　With borrowed locks in rosy chaplets bound,
　　Clothes her dim eye, parched lip, and skinny cheek
　　In most unlovely softness.
　　And youthful age, with fat round trackless face,　145
　　The down-cast look of contemplation deep,
　　Most pensively assumes.
　　Is it not even so? The native prude,°
　　With forcèd laugh, and merriment uncouth,
　　Plays off the wild coquette's successful charms　150
　　With most unskilful pains; and the coquette,
　　In temporary crust of cold reserve,
　　Fixes her studied looks upon the ground
　　Forbiddingly demure.

FREBERG Fie! thou art too severe.

REZENVELT　　　　　　　　　　Say, rather, gentle.　　155
　　I'faith! the very dwarfs attempt to charm
　　With lofty airs of puny majesty,
　　Whilst potent damsels, of a portly make,
　　Totter like nurselings, and demand the aid
　　Of gentle sympathy.　　　　　　　　　　　160
　　From all those diverse modes of dire assault,
　　He owns a heart of hardest adamant,
　　Who shall escape tonight.

　　　　　*De Monfort has entered during Rezenvelt's speech, and heard the
　　　　　greatest part of it*

FREBERG (*to De Monfort*)   Ha, ha, ha, ha!
  How pleasantly he gives his wit the rein,
  Yet guides its wild career!   165
     De Monfort is silent
REZENVELT (*smiling archly*) What, think you, Freberg, the same
    powerful spell
  Of transformation reigns o'er all to–night?
  Or that De Monfort is a woman turned,
  So widely from his native self to swerve,
  As grace my gai'ty with a smile of his?   170
DE MONFORT Nay, think not, Rezenvelt, there is no smile
  I can bestow on thee. There is a smile,
  A smile of nature too, which I can spare,
  And yet, perhaps, thou wilt not thank me for it.
     [De Monfort] smiles contemptuously
REZENVELT Not thank thee! It were surely most ungrateful   175
  No thanks to pay for nobly giving me
  What, well we see, has cost thee so much pain.
  For nature hath her smiles, of birth more painful
  Than bitt'rest execrations.
FREBERG These idle words will lead us to disquiet:°   180
  Forbear, forbear, my friends. Go, Rezenvelt,
  Accept the challenge of those lovely dames,
  Who through the portal come with bolder steps
  To claim your notice.
     Enter a group of Ladies from the other apartment. Rezenvelt
     shrugs up his shoulders, as if unwilling to go
FIRST GENTLEMAN (*to Rezenvelt*) Behold in sable veil a lady comes,   185
  Whose noble air doth challenge fancy's skill
  To suit it with a countenance as goodly.
     [First Gentleman] points to Jane, who now enters in a thick black
     veil
REZENVELT Yes, this way lies attraction. (*To Freberg*) With
    permission—
  (*Going up to Jane*) Fair lady, though within that envious shroud°
  Your beauty deigns not to enlighten us,   190
  We bid you welcome, and our beauties here
  Will welcome you the more for such concealment.
  With the permission of our noble host—
     Rezenvelt takes Jane's hand, and leads her to the front of the
     stage

JANE (*to Freberg*) Pardon me this presumption, courteous sir:
    I thus appear, (*pointing to her veil*) not careless of respect   195
    Unto the gen'rous lady of the feast.
    Beneath this veil no beauty shrouded is,
    That, now, or pain or pleasure can bestow.°
    Within the friendly cover of its shade
    I only wish, unknown, again to see   200
    One who, alas! is heedless of my pain.
DE MONFORT Yes, it is ever thus. Undo that veil,
    And give thy count'nance to the cheerful light.
    Men now all soft and female beauty scorn,
    And mock the gentle cares which aim to please.   205
    It is most damnable! undo thy veil,
    And think of him no more.
JANE I know it well, even to a proverb grown
    Is lovers' faith, and I had borne such slight:°
    But he who has, alas! forsaken me   210
    Was the companion of my early days,
    My cradle's mate, mine infant play-fellow.
    Within our op'ning minds with riper years
    The love of praise and gen'rous virtue sprung:
    Through varied life our pride, our joys, were one;   215
    At the same tale we wept: he is my brother.
DE MONFORT And he forsook thee?—No, I dare not curse him:
    My heart upbraids me with a crime like his.
JANE Ah! do not thus distress a feeling heart.
    All sisters are not to the soul entwined   220
    With equal bands; thine has not watched for thee,
    Weeped for thee, cheered thee, shared thy weal and woe,
    As I have done for him.
DE MONFORT (*eagerly*)   Ha! has she not?
    By heaven! the sum of all thy kindly deeds
    Were but as chaff poised against the massy gold,°   225
    Compared to that which I do owe her love.
    Oh pardon me! I mean not to offend—
    I am too warm—But she of whom I speak
    Is the dear sister of my earliest love;
    In noble virtuous worth to none a second: 230
    And though behind those sable folds were hid
    As fair a face as ever woman owned,
    Still would I say she is as fair as thee.

How oft amidst the beauty-blazing throng,
I've proudly to th'inquiring stranger told   235
Her name and lineage! yet within her house,
The virgin mother of an orphan race
Her dying parents left, this noble woman
Did, like a Roman matron, proudly sit,°
Despising all the blandishments of love;   240
Whilst many a youth his hopeless love concealed,
Or, humbly distant, wooed her like a queen.
Forgive, I pray you! Oh forgive this boasting!
In faith! I mean you no discourtesy.

JANE (*off her guard, in a soft natural tone of voice*) Oh no! nor do me
    any.   245

DE MONFORT What voice speaks now? Withdraw, withdraw this
    shade!
For if thy face bear semblance to thy voice,
I'll fall and worship thee. Pray! pray undo!
> [*De Monfort*] *puts forth his hand eagerly to snatch away the veil,*
> *whilst Jane shrinks back, and Rezenvelt steps between to prevent*
> *him*

REZENVELT Stand off: no hand shall lift this sacred veil.

DE MONFORT What, dost thou think De Monfort fall'n so low,   250
That there may live a man beneath heav'n's roof
Who dares to say he shall not?

REZENVELT He lives who dares to say—
> *Jane throws back her veil, very much alarmed, and rushes*
> *between De Monfort and Rezenvelt*

JANE   Forbear, forbear!
> *Rezenvelt, very much struck, steps back respectfully, and makes*
> *Jane a very low bow. De Monfort stands for a while motionless,*
> *gazing upon her, till she, looking expressively to him, extends her*
> *arms, and he, rushing into them, bursts into tears. Freberg seems*
> *very much pleased. The company then gather about them, and*
> *the scene closes*°

2.2

De Monfort's apartments

*Enter De Monfort, with a disordered air, and his hand pressed
upon his forehead, followed by Jane*

DE MONFORT No more, my sister, urge me not again:
My secret troubles cannot be revealed.
From all participation of its thoughts°
My heart recoils: I pray thee be contented.
JANE What, must I, like a distant humble friend,   5
Observe thy restless eye, and gait disturbed,
In timid silence, whilst with yearning heart
I turn aside to weep? Oh no! De Monfort!
A nobler task thy noble mind will give;
Thy true entrusted friend I still shall be.   10
DE MONFORT Ah, Jane, forbear! I cannot e'en to thee.
JANE Then fie upon it! fie upon it, Monfort!
There was a time when e'en with murder stained,
Had it been possible that such dire deed
Could e'er have been the crime of one so piteous,°   15
Thou wouldst have told it me.
DE MONFORT So would I now—but ask of this no more.
All other trouble but the one I feel
I had disclosed to thee. I pray thee spare me.°
It is the secret weakness of my nature.   20
JANE Then secret let it be; I urge no farther.
The eldest of our valiant father's hopes,
So sadly orphaned, side by side we stood,
Like two young trees, whose boughs, in early strength,
Screen the weak saplings of the rising grove,°   25
And brave the storm together—
I have so long, as if by nature's right,
Thy bosom's inmate and adviser been,
I thought through life I should have so remained,
Nor ever known a change. Forgive me, Monfort,   30
A humbler station will I take by thee:
The close attendant of thy wand'ring steps;
The cheerer of this home, by strangers sought;
The soother of those griefs I must not know,

This is mine office now: I ask no more.   35
DE MONFORT Oh Jane! thou dost constrain me with thy love!
  Would I could tell it thee!
JANE Thou shalt not tell me. Nay, I'll stop mine ears,
  Nor from the yearnings of affection wring
  What shrinks from utt'rance. Let it pass, my brother.   40
  I'll stay by thee; I'll cheer thee, comfort thee:
  Pursue with thee the study of some art,
  Or nobler science, that compels the mind
  To steady thought progressive, driving forth
  All floating, wild, unhappy fantasies;   45
  Till thou, with brow unclouded, smil'st again,
  Like one who from dark visions of the night,
  When th'active soul within its lifeless cell
  Holds its own world, with dreadful fancy pressed
  Of some dire, terrible, or murd'rous deed,   50
  Wakes to the dawning morn, and blesses heaven.
DE MONFORT It will not pass away: 'twill haunt me still.
JANE Ah! say not so, for I will haunt thee too;
  And be to it so close an adversary,
  That, though I wrestle darkling with the fiend,   55
  I shall o'ercome it.
DE MONFORT   Thou most gen'rous woman!
  Why do I treat thee thus? It should not be—
  And yet I cannot—Oh that cursèd villain!
  He will not let me be the man I would.
JANE What say'st thou, Monfort? Oh! what words are these?   60
  They have awaked my soul to dreadful thoughts.
  I do beseech thee speak!
        De Monfort shakes his head and turns from Jane; she following him
  By the affection thou didst ever bear me,
  By the dear mem'ry of our infant days;
  By kindred living ties, aye, and by those°   65
  Who sleep i'the tomb, and cannot call to thee,
  I do conjure thee speak.
        De Monfort waves Jane off with his hand, and covers his face
        with the other, still turning from her
                    Ha! wilt thou not?°
  (*Assuming dignity*) Then, if affection, most unwearied love,
  Tried early, long, and never wanting found,
  O'er gen'rous man hath more authority,   70

More rightful power than crown and sceptre give,
I do command thee.
    De Monfort throws himself into a chair greatly agitated
De Monfort, do not thus resist my love.
(*Kneeling*) Here I entreat thee on my bended knees.
Alas! my brother!   75
    De Monfort starts up, and, catching Jane in his arms, raises her
    up, then placing her in the chair, kneels at her feet
DE MONFORT Thus let him kneel who should th'abasèd be,
And at thine honoured feet confession make.
I'll tell thee all—but oh! thou wilt despise me.
For in my breast a raging passion burns,
To which thy soul no sympathy will own.   80
A passion which hath made my nightly couch
A place of torment; and the light of day,
With the gay intercourse of social man,
Feel like th'oppressive airless pestilence.
Oh Jane! thou wilt despise me.
JANE   Say not so: 85
I never can despise thee, gentle brother.
A lover's jealousy and hopeless pangs
No kindly heart contemns.
DE MONFORT   A lover, say'st thou?
No, it is hate! black, lasting, deadly hate;
Which thus hath driv'n me forth from kindred peace,°   90
From social pleasure, from my native home,
To be a sullen wand'rer on the earth,
Avoiding all men, cursing and accursed.
JANE De Monfort, this is fiend-like, frightful, terrible!
What being, by th'Almighty Father formed,   95
Of flesh and blood, created ev'n as thou,
Could in thy breast such horrid tempest wake,
Who art thyself his fellow?
Unknit thy brows, and spread those wrath-clenched hands:
Some sprite accursed within thy bosom mates°   100
To work thy ruin. Strive with it, my brother!
Strive bravely with it; drive it from thy breast:
'Tis the degrader of a noble heart;
Curse it, and bid it part.
DE MONFORT It will not part. ([*With*] *his hand on his breast*) I've
    lodged it here too long;   105

With my first cares I felt its rankling touch,
I loathed him when a boy.
JANE Who didst thou say?
DE MONFORT   Oh! that detested Rezenvelt!
   E'en in our early sports, like two young whelps
   Of hostile breed, instinctively reverse,°   110
   Each 'gainst the other pitched his ready pledge,°
   And frowned defiance. As we onward passed
   From youth to man's estate, his narrow art,
   And envious gibing malice, poorly veiled
   In the affected carelessness of mirth,   115
   Still more detestable and odious grew.
   There is no living being on this earth
   Who can conceive the malice of his soul,
   With all his gay and damnèd merriment,
   To those, by fortune or by merit placed   120
   Above his paltry self. When, low in fortune,
   He looked upon the state of prosp'rous men,
   As nightly birds, roused from their murky holes,
   Do scowl and chatter at the light of day,
   I could endure it; even as we bear   125
   Th'impotent bite of some half-trodden worm,
   I could endure it. But when honours came,
   And wealth and new-got titles fed his pride;
   Whilst flatt'ring knaves did trumpet forth his praise,
   And grov'ling idiots grinned applauses on him;   130
   Oh! then I could no longer suffer it!
   It drove me frantic.—What! what would I give!
   What would I give to crush the bloated toad,
   So rankly do I loathe him!
JANE And would thy hatred crush the very man   135
   Who gave to thee that life he might have ta'en?
   That life which thou so rashly didst expose
   To aim at his! Oh! this is horrible!
DE MONFORT Ha! thou hast heard it, then? From all the
        world,
   But most of all from thee, I thought it hid.   140
JANE I heard a secret whisper, and resolved
   Upon the instant to return to thee.
   Didst thou receive my letter?
DE MONFORT I did! I did! 'twas that which drove me hither.

I could not bear to meet thine eye again.   145
JANE Alas! that, tempted by a sister's tears,
    I ever left thy house! these few past months,
    These absent months, have brought us all this woe.
    Had I remained with thee it had not been.
    And yet, methinks, it should not move you thus.   150
    You dared him to the field; both bravely fought;
    He, more adroit, disarmed you; courteously
    Returned the forfeit sword, which, so returned,
    You did refuse to use against him more;
    And then, as says report, you parted friends.   155
DE MONFORT When he disarmed this cursed, this worthless hand
    Of its most worthless weapon, he but spared
    From dev'lish pride, which now derives a bliss
    In seeing me thus fettered, shamed, subjected
    With the vile favour of his poor forbearance;   160
    Whilst he securely sits with gibing brow
    And basely bates me, like a muzzled cur
    Who cannot turn again.—
    Until that day, till that accursèd day,
    I knew not half the torment of this hell,   165
    Which burns within my breast. Heaven's lightning blast him!
JANE Oh this is horrible! Forbear, forbear!
    Lest heaven's vengeance light upon thy head,°
    For this most impious wish.
DE MONFORT   Then let it light.
    Torments more fell than I have felt already   170
    It cannot send. To be annihilated;
    What all men shrink from; to be dust, be nothing,
    Were bliss to me, compared to what I am.
JANE Oh! wouldst thou kill me with these dreadful words?
DE MONFORT (*raising his arms to heaven*) Let me but once upon his
        ruin look,   175
    Then close mine eyes for ever!
        Jane, in great distress, staggers back, and supports herself upon
        the side scene.° De Monfort, alarmed, runs up to her with a
        softened voice
    Ha! how is this? thou'rt ill; thou'rt very pale.
    What have I done to thee? Alas, alas!
    I meant not to distress thee.—Oh my sister!
JANE (*shaking her head*) I cannot speak to thee.

DE MONFORT   I have killed thee.   180
   Turn, turn thee not away! look on me still!
   Oh! droop not thus, my life, my pride, my sister!
   Look on me yet again.
JANE   Thou too, De Monfort,
   In better days, wert wont to be my pride.
DE MONFORT I am a wretch, most wretched in myself,   185
   And still more wretched in the pain I give.
   Oh curse that villain! that detested villain!
   He hath spread mis'ry o'er my fated life:
   He will undo us all.
JANE I've held my warfare through a troubled world,   190
   And borne with steady mind my share of ill;
   For then the helpmate of my toil wert thou.
   But now the wane of life comes darkly on,
   And hideous passion tears thee from my heart,
   Blasting thy worth.—I cannot strive with this.   195
DE MONFORT (*affectionately*) What shall I do?
JANE   Call up thy noble spirit,
   Rouse all the gen'rous energy of virtue;
   And with the strength of heav'n-enduèd man,°
   Repel the hideous foe. Be great; be valiant.
   Oh, if thou couldst! E'en shrouded as thou art   200
   In all the sad infirmities of nature,
   What a most noble creature wouldst thou be!
DE MONFORT Aye, if I could: alas! alas! I cannot.
JANE Thou canst, thou may'st, thou wilt.
   We shall not part till I have turned thy soul.   205
     Enter Manuel
DE MONFORT Ha! someone enters. Wherefore com'st thou here?
MANUEL Count Freberg waits your leisure.
DE MONFORT (*angrily*) Be gone, be gone.—I cannot see him now.
     Exit Manuel
JANE Come to my closet; free from all intrusion,°
   I'll school thee there; and thou again shalt be   210
   My willing pupil, and my gen'rous friend;
   The noble Monfort I have loved so long,
   And must not, will not lose.
DE MONFORT Do as thou wilt; I will not grieve thee more.
     Exeunt

2.3°

Freberg's house

Enter Countess Freberg, followed by the Page, and speaking as she enters

COUNTESS FREBERG (*giving [the Page] two packets*) Take this and this.
    And tell my gentle friend,°
I hope to see her ere the day be done.
PAGE Is there no message for the Lady Jane?
COUNTESS FREBERG No, foolish boy, that would too far extend
    Your morning's route, and keep you absent long. 5
PAGE Oh no, dear madam! I'll the swifter run.
    The summer's lightning moves not as I'll move,
If you will send me to the Lady Jane.
COUNTESS FREBERG No, not so slow, I ween. The summer's
    lightning!
Thou art a lad of taste and letters grown: 10
Wouldst poetry admire, and ape thy master.
Go, go; my little spaniels are unkempt;
My cards unwritten, and my china broke:°
Thou art too learnèd for a lady's page.
Did I not bid thee call Theresa here? 15
PAGE Madam, she comes.
    Enter Theresa, carrying a robe over her arm
COUNTESS FREBERG (*to Theresa*) What has employed you all this
    dreary while?
I've waited long.
THERESA   Madam, the robe is finished.
COUNTESS FREBERG Well, let me see it.
    Theresa spreads out the robe
(*Impatiently to the Page*) Boy, hast thou ne'er a hand to lift that fold? 20
See where it hangs.
    *Page takes the other side of the robe, and spreads it out to its full
    extent before her, whilst she sits down and looks at it with much
    dissatisfaction*
THERESA Does not my lady like this easy form?
COUNTESS FREBERG That sleeve is all awry.
THERESA   Your pardon, madam;
'Tis but the empty fold that shades it thus.

I took the pattern from a graceful shape;   25
  The Lady Jane De Monfort wears it so.
COUNTESS FREBERG Yes, yes, I see 'tis thus with all of you.
  Whate'er she wears is elegance and grace,
  Whil'st ev'ry ornament of mine, forsooth,
  Must hang like trappings on a May Day queen.   30
  (*Angrily to the Page, who is smiling to himself*) Youngster be gone.
    Why do you loiter here?
        Exit Page
THERESA What would you, madam, choose to wear tonight?
  One of your newest robes?
COUNTESS FREBERG   I hate them all.
THERESA Surely, that purple scarf became you well,
  With all those wreaths of richly hanging flowers.   35
  Did I not overhear them say, last night,
  As from the crowded ball–room ladies passed,
  How gay and handsome, in her costly dress,
  The Countess Freberg looked?
COUNTESS FREBERG   Didst thou o'erhear it?
THERESA I did, and more than this.   40
COUNTESS FREBERG Well, all are not so greatly prejudiced;
  All do not think me like a May Day queen,
  Which peasants deck in sport.
THERESA   And who said this?
COUNTESS FREBERG (*putting her handkerchief to her eyes*) E'en my
    good lord, Theresa.
THERESA He said it but in jest. He loves you well.   45
COUNTESS FREBERG I know as well as thee he loves me well;
  But what of that? he takes no pride in me.
  Elsewhere his praise and admiration go,
  And Jane De Monfort is not mortal woman.
THERESA The wond'rous character this lady bears°   50
  For worth and excellence; from early youth
  The friend and mother of her younger sisters
  (Now greatly married, as I have been told,
  From her most prudent care), may well excuse
  The admiration of so good a man   55
  As my good master is. And then, dear madam,
  I must confess, when I myself did hear
  How she was come through the rough winter's storm,
  To seek and comfort an unhappy brother,

My heart beat kindly to her.   60
COUNTESS FREBERG Aye, aye, there is a charm in this I find:
    But wherefore may she not have come as well
    Through wintry storms to seek a lover too?
THERESA No, madam, no, I could not think of this.
COUNTESS FREBERG That would reduce her in your eyes, mayhap, 65
    To woman's level.—Now I see my vengeance!
    I'll tell it round that she is hither come,
    Under pretence of finding out De Monfort,
    To meet with Rezenvelt. When Freberg hears it
    'Twill help, I ween, to break this magic charm.   70
THERESA And say what is not, madam?
COUNTESS FREBERG How canst thou know that I shall say what is
        not?
    'Tis like enough I shall but speak the truth.
THERESA Ah no! there is—
COUNTESS FREBERG   Well, hold thy foolish tongue.
    Carry that robe into my chamber, do: 75
    I'll try it there myself.
        Exeunt

3.1

[De Monfort's apartments]°

*De Monfort discovered sitting by a table reading. After a little
time he lays down his book, and continues in a thoughtful posture.
Enter to him Jane*

JANE Thanks, gentle brother.—(*Pointing to the book*)
Thy willing mind has been right well employed.
Did not thy heart warm at the fair display
Of peace and concord and forgiving love?

DE MONFORT I know resentment may to love be turned;   5
Though keen and lasting, into love as strong:
And fiercest rivals in th'ensanguined field
Have cast their brandished weapons to the ground,
Joining their mailèd breasts in close embrace,
With gen'rous impulse fired. I know right well   10
The darkest, fellest wrongs have been forgiven
Seventy times o'er from blessed heavenly love:
I've heard of things like these; I've heard and wept.
But what is this to me?

JANE   All, all, my brother!
It bids thee too that noble precept learn,   15
To love thine enemy.°

DE MONFORT Th'uplifted stroke that would a wretch destroy
Gorged with my richest spoil, stained with my blood,
I would arrest and cry, 'Hold! hold! have mercy':°
But when the man most adverse to my nature,°   20
Who e'en from childhood hath, with rude malevolence,
Withheld the fair respect all paid beside,
Turning my very praise into derision;
Who galls and presses me where'er I go,
Would claim the gen'rous feelings of my heart,   25
Nature herself doth lift her voice aloud,
And cries, 'It is impossible.'

JANE (*shaking her head*)—Ah Monfort, Monfort!

DE MONFORT I can forgive th'envenomed reptile's sting,
But hate his loathsome self.   30

JANE And canst thou do no more for love of heaven?

140

DE MONFORT Alas! I cannot now so school my mind
　　As holy men have taught, nor search it truly:
　　But this, my Jane, I'll do for love of thee;
　　And more it is than crowns could win me to,　　　　　35
　　Or any power but thine. I'll see the man.
　　Th'indignant risings of abhorrent nature;
　　The stern contraction of my scowling brows,
　　That, like the plant, whose closing leaves do shrink°
　　At hostile touch, still knit at his approach;　　　　　40
　　The crookèd curving lip, by instinct taught,
　　In imitation of disgustful things
　　To pout and swell, I strictly will repress;
　　And meet him with a tamèd countenance,
　　E'en as a townsman, who would live at peace,　　　　　45
　　And pay him the respect his station claims.
　　I'll crave his pardon too for all offence
　　My dark and wayward temper may have done;
　　Nay more, I will confess myself his debtor
　　For the forbearance I have cursed so oft.　　　　　50
　　Life spared by him, more horrid than the grave
　　With all its dark corruption! This I'll do.
　　Will it suffice thee? More than this I cannot.
JANE No more than this do I require of thee
　　In outward act, though in thy heart, my friend,　　　　　55
　　I hoped a better change, and still will hope.
　　I told thee Freberg had proposed a meeting.
DE MONFORT I know it well.
JANE　　　　　　　　　　And Rezenvelt consents.
　　He meets you here; so far he shows respect.
DE MONFORT Well, let it be; the sooner past the better.　　60
JANE I'm glad to hear you say so, for, in truth,
　　He has proposed it for an early hour.
　　'Tis almost near his time; I came to tell you.
DE MONFORT What, comes he here so soon? shame on his speed!
　　It is not decent thus to rush upon me.　　　　　65
　　He loves the secret pleasure he will feel
　　To see me thus subdued.
JANE Oh say not so! he comes with heart sincere.
DE MONFORT Could we not meet elsewhere? from home—
　　　i'the fields,
　　Where other men—must I alone receive him?　　　　　70

Where is your agent, Freberg, and his friends,
That I must meet him here?
        [*De Monfort*] *walks up and down very much disturbed*
Now didst thou say?—how goes the hour?—e'en now!
I would some other friend were first arrived.
JANE See, to thy wish comes Freberg and his dame.   75
DE MONFORT His lady too! why comes he not alone?
        Must all the world stare upon our meeting?
        Enter Freberg and Countess Freberg
FREBERG A happy morrow to my noble marquis
        And his most noble sister.
JANE   Gen'rous Freberg,
        Your face, methinks, forebodes a happy morn   80
        Open and cheerful. What of Rezenvelt?
FREBERG I left him at his home, prepared to follow:
        He'll soon appear. (*To De Monfort*) And now, my worthy friend,
        Give me your hand; this happy change delights me.
                De Monfort gives him his hand coldly, and they walk to the
                [*back*] *of the stage together, in earnest discourse, whilst Jane and*
                Countess Freberg remain in the front
COUNTESS FREBERG My dearest madam, will you pardon me?   85
        I know Count Freberg's bus'ness with De Monfort,
        And had a strong desire to visit you,
        So much I wish the honour of your friendship.
        For he retains no secret from mine ear.
JANE (*archly*) Knowing your prudence.—You are welcome, madam,   90
        So shall Count Freberg's lady ever be.
                De Monfort and Freberg return towards the front of the stage,
                still engaged in discourse
FREBERG He is indeed a man, within whose breast,
        Firm rectitude and honour hold their seat,
        Though unadornèd with that dignity
        Which were their fittest garb. Now, on my life!   95
        I know no truer heart than Rezenvelt.
DE MONFORT Well, Freberg, well, there needs not all this pains
        To garnish out his worth; let it suffice.°
        I am resolved I will respect the man,
        As his fair station and repute demand.   100
        Methinks I see not at your jolly feasts
        The youthful knight, who sung so pleasantly.
FREBERG A pleasant circumstance detains him hence;

Pleasant to those who love high gen'rous deeds
Above the middle pitch of common minds;   105
And, though I have been sworn to secrecy,
Yet must I tell it thee.
This knight is near akin to Rezenvelt
To whom an old relation, short while dead,°
Bequeathed a good estate, some leagues distant.   110
But Rezenvelt, now rich in fortune's store,
Disdained the sordid love of further gain,
And gen'rously the rich bequest resigned
To this young man, blood of the same degree
To the deceased, and low in fortune's gifts,   115
Who is from hence to take possession of it.
Was it not nobly done?

DE MONFORT   'Twas right, and honourable.
This morning is oppressive, warm, and heavy:
There hangs a foggy closeness in the air;
Dost thou not feel it?   120

FREBERG Oh no! to think upon a gen'rous deed
Expands my soul, and makes me lightly breathe.

DE MONFORT Who gives the feast tonight? His name escapes me.
You say I am invited.

FREBERG   Old Count Waterlan.
In honour of your townsman's gen'rous gift   125
He spreads the board.°

DE MONFORT He is too old to revel with the gay.

FREBERG But not too old is he to honour virtue.
I shall partake of it with open soul;
For, on my honest faith, of living men   130
I know not one, for talents, honour, worth,
That I should rank superior to Rezenvelt.

DE MONFORT How virtuous he hath been in three short days!

FREBERG Nay, longer, marquis, but my friendship rests
Upon the good report of other men;   135
And that has told me much.

> *De Monfort goes some steps hastily from Freberg, and rends his*
> *cloak with agitation as he goes*

DE MONFORT (*aside*) Would he were come! by heaven I would he
    were!
This fool besets me so.

> [*De Monfort*] *suddenly corrects himself, and joining Jane and*

Countess Freberg, who have retired to the [back] of the stage, he
speaks to Countess Freberg with affected cheerfulness
The sprightly dames of Amberg rise by times°
Untarnished with the vigils of the night.   140
COUNTESS FREBERG Praise us not rashly, 'tis not always so.
DE MONFORT He does not rashly praise who praises you;
    For he were dull indeed—
    [De Monfort] stops short, as if he heard something
COUNTESS FREBERG   How dull indeed?
DE MONFORT I should have said—It has escaped me now.
    [De Monfort] listens again, as if he heard something
JANE (*to De Monfort*) What, hear you aught?
DE MONFORT (*hastily*)   'Tis nothing.   145
COUNTESS FREBERG (*to De Monfort*) Nay, do not let me lose it so, my
    lord.
    Some fair one has bewitched your memory,
    And robs me of the half-formed compliment.
JANE Half-uttered praise is to the curious mind,
    As to the eye half-veilèd beauty is,   150
    More precious than the whole. Pray pardon him.
    (*Listening*) Some one approaches.
FREBERG No, no, it is a servant who ascends;
    He will not come so soon.
DE MONFORT (*off his guard*) 'Tis Rezenvelt: I heard his well-known
    foot!   155
    From the first stair-case, mounting step by step.
FREBERG How quick an ear thou hast for distant sound!
    I heard him not.
            De Monfort looks embarrassed, and is silent. Enter Rezenvelt.
            De Monfort, recovering himself, goes up to receive Rezenvelt,
            who meets him with a cheerful countenance
DE MONFORT (*to Rezenvelt*) I am, my lord, beholden to you greatly.
    This ready visit makes me much your debtor.   160
REZENVELT Then may such debts between us, noble marquis,
    Be oft incurred, and often paid again.
    (*To Jane*) Madam, I am devoted to your service,
    And ev'ry wish of yours commands my will.
    (*To Countess Freberg*) Lady, good morning. (*To Freberg*) Well, my
    gentle friend,   165
    You see I have not lingered long behind.
FREBERG No, thou art sooner than I looked for thee.

REZENVELT A willing heart adds feather to the heel,
 And makes the clown a wingèd mercury.°
DE MONFORT Then let me say, that with a grateful mind   170
 I do receive these tokens of good will;
 And must regret that, in my wayward moods,
 I have too oft forgot the due regard
 Your rank and talents claim.
REZENVELT   No, no, De Monfort,
 You have but rightly curbed a wanton spirit,   175
 Which makes me, too, neglectful of respect.
 Let us be friends, and think of this no more.
FREBERG Aye, let it rest with the departed shades
 Of things which are no more; whilst lovely concord,
 Followed by friendship sweet, and firm esteem,   180
 Your future days enrich. Oh heavenly friendship!
 Thou dost exalt the sluggish souls of men,
 By thee conjoined, to great and glorious deeds;
 As two dark clouds, when mixed in middle air,
 The vivid lightning's flash, and roar sublime.   185
 Talk not of what is past, but future love.
DE MONFORT (*with dignity*) No, Freberg, no, it must not. (*To
 Rezenvelt*) No, my lord.
 I will not offer you an hand of concord
 And poorly hide the motives which constrain me.
 I would that, not alone these present friends,   190
 But ev'ry soul in Amberg were assembled,
 That I, before them all, might here declare
 I owe my spared life to your forbearance.
 (*Holding out his hand*) Take this from one who boasts no feeling
  warmth,
 But never will deceive.   195
   Jane smiles upon De Monfort with great approbation, and
   Rezenvelt runs up to him with open arms
REZENVELT Away with hands! I'll have thee to my breast.
 Thou art, upon my faith, a noble spirit!
DE MONFORT (*shrinking back from him*) Nay, if you please, I am not so
 prepared—
 My nature is of temp'rature too cold—
 I pray you pardon me.   200
   Jane's countenance changes
 But take this hand, the token of respect;

The token of a will inclined to concord;
The token of a mind that bears within
A sense impressive of the debt it owes you;
And cursèd be its power, unnerved its strength,   205
If e'er again it shall be lifted up
To do you any harm.
REZENVELT Well, be it so, De Monfort, I'm contented;
I'll take thy hand since I can have no more.
(*Carelessly*) I take of worthy men whate'er they give.°   210
Their heart I gladly take; if not, their hand:
If that too is withheld, a courteous word,
Or the civility of placid looks;
And, if e'en these are too great favours deemed,
'Faith, I can set me down contentedly   215
With plain and homely greeting, or, 'God save ye!'
    De Monfort starts away from Rezenvelt some paces
DE MONFORT (*aside*) By the good light, he makes a jest of it!°
    *Jane seems greatly distressed, and Freberg endeavours to cheer
    her*
FREBERG (*To Jane*) Cheer up, my noble friend; all will go well;
For friendship is no plant of hasty growth.
Though planted in esteem's deep-fixèd soil,   220
The gradual culture of kind intercourse
Must bring it to perfection.
(*To Countess Freberg*) My love, the morning, now, is far advanced;
Our friends elsewhere expect us; take your leave.
COUNTESS FREBERG (*to Jane*) Farewell! dear madam, till the ev'ning
    hour.   225
FREBERG (*to De Monfort*) Good day, De Monfort. (*To Jane*) Most
    devoutly yours.
REZENVELT (*to Freberg*) Go not too fast, for I will follow you.
    Exeunt Freberg and Countess Freberg
(*To Jane*) The Lady Jane is yet a stranger here:
She might, perhaps, in the purlieus of Amberg
Find somewhat worth her notice.   230
JANE I thank you, marquis, I am much engaged;
I go not out today.
REZENVELT Then fare ye well! I see I cannot now
Be the proud man who shall escort you forth,
And show to all the world my proudest boast,   235
The notice and respect of Jane De Monfort.

146

DE MONFORT (*aside, impatiently*) He says farewell, and goes not!
JANE (*to Rezenvelt*)   You do me honour.
REZENVELT (*to Jane*) Madam, adieu! [*To De Monfort*] Good morning,
    noble marquis.
        Exit [Rezenvelt]. Jane and De Monfort look expressively to one
        another, without speaking, and then exeunt, severally

3.2°

A splendid banqueting room

De Monfort, Rezenvelt, Freberg, Count Waterlan, and Guests,
are discovered sitting at table, with wine, &c. before them

SONG.—A GLEE.°

> *Pleasant is the mantling bowl,*
> *And the song of merry soul;*
> *And the red lamps' cheery light.*
> *And the goblet glancing bright;°*
> *Whilst many a cheerful face, around,*   5
> *Listens to the jovial sound.*
> *Social spirits, join with me;*
> *Bless the God of jollity.*

FREBERG (*to De Monfort, who rises to go away*) Thou wilt not leave us,
    Monfort? wherefore so?
DE MONFORT (*aside to Freberg*) I pray thee take no notice of me now.   10
    Mine ears are stunnèd with these noisy fools;
    Let me escape.
        Exit [De Monfort] hastily
COUNT WATERLAN What, is De Monfort gone?
FREBERG   Time presses him.
REZENVELT It seemed to sit right heavily upon him,
    We must confess.   15
COUNT WATERLAN (*to Freberg*) How is your friend? He wears a noble
    mien,
    But most averse, methinks, from social pleasure.
    Is this his nature?

FREBERG   No, I've seen him cheerful,
　　And at the board, with soul-enlivened face,
　　Push the gay goblet round.—But it wears late.   20
　　We shall seem topers more than social friends,
　　If the returning sun surprise us here.
　　(*To Count Waterlan*) Good rest, my gen'rous host; we will retire.
　　You wrestle with your age most manfully,
　　But brave it not too far. Retire to sleep.   25
COUNT WATERLAN I will, my friend, but do you still remain,
　　With noble Rezenvelt, and all my guests.
　　Ye have not fourscore years upon your head;
　　Do not depart so soon. God save you all!
　　　　Exit Count Waterlan, leaning upon a Servant
FREBERG (*to Guests*) Shall we resume?
GUESTS   The night is too far spent.   30
FREBERG Well then, good rest to you.
REZENVELT (*to Guests*)   Good rest, my friends.
　　　　Exeunt all but Freberg and Rezenvelt
FREBERG Alas! my Rezenvelt!
　　I vainly hoped the hand of gentle peace,
　　From this day's reconciliation sprung,
　　These rude unseemly jarrings had subdued: 35
　　But I have marked, e'en at the social board,
　　Such looks, such words, such tones, such untold things,
　　Too plainly told, 'twixt you and Monfort pass,
　　That I must now despair.
　　Yet who could think, two minds so much refined,   40
　　So near in excellence, should be removed,
　　So far removed, in gen'rous sympathy.
REZENVELT Aye, far removed indeed.
FREBERG And yet, methought, he made a noble effort,
　　And with a manly plainness bravely told   45
　　The galling debt he owes to your forbearance.
REZENVELT 'Faith! so he did, and so did I receive it;
　　When, with spread arms, and heart e'en moved to tears,
　　I frankly proffered him a friend's embrace:
　　And, I declare, had he as such received it,   50
　　I from that very moment had forborne
　　All opposition, pride-provoking jest,
　　Contemning carelessness, and all offence;
　　And had caressed him as a worthy heart,°

From native weakness such indulgence claiming: 55
But since he proudly thinks that cold respect,
The formal tokens of his lordly favour,
So precious are, that I would sue for them
As fair distinction in the world's eye,
Forgetting former wrongs, I spurn it all;   60
And but that I do bear the noble woman,
His worthy, his incomparable sister,
Such fixed profound regard, I would expose him;
And as a mighty bull, in senseless rage,
Roused at the baiter's will, with wretched rags   65
Of ire-provoking scarlet, chaffs and bellows,
I'd make him at small cost of paltry wit,
With all his deep and manly faculties,
The scorn and laugh of fools.
FREBERG For heaven's sake, my friend! restrain your wrath;   70
For what has Monfort done of wrong to you,
Or you to him, bating one foolish quarrel,
Which you confess from slight occasion rose,
That in your breasts such dark resentment dwells,
So fixed, so hopeless?   75
REZENVELT Oh! from our youth he has distinguished me
With ev'ry mark of hatred and disgust.
For e'en in boyish sports I still opposed
His proud pretensions to pre-eminence;
Nor would I to his ripened greatness give   80
That fulsome adulation of applause
A senseless crowd bestowed. Though poor in fortune,
I still would smile at vain-assuming wealth:°
But when unlooked-for fate on me bestowed
Riches and splendour equal to his own,   85
Though I, in truth, despise such poor distinction,
Feeling inclined to be at peace with him,
And with all men beside, I curbed my spirit,
And sought to soothe him. Then, with spiteful rage,
From small offence he reared a quarrel with me,   90
And dared me to the field. The rest you know.
In short, I still have been th'opposing rock,
O'er which the stream of his o'erflowing pride
Hath foamed and bellowed. See'st thou how it is?
FREBERG Too well I see, and warn thee to beware.   95

Such streams have oft, by swelling floods surcharged,
Borne down with sudden and impetuous force
The yet unshaken stone of opposition,
Which had for ages stopped their flowing course.
I pray thee, friend, beware.   100
REZENVELT Thou canst not mean—he will not murder me?
FREBERG What a proud heart, with such dark passion tossed,
   May, in anguish of its thoughts, conceive,
   I will not dare to say.
REZENVELT   Ha, ha! thou know'st him not.
   Full often have I marked it in his youth,   105
   And could have almost loved him for the weakness;
   He's formed with such antipathy, by nature,
   To all infliction of corporeal pain,
   To wounding life, e'en to the sight of blood,
   He cannot if he would.
FREBERG   Then fie upon thee!   110
   It is not gen'rous to provoke him thus.
   But let us part; we'll talk of this again.
   Something approaches.—We are here too long.
REZENVELT Well, then, tomorrow I'll attend your call.
   Here lies my way. Good night.   115
     Exit [Rezenvelt]. Enter Grimbald
GRIMBALD Forgive, I pray, my lord, a stranger's boldness.
   I have presumed to wait your leisure here,
   Though at so late an hour.
FREBERG   But who art thou?
GRIMBALD My name is Grimbald, sir,
   A humble suitor to your honour's goodness,   120
   Who is the more emboldened to presume,
   In that the noble Marquis of De Monfort
   Is so much famed for good and gen'rous deeds.
FREBERG You are mistaken, I am not the man.
GRIMBALD Then, pardon me; I thought I could not err.   125
   That mien so dignified, that piercing eye
   Assured me it was he.
FREBERG My name is not De Monfort, courteous stranger;
   But, if you have a favour to request,
   I may, perhaps, with him befriend your suit.   130
GRIMBALD I thank your honour, but I have a friend
   Who will commend me to De Monfort's favour:

The Marquis Rezenvelt has known me long,
Who, says report, will soon become his brother.

FREBERG If thou wouldst seek thy ruin from De Monfort,   135
The name of Rezenvelt employ, and prosper;
But, if aught good, use any name but his.

GRIMBALD How may this be?

FREBERG   I cannot now explain.
Early tomorrow call upon Count Freberg;
So am I called, each burgher knows my house,   140
And there instruct me how to do you service.
Good-night.
    Exit [Freberg]

GRIMBALD (*alone*) Well, this mistake may be of service to me;
And yet my business I will not unfold
To this mild, ready, promise-making courtier;   145
I've been by such too oft deceived already:
But if such violent enmity exists
Between De Monfort and this Rezenvelt,
He'll prove my advocate by opposition.
For, if De Monfort would reject my suit,   150
Being the man whom Rezenvelt esteems,
Being the man he hates, a cord as strong,
Will he not favour me? I'll think of this.
    Exit

3.3

*A lower apartment in Jerome's house, with a wide folding glass
door, looking into a garden, where the trees and shrubs are brown
and leafless*

*Enter De Monfort with his arms crossed, with a thoughtful
frowning aspect, and paces slowly across the stage, Jerome
following behind him with a timid step. De Monfort hearing him,
turns suddenly about*

DE MONFORT (*angrily*) Who follows me to this sequestered room?

JEROME I have presumed, my lord. 'Tis somewhat late:
I am informed you eat at home tonight;
Here is a list of all the dainty fare°

My busy search has found; please to peruse it.   5
DE MONFORT Leave me: begone! Put hemlock in thy soup,
  Or deadly night-shade, or rank hellebore,°
  And I will mess upon it.
JEROME   Heaven forbid!°
  Your honour's life is all too precious, sure—
DE MONFORT (*sternly*) Did I not say begone?   10
JEROME Pardon, my lord, I'm old, and oft forget.
    Exit [Jerome]
DE MONFORT (*looking after him, as if his heart smote him*) Why will
  they thus mistime their foolish zeal,
  That I must be so stern?
  Oh! that I were upon some desert coast!
  Where howling tempests and the lashing tide   15
  Would stun me into deep and senseless quiet;
  As the storm-beaten trav'ller droops his head,
  In heavy, dull, lethargic weariness,
  And, midst the roar of jarring elements,
  Sleeps to awake no more.   20
  What am I grown? All things are hateful to me.
    Enter Manuel
  (*Stamping with his foot*) Who bids thee break upon my privacy?
MANUEL Nay, good, my lord! I heard you speak aloud,
  And dreamt not, surely, that you were alone.
DE MONFORT What, dost thou watch, and pin thine ear to holes,   25
  To catch those exclamations of the soul,
  Which heaven alone should hear? Who hired thee, pray?°
  Who basely hired thee for a task like this?
MANUEL My lord, I cannot hold. For fifteen years,°
  Long-troubled years, I have your servant been,   30
  Nor hath the proudest lord in all the realm,
  With firmer, with more honourable faith
  His sov'reign served, than I have servèd you;
  But, if my honesty is doubted now,
  Let him who is more faithful take my place,   35
  And serve you better.
DE MONFORT Well, be it as thou wilt. Away with thee.
  Thy loud-mouthed boasting is no rule for me
  To judge thy merit by.
    Enter Jerome hastily, and pulls Manuel away
JEROME Come, Manuel, come away; thou art not wise.   40

The stranger must depart and come again,
For now his honour will not be disturbed.
  Exit Manuel sulkily
DE MONFORT A stranger, said'st thou?
  [De Monfort] drops his handkerchief
JEROME I did, good sir, but he shall go away;
 You shall not be disturbed. (*Stooping to lift the handkerchief*) You
 have dropped somewhat.   45
DE MONFORT (*preventing him*) Nay, do not stoop, my friend! I pray
 thee not!
 Thou art too old to stoop.—
 I am much indebted to thee.—Take this ring—
 I love thee better than I seem to do.
 I pray thee do it—thank me not.—What stranger?   50
JEROME A man who does most earnestly entreat
 To see your honour, but I know him not.
DE MONFORT Then let him enter.
  Exit Jerome. A pause. Enter Grimbald
DE MONFORT You are the stranger who would speak with me?
GRIMBALD I am so far unfortunate, my lord,   55
 That, though my fortune on your favour hangs,
 I am to you a stranger.
DE MONFORT How may this be? What can I do for you?
GRIMBALD Since thus your lordship does so frankly ask,
 The tiresome preface of apology   60
 I will forbear, and tell my tale at once.—
 In plodding drudgery I've spent my youth,
 A careful penman in another's office;
 And now, my master and employer dead,
 They seek to set a stripling o'er my head,   65
 And leave me on to drudge, e'en to old age,
 Because I have no friend to take my part.
 It is an office in your native town,
 For I am come from thence, and I am told
 You can procure it for me. Thus, my lord,   70
 From the repute of goodness which you bear,
 I have presumed to beg.
DE MONFORT They have befooled thee with a false report.
GRIMBALD Alas! I see it is in vain to plead.
 Your mind is pre-possessed against a wretch,   75
 Who has, unfortunately for his weal,

Offended the revengeful Rezenvelt.
DE MONFORT What dost thou say?
GRIMBALD What I, perhaps, had better leave unsaid.
Who will believe my wrongs if I complain?   80
I am a stranger, Rezenvelt my foe,
Who will believe my wrongs?
DE MONFORT (*eagerly catching him by the coat*)   I will believe them!
Though they were base as basest, vilest deeds,
In ancient record told, I would believe them.
Let not the smallest atom of unworthiness   85
That he has put upon thee be concealed.
Speak boldly, tell it all; for, by the light!
I'll be thy friend, I'll be thy warmest friend,
If he has done thee wrong.
GRIMBALD Nay, pardon me, it were not well advised,   90
If I should speak so freely of the man,
Who will so soon your nearest kinsman be.
DE MONFORT What canst thou mean by this?
GRIMBALD   That Marquis Rezenvelt
Has pledged his faith unto your noble sister,
And soon will be the husband of her choice.   95
So, I am told, and so the world believes.
DE MONFORT 'Tis false! 'tis basely false!
What wretch could drop from his envenomed tongue
A tale so damned?—It chokes my breath—
(*Stamping with his foot*) What wretch did tell it thee?   100
GRIMBALD Nay, everyone with whom I have conversed
Has held the same discourse. I judge it not.
But you, my lord, who with the lady dwell,
You best can tell what her deportment speaks;°
Whether her conduct and unguarded words   105
Belie such rumour.
        De Monfort pauses, staggers backwards, and sinks into a chair;
        then, starting up hastily—
DE MONFORT Where am I now? 'midst all the cursèd thoughts
That on my soul like stinging scorpions preyed,
This never came before—Oh, if it be!
The thought will drive me mad.—Was it for this   110
She urged her warm request on bended knee?
Alas! I wept, and thought of sister's love,
No damnèd love like this.

154

Fell devil! 'tis hell itself has lent thee aid
To work such sorcery! (*Pauses*) I'll not believe it.   115
I must have proof clear as the noon–day sun
For such foul charge as this! [*Calling offstage*] Who waits without?°
    [*De Monfort*] *paces up and down furiously agitated*
GRIMBALD (*aside*) What have I done? I've carried this too far.
I've roused a fierce ungovernable madman.
    Enter Jerome
DE MONFORT ([*to Jerome*] *in a loud angry voice*) Where did she go, at
    such an early hour,   120
And with such slight attendance?
JEROME Of whom inquires your honour?
DE MONFORT Why, of your lady. Said I not my sister?
JEROME The Lady Jane, your sister?
DE MONFORT (*in a faltering voice*) Yes, I did call her so.   125
JEROME In truth, I cannot tell you where she went.
E'en now, from the short–beechen walk hard–by,°
I saw her through the garden–gate return.
The Marquis Rezenvelt, and Freberg's Countess
Are in her company. This way they come,   130
As being nearer to the back apartments;
But I shall stop them, if it be your will,
And bid them enter here.
DE MONFORT No, stop them not. I will remain unseen,
And mark them as they pass. Draw back a little.   135
    Grimbald seems alarmed, and steals off unnoticed. De Monfort
    grasps Jerome tightly by the hand, and drawing back with him
    two or three steps, not to be seen from the garden, waits in silence
    with his eyes fixed on the glass–door
DE MONFORT I hear their footsteps on the grating sand.
How like the croaking of a carrion bird,
That hateful voice sounds to the distant ear!
And now she speaks—her voice sounds cheerly too—
Oh curse their mirth!—   140
Now, now, they come, keep closer still! keep steady!
    [*De Monfort*] *takes hold of Jerome with both hands*
JEROME My lord, you tremble much.
DE MONFORT   What, do I shake?
JEROME You do, in truth, and your teeth chatter too.
DE MONFORT See! see they come! he strutting by her side.
    Jane, Rezenvelt, and Countess Freberg appear through the

> *glass-door, pursuing their way up a short walk leading to the*
> *other wing of the house*

See how he turns his odious face to hers!   145
Utt'ring with confidence some nauseous jest.
And she endures it too—Oh! this looks vilely!
Ha! mark that courteous motion of his arm—
What does he mean?—He dares not take her hand!
(*Pauses and looks eagerly*) By heaven and hell he does!   150
> *Letting go his hold of Jerome, De Monfort throws out his hands*
> *vehemently, and thereby pushes him against the scene*°

JEROME   Oh! I am stunned! my head is cracked in twain:
Your honour does forget how old I am.
DE MONFORT   Well, well, the wall is harder than I wist.
Begone! and whine within.
> *Exit Jerome, with a sad rueful countenance. De Monfort comes*
> *forward to the front of the stage, and makes a long pause,*
> *expressive of great agony of mind*

It must be so; each passing circumstance;   155
Her hasty journey here; her keen distress
Whene'er my soul's abhorrence I expressed;
Aye, and that damned reconciliation,
With tears extorted from me: Oh, too well!
All, all too well bespeak the shameful tale.   160
I should have thought of heav'n and hell conjoined,
The morning star mixed with infernal fire,
Ere I had thought of this—
Hell's blackest magic, in the midnight hour,
With horrid spells and incantation dire,   165
Such combination opposite, unseemly,
Of fair and loathsome, excellent and base,
Did ne'er produce.—But every thing is possible,
So as it may my misery enhance!
Oh! I did love her with such pride of soul!   170
When other men, in gay'st pursuit of love,
Each beauty followed, by her side I stayed;
Far prouder of a brother's station there,
Than all the favours favoured lovers boast.
We quarrelled once, and when I could no more   175
The altered coldness of her eye endure,
I slipped o'tip-toe to her chamber door;
And when she asked who gently knocked—Oh! oh!

Who could have thought of this?

> [*De Monfort*] *throws himself into a chair, covers his face with his hand, and bursts into tears. After some time he starts up from his seat furiously*

Hell's direst torment seize th'infernal villain!   180
Detested of my soul! I will have vengeance!
I'll crush thy swelling pride!—I'll still thy vaunting—
I'll do a deed of blood—Why shrink I thus?
If, by some spell or magic sympathy,
Piercing the lifeless figure on that wall   185
Could pierce his bosom too, would I not cast it?

> (*Throwing a dagger against the wall*)

Shall groans and blood affright me? No, I'll do it.
Though gasping life beneath my pressure heaved,
And my soul shuddered at the horrid brink,
I would not flinch.—Fie, this recoiling nature!   190
Oh that his severed limbs were strewed in air,
So as I saw him not!

> *Enter Rezenvelt behind, from the glass door. De Monfort turns round, and on seeing him starts back, then drawing his sword, rushes furiously upon him*

Detested robber; now all forms are over:°
Now open villainy, now open hate!
Defend thy life.
REZENVELT   De Monfort, thou art mad.   195
DE MONFORT Speak not, but draw. Now for thy hated life!

> *They fight: Rezenvelt parries his thrusts with great skill, and at last disarms him*

Then take my life, black fiend, for hell assists thee.
REZENVELT No, Monfort, but I'll take away your sword.
Not as a mark of disrespect to you,
But for your safety. By tomorrow's eve   200
I'll call on you myself and give it back:
And then, if I am charged with any wrong,
I'll justify myself. Farewell, strange man!

> *Exit [Rezenvelt]. De Monfort stands for some time quite motionless, like one stupefied. Enter to him Jacques: he starts*

DE MONFORT Ha! who art thou?
JACQUES   'Tis I, an please your honour.
DE MONFORT (*staring wildly at him*) Who art thou?   205
JACQUES Your servant Jacques.

157

DE MONFORT   Indeed I know thee not.
  Leave me, and when Rezenvelt is gone,
  Return and let me know.
JACQUES   He's gone already, sir.
DE MONFORT How, gone so soon?
JACQUES   Yes, as his servant told me,
  He was in haste to go, for night comes on,   210
  And at the ev'ning hour he must take horse,
  To visit some old friend whose lonely mansion
  Stands a short mile beyond the farther wood;
  And, as he loves to wander through those wilds
  Whilst yet the early moon may light his way,   215
  He sends his horses round the usual road,
  And crosses it alone.°
  I would not walk through those wild dens alone
  For all his wealth. For there, as I have heard,
  Foul murders have been done, and ravens scream;   220
  And things unearthly, stalking through the night,
  Have scared the lonely trav'ller from his wits.
          De Monfort stands fixed in thought
  I've ta'en your mare, an please you, from her field,
  And wait your farther orders.
          De Monfort heeds him not
  Her hoofs are sound, and where the saddle galled   225
  Begins to mend. What further must be done?
          De Monfort still heeds him not
  His honour heeds me not. Why should I stay?
DE MONFORT (*eagerly, as Jacques is going*) He goes alone, said'st thou?
JACQUES His servant told me so.
DE MONFORT   And at what hour?
JACQUES He parts from Amberg by the fall of eve.   230
  Save you, my lord! how changed your count'nance is!°
  Are you not well?
DE MONFORT   Yes, I am well: begone!
  And wait my orders by the city wall:
  I'll that way bend, and speak to thee again.
          *Exit Jacques. De Monfort walks rapidly two or three times across
          the stage; then seizes his dagger from the wall; looks steadfastly
          at its point, and exit, hastily*

4.1

Moonlight. A wild path in a wood, shaded with trees

Enter De Monfort, with a strong expression of disquiet, mixed with fear, upon his face, looking behind him, and bending his ear to the ground, as if he listened to something

DE MONFORT How hollow groans the earth beneath my tread!°
Is there an echo here? Methink it sounds
As though some heavy footstep followed me.
I will advance no farther.
Deep settled shadows rest across the path,   5
And thickly-tangled boughs o'er-hang this spot.
Oh that a tenfold gloom did cover it!
That 'midst the murky darkness I might strike;
As in the wild confusion of a dream,
Things horrid, bloody, terrible, do pass,   10
As though they passed not; nor impress the mind
With the fixed clearness of reality.
        An owl is heard screaming near him
(*Starting*) What sound is that?
        [*De Monfort*] *listens, and the owl cries again*
                        It is the screech-owl's cry.°
Foul bird of night! what spirit guides thee here?
Art thou instinctive drawn to scenes of horror?°   15
I've heard of this.
        (*Pauses and listens*)
How those fall'n leaves so rustle on the path,
With whisp'ring noise, as though the earth around me
Did utter secret things!
The distant river, too, bears to mine ear   20
A dismal wailing. Oh mysterious night!
Thou art not silent; many tongues hast thou.
A distant gath'ring blast sounds through the wood,
And dark clouds fleetly hasten o'er the sky:
Oh! that a storm would rise, a raging storm;   25
Amidst the roar of warring elements
I'd lift my hand and strike: but this pale light,
The calm distinctness of each stilly thing,

Is terrible. (*Starting*) Footsteps are near—
He comes, he comes! I'll watch him farther on—   30
I cannot do it here.
      Exit [*De Monfort*]. *Enter Rezenvelt, and continues his way*
    · *slowly across the stage, but just as he is going off the owl screams,*
     he stops and listens, and the owl screams again
REZENVELT Ha! does the night bird greet me on my way?
How much his hooting is in harmony
With such a scene as this! I like it well.
Oft when a boy, at the still twilight hour,   35
I've leant my back against some knotted oak,
And loudly mimicked him, till to my call
He answer would return, and through the gloom
We friendly converse held.°
Between me and the star-bespangled sky   40
Those agèd oaks their crossing branches wave,
And through them looks the pale and placid moon.
How like a crocodile, or wingèd snake,
Yon sailing cloud bears on its dusky length!
And now transformèd by the passing wind,   45
Methinks it seems a flying Pegasus.°
Aye, but a shapeless band of blacker hue
Come swiftly after.—
A hollow murm'ring wind comes through the trees;
I hear it from afar; this bodes a storm.   50
I must not linger here—
    A bell heard at some distance
               What bell is this?
It sends a solemn sound upon the breeze.
Now, to a fearful superstitious mind,
In such a scene, 'twould like a death-knell come:
For me it tells but of a shelter near,   55
And so I bid it welcome.
    Exit

4.2

*The inside of a convent chapel, of old Gothic architecture, almost
dark; two torches only are seen at a distance, burning over a new-
made grave. The noise of loud wind, beating upon the windows
and roof, is heard*

Enter two Monks

FIRST MONK The storm increases: hark how dismally
  It howls along the cloisters. How goes time?
SECOND MONK It is the hour: I hear them near at hand;
  And when the solemn requiem has been sung
  For the departed sister, we'll retire.   5
  Yet, should this tempest still more violent grow,
  We'll beg a friendly shelter till the morn.
FIRST MONK See, the procession enters: let us join.
      *The organ strikes up a solemn prelude. Enter a procession of
      Nuns, with the Abbess, bearing torches. After compassing the
      grave twice, and remaining there some time, whilst the organ
      plays a grand dirge, they advance to the front of the stage*
NUNS (*sing*)
            Departed soul, whose poor remains
            This hallowed lowly grave contains   10
            Whose passing storm of life is o'er
            Whose pains and sorrows are no more!
            Blessed by thou with the blessed above!
            Where all is joy, and purity, and love.

            Let him, in might and mercy dread,   15
            Lord of the living and the dead;
            In whom the stars of heav'n rejoice,
            To whom the ocean lifts his voice,
            Thy spirit purified to glory raise,
            To sing with holy saints his everlasting praise. 20
            Departed soul, who in this earthly scene
            Hast our lowly sister been,
            Swift be thy way to where the blessèd dwell!°
            Until we meet thee there, farewell! farewell!

*Enter a Lay Sister, with a wild terrified look, her hair and dress
all scattered, and rushes forward amongst them*

ABBESS Why com'st thou here, with such disordered looks,   25
    To break upon our sad solemnity?
LAY SISTER Oh! I did hear, through the receding blast,
    Such horrid cries! it made my blood run chill.
ABBESS 'Tis but the varied voices of the storm,
    Which many times will sound like distant screams: 30
    It has deceived thee.
LAY SISTER Oh no, for twice it called, so loudly called,
    With horrid strength, beyond the pitch of nature.
    And 'Murder! murder!' was the dreadful cry.
    A third time it returned with feeble strength,   35
    But o'the sudden ceased, as though the words
    Were rudely smothered in the graspèd throat;
    And all was still again, save the wild blast
    Which at a distance growled—
    Oh! it will never from my mind depart!   40
    That dreadful cry all i'the instant stilled,
    For then, so near, some horrid deed was done,
    And none to rescue.
ABBESS Where didst thou hear it?
LAY SISTER   In the higher cells,
    As now a window, opened by the storm,   45
    I did attempt to close.
FIRST MONK I wish our brother Bernard were arrived;
    He is upon his way.
ABBESS Be not alarmed; it still may be deception.
    'Tis meet we finish our solemnity,   50
    Nor show neglect unto the honoured dead.
        [*Abbess*] *gives a sign, and the organ plays again: just as it ceases*
        a loud knocking is heard offstage°
    Ha! who may this be? hush!
        Knocking heard again
SECOND MONK It is the knock of one in furious haste.
    Hush, hush! What footsteps come? Ha! brother Bernard.
        Enter Bernard bearing a lantern
FIRST MONK See, what a look he wears of stiffened fear!   55
    Where hast thou been, good brother?
BERNARD I've seen a horrid sight!
ALL (*gathering round him and speaking at once*)
                            What has thou seen?
BERNARD As on I hastened, bearing thus my light,

162

Across the path, not fifty paces off,
I saw a murdered corpse stretched on its back,   60
Smeared with new blood, as though but freshly slain.

ABBESS A man or woman?

BERNARD   A man, a man!

ABBESS Didst thou examine if within its breast
There yet is lodged some small remains of life?
Was it quite dead?

BERNARD   Nought in the grave is deader.   65
I looked but once, yet life did never lodge
In any form so laid.—
A chilly horror seized me, and I fled.

FIRST MONK And does the face seem all unknown to thee?

BERNARD The face! I would not on the face have looked   70
For e'en a kingdom's wealth, for all the world.
            (*Shaking his head, and shuddering with horror*)
O no! the bloody neck, the bloody neck!
            Loud knocking heard offstage

LAY SISTER Good mercy! who comes next?

BERNARD   Not far behind
I left our brother Thomas on the road;
But then he did repent him as he went,   75
And threatened to return.

SECOND MONK   See, here he comes.
            Enter Thomas, with a wild terrified look

FIRST MONK How wild he looks!

BERNARD (*going up to him eagerly*)
                              What, hast thou seen it too?

THOMAS Yes, yes! it glared upon me as it passed.

BERNARD What glared upon thee?

ALL (*gathering round Thomas and speaking at once*)
                              Oh! what hast thou seen?

THOMAS As, striving with the blast, I onward came,   80
Turning my feeble lantern from the wind,
Its light upon a dreadful visage gleamed,
Which paused, and looked upon me as it passed.
But such a look, such wildness of despair,
Such horror-strainèd features never yet   85
Did earthly visage show. I shrunk and shuddered.
If damnèd spirits may to earth return
I've seen it.

BERNARD   Was there blood upon it?°
THOMAS Nay, as it passed, I did not see its form;
   Nought but the horrid face.   90
BERNARD It is the murderer.
FIRST MONK   What way went it?
THOMAS I durst not look till I had passed it far,
   Then turning round, upon the rising bank,
   I saw, between me and the paly sky,
   A dusky form, tossing and agitated.   95
   I stopped to mark it, but, in truth, I found
   'Twas but a sapling bending to the wind,
   And so I onward hied, and looked no more.
FIRST MONK But we must look to't; we must follow it:
   Our duty so commands. (*To Second Monk*) Will you go, brother?   100
   (*To Bernard*) And you, good Bernard?
BERNARD   If I needs must go.
FIRST MONK Come, we must all go.
ABBESS   Heaven be with you, then!
    Exeunt [Bernard, Thomas, and the other] Monks
LAY SISTER Amen, amen! Good heaven be with us all!
   Oh what a dreadful night!
ABBESS Daughters retire; peace to the peaceful dead!   105
   Our solemn ceremony now is finished.
    Exeunt

4.3

A large room in the convent, very dark

Enter the Abbess, Lay Sister bearing a light, and several Nuns.
Lay Sister sets down the light on a table at the [back] of the stage,
so that the room is still very gloomy

ABBESS They have been longer absent than I thought;
   I fear he has escaped them.
FIRST NUN   Heaven forbid!
LAY SISTER No no, found out foul murder ever is,
   And the foul murd'rer too.
SECOND NUN The good St. Francis will direct their search;   5
   The blood so near his holy convent shed

For threefold vengeance calls.

ABBESS I hear a noise within the inner court,
They are returned; (*listening*) and Bernard's voice I hear:
They are returned.

LAY SISTER   Why do I tremble so?   10
It is not I who ought to tremble thus.

SECOND NUN I hear them at the door.

BERNARD (*offstage*) Open the door, I pray thee brother Thomas;
I cannot now unhand the prisoner.

ALL (*speaking together, shrinking back from the door, and staring upon one
     another*) He is with them.

> *A folding door at the [back] of the stage is opened, and enter
> Bernard, Thomas, and the other two Monks, carrying lanterns in
> their hands, and bringing in De Monfort. They are likewise
> followed by other Monks. As they lead forward De Monfort the
> light is turned away, so that he is seen obscurely; but when they
> come to the front of the stage they all turn the light side of their
> lanterns on him at once, and his face is seen in all the strengthened
> horror of despair, with his hands and clothes bloody*

ABBESS *and* NUNS (*speaking together, and starting back*)
                              Holy saints be with us!   15

BERNARD (*to Abbess*) Behold the man of blood!

ABBESS Of misery too; I cannot look upon him.

BERNARD (*to Nuns*) Nay, holy sisters, turn not thus away.
Speak to him, if, perchance, he will regard you:
For from his mouth we have no utt'rance heard,   20
Save one deep and smothered exclamation,
When first we seized him.

ABBESS (*to De Monfort*) Most miserable man, how art thou thus?
(*Pauses*)
Thy tongue is silent, but those bloody hands
Do witness horrid things. What is thy name?   25

> *De Monfort, roused, looks steadfastly at the Abbess for some time,
> then speaking in a short hurried voice—*

DE MONFORT I have no name.

ABBESS (*to Bernard*) Do it thyself: I'll speak to him no more.

LAY SISTER Oh holy saints! that this should be the man,
Who did against his fellow lift the stroke,
Whilst he so loudly called.—   30
Still in mine ear it sounds: 'Oh murder! murder!'

DE MONFORT (*starting*) He calls again!

LAY SISTER No, he did call, but now his voice is stilled.
  'Tis past.
DE MONFORT (*in great anguish*) 'Tis past!
LAY SISTER Yes it is past, art thou not he who did it?   35
      De Monfort utters a deep groan, and is supported from falling by
      the Monks. A noise is heard offstage
ABBESS What noise is this of heavy lumb'ring steps,
  Like men who with a weighty burden come?
BERNARD It is the body: I have orders given
  That here it should be laid.
      Enter Men bearing the body of Rezenvelt, covered with a white
      cloth, and set it down in the middle of the room: they then
      uncover it. De Monfort stands fixed and motionless with horror,
      only that a sudden shivering seems to pass over him when they
      uncover the corpse. The Abbess and Nuns shrink back and retire
      to some distance; all the rest fixing their eyes steadfastly upon De
      Monfort. A long pause
BERNARD (*to De Monfort*) See'st thou that lifeless corpse, those
    bloody wounds,   40
  See how he lies, who but so shortly since
  A living creature was, with all the powers
  Of sense, and motion, and humanity?
  Oh! what a heart had he who did this deed!
FIRST MONK (*looking at the body*) How hard those teeth against the
    lips are pressed,   45
  As though he struggled still!
SECOND MONK The hands, too, clenched: the last efforts of nature.
      De Monfort still stands motionless. Thomas then goes to the body,
      and raising up the head little, turns it towards De Monfort
THOMAS Know'st thou this ghastly face?
DE MONFORT (*putting his hands before his face in violent*
    perturbation) Oh do not! do not! veil it from my sight!
  Put me to any agony but this!   50
THOMAS Ha! dost thou then confess the dreadful deed?
  Hast thou against the laws of awful heav'n
  Such horrid murder done? What fiend could tempt thee?
      [*Thomas*] *pauses and looks steadfastly at De Monfort*
DE MONFORT I hear thy words but do not hear their sense—
  Hast thou not covered it?   55
BERNARD (*to Thomas*) Forbear, my brother, for thou see'st right well
  He is not in a state to answer thee.

Let us retire and leave him for a while.
These windows are with iron grated o'er;
He cannot 'scape, and other duty calls.   60
THOMAS Then let it be.
BERNARD (*to Monks, [Abbess, Lay Sister, and Nuns]*) Come, let us all
    depart.
        Exeunt Abbess, [Lay Sister] and Nuns, followed by [Bernard,
        Thomas, and] the Monks. One Monk lingering a little behind
DE MONFORT All gone! (*Perceiving the Monk*) Oh stay thou here!
MONK   It must not be.
DE MONFORT I'll give thee gold; I'll make thee rich in gold,
If thou wilt stay e'en but a little while.
MONK I must not, must not stay.
DE MONFORT   I do conjure thee!   65
MONK I dare not stay with thee. (*Going*)
DE MONFORT   And wilt thou go?
        (*Catching hold of him eagerly*)
Oh! throw thy cloak upon this grisly form!
The unclosed eyes do stare upon me still.
Oh do not leave me thus!
        Monk covers the body, and exit
DE MONFORT (*alone, looking at the covered body, but at a*
    distance) Alone with thee! but thou art nothing now,   70
'Tis done, 'tis numbered with the things o'erpassed,
Would! would it were to come!
What fated end, what darkly gath'ring cloud
Will close on all this horror?
Oh that dire madness would unloose my thoughts,   75
And fill my mind with wildest fantasies,
Dark, restless, terrible! aught, aught but this!
        (*Pauses and shudders*)
How with convulsive life he heaved beneath me,
E'en with the death's wound gored. Oh horrid, horrid!
Methinks I feel him still—What sound is that?   80
I heard a smothered groan.—It is impossible!
        (*Looking steadfastly at the body*)
It moves! it moves! the cloth doth heave and swell.
It moves again.—I cannot suffer this—
Whate'er it be I will uncover it.
        (*Runs to the corpse and tears off the cloth in despair*)
All still beneath.   85

Nought is there here but fixed and grisly death.
How sternly fixèd! Oh! those glazèd eyes!
They look me still.°
        (*Shrinks back with horror*)
Come, madness! come unto me senseless death!
I cannot suffer this! Here, rocky wall,   90
Scatter these brains, or dull them.
        [*De Monfort*] *runs furiously, and, dashing his head against the*
        wall, falls upon the floor.°
        Enter First Monk and Second Monk, hastily
FIRST MONK See; wretched man, he hath destroyed himself.
SECOND MONK He does but faint. Let us remove him hence.
FIRST MONK We did not well to leave him here alone.
SECOND MONK Come, let us bear him to the open air.   95
        Exeunt [*First Monk and Second Monk*], *bearing out De Monfort*

5.1

Before the gates of the convent

*Enter Jane, Freberg, and Manuel. As they are proceeding
towards the gate, Jane stops short and shrinks back*

FREBERG Ha! wherefore? has a sudden illness seized thee?

JANE No, no, my friend.—And yet I am very faint—
I dread to enter here!

MANUEL   Aye! so I thought:
For, when between the trees, that abbey tower
First showed its top, I saw your count'nance change.   5
But breathe a little here; I'll go before,
And make enquiry at the nearest gate.

FREBERG Do so, good Manuel.

Manuel goes and knocks at the gate

Courage, dear madam: all may yet be well.
Rezenvelt's servant, frightened with the storm,   10
And seeing that his master joined him not,
As by appointment, at the forest's edge,
Might be alarmed, and give too ready ear
To an unfounded rumour.
He saw it not; he came not here himself.   15

JANE (*looking eagerly to the gate, where Manuel talks with the
porter*) Ha! see, he talks with someone earnestly.
And see'st thou not that motion of his hands?
He stands like one who hears a horrid tale.
Almighty God!

Manuel goes into the convent

                  He comes not back; he enters.

FREBERG Bear up, my noble friend.   20

JANE I will, I will! But this suspense is dreadful.

*A long pause. Manuel re-enters from the convent, and comes
forward slowly, with a sad countenance*

Is this the pace of one who bears good tidings?
Oh God! his face doth tell the horrid fact;°
There is nought doubtful here.

FREBERG   How is it, Manuel?

MANUEL I've seen him through a crevice in his door: 25

169

It is indeed my master. (*Bursting into tears*)
    Jane faints, and is supported by Freberg. Enter Abbess and
    several Nuns from the convent, who gather about her, and apply
    remedies. Jane recovers

FIRST NUN The life returns again.

SECOND NUN   Yes, she revives.

ABBESS (*to Freberg*) Let me entreat this noble lady's leave
To lead her in. She seems in great distress:
We would with holy kindness soothe her woe,   30
And do by her the deeds of Christian love.

FREBERG Madam, your goodness has my grateful thanks.
    Exeunt, supporting Jane into the convent

5.2

[*A cell*]

De Monfort is discovered sitting in a thoughtful posture. He
remains so for some time. His face afterwards begins to appear
agitated, like one whose mind is harrowed with severest thoughts;
then, starting from his seat, he clasps his hands together, and holds
them up to heaven

DE MONFORT Oh that I had ne'er known the light of day!
That filmy darkness on mine eyes had hung,
And closed me out from the fair face of nature!
Oh that my mind, in mental darkness pent,
Had no perception, no distinction known,   5
Of fair or foul, perfection nor defect;
Nor thought conceived of proud pre-eminence!
Oh that it had! Oh that I had been formed
An idiot from the birth! a senseless changeling,
Who eats his glutton's meal with greedy haste,   10
Nor knows the hand who feeds him.—
    (*Pauses; then, in a calmer sorrowful voice*)
What am I now? how ends the day of life?
For end it must; and terrible this gloom,
The storm of horrors that surround its close.
This little term of nature's agony   15

Will soon be o'er, and what is past is past:
But shall I then, on the dark lap of earth
Lay me to rest, in still unconsciousness,
Like senseless clod that doth no pressure feel
From wearing foot of daily passenger;   20
Like steepèd rock o'er which the breaking waves
Bellow and foam unheard? Oh would I could!°
     Enter Manuel, who springs forward to his master, but is checked
     upon perceiving De Monfort draw back and look sternly upon him
MANUEL My lord, my master! Oh my dearest master!
     De Monfort still looks at him without speaking
Nay, do not thus regard me; good my lord!
Speak to me: am I not your faithful Manuel?   25
DE MONFORT (*in a hasty broken voice*) Art thou alone?
MANUEL No, sir, the Lady Jane is on her way;
  She is not far behind.
DE MONFORT (*tossing his arm over his head in an agony*) This is too
    much! All I can bear but this!
It must not be.—Run and prevent her coming.   30
Say, he who is detained a pris'ner here
Is one to her unknown. I now am nothing.
I am a man, of holy claims bereft;
Out from the pale of social kindred cast;
Nameless and horrible.—   35
Tell her De Monfort far from hence is gone
Into a desolate, and distant land,
Ne'er to return again. Fly, tell her this;
For we must meet no more.
     Enter Jane, bursting into the chamber, and followed by Freberg,
     Abbess, and several Nuns
JANE We must! we must! My brother, oh my brother!   40
     De Monfort turns away his head and hides his face with his arm.
     Jane stops short, and, making a great effort, turns to Freberg,
     and the others who followed her; and with an air of dignity
     stretches out her hand, beckoning them to retire. Exeunt all but
     Freberg, who seems to hesitate
And thou too, Freberg: call it not unkind.
     Exit Freberg; Jane and De Monfort only remain
JANE My hapless Monfort!
     De Monfort turns round and looks sorrowfully upon her; she

opens her arms to him, and he, rushing into them, hides his face
upon her breast and weeps

JANE Aye, give thy sorrow vent: here may'st thou weep.

DE MONFORT (*in broken accents*) Oh! this, my sister, makes me feel
   again°
  The kindness of affection.   45
  My mind has in a dreadful storm been tossed;
  Horrid and dark.—I thought to weep no more.—
  I've done a deed—But I am human still.

JANE I know thy suff'rings: leave thy sorrow free:
  Thou art with one who never did upbraid;   50
  Who mourns, who loves thee still.

DE MONFORT Ah! say'st thou so? no, no; it should not be.
  (*Shrinking from her*) I am a foul and bloody murderer,
  For such embrace unmeet. Oh leave me! leave me!
  Disgrace and public shame abide me now;   55
  And all, alas! who do my kindred own
  The direful portion share.—Away, away!
  Shall a disgraced and public criminal
  Degrade thy name, and claim affinity
  To noble worth like thine?—I have no name—   60
  I am nothing, now, not e'en to thee; depart.
     Jane takes De Monfort's hand, and grasping it firmly, speaks
     with a determined voice

JANE De Monfort, hand in hand we have enjoyed
  The playful term of infancy together;
  And in the rougher path of ripened years
  We've been each other's stay. Dark lowers our fate,°   65
  And terrible the storm that gathers over us;
  But nothing, till that latest agony
  Which severs thee from nature, shall unloose
  This fixed and sacred hold. In thy dark prison-house;
  In the terrific face of armèd law;   70
  Yea, on the scaffold, if it needs must be,
  I never will forsake thee.

DE MONFORT (*looking at her with admiration*) Heav'n bless thy
   gen'rous soul, my noble Jane!
  I thought to sink beneath this load of ill,
  Depressed with infamy and open shame;   75
  I thought to sink in abject wretchedness:
  But for thy sake I'll rouse my manhood up,

And meet it bravely; no unseemly weakness,
I feel my rising strength, shall blot my end,
To clothe thy cheek with shame.   80
JANE Yes, thou art noble still.
DE MONFORT With thee I am; who were not so with thee?
But, ah, my sister! short will be the term:
Death's stroke will come, and in that state beyond,
Where things unutterable wait the soul,   85
New from its earthly tenement discharged,
We shall be severed far.
Far as the spotless purity of virtue
Is from the murd'rer's guilt, far shall we be.
This is the gulf of dread uncertainty   90
From which the soul recoils.°
JANE The God who made thee is a God of mercy;
Think upon this.
DE MONFORT (*shaking his head*) No, no! this blood! this blood!
JANE Yea, e'en the sin of blood may be forgiv'n,
When humble penitence hath once atoned.   95
DE MONFORT (*eagerly*) What, after terms of lengthened misery,
Imprisoned anguish of tormented spirits,
Shall I again, a renovated soul,
Into the blessèd family of the good
Admittance have? Think'st thou that this may be?   100
Speak if thou canst: Oh speak me comfort here!
For dreadful fancies, like an armèd host,
Have pushed me to despair. It is most horrible—
O speak of hope! if any hope there be.
        Jane is silent and looks sorrowfully upon De Monfort; then
        clasping her hands, and turning her eyes to heaven, seems to
        mutter a prayer
DE MONFORT Ha! dost thou pray for me? heav'n hear thy prayer! 105
I fain would kneel—Alas! I dare not do it.
JANE Not so; all by th'Almighty Father formed
May in their deepest mis'ry call on him.
Come kneel with me, my brother.
        Jane kneels and prays to herself;° De Monfort kneels by her,
        and clasps his hands fervently, but speaks not. A noise of
        chains clanking is heard offstage, and they both rise
DE MONFORT Hear'st thou that noise? They come to interrupt us. 110
JANE (*moving towards a side door*) Then let us enter here.

DE MONFORT (*catching hold of her with a look of horror*) Not there—
    not there—the corpse—the bloody corpse.
JANE What, lies he there?—Unhappy Rezenvelt!
DE MONFORT A sudden thought has come across my mind;
    How came it not before? Unhappy Rezenvelt!   115
    Say'st thou but this?
JANE What should I say? he was an honest man;
    I still have thought him such, as such lament him.
        De Monfort utters a deep groan
    What means this heavy groan?
DE MONFORT   It hath a meaning.
        Enter Abbess and Monks, with two Officers of justice carrying
        fetters in their hands to put upon De Monfort
JANE (*starting*) What men are these?   120
FIRST OFFICER Lady, we are the servants of the law,
    And bear with us a power, which doth constrain
    To bind with fetters this our prisoner. (*Pointing to De Monfort*)
JANE A stranger uncondemned? this cannot be.
FIRST OFFICER As yet, indeed, he is by law unjudged,   125
    But is so far condemned by circumstance,
    That law, or custom sacred held as law,
    Doth fully warrant us, and it must be.
JANE Nay, say not so; he has no power to escape:
    Distress hath bound him with a heavy chain;   130
    There is no need of yours.
FIRST OFFICER We must perform our office.
JANE Oh! do not offer this indignity!°
FIRST OFFICER Is it indignity in sacred law
    To bind a murderer? (*To Second Officer*) Come, do thy work.   135
JANE Harsh are thy words, and stern thy hardened brow;
    Dark is thine eye; but all some pity have
    Unto the last extreme of misery.
    I do beseech thee! if thou art a man—(*Kneeling to First Officer*)
        De Monfort, roused at this, runs up to Jane, and raises her
        hastily from the ground; then stretches himself up proudly
DE MONFORT (*to Jane*) Stand thou erect in native dignity;   140
    And bend to none on earth the suppliant knee,
    Though clothed in power imperial. To my heart
    It gives a feller gripe than many irons.
    (*Holding out his hands*) Here, officers of law, bind on those
    shackles,

And if they are too light bring heavier chains.   145
Add iron to iron, load, crush me to the ground;
Nay, heap ten thousand weight upon my breast,
For that were best of all.

> *A long pause, whilst they put irons upon him. After they are on,
> Jane looks at him sorrowfully, and lets her head sink on her
> breast. De Monfort stretches out his hands, looks at them, and
> then at Jane; crosses them over his breast, and endeavours to
> suppress his feelings*

FIRST OFFICER (*to De Monfort*) I have it, too, in charge to move you
    hence,
Into another chamber, more secure.   150
DE MONFORT Well, I am ready, sir.

> *[De Monfort] approaches Jane, whom the Abbess is endeavouring
> to comfort, but to no purpose*

Ah! wherefore thus! most honoured and most dear?
Shrink not at the accoutrements of ill,
Daring the thing itself.

> (*Endeavouring to look cheerful*)

Wilt thou permit me with a gyvèd hand?   155

> *Jane gives De Monfort her hand, which he raises to his lips*

This was my proudest office.

> *Exeunt, De Monfort leading out Jane*

5.3°

> *A long narrow gallery in the convent, with the doors of the cells
> on each side. The stage darkened. First Nun is discovered at a
> distance listening.*

> *Enter Second Nun at the front of the stage, and starts back*

FIRST NUN Ha! who is this not yet retired to rest?
(*To the other, who advances*) My sister, is it you?
SECOND NUN Returning from the sister Nina's cell,
Passing yon door where the poor pris'ner lies,
The sound of one who struggled with despair   5
Struck on me as I went: I stopped and listened;
Oh God! such piteous groans!

FIRST NUN Yes, since the ev'ning sun it hath been so.
   The voice of mis'ry oft hath reached mine ear,
   E'en in the cell above.

SECOND NUN   How is it thus?   10
   Methought he braved it with a manly spirit,
   And led, with shackled hands, his sister forth,
   Like one resolved to bear misfortune boldly.

FIRST NUN Yes, with heroic courage, for a while
   He seemed inspired; but, soon depressed again,   15
   Remorse and dark despair o'erwhelmed his soul,
   And so he hath remained.

      Enter Bernard, advancing from the further end of the gallery,
      bearing a crucifix

FIRST NUN How goes it, father, with your penitent?
   We've heard his heavy groans.

BERNARD Retire, my daughters; many a bed of death,   20
   With all its pangs and horror I have seen,
   But never aught like this.

SECOND NUN He's dying, then?

BERNARD   Yes, death is dealing with him.
   From violent agitation of the mind,
   Some stream of life within his breast has burst;   25
   For many times, within a little space,
   The ruddy-tide has rushed into his mouth.°
   God, grant his pains be short!

FIRST NUN   Amen, amen!

SECOND NUN How does the lady?

BERNARD She sits and bears his head upon her lap;   30
   And like a heaven-inspired angel, speaks
   The word of comfort to his troubled soul:
   Then does she wipe the cold drops from his brow,
   With such a look of tender wretchedness,
   It wrings the heart to see her.   35

FIRST NUN Ha! hear ye nothing?

SECOND NUN (*alarmed*)   Yes, I heard a noise.

FIRST NUN And see'st thou nothing? (*Creeping close to her sister*)

BERNARD   'Tis a nun in white.

      Enter Lay Sister in her night clothes, advancing from the dark
      end of the gallery

  (*To Lay Sister*) Wherefore, my daughter, hast thou left thy
   cell?

It is not meet at this untimely hour.

LAY SISTER I cannot rest. I hear such dismal sounds,   40
Such wailings in the air, such shrilly shrieks,
As though the cry of murder rose again
From the deep gloom of night. I cannot rest;
I pray you let me stay with you, good sisters!
    Bell tolls

NUNS (*starting*) What bell is that?

BERNARD   It is the bell of death.   45
A holy sister was upon the watch
To give this notice.
    Bell tolls again
                Hark! another knell!
The wretched struggler hath his warfare closed;
May heaven have mercy on him.
    Bell tolls again
Retire, my daughters; let us all retire,   50
For scenes like this to meditation call.
    Exeunt, bell tolling again

5.4

*A hall or large room in the convent. The bodies of De Monfort
and Rezenvelt are discovered laid out upon a low table or
platform, covered with black. Freberg, Bernard, Abbess, Monks
and Nuns attending*

ABBESS (*to Freberg*) Here must they lie, my lord, until we know
Respecting this the order of the law.

FREBERG And you have wisely done, my rev'rend mother.
    [*Freberg*] *goes to the table, and looks at the bodies, but without
    uncovering them*
Unhappy men! ye, both in nature rich,
With talents and with virtues were endued.   5
Ye should have loved, yet deadly rancour came,
And in the prime and manhood of your days
Ye sleep in horrid death. Oh direful hate!
What shame and wretchedness his portion is
Who, for a secret inmate, harbours thee!   10
And who shall call him blameless who excites,

Ungen'rously excites, with careless scorn,
Such baleful passion in a brother's breast,
Whom heav'n commands to love. Low are ye laid:
Still all contention now.—Low are ye laid.   15
I loved you both, and mourn your hapless fall.
ABBESS They were your friends, my lord?
FREBERG I loved them both. How does the Lady Jane?
ABBESS She bears misfortune with intrepid soul.
I never saw in woman bowed with grief   20
Such moving dignity.
FREBERG   Aye, still the same.
I've known her long; of worth most excellent;
But, in the day of woe, she ever rose
Upon the mind with added majesty,
As the dark mountain more sublimely tow'rs   25
Mantled in clouds and storm.
            Enter Manuel and Jerome
MANUEL (*pointing*) Here, my good Jerome, there's a piteous sight.
JEROME A piteous sight! yet I will look upon him:
I'll see his face in death. Alas, alas!
I've seen him move a noble gentleman;°   30
And when with vexing passion undisturbed,
He looked most graciously.
            [*Jerome*] *lifts up in mistake the cloth from the body of Rezenvelt,*
            and starts back with horror
Oh! this was bloody work! Oh, oh! oh, oh!
That human hands could do it!
            [*Jerome*] *drops the cloth again*
MANUEL That is the murdered corpse; here lies De Monfort.   35
            [*Manuel*] *goes to uncover the other body*
JEROME (*turning away his head*) No, no! I cannot look upon him now.
MANUEL Didst thou not come to see him?
JEROME Fie! cover him—inter him in the dark—
Let no one look upon him.
BERNARD (*to Jerome*) Well dost thou show the abhorrence nature feels   40
For deeds of blood, and I commend thee well.
In the most ruthless heart compassion wakes
For one who, from the hand of fellow man,
Hath felt such cruelty.
(*Uncovering the body of Rezenvelt*)
This is the murdered corpse.

(*Uncovering the body of De Monfort*) But see, I pray!   45
Here lies the murderer. What think'st thou here?
Look on those features, thou hast seen them oft,
With the last dreadful conflict of despair,
So fixed in horrid strength.
See those knit brows, those hollow sunken eyes;   50
The sharpened nose, with nostrils all distent;
That writhèd mouth, where yet the teeth appear,
In agony, to gnash the nether lip.
Think'st thou, less painful than the murd'rer's knife
Was such a death as this?   55
Aye, and how changèd too those matted locks!
JEROME Merciful heaven! his hair is grizzly grown,°
Changed to white age, what was, but two days since,
Black as the raven's plume. How may this be?
BERNARD Such change, from violent conflict of the mind,   60
Will sometimes come.
JEROME   Alas, alas! most wretched!
Thou wert too good to do a cruel deed,
And so it killed thee. Thou hast suffered for it.
God rest thy soul! I needs must touch thy hand,
And bid thee long farewell. (*Laying his hand on De Monfort*)   65
BERNARD [*covering the bodies*] Draw back, draw back! see where the
    lady comes.°
          Enter Jane. Freberg, who has been for some time retired by
          himself to the [back] of the stage, now steps forward to lead her
          in, but checks himself on seeing the fixed sorrow of her
          countenance, and draws back respectfully. Jane advances to the
          table, and looks attentively at the covered bodies. Manuel points
          out the body of De Monfort, and she gives a gentle inclination of
          the head, to signify that she understands him. She then bends
          tenderly over it, without speaking
MANUEL (*to Jane, as she raises her head*) Oh, madam! my good lord.
JANE Well says thy love, my good and faithful Manuel;
But we must mourn in silence.
MANUEL Alas! the times that I have followed him!   70
JANE Forbear, my faithful Manuel. For this love
'Thou hast my grateful thanks; and here's my hand:
Thou hast loved him, and I'll remember thee:
Where'er I am; in whate'er spot of earth
I linger out the remnant of my days,   75

179

I'll remember thee.

MANUEL Nay, by the living God! where'er you are,
There will I be. I'll prove a trusty servant:
I'll follow you, e'en to the world's end.
My master's gone, and I, indeed, am mean,°   80
Yet will I show the strength of nobler men,
Should any dare upon your honoured worth
To put the slightest wrong. Leave you, dear lady!
Kill me, but say not this! (*Throwing himself at Jane's feet*)

JANE (*raising him*) Well then! be thou my servant, and my friend.   85
Art thou, good Jerome, too, in kindness come?
I see thou art. How goes it with thine age?

JEROME Ah, madam! woe and weakness dwell with age:
Would I could serve you with a young man's strength!
I'd spend my life for you.

JANE   Thanks, worthy Jerome.   90
Oh! who hath said, 'The wretched have no friends'!°

FREBERG In every sensible and gen'rous breast°
Affliction finds a friend; but unto thee,
Thou most exalted and most honourable,
The heart in warmest adoration bows,   95
And even a worship pays.

JANE Nay, Freberg, Freberg! grieve me not, my friend.
He to whose ear my praise most welcome was,
Hears it no more; and, oh our piteous lot!
What tongue will talk of him? Alas, alas!   100
This more than all will bow me to the earth;
I feel my misery here.
The voice of praise was wont to name us both:
I had no greater pride.

> [*Jane*] *covers her face with her hands, and bursts into tears. Here*
> *they all hang about her: Freberg supporting her tenderly;*
> *Manuel embracing her knees, and old Jerome catching hold of*
> *her robe affectionately. Bernard, Abbess, Monks, and Nuns,*
> *likewise, gather round her, with looks of sympathy. Enter two*
> *Officers of Law*

FIRST OFFICER   Where is the prisoner?
Into our hands he straight must be consigned.   105

BERNARD He is not subject now to human laws;
The prison that awaits him is the grave.

FIRST OFFICER Ha! say'st thou so? there is foul play in this.

MANUEL (*to First Officer*) Hold thy unrighteous tongue, or hie thee
    hence,
    Nor, in the presence of this honoured dame 110
    Utter the slightest meaning of reproach.
FIRST OFFICER I am an officer on duty called,
    And have authority to say, how died he?°
        Here Jane shakes off the weakness of grief, and repressing°
        Manuel, who is about to reply to First Officer, steps forward with
        dignity
JANE Tell them by whose authority you come,
    He died that death which best becomes a man 115
    Who is with keenest sense of conscious ill
    And deep remorse assailed, a wounded spirit.
    A death that kills the noble and the brave,
    And only them. He had no other wound.
FIRST OFFICER And shall I trust to this?
JANE   Do as thou wilt: 120
    To one who can suspect my simple word
    I have no more reply. Fulfil thine office.
FIRST OFFICER No, lady, I believe your honoured word,
    And will no farther search.
JANE I thank your courtesy: thanks, thanks to all! 125
    My rev'rend mother, and ye honoured maids;
    Ye holy men; and you, my faithful friends,
    The blessing of the afflicted rest with you:
    And he, who to the wretched is most piteous,
    Will recompense you.—Freberg, thou art good, 130
    Remove the body of the friend you loved,
    'Tis Rezenvelt I mean. Take thou this charge:
    'Tis meet that, with his noble ancestors,
    He lie entombed in honourable state.
    And now, I have a sad request to make, 135
    Nor will these holy sisters scorn my boon;
    That I, within these sacred cloister walls
    May raise a humble, nameless tomb to him,
    Who, but for one dark passion, one dire deed,
    Had claimed a record of as noble worth, 140
    As e'er enriched the sculptured pedestal.°
        Exeunt

APPENDIX TO *DE MONFORT*

[3.1, replacing 2.3: from *A Series of Plays*, 4th edn. (1802).]

> *Countess Freberg's dressing-room. Enter Countess Freberg dispirited and out of humour, and throws herself into a chair*

THERESA Madam, I am afraid you are unwell:
What is the matter? does your head ache?

COUNTESS FREBERG (*peevishly*)   No,
'Tis not my head: concern thyself no more
With what concerns not thee.

THERESA Go you abroad tonight?   5

COUNTESS FREBERG Yes, thinkest thou I'll stay and fret at home?

THERESA Then please to say what you would choose to wear:—
One of your newest robes?

COUNTESS FREBERG   I hate them all.

THERESA Surely, that purple scarf became you well,
With all those wreaths of richly hanging flowers.   10
Did I not overhear them say, last night,
As from the crowded ball-room past,
How gay and handsome, in her costly dress,
The Countess Freberg looked?

LADY   Did'st thou o'erhear it?

THERESA I did, and more than this.   15

COUNTESS FREBERG Well, all are not so greatly prejudiced;
All do not think me like a May Day queen,
Which peasants deck in sport.

THERESA   And who said this?

COUNTESS FREBERG (*putting her handkerchief to her eyes*) E'en my good lord,
Theresa.

THERESA He said it but in jest. He loves you well.   20

COUNTESS FREBERG I know as well as thee he loves me well;
But what of that! he takes no pride in me:
Elsewhere his praise and admiration go,
And Jane De Monfort is not mortal woman.

THERESA The wond'rous character this lady bears   25
For worth and excellence; from early youth
The friend and mother of her younger sisters,
Now greatly married, as I have been told,
From her most prudent care, may well excuse
The admiration of so good a man   30
As my good master is. And then, dear Madam,

I must confess, when I myself did hear
How she was come through the rough winter's storm,
To seek and comfort an unhappy brother,
My heart beat kindly to her.   35
COUNTESS FREBERG Aye, aye, there is a charm in this I find:
But wherefore may she not have come as well
Through wintry storms to seek a lover too?
THERESA No, Madam, no, I could not think of this.
COUNTESS FREBERG That would reduce her in your eyes, mayhap,   40
To woman's level—Now I see my vengeance!
I'll tell it round that she is hither come,
Under pretence of finding out De Monfort,
To meet with Rezenvelt. When Freberg hears it,
'Twill help, I ween, to break this magic charm.   45
THERESA And say what is not, madam?
COUNTESS FREBERG How can'st thou know that I shall say what is not?
'Tis like enough I shall but speak the truth.
THERESA Ah no! there is—
COUNTESS FREBERG   Well, hold thy foolish tongue.
        Freberg's voice is heard offstage
(*After hesitating*) I will not see him now.   50
        *Exit Countess Freberg. Enter Freberg by the opposite side, passing on
        hastily*
THERESA Pardon, my lord; I fear you are in haste,
Yet must I crave that you will give to me
The books my lady mentioned to you: she
Has charged me to remind you.
FREBERG (*passing on*)   I'm in haste.
THERESA Pray you, my lord; your countess wants them much;   55
The Lady Jane De Monfort asked them of her.
FREBERG (*returning instantly*) Are they for her? I knew not this
    before.
I will, then, search them out immediately.
There is nought good or precious in my keeping,
That is not dearly honoured by her use.   60
THERESA My Lord, what would your gentle countess say
If she o'erheard her own request neglected,
Until supported by a name more potent?
FREBERG Think'st thou she is a fool, my good Theresa,
Vainly to please herself with childish thoughts   65
Of matching what is matchless—Jane De Monfort?
Think'st thou she is a fool, and cannot see,
That love and admiration often thrive
Though far apart?
        Enter Countess Freberg with great violence

COUNTESS FREBERG I am not a fool, not to have seen full well,   70
  That thy best pleasure in o'errating so
  This lofty stranger is to humble me,
  And cast a dark'ning shadow o'er my head.
  Aye, wherefore dost thou stare upon me thus?
  Art thou ashamed that I have thus surprised thee?   75
  Well may'st thou be so!
FREBERG   True; thou rightly say'st.
  Well may I be ashamed; not for the praise
  Which I have ever openly bestowed
  On Monfort's noble sister; but that thus,
  Like a poor mean and jealous listener,   80
  She should be found, who is Count Freberg's wife.
COUNTESS FREBERG (*pretending to faint*) Oh I am lost and ruined! hated,
  scorned!
FREBERG Alas, I've been too rough!
    (*Taking her hand and kissing it tenderly*)
  My gentle love! my own, my only love!
  See she revives again. How art thou, love?   85
  Support her to her chamber, good Theresa.
  I'll sit and watch by her. I've been too rough.
    Exeunt, Countess Freberg supported by Freberg and Theresa

LOVERS' VOWS

A PLAY, IN FIVE ACTS

by
ELIZABETH INCHBALD

PREFACE

It would appear like affectation to offer an apology for any scenes or passages omitted or added, in this play, different from the original: its reception has given me confidence to suppose what I have done is right; for Kotzebue's *Child of Love*° in Germany, was never more attractive than *Lovers' Vows* has been in England.　　　　　　5

I could trouble my reader with many pages to disclose the motives which induced me to alter, with the exception of a few commonplace sentences only, the characters of Count Cassel, Amelia, and Verdun the Butler—I could explain why the part of the Count, as in the original, would inevitably have condemned the whole play—I could　10 inform my reader why I have portrayed the Baron in many particulars different from the German author, and carefully prepared the audience for the grand effect of the last scene in the fourth act, by totally changing his conduct towards his son as a robber—why I gave sentences of a humorous kind to the parts of the two Cottagers—why I　15 was compelled, on many occasions, to compress the matter of a speech of three or four pages into one of three or four lines—and why, in no one instance, I would suffer my respect for Kotzebue to interfere with my profound respect for the judgment of a British audience. But I flatter myself such a vindication is not requisite to the enlightened　20 reader, who, I trust, on comparing this drama with the original, will at once see all my motives—and the dull admirer of mere verbal translation, it would be vain to endeavour to inspire with taste by instruction.

Wholly unacquainted with the German language, a literal transla-　25 tion of the *Child of Love* was given to me by the manager of Covent Garden Theatre° to be fitted, as my opinion should direct, for his stage. This translation, tedious and vapid as most literal translations are, had the peculiar disadvantage of having been put into our language by a German—of course it came to me in broken English. It was　30 no slight misfortune to have an example of bad grammar, false metaphors and similes, with all the usual errors of feminine diction, placed before a female writer. But if, disdaining the construction of sentences, the precise decorum of the cold grammarian, she has caught the spirit of her author—if, in every altered scene, still adhering to the nice　35 propriety of his meaning, and still keeping in view his great catastrophe°—she has agitated her audience with all the various passions he depicted, the rigid criticism of the closet will be but a slender abatement of the pleasure resulting from the sanction° of an applauding theatre. 40

It has not been one of the least gratifications I have received from the success of this play, that the original German, from which it is taken, was printed in the year 1791;° and yet, that during all the period which has intervened, no person of talents or literary knowledge (though there are in this country many of that description, who profess to search for German dramas) has thought it worth employment to make a translation of the work. I can only account for such an apparent neglect of Kotzebue's *Child of Love*, by the consideration of its original unfitness for an English stage, and the difficulty of making it otherwise—a difficulty which once appeared so formidable, that I seriously thought I must have declined it even after I had proceeded some length in the undertaking. 50

Independently of objections to the character of the Count, the dangerous insignificance of the Butler, in the original, embarrassed me much. I found, if he was retained in the *Dramatis Personae*,° something more must be supplied than the author had assigned him: I suggested the verses I have introduced; but not being blessed with the Butler's happy art of rhyming, I am indebted for them, except the seventh and eleventh stanzas in the first of his poetic stories, to the author of the prologue. 55 60

The part of Amelia has been a very particular object of my solicitude and alteration: the same situations which the author gave her remain, but almost all the dialogue of the character I have changed: the forward and unequivocal manner in which she announces her affection to her lover, in the original, would have been revolting to an English audience: the passion of love, represented on the stage, is certain to be insipid or disgusting, unless it creates smiles or tears: Amelia's love, by Kotzebue, is indelicately blunt, and yet void of mirth or sadness: I have endeavoured to attach the attention and sympathy of the audience by whimsical insinuations, rather than coarse abruptness—the same woman, I conceive, whom the author drew, with the self-same sentiments, but with manners adapted to the English rather than the German taste; and if the favour in which this character is held by the audience, together with every sentence and incident which I have presumed to introduce in the play, may be offered as the criterion of my skill, I am sufficiently rewarded for the task I have performed. 65 70 75

In stating the foregoing circumstances relating to this production, I hope not to be suspected of arrogating to my own exertions only, the

popularity which has attended *The Child of Love*, under the title of
Lovers' Vows—the exertions of every performer engaged in the play   80
deservedly claim a share in its success; and I most sincerely thank
them for the high importance of their aid.

Prologue

Written by John Taylor, Esq.°
Spoken by Mr Murray°

Poets have oft declared, in doleful strain,
That o'er dramatic tracks they beat in vain,
Hopeless that novelty will spring to sight;
For life and nature are exhausted quite.
Though plaints like these have rung from age to age,   5
Too kind are writers to desert the stage;
And if they, fruitless, search for unknown prey,
At least they dress *old game* a *novel way*;
But such lamentings should be heard no more,
For modern taste turns Nature out of door;   10
Who ne'er again her former sway will boast,
Till, to complete her works, *she starts a ghost.*°
If such the mode, what can we hope to-night,
Who rashly dare approach without a sprite?
No dreadful cavern, and no midnight scream,   15
No rosin flames, nor e'en one flitting gleam.°
Nought of the charms so potent to invite
The monstrous charms of terrible delight.
Our present theme the German Muse supplies,°
But rather aims to soften than surprise.   20
Yet, with her woes she strives some smiles to blend,
Intent as well to cheer as to amend:
On her own native soil she knows the art
To charm the fancy, and to touch the heart.
If, then, she mirth and pathos can express,   25
Though less engaging in an English dress,
Let her from British hearts no peril fear,
But, as a STRANGER, find a welcome here.°

THE CHARACTERS OF THE PLAY°

MEN

Baron Wildenhaim
Count Cassel, [*suitor to Amelia*]
Anhalt, [*a clergyman*]
Frederick, [*Agatha's son*]
Verdun, *the butler*
Landlord
Cottager
Farmer
Countryman
[Gentleman in Waiting]
Huntsmen
[Gamekeepers]
[Sportsmen]
Servants

WOMEN

Agatha Friburg
Amelia Wildenhaim, [*the Baron's daughter*]
Wife *of the Cottager*
Country Girl

SCENE: GERMANY
TIME OF REPRESENTATION: ONE DAY

1.1

A high road, a town at a distance—A small inn on one side the road—A cottage on the other

The Landlord of the inn leads Agatha by the hand out of his house

LANDLORD No, no! no room for you any longer—It is the fair today in the next village; as great a fair as any in the German dominions. The country people with their wives and children take up every corner we have.

AGATHA You will turn a poor sick woman out of doors who has spent her last farthing in your house. 5

LANDLORD For that very reason; because she *has* spent her last farthing.

AGATHA I can work.

LANDLORD You can hardly move your hands. 10

AGATHA My strength will come again.

LANDLORD Then *you* may come again.

AGATHA What am I to do? Where shall I go?

LANDLORD It is fine weather—you may go anywhere.

AGATHA Who will give me a morsel of bread to satisfy my hunger? 15

LANDLORD Sick people eat but little.

AGATHA Hard, unfeeling man, have pity.

LANDLORD When times are hard, pity is too expensive for a poor man. Ask alms of the different people that go by.

AGATHA Beg! I would rather starve. 20

LANDLORD You may beg, and starve too. What a fine lady you are! Many an honest woman has been obliged to beg. Why should not you?

Agatha sits down upon a large stone under a tree

For instance, here comes somebody; and I will teach you how to begin. 25

A Countryman, with working tools, crosses the road

Good day, neighbour Nicholas.

COUNTRYMAN (*stops*) Good day.

LANDLORD Won't you give a trifle to this poor woman?

Countryman takes no notice, but walks off

That would not do—the poor man has nothing himself but what he

gets by hard labour. Here comes a rich farmer; perhaps he will give   30
you something.

Enter Farmer

Good morning to you, sir. Under yon tree sits a poor woman in
distress, who is in need of your charity.

FARMER Is she not ashamed of herself? Why don't she work?

LANDLORD She has had a fever.—If you would but pay for one   35
dinner—

FARMER The harvest has been but indifferent, and my cattle and
sheep have suffered by a distemper.

Exit [Farmer]

LANDLORD My fat, smiling face was not made for begging: you'll
have more luck with your thin, sour one—so, I'll leave you to   40
yourself.

Exit [Landlord]. Agatha rises and comes forward

AGATHA Oh providence! thou hast till this hour protected me, and
hast given me fortitude not to despair. Receive my humble thanks,
and restore me to health, for the sake of my poor son, the innocent
cause of my sufferings, and yet my only comfort. (*Kneeling*) Oh,   45
grant that I may see him once more! See him improved in strength
of mind and body; and that by thy gracious mercy he may never be
visited with afflictions great as mine. (*After a pause*) Protect his
father too, merciful providence, and pardon his crime of perjury to
me! Here, in the face of heaven (supposing my end approaching,   50
and that I can but a few days longer struggle with want and sorrow), here, I solemnly forgive my seducer for all the ills, the
accumulated evils which his allurements, his deceit, and cruelty,
have for twenty years past drawn upon me.

Enter a Country Girl with a basket

AGATHA (*near fainting*) My dear child, if you could spare me a trifle—   55

COUNTRY GIRL I have not a farthing in the world—But I am going to
market to sell my eggs, and as I come back I'll give you
threepence—And I'll be back as soon as ever I can.

Exit [Country Girl]

AGATHA There was a time when I was as happy as this country girl,
and as willing to assist the poor in distress.   60

*[Agatha] retires to the tree and sits down. Enter Frederick—He
is dressed in a German soldier's uniform, has a knapsack on his
shoulders, appears in high spirits, and stops at the door of the inn*

FREDERICK Halt! Stand at ease! It is a very hot day—A draught of
good wine will not be amiss. But first let me consult my purse.

(*Takes out a couple of pieces of money, which he turns about in his hand*) This will do for a breakfast—the other remains for my dinner; and in the evening I shall be at home. (*Calls out*) Ha! Halloo! Landlord! (*Takes notice of Agatha, who is leaning against the tree*) 65
Who is that? A poor sick woman! She don't beg; but her appearance makes me think she is in want. Must one always wait to give till one is asked? Shall I go without my breakfast now, or lose my dinner? The first I think is the best. Aye, I don't want a breakfast, for dinner time will soon be here. To do good satisfies both hunger 70
and thirst. (*Going towards her with the money in his hand*) Take this, good woman.

> *Agatha stretches her hand for the gift, looks steadfastly at*
> *Frederick, and cries out with astonishment and joy*

AGATHA Frederick!

FREDERICK Mother! (*With amazement and grief*) Mother! For God's sake what is this! How is this! And why do I find my mother thus? 75
Speak!

AGATHA I cannot speak, dear son! (*Rising and embracing him*) My dear Frederick! The joy is too great—I was not prepared—

FREDERICK Dear mother, compose yourself: (*leans her head against his breast*) now, then, be comforted. How she trembles! She is fainting. 80

AGATHA I am so weak, and my head so giddy—I had nothing to eat all yesterday.

FREDERICK Good heavens! Here is my little money, take it all! Oh mother! mother! (*Runs to the inn*) Landlord! Landlord! (*Knocking violently at the door*)

> [*Enter Landlord*]

LANDLORD What is the matter? 85

FREDERICK A bottle of wine—quick, quick!

LANDLORD (*surprised*) A bottle of wine! For who?

FREDERICK For me. Why do you ask? Why don't you make haste?

LANDLORD Well, well, Mr Soldier: but can you pay for it?

FREDERICK Here is money—make haste, or I'll break every window 90
in your house.

LANDLORD Patience! Patience!

> [*Landlord*] *goes off*

FREDERICK (*to Agatha*) You were hungry yesterday when I sat down to a comfortable dinner. You were hungry when I partook of a good supper. Oh! why is so much bitter mixed with the joy of my 95
return?

AGATHA Be patient, my dear Frederick. Since I see you, I am well.

193

But I *have been* very ill: so ill, that I despaired of ever beholding you again.

FREDERICK Ill, and I was not with you? I will, now, never leave you 100 more. Look, mother, how tall and strong I am grown. These arms can now afford you support. They can, and shall, procure you subsistence.

Enter Landlord out of the house with a small pitcher

LANDLORD Here is wine—a most delicious nectar. (*Aside*) It is only Rhenish; but it will pass for the best old Hock. 105

FREDERICK (*impatiently snatching the pitcher*) Give it me.

LANDLORD No, no—the money first. One shilling and twopence, if you please.

Frederick gives Landlord money

FREDERICK This is all I have.—Here, here, mother.

While Agatha drinks Landlord counts the money

LANDLORD Three halfpence too short! However, one must be 110 charitable.

Exit Landlord

AGATHA I thank you, my dear Frederick—Wine revives me—Wine from the hand of my son gives me almost a new life.

FREDERICK Don't speak too much, mother.—Take your time.

AGATHA Tell me, dear child, how you have passed the five years since 115 you left me.

FREDERICK Both good and bad, mother. Today plenty—tomorrow not so much—And sometimes nothing at all.

AGATHA You have not written to me this long while.

FREDERICK Dear mother, consider the great distance I was from 120 you!—And then, in time of war, how often letters miscarry.— Besides—

AGATHA No matter now I see you. But have you obtained your discharge?

FREDERICK Oh, no, mother—I have leave of absence only for two 125 months; and that for a particular reason. But I will not quit you so soon, now I find you are in want of my assistance.

AGATHA No, no, Frederick; your visit will make me so well, that I shall in a very short time recover strength to work again; and you must return to your regiment when your furlough is expired. But 130 you told me leave of absence was granted you for a particular reason.—What reason?

FREDERICK Whcn I left you five years ago, you gave me everything you could afford, and all you thought would be necessary for me.

But one trifle you forgot, which was, the certificate of my birth   135
from the church-book.—You know in this country there is nothing
to be done without it. At the time of parting from you, I little
thought it could be of that consequence to me which I have since
found it would have been. Once I became tired of a soldier's life, and
in the hope I should obtain my discharge, offered myself to a master   140
to learn a profession;° but his question was, 'Where is your certificate from the church-book of the parish in which you were born?'
It vexed me that I had not it to produce, for my comrades laughed
at my disappointment. My captain behaved kinder, for he gave me
leave to come home to fetch it—and you see, mother, here I am.   145
        During this speech Agatha is confused and agitated
AGATHA So, you are come for the purpose of fetching your certificate
    from the church-book.
FREDERICK Yes, mother.
AGATHA Oh! oh!
FREDERICK What is the matter?   150
        Agatha bursts into tears
    For heaven's sake, mother, tell me what's the matter?
AGATHA You have no certificate.
FREDERICK No!
AGATHA No.—The laws of Germany excluded you from being regis-
    tered at your birth—for—you are a natural° son!   155
FREDERICK (*starts—after a pause*) So!—And who is my father?
AGATHA Oh Frederick, your wild looks are daggers to my heart.
    Another time.
FREDERICK (*endeavouring to conceal his emotion*) No, no—I am still
    your son—and you are still my mother. Only tell me, who is my   160
    father?
AGATHA When we parted five years ago, you were too young to be
    entrusted with a secret of so much importance.—But the time is
    come when I can, in confidence, open my heart, and unload that
    burden with which it has been long oppressed. And yet, to reveal   165
    my errors to my child, and sue for his mild judgment on my
    conduct—
FREDERICK You have nothing to sue for; only explain this mystery.
AGATHA I will, I will. But—my tongue is locked with remorse and
    shame. You must not look at me.   170
FREDERICK Not look at you! Cursed be that son who could find his
    mother guilty, although the world should call her so.
AGATHA Then listen to me, and take notice of that village, (*pointing*)

of that castle, and of that church. In that village I was born—in that church I was baptized. My parents were poor, but reputable 175
farmers.—The lady of that castle and estate requested them to let me live with her, and she would provide for me through life. They resigned me; and at the age of fourteen I went to my patroness. She took pleasure to instruct me in all kinds of female literature and accomplishments, and three happy years had passed under her pro- 180
tection, when her only son, who was an officer in the Saxon service, obtained permission to come home. I had never seen him before— he was a handsome young man—in my eyes a prodigy; for he talked of love, and promised me marriage. He was the first man who had ever spoken to me on such a subject.—His flattery made me vain, 185
and his repeated vows—Don't look at me, dear Frederick!—I can say no more.

> *Frederick, with his eyes cast down, takes Agatha's hand, and puts it to his heart*

Oh! oh! my son! I was intoxicated by the fervent caresses of a young, inexperienced, capricious man, and did not recover from the delirium till it was too late. 190

FREDERICK (*after a pause*) Go on.—Let me know more of my father.

AGATHA When the time drew near that I could no longer conceal my guilt and shame, my seducer prevailed on me not to expose him to the resentment of his mother. He renewed his former promises of marriage at her death;—on which relying, I gave him my word to 195
be secret—and I have to this hour buried his name deep in my heart.

FREDERICK Proceed, proceed! Give me full information—I will have courage to hear it all. (*Greatly agitated*)

AGATHA His leave of absence expired, he returned to his regiment, 200
depending on my promise, and well assured of my esteem. As soon as my situation became known, I was questioned, and received many severe reproaches: but I refused to confess who was my undoer; and for that obstinacy was turned from the castle.—I went to my parents; but their door was shut against me. My mother, 205
indeed, wept as she bade me quit her sight for ever; but my father wished increased affliction might befall me.

FREDERICK (*weeping*) Be quick with your narrative, or you'll break my heart.

AGATHA I now sought protection from the old clergyman of the par- 210
ish. He received me with compassion. On my knees I begged for- giveness for the scandal I had caused to his parishioners; promised

amendment; and he said he did not doubt me. Through his rec- ommendation I went to town; and, hid in humble lodgings, pro- cured the means of subsistence by teaching to the neighbouring 215 children what I had learnt under the tuition of my benefactress.— To instruct you, my Frederick, was my care and my delight; and in return for your filial love I would not thwart your wishes when they led to a soldier's life: but I saw you go from me with an aching heart. Soon after, my health declined, I was compelled to give up 220 my employment, and, by degrees, became the object you now see me. But, let me add, before I close my calamitous story, that—when I left the good old clergyman, taking along with me his kind advice and his blessing, I left him with a firm determination to fulfil the vow I had made of repentance and amendment. I *have* fulfilled it— 225 and now, Frederick, you may look at me again.

    Frederick embraces Agatha

FREDERICK But my father all this time? (*Mournfully*) I apprehend he died.

AGATHA No—he married.

FREDERICK Married!

AGATHA A woman of virtue—of noble birth and immense fortune. 230 Yet, (*weeps*) I had written to him many times; had described your infant innocence and wants; had glanced obliquely at former promises—

FREDERICK (*rapidly*) No answer to these letters?

AGATHA Not a word.—But in the time of war, you know, letters 235 miscarry.

FREDERICK Nor did he ever return to his estate?

AGATHA No—since the death of his mother this castle has only been inhabited by servants—for he settled as far off as Alsace,° upon the estate of his wife. 240

FREDERICK I will carry you in my arms to Alsace. No—why should I ever know my father, if he is a villain! My heart is satisfied with a mother.—No—I will not go to him. I will not disturb his peace—I leave that task to his conscience. What say you, mother, can't we do without him? (*Struggling between his tears and his pride*) We don't 245 want him. I will write directly to my captain. Let the consequence be what it will, leave you again I cannot. Should I be able to get my discharge, I will work all day at the plough, and all the night with my pen. It will do, mother, it will do! Heaven's goodness will assist me—it will prosper the endeavours of a dutiful son for the sake of a 250 helpless mother.

AGATHA (*presses him to her breast*) Where could be found such another
son?

FREDERICK But tell me my father's name, that I may know how to
shun him.   255

AGATHA Baron Wildenhaim.

FREDERICK Baron Wildenhaim! I shall never forget it.—Oh! you are
near fainting. Your eyes are cast down. What's the matter? Speak,
mother!

AGATHA Nothing particular.—Only fatigued with talking. I wish to   260
take a little rest.

FREDERICK I did not consider that we have been all this time in the
open road.
        [*Frederick*] *goes to the inn, and knocks at the door*
Here, landlord!
        Enter Landlord

LANDLORD Well, what is the matter now?   265

FREDERICK Make haste, and get a bed ready for this good woman.

LANDLORD (*with a sneer*) A bed for this good woman! ha, ha, ha! She
slept last night in that pent-house;° so she may tonight.
        Exit [*Landlord,*] *shutting the door*

FREDERICK You are an infamous—
        [*Frederick*] *goes back to Agatha*
Oh! my poor mother—   270
        [*Frederick*] *runs to the cottage at a little distance, and knocks*
Ha! halloo! Who is there?
        Enter Cottager

COTTAGER Good day, young soldier.—What is it you want?

FREDERICK Good friend, look at that poor woman. She is perishing
in the public road! It is my mother.—Will you give her a small
corner in your hut? I beg for mercy's sake—Heaven will reward   275
you.

COTTAGER Can't you speak quietly? I understand you very well.
(*Calls at the door of the hut*) Wife, shake up our bed—here's a poor
sick woman wants it.
        Enter Wife
Why could not you say all this in fewer words? Why such a long   280
preamble? Why for mercy's sake, and heaven's reward? Why talk
about reward for such trifles as these? Come, let us lead her in; and
welcome she shall be to a bed, as good as I can give her; and to our
homely fare.

FREDERICK Ten thousand thanks, and blessings on you!   285

WIFE Thanks and blessings! Here's a piece of work indeed about nothing! Good sick lady, lean on my shoulder. (*To Frederick*) Thanks and reward indeed! Do you think husband and I have lived to these years, and don't know our duty? [*To Agatha*] Lean on my shoulder.   290

    Exeunt into the cottage

2.1

A room in the cottage

> *Agatha, Cottager, his Wife, and Frederick discovered—Agatha*
> *reclined upon a wooden bench, Frederick leaning over her*

FREDERICK Good people, have you nothing to give her? Nothing that's nourishing?

WIFE Run, husband, run, and fetch a bottle of wine from the landlord of the inn.

FREDERICK No, no—his wine is as bad as his heart: she has drank   5
some of it, which I am afraid has turned to poison.

COTTAGER Suppose, wife, you look for a new-laid egg?

WIFE Or a drop of brandy, husband—that mostly cures me.

FREDERICK Do you hear, mother—will you, mother?

> *Agatha makes a sign with her hand as if she could not take*
> *anything*

She will not. Is there no doctor in this neighbourhood?   10

WIFE At the end of the village there lives a horse-doctor. I have never heard of any other.

FREDERICK What shall I do? She is dying. My mother is dying—Pray for her, good people!

AGATHA Make yourself easy, dear Frederick, I am well, only weak—   15
Some wholesome nourishment—

FREDERICK Yes, mother, directly—directly. (*Aside*) Oh where shall I—no money—not a farthing left.

WIFE Oh, dear me! Had you not paid the rent yesterday, husband—

COTTAGER I then, should know what to do. But as I hope for mercy, I   20
have not a penny in my house.

FREDERICK Then I must—(*aside, coming forward*)—Yes, I will go, and beg.—But should I be refused—I will then—[*To Cottager and Wife*] I leave my mother in your care, good people—Do all you can for her, I beseech you! I shall soon be with you again.   25

> [*Frederick*] *goes off in haste and confusion*

COTTAGER If he should go to our parson, I am sure he would give him something.

> *Agatha, having revived by degrees during the scene, rises*

AGATHA Is that good old man still living, who was minister here some time ago?

WIFE No—It pleased providence to take that worthy man to heaven   30
two years ago.—We have lost in him both a friend and a father. We
shall never get such another.

COTTAGER Wife, wife, our present rector is likewise a very good man.

WIFE Yes! But he is so very young.

COTTAGER Our late parson was once young too.   35

WIFE (*to Agatha*) This young man being tutor in our Baron's family,
he was very much beloved by them all; and so the Baron gave him
this living° in consequence.

COTTAGER And well he deserved it, for his pious instructions to our
young lady: who is, in consequence, good, and friendly to   40
everybody.

AGATHA What young lady do you mean?

COTTAGER Our Baron's daughter.

AGATHA Is she here?

WIFE Dear me! Don't you know that? I thought everybody had known   45
that. It is almost five weeks since the Baron and all his family
arrived at the castle.

AGATHA Baron Wildenhaim?

WIFE Yes, Baron Wildenhaim.

AGATHA And his lady?   50

COTTAGER His lady died in France many miles from hence, and her
death, I suppose, was the cause of his coming to this estate—For
the Baron has not been here till within these five weeks ever since
he was married. We regretted his absence much, and his arrival has
caused great joy.   55

WIFE (*addressing her discourse to Agatha*)° By all accounts the Baroness
was very haughty; and very whimsical.

COTTAGER Wife, wife, never speak ill of the dead. Say what you
please against the living, but not a word against the dead.

WIFE And yet, husband, I believe the dead care the least what is said   60
against them—And so, if you please, I'll tell my story. The late
Baroness was, they say, haughty and proud; and they do say, the
Baron was not so happy as he might have been; but he, bless him,
our good Baron is still the same as when a boy. Soon after Madam
had closed her eyes, he left France, and came to Wildenhaim, his   65
native country.

COTTAGER Many times has he joined in our village dances. Afterwards, when he became an officer, he was rather wild, as most
young men are.

WIFE Yes, I remember when he fell in love with poor Agatha,   70

Friburg's daughter: what a piece of work that was—It did not do him much credit. That was a wicked thing.

COTTAGER Have done—no more of this—It is not well to stir up old grievances.

WIFE Why, you said I might speak ill of the living. 'Tis very hard   75
indeed, if one must not speak ill of one's neighbours, dead, nor alive.

COTTAGER Who knows whether he was the father of Agatha's child? She never said he was.

WIFE Nobody but him—that I am sure—I would lay a wager—no, no,   80
husband—you must not take his part—it was very wicked! Who knows what is now become of that poor creature? She has not been heard of this many a year. Maybe she is starving for hunger. Her father might have lived longer too, if that misfortune had not happened.   85

Agatha faints

COTTAGER See here! Help! She is fainting—take hold!

WIFE Oh, poor woman!

COTTAGER Let us take her into the next room.

WIFE Oh poor woman!—[*To Cottager*] I am afraid she will not live.
[*To Agatha*] Come, cheer up, cheer up. You are with those who feel   90
for you.

Cottager and Wife lead Agatha off

2.2

An apartment in the castle

*A table spread for breakfast—Several Servants in livery
disposing the equipage—Baron enters, attended by a Gentleman
in Waiting°*

BARON Has not Count Cassel left his chamber yet?

GENTLEMAN No, my lord, he has but now rung for his valet.

BARON The whole castle smells of his perfumery. Go, call my daughter hither.

Exit Gentleman

And am I after all to have an ape° for a son-in-law? No, I shall not be   5
in a hurry—I love my daughter too well. We must be better acquainted before I give her to him. I shall not sacrifice my Amelia

to the will of others, as I myself was sacrificed. The poor girl might,
in thoughtlessness, say yes, and afterwards be miserable. What a
pity she is not a boy! The name of Wildenhaim will die with me.   10
My fine estates, my good peasants, all will fall into the hands of
strangers. Oh! why was not my Amelia a boy?

Enter Amelia. She kisses the Baron's hand

AMELIA Good morning, dear my lord.

BARON Good morning, Amelia. Have you slept well?

AMELIA Oh! yes, papa. I always sleep well.   15

BARON Not a little restless last night?

AMELIA No.

BARON Amelia, you know you have a father who loves you, and I
believe you know you have a suitor who is come to ask permission
to love you. Tell me candidly how you like Count Cassel?   20

AMELIA Very well.

BARON Do not you blush when I talk of him?

AMELIA No.

BARON No—(*Aside*) I am sorry for that. [*To Amelia*] Have you dreamt
of him?   25

AMELIA No.

BARON Have you not dreamt at all tonight?

AMELIA Oh yes—I have dreamt of our chaplain, Mr Anhalt.

BARON Ah ha! As if he stood before you and the Count to ask for the
ring.°   30

AMELIA No: not that—I dreamt we were all still in France, and he, my
tutor, just going to take his leave of us for ever—I woke with the
fright, and found my eyes full of tears.

BARON Psha! I want to know if you can love the Count. You saw him
at the last ball we were at in France: when he capered° round you;   35
when he danced minuets; when he—. But I cannot say what his
conversation was.

AMELIA Nor I either—I do not remember a syllable of it.

BARON No? Then I do not think you like him.

AMELIA I believe not.   40

BARON But I think proper to acquaint you he is rich, and of great
consequence: rich, and of consequence; do you hear?

AMELIA Yes, dear papa. But my tutor has always told me that birth
and fortune are inconsiderable things, and cannot give happiness.

BARON There he is right—But what if it happens that birth and   45
fortune are joined with sense and virtue—

AMELIA But is it so with Count Cassel?

BARON (*aside*) Hem! Hem! [*To Amelia*] I will ask you a few questions on this subject; but be sure to answer me honestly—Speak truth.   50

AMELIA I never told an untruth in my life.

BARON Nor ever *conceal* the truth from me, I command you.

AMELIA (*earnestly*) Indeed, my lord, I never will.

BARON I take you at your word—And now reply to me truly—Do you like to hear the Count spoken of?   55

AMELIA Good, or bad?

BARON Good. Good.

AMELIA Oh yes; I like to hear good of everybody.

BARON But do not you feel a little fluttered when he is talked of?

AMELIA (*shaking her head*) No.   60

BARON Are not you a little embarrassed?

AMELIA No.

BARON Don't you wish sometimes to speak to him, and have not the courage to begin?

AMELIA No.   65

BARON Do not you wish to take his part when his companions laugh at him?

AMELIA No—I love to laugh at him myself.

BARON (*aside*) Provoking! [*To Amelia*] Are not you afraid of him when he comes near you?   70

AMELIA No, not at all.—(*Recollecting herself*) Oh yes—once.

BARON Ah! Now it comes!

AMELIA Once at a ball he trod on my foot; and I was so afraid he should tread on me again.

BARON You put me out of patience. Hear, Amelia! (*Stops short, and   75
speaks softer*) To see you happy is my wish. But matrimony, without concord, is like a duetto badly performed; for that reason, nature, the great composer of all harmony, has ordained, that, when bodies are allied, hearts should be in perfect unison. However, I will send Mr Anhalt to you—   80

AMELIA (*much pleased*) Do, papa.

BARON —He shall explain to you my sentiments. (*Rings*) A clergyman can do this better than—
          Enter Servant
Go directly to Mr Anhalt, tell him that I shall be glad to see him for a quarter of an hour if he is not engaged.   85
          Exit Servant

AMELIA (*calls after Servant*) Wish him a good morning from me.

BARON (*looking at his watch*) The Count is a tedious time dressing.—
Have you breakfasted, Amelia?

AMELIA No, papa.

Baron and Amelia sit down to breakfast

BARON How is the weather? Have you walked this morning? 90

AMELIA Oh, yes—I was in the garden at five o'clock; it is very fine.

BARON Then I'll go out shooting. I do not know in what other way to
amuse my guest.

Enter Count

COUNT Ah, my dear Colonel!° Miss Wildenhaim, I kiss your hand.

BARON Good morning! Good morning! though it is late in the day, 95
Count. In the country we should rise earlier.

Amelia offers the Count a cup of tea

COUNT Is it Hebe herself, or Venus,° or—

AMELIA Ha, ha, ha! Who can help laughing at his nonsense?

BARON (*rather angry*) Neither Venus, nor Hebe; but Amelia Wildenhaim, if you please. 100

COUNT (*sitting down to breakfast*) You are beautiful, Miss
Wildenhaim.—Upon my honour, I think so. I have travelled, and
seen much of the world, and yet I can positively admire you.

AMELIA I am sorry I have not seen the world.

COUNT Wherefore? 105

AMELIA Because I might then, perhaps, admire you.

COUNT True;—for I am an epitome of the world. In my travels I
learnt delicacy in Italy—hauteur, in Spain—in France,
enterprise—in Russia, prudence—in England, sincerity—in Scotland, frugality—and in the wilds of America, I learnt love. 110

AMELIA Is there any country where love is taught?

COUNT In all barbarous countries. But the whole system is exploded°
in places that are civilized.

AMELIA And what is substituted in its stead?

COUNT Intrigue.° 115

AMELIA What a poor, uncomfortable substitute!

COUNT There are other things—Song, dance, the opera, and war.

*Since the entrance of the Count the Baron has removed to a table
at a little distance*

BARON What are you talking of there?

COUNT Of war, Colonel.

BARON (*rising*) Aye, we like to talk on what we don't understand. 120

COUNT (*rising*) Therefore, to a lady, I always speak of politics; and to
her father, on love.

BARON I believe, Count, notwithstanding your sneer, I am still as much of a proficient in that art as yourself.

COUNT I do not doubt it, my dear Colonel, for you are a soldier: and since the days of Alexander,° whoever conquers men is certain to overcome women.   125

BARON An achievement to animate a poltroon.

COUNT And, I verily believe, gains more recruits than the king's pay.

BARON Now we are on the subject of arms, should you like to go out a shooting with me for an hour before dinner?   130

COUNT Bravo, Colonel! A charming thought! This will give me an opportunity to use my elegant gun: the butt is inlaid with mother-of-pearl. You cannot find better work, or better taste.—Even my coat of arms is engraved.   135

BARON But can you shoot?

COUNT That I have never tried—except, with my eyes, at a fine woman.

BARON I am not particular what game I pursue.—I have an old gun; it does not look fine; but I can always bring down my bird.   140

Enter Servant

SERVANT Mr Anhalt begs leave—

BARON Tell him to come in.—I shall be ready in a moment.

Exit Servant

COUNT Who is Mr Anhalt?

AMELIA (*with warmth*) Oh, a very good man.

COUNT 'A good man'. In Italy, that means a religious man; in France,   145
it means a cheerful man; in Spain, it means a wise man; and in England, it means a rich man.—Which good man of all these is Mr Anhalt?

AMELIA A good man in every country, except England.

COUNT And give me the English good man, before that of any other   150
nation.

BARON And of what nation would you prefer your good woman to be, Count?

COUNT (*bowing to Amelia*) Of Germany.

AMELIA In compliment to me?   155

COUNT In justice to my own judgment.

BARON Certainly. For have we not an instance of one German woman, who possesses every virtue that ornaments the whole sex; whether as a woman of illustrious rank, or in the more exalted character of a wife, and a mother?°   160

Enter Anhalt

ANHALT I come by your command, Baron—

BARON Quick, Count.—Get your elegant gun—I pass your apartments, and will soon call for you.

COUNT I fly.—Beautiful Amelia, it is a sacrifice I make to your father, that I leave for a few hours his amiable daughter.   165

  Exit [Count]

BARON My dear Amelia, I think it scarcely necessary to speak to Mr Anhalt, or that he should speak to you, on the subject of the Count; but as he is here, leave us alone.

AMELIA (*as she retires*) Good morning, Mr Anhalt.—I hope you are very well.   170

  Exit [Amelia]

BARON I'll tell you in a few words why I sent for you. Count Cassel is here, and wishes to marry my daughter.

ANHALT (*much concerned*) Really!

BARON He is—he—in a word I don't like him.

ANHALT (*with emotion*) And Miss Wildenhaim—   175

BARON I shall not command, neither persuade her to the marriage—I know too well the fatal influence of parents on such a subject. Objections to be sure, if they could be removed—But when you find a man's head without brains, and his bosom without a heart, these are important articles to supply. Young as you are, Anhalt, I   180
know no one so able to restore, or to bestow those blessings on his fellow-creatures, as you.

  Anhalt bows

The Count wants a little of my daughter's simplicity and sensibility.°—Take him under your care while he is here, and make him something like yourself.—You have succeeded to my wish in   185
the education of my daughter.—Form the Count after your own manner.—I shall then have what I have sighed for all my life—a son.

ANHALT With your permission, Baron, I will ask one question. What remains to interest you in favour of° a man, whose head and heart   190
are good for nothing?

BARON Birth and fortune. Yet, if I thought my daughter absolutely disliked him, or that she loved another, I would not thwart a first affection;—no, for the world, I would not. (*Sighing*) But that her affections are already bestowed, is not probable.   195

ANHALT Are you of opinion that she will never fall in love?

BARON Oh! no. I am of opinion that no woman ever arrived at the age of twenty without that misfortune.—But this is another subject.—

Go to Amelia—explain to her the duties of a wife and of a mother.—If she comprehends them, as she ought, then ask her if she thinks she could fulfil those duties, as the wife of Count Cassel. 200

ANHALT I will.—But—I—Miss Wildenhaim—(*confused*) I—I shall —I—I shall obey your commands.

BARON Do so. (*Gives a deep sigh*) Ah! so far this weight is removed; but there lies still a heavier next my heart.—You understand me.— 205 How is it, Mr Anhalt? Have you not yet been able to make any discoveries on that unfortunate subject?

ANHALT I have taken infinite pains; but in vain. No such person is to be found.

BARON Believe me, this burden presses on my thoughts so much, that 210 many nights I go without sleep. A man is sometimes tempted to commit such depravity when young.—Oh, Anhalt! had I, in my youth, had you for a tutor;—but I had no instructor but my passions; no governor but my own will.

Exit Baron

ANHALT This commission of the Baron's in respect to his daughter, I 215 am—(*Looks about*)—If I should meet her now, I cannot—I must recover myself first, and then prepare.—A walk in the fields, and a fervent prayer—After these, I trust, I shall return, as a man whose views are solely placed on a future world; all hopes in this, with fortitude resigned. 220

Exit

3.1

An open field

Frederick alone, with a few pieces of money which he turns about in his hands

FREDERICK To return with this trifle for which I have stooped to beg! return to see my mother dying! I would rather fly to the world's end. (*Looking at the money*) What can I buy with this? It is hardly enough to pay for the nails that will be wanted for her coffin. My great anxiety will drive me to distraction. However, let the con- 5
sequence of our affliction be what it may, all will fall upon my father's head; and may he pant for heaven's forgiveness, as my poor mother—

At a distance is heard the firing of a gun, then the cry of 'Halloo, halloo'°—*Gamekeepers and Sportsmen run across the stage*—*Frederick looks about*

Here they come—a nobleman, I suppose, or a man of fortune. Yes, yes—and I will once more beg for my mother.—May heaven send 10
relief!

Enter the Baron followed slowly by the Count. The Baron stops

BARON Quick, quick, Count! Aye, aye, that was a blunder indeed. Don't you see the dogs? There they run—they have lost the scent.

Exit Baron looking after the dogs°

COUNT So much the better, Colonel, for I must take a little breath.

Count leans on his gun—*Frederick goes up to him with great modesty*

FREDERICK Gentleman, I beg you will bestow from your superfluous 15
wants something to relieve the pain, and nourish the weak frame, of an expiring woman.

Enter the Baron

COUNT What police is here!° that a nobleman's amusements should be interrupted by the attack of vagrants.

FREDERICK (*to the Baron*) Have pity, noble sir, and relieve the distress 20
of an unfortunate son, who supplicates for his dying mother.

BARON (*taking out his purse*) I think, young soldier, it would be better if you were with your regiment on duty, instead of begging.

FREDERICK I would with all my heart: but at this present moment my sorrows are too great.— 25

Baron gives something

I entreat your pardon. What you have been so good as to give me is not enough.

BARON (*surprised*) Not enough!

FREDERICK No, it is not enough.

COUNT The most singular beggar I ever met in all my travels.   30

FREDERICK If you have a charitable heart, give me one dollar.°

BARON This is the first time I was ever dictated by a beggar what to give him.

FREDERICK With one dollar you will save a distracted man.

BARON I don't choose to give any more. Count, go on.   35

Exit Count—as the Baron follows, Frederick seizes him by the breast and draws his sword

FREDERICK Your purse, or your life.

BARON (*calling*) Here! here! seize and secure him.

Some of the Gamekeepers run on, lay hold of Frederick, and disarm him

FREDERICK What have I done!

BARON Take him to the castle, and confine him in one of the towers. I shall follow you immediately.   40

FREDERICK One favour I have to beg, one favour only.—I know that I am guilty, and am ready to receive the punishment my crime deserves. But I have a mother, who is expiring for want—pity her, if you cannot pity me—bestow on her relief. If you will send to yonder hut, you will find that I do not impose on you a falsehood. For   45 her it was I drew my sword—for her I am ready to die.

BARON Take him away, and imprison him where I told you.

FREDERICK (*as he is forced off by the Gamekeepers*) Woe to that man to whom I owe my birth!

[Exeunt Frederick and Gamekeepers]

BARON (*calls another Gamekeeper*) Here, Frank, run directly to yonder   50 hamlet, inquire in the first, second and third cottage for a poor sick woman—and if you really find such a person, give her this purse.

Exit Gamekeeper

A most extraordinary event!—and what a well-looking youth! something in his countenance and address which struck me inconceivably!—If it is true that he begged for his mother—But if   55 he did—for the attempt upon my life, he must die. Vice is never half so dangerous, as when it assumes the garb of morality.

Exit

3.2

A room in the castle

AMELIA (*alone*) Why am I so uneasy; so peevish; who has offended me? I did not mean to come into this room. In the garden I intended to go. (*Going, turns back*) No, I will not—yes, I will—just go, and look if my auriculas° are still in blossom; and if the apple tree is grown which Mr Anhalt planted.—I feel very low-spirited— something must be the matter.—Why do I cry?—Am I not well? 5

Enter Anhalt

Ah! good morning, my dear sir—Mr Anhalt, I meant to say—I beg pardon.

ANHALT Never mind, Miss Wildenhaim—I don't dislike to hear you call me as you did. 10

AMELIA In earnest?

ANHALT Really. You have been crying. May I know the reason? The loss of your mother, still?—

AMELIA No—I have left off crying for her.

ANHALT I beg pardon if I have come at an improper hour; but I wait 15 upon you by the commands of your father.

AMELIA You are welcome at all hours. My father has more than once told me that he who forms my mind I should always consider as my greatest benefactor. (*Looking down*) And my heart tells me the same. 20

ANHALT I think myself amply rewarded by the good opinion you have of me.

AMELIA When I remember what trouble I have sometimes given you, I cannot be too grateful.

ANHALT (*aside*) Oh! Heavens!—(*To Amelia*) I—I come from your 25 father with a commission.—If you please, we will sit down.

Anhalt places chairs, and he and Amelia sit

Count Cassel is arrived.

AMELIA Yes, I know.

ANHALT And do you know for what reason?

AMELIA He wishes to marry me. 30

ANHALT (*hastily*) Does he? But believe me, the Baron will not per- suade you—No, I am sure he will not.

AMELIA I know that.

ANHALT He wishes that I should ascertain whether you have an inclination— 35

AMELIA For the Count, or for matrimony do you mean?

ANHALT For matrimony.

AMELIA All things that I don't know, and don't understand, are quite indifferent to me.

ANHALT For that very reason I am sent to you to explain the good and   40
the bad of which matrimony is composed.

AMELIA Then I beg to be acquainted with the good.

ANHALT When two sympathetic hearts meet in the marriage state, matrimony may be called a happy life. When such a wedded pair find thorns in their path, each will be eager, for the sake of the   45
other, to tear them from the root.° Where they have to mount hills, or wind a labyrinth, the most experienced will lead the way, and be a guide to his companion. Patience and love will accompany them in their journey, while melancholy and discord they leave far behind.—Hand in hand they pass on from morning till evening,   50
through their summer's day, till the night of age draws on, and the sleep of death overtakes the one. The other, weeping and mourning, yet looks forward to the bright region where he shall meet his still surviving partner, among trees and flowers which themselves have planted, in fields of eternal verdure.   55

AMELIA You may tell my father—I'll marry. (*Rises*)

ANHALT (*rising*) This picture is pleasing; but I must beg you not to forget that there is another on the same subject.—When convenience, and fair appearance joined to folly and ill-humour, forge the fetters of matrimony, they gall with their weight the married pair.   60
Discontented with each other—at variance in opinions—their mutual aversion increases with the years they live together. They contend most, where they should most unite; torment, where they should most soothe. In this rugged way, choked with the weeds of suspicion, jealousy, anger, and hatred, they take their daily journey,   65
till one of these *also* sleep in death. The other then lifts up his dejected head, and calls out in acclamations of joy—'Oh, liberty! dear liberty!'

AMELIA I will not marry.

ANHALT You mean to say, you will not fall in love.   70

AMELIA Oh no! (*Ashamed*) I am in love.

ANHALT Are in love! (*Starting*) And with the Count?

AMELIA I wish I was.

ANHALT Why so?

AMELIA Because *he* would, perhaps, love me again.   75

ANHALT (*warmly*) Who is there that would not?

AMELIA Would you?

ANHALT I—I—me—I—I am out of the question.

AMELIA No; you are the very person to whom I have put the question.

ANHALT What do you mean?   80

AMELIA I am glad you don't understand me. I was afraid I had spoken too plain. (*In confusion*)

ANHALT Understand you!—As to that—I am not dull.°

AMELIA I know you are not—And as you have for a long time instructed me, why should not I now begin to teach you?   85

ANHALT Teach me what?

AMELIA Whatever I know, and you don't.

ANHALT There are some things I had rather never know.

AMELIA So you may remember I said when you began to teach me mathematics. I said I had rather not know it—But now I have learnt   90
it gives me a great deal of pleasure—and (*hesitating*) perhaps, who can tell, but that I might teach something as pleasant to you, as resolving a problem° is to me.

ANHALT Woman herself is a problem.

AMELIA And I'll teach you to make her out.   95

ANHALT *You* teach?

AMELIA Why not? None but a woman can teach the science of herself: and though I own I am very young, a young woman may be as agreeable for a tutoress as an old one.—I am sure I always learnt faster from you than from the old clergyman who taught me before   100
you came.

ANHALT This is nothing to the subject.

AMELIA What is the subject?

ANHALT ——Love.

AMELIA (*going up to him*) Come, then, teach it me—teach it me as you   105
taught me geography, languages, and other important things.

ANHALT (*turning from her*) Psha!

AMELIA Ah! you won't—You know you have already taught me that, and you won't begin again.

ANHALT You misconstrue—you misconceive everything I say or do.   110
The subject I came to you upon was marriage.

AMELIA A very proper subject from the man who has taught me love, and I accept the proposal. (*Curtsying*)

ANHALT Again you misconceive and confound me.

AMELIA Aye, I see how it is—You have no inclination to experience   115
with me 'the good part of matrimony': I am not the female with whom you would like to go 'hand in hand up hills, and through

labyrinths'—with whom you would like to 'root up thorns'; and with whom you would delight to 'plant lilies and roses'. No, you had rather call out, 'Oh liberty, dear liberty'.   120

ANHALT Why do you force from me, what it is villainous to own?—I love you more than life—Oh, Amelia! had we lived in those golden times, which the poets picture, no one but you——But as the world is changed, your birth and fortune make our union impossible—To preserve the character, and more the feelings of an honest man, I   125 would not marry you without the consent of your father—And could I, dare I propose it to him?

AMELIA He has commanded me never to conceal or disguise the truth. I will propose it to him. The subject of the Count will force me to speak plainly, and this will be the most proper time, while he   130 can compare the merit of you both.

ANHALT I conjure you not to think of exposing yourself and me to his resentment.

AMELIA It is my father's will that I should marry—It is my father's wish to see me happy—If then you love me as you say, I will marry;   135 and will be happy—but only with you.—I will tell him this.—At first he will start; then grow angry; then be in a passion—In his passion he will call me 'undutiful': but he will soon recollect himself, and resume his usual smiles, saying 'Well, well, if he love you, and you love him, in the name of heaven, let it be'.—Then I shall   140 hug him round the neck, kiss his hands, run away from him, and fly to you; it will soon be known that I am your bride, the whole village will come to wish me joy, and heaven's blessing will follow.

    Enter Verdun

AMELIA (*discontented*) Ah! is it you?

VERDUN Without vanity, I have taken the liberty to enter this apart-   145 ment the moment the good news reached my ears.

AMELIA What news?

VERDUN Pardon an old servant, your father's old butler, gracious lady, who has had the honour to carry the Baron in his arms—and afterwards with humble submission to receive many a box o'the ear   150 from you—if he thinks it his duty to make his congratulations with due reverence on this happy day, and to join with the muses in harmonious tunes on the lyre.°

AMELIA Oh! my good butler, I am not in a humour to listen to the muses, and your lyre.   155

VERDUN There has never been a birthday, nor wedding-day, nor christening-day, celebrated in your family, in which I have not

214

joined with the muses in full chorus.—In forty-six years, three hundred and ninety-seven congratulations on different occasions have dropped from my pen. Today, the three hundred and ninety— 160 eighth is coming forth;—for heaven has protected our noble master, who has been in great danger.

AMELIA Danger! My father in danger! What do you mean?

VERDUN One of the gamekeepers has returned to inform the whole castle of a base and knavish trick, of which the world will talk, and 165 my poetry hand down to posterity.

AMELIA What, what is all this?

VERDUN The Baron, my lord and master, in company with the strange Count, had not been gone a mile beyond the lawn, when one of them— 170

AMELIA What happened? Speak for heaven's sake.

VERDUN My verse shall tell you.

AMELIA No, no; tell us in prose.

ANHALT Yes, in prose.

VERDUN Ah, you have neither of you ever been in love, or you would 175 prefer poetry to prose. But excuse (*pulls out a paper*) the haste in which it was written. I heard the news in the fields—always have paper and a pencil about me, and composed the whole forty lines crossing the meadows and the park in my way home. (*Reads*)

> Oh Muse, ascend the forkèd mount,°   180
>   And lofty strains prepare,
> About a Baron and a Count,
>   Who went to hunt the hare.
>
> The hare she ran with utmost speed,
>   And sad, and anxious looks,   185
> Because the furious hounds indeed,
>   Were near to her, gadzooks.°
>
> At length, the Count and Baron bold
>   Their footsteps homeward bended;
> For why, because, as you were told,°   190
>   The hunting it was ended.
>
> Before them straight a youth appears,
>   Who made a piteous pother,
> And told a tale with many tears,
>   About his dying mother.   195

215

The youth was in severe distress,
    And seemed as he had spent all,
He looked a soldier by his dress;
    For that was regimental.

The Baron's heart was full of ruth,   200
    While from his eye fell brine oh!
And soon he gave the mournful youth
    A little ready rhino.

He gave a shilling as I live,
    Which, sure, was mighty well;   205
But to some people if you give
    An inch—they'll take an ell.

The youth then drew his martial knife,
    And seized the Baron's collar,
He swore he'd have the Baron's life,   210
    Or else another dollar.

Then did the Baron in a fume,
    Soon raise a mighty din,
Whereon came butler, huntsman, groom,
    And eke the whipper-in.   215

Maugre this young man's warlike coat,
    They bore him off to prison;
And held so strongly by his throat,
    They almost stopped his whizzen.

Soon may a neckcloth, called a rope,   220
    Of robbing cure this elf;
If so I'll write, without a trope,
    His dying speech myself.°

And had the Baron chanced to die,
    Oh! grief to all the nation,   225
I must have made an elegy,
    And not this fine narration.

MORAL

Henceforth let those who all have spent,
    And would by begging live,   230
Take warning here, and be content,
    With what folks choose to give.

AMELIA Your muse, Mr Butler, is in a very inventive humour this morning.

ANHALT And your tale too improbable, even for fiction. 235

VERDUN Improbable! It's a real fact.

AMELIA What, a robber in our grounds at noonday? Very likely indeed!

VERDUN I don't say it was likely—I only say it is true.

ANHALT No, no, Mr Verdun, we find no fault with your poetry; but 240 don't attempt to impose it upon us for truth.

AMELIA Poets are allowed to speak falsehood, and we forgive yours.

VERDUN I won't be forgiven, for I speak truth—And here the robber comes, in custody, to prove my words.

Verdun goes off, repeating, 'I'll write his dying speech myself'. 245

AMELIA Look! as I live, so he does—They come nearer; he's a young man, and has something interesting in his figure. An honest countenance, with grief and sorrow in his face. No, he is no robber—I pity him! Oh! look how the keepers drag him unmercifully into the tower—Now they lock it—Oh! how that poor, unfortunate man 250 must feel!

ANHALT (*aside*) Hardly worse than I do.

Enter the Baron. Amelia runs up to him

AMELIA A thousand congratulations, my dear papa.

BARON For heaven's sake spare your congratulations. The old butler, in coming up stairs, has already overwhelmed me with them. 255

ANHALT Then, it is true, my lord? I could hardly believe the old man.

AMELIA And the young prisoner, with all his honest looks, is a robber?

BARON He is; but I verily believe for the first and last time. A most extraordinary event, Mr Anhalt. This young man begged; then drew his sword upon me; but he trembled so, when he seized me by 260 the breast, a child might have overpowered him. I almost wish he had made his escape—this adventure may cost him his life, and I might have preserved it with one dollar: but, now, to save him would set a bad example.

AMELIA Oh no! my lord, have pity on him! Plead for him, Mr Anhalt! 265

BARON Amelia, have you had any conversation with Mr Anhalt?

AMELIA Yes, my lord.

BARON Respecting matrimony?

AMELIA Yes; and I have told him——

ANHALT (*very hastily*) According to your commands, Baron—— 270

AMELIA But he has conjured me——

ANHALT I have endeavoured, my lord, to find out——

AMELIA Yet, I am sure, dear papa, your affection for me——

ANHALT You wish to say something to me in your closet, my lord?

BARON What the devil is all this conversation? You will not let one 275
another speak—I don't understand either of you.

AMELIA Dear father, have you not promised you will not thwart my
affections when I marry, but suffer me to follow their dictates?

BARON Certainly.

AMELIA Do you hear, Mr Anhalt? 280

ANHALT I beg pardon—I have a person who is waiting for me—I am
obliged to retire.

     Exit [Anhalt] in confusion

BARON (*calls after Anhalt*) I shall expect you in my closet. I am going
there immediately.

     The Baron retires towards the opposite door

AMELIA Pray, my lord, stop a few minutes longer: I have something of 285
great importance to say to you.

BARON Something of importance! to plead for the young man, I suppose! But that's a subject I must not listen to.

     Exit [Baron]

AMELIA I wish to plead for two young men—For one, that he may be
let out of prison: for the other, that he may be made a prisoner for 290
life. (*Looks out*) The tower is still locked. How dismal it must be to
be shut up in such a place; and perhaps—(*Calls*) Butler! Butler!
Come this way. I wish to speak to you. [*Aside*] This young soldier
has risked his life for his mother, and that accounts for the interest I
take in his misfortunes. 295

     Enter Verdun

Pray, have you carried anything to the prisoner to eat?

VERDUN Yes.

AMELIA What was it?

VERDUN Some fine black bread; and water as clear as crystal.

AMELIA Are you not ashamed! Even my father pities him. Go directly 300
down to the kitchen, and desire the cook to give you something
good and comfortable;° and then go into the cellar for a bottle of
wine.

VERDUN Good and comfortable indeed!

AMELIA And carry both to the tower. 305

VERDUN I am willing at any time, dear lady, to obey your orders; but,
on this occasion, the prisoner's food must remain bread and
water—It is the Baron's particular command.

AMELIA Ah! My father was in the height of passion when he gave it.

VERDUN Whatsoever his passion might be, it is the duty of a true and   310
honest dependant to obey his lord's mandates. I will not suffer a
servant in this house, nor will I, myself, give the young man any
thing except bread and water—But I'll tell you what I'll do—I'll
read my verses to him.

AMELIA Give me the key of the cellar—I'll go myself.   315

VERDUN (*gives the key*) And there's my verses—(*Taking them from his
pocket*) Carry them with you, they may comfort him as much as the
wine.

> *Amelia throws them down. Exit Amelia*

VERDUN (*in amazement*) Not take them! Refuse to take them—
> *Verdun lifts them from the floor with the utmost respect*

> '*I must have made an elegy,*
> > *And not this fine narration.*'   320

> *Exit*

4.1

A prison in one of the towers of the castle

FREDERICK (*alone*) How a few moments destroy the happiness of man! When I, this morning, set out from my inn, and saw the sun rise, I sung with joy.—Flattered with the hope of seeing my mother, I formed a scheme how I would with joy surprise her. But, farewell all pleasant prospects—I return to my native country, and the first object I behold, is my dying parent; my first lodging, a prison; and my next walk will perhaps be—oh, merciful providence! have I deserved all this?

Enter Amelia with a small basket covered with a napkin.—She speaks to someone offstage

AMELIA Wait there, Francis, I shall soon be back.

FREDERICK (*hearing the door open, and turning round*) Who's there?

AMELIA You must be both hungry and thirsty, I fear.

FREDERICK Oh, no! neither.

AMELIA Here is a bottle of wine, and something to eat. (*Places the basket on the table*) I have often heard my father say, that wine is quite a cordial° to the heart.

FREDERICK A thousand thanks, dear stranger. Ah! could I prevail on you to have it sent to my mother, who is upon her death-bed, under the roof of an honest peasant, called Hubert! Take it hence, my kind benefactress, and save my mother.

AMELIA But first assure me that you did not intend to murder my father.

FREDERICK Your father! heaven forbid.—I meant but to preserve her life, who gave me mine.—Murder your father! No, no—I hope not.

AMELIA And I thought not—Or, if you had murdered anyone, you had better have killed the Count; nobody would have missed him.

FREDERICK Who, may I enquire, were those gentlemen, whom I hoped to frighten into charity?

AMELIA Aye, if you only intended to frighten them, the Count was the very person for your purpose. But you caught hold of the other gentleman.—And could you hope to intimidate Baron Wildenhaim?

FREDERICK Baron Wildenhaim!—Almighty powers!

AMELIA What's the matter?

FREDERICK The man to whose breast I held my sword—(*trembling*)   35
AMELIA Was Baron Wildenhaim—the owner of this estate—my father!
FREDERICK (*with the greatest emotion*) *My* father!
AMELIA Good heaven, how he looks! I am afraid he's mad. Here! Francis, Francis.   40
       Exit [*Amelia*], *calling*
FREDERICK (*all agitation*) My *father*! Eternal judge! thou dost not slumber! The man, against whom I drew my sword this day, was my father! One moment longer, and provoked, I might have been the murderer of my father! My hair stands on end! My eyes are clouded! I cannot see any thing before me. (*Sinks down on a chair*).   45
If providence had ordained that I should give the fatal blow, who would have been in most fault?—I dare not pronounce——(*After a pause*) That benevolent young female who left me just now, is, then, my sister—and I suppose that fop, who accompanied my father—
       Enter Anhalt
Welcome, sir! By your dress you are of the church, and consequently   50
a messenger of comfort. You are most welcome, sir.
ANHALT I wish to bring comfort and avoid upbraidings; for your own conscience will reproach you more than the voice of a preacher. From the sensibility of your countenance, together with a language, and address superior to the vulgar, it appears, young man, you have   55
had an education, which should have preserved you from a state like this.
FREDERICK My education I owe to my mother. Filial love, in return, has plunged me into the state you see. A civil magistrate will condemn according to the law—A priest, in judgment, is not to   60
consider the act itself, but the impulse which led to the act.
ANHALT I shall judge with all the lenity my religion dictates: and you are the prisoner of a nobleman, who compassionates you for the affection which you bear towards your mother; for he has sent to the village where you directed him, and has found the account you   65
gave relating to her true.—With this impression in your favour, it is my advice, that you endeavour to see and supplicate the Baron for your release from prison, and all the peril of his justice.
FREDERICK (*starting*) I—I see the Baron! I!—I supplicate for my deliverance!—Will you favour me with his name?—Is it not   70
Baron—
ANHALT Baron Wildenhaim.
FREDERICK Baron Wildenhaim! He lived formerly in Alsace.

ANHALT The same.—About a year after the death of his wife, he left
Alsace; and arrived here a few weeks ago to take possession of this   75
his paternal estate.

FREDERICK So! his wife is dead;—and that generous young lady who
came to my prison just now is his daughter?

ANHALT Miss Wildenhaim, his daughter.

FREDERICK And that young gentleman, I saw with him this morning,   80
is his son?

ANHALT He has no son.

FREDERICK (*hastily*) Oh, yes, he has—(*recollecting himself*)—I mean
him that was out shooting today.

ANHALT He is not his son.   85

FREDERICK (*to himself*) Thank heaven!

ANHALT He is only a visitor.

FREDERICK I thank you for this information; and if you will under-
take to procure me a private interview with Baron Wildenhaim—

ANHALT Why private? However, I will venture to take you for a short   90
time from this place, and introduce you; depending on your innocence, or your repentance—on his conviction in your favour, or his
mercy towards your guilt. Follow me.

    Exit [*Anhalt*]

FREDERICK (*following*) I have beheld an affectionate parent in deep
adversity.—Why should I tremble thus?—Why doubt my fortitude,   95
in the presence of an unnatural parent in prosperity?

    Exit

4.2

A room in the castle

Enter Baron and Amelia

BARON I hope you judge more favourably of Count Cassel's understanding since the private interview you have had with him.
Confess to me the exact effect of the long conference between you.

AMELIA To make me hate him.

BARON What has he done?   5

AMELIA Oh! told me of such barbarous deeds he has committed.

BARON What deeds?

AMELIA Made vows of love to so many women, that, on his marriage with me, a hundred female hearts will at least be broken.°

BARON Psha! do you believe him?   10

AMELIA Suppose I do not; is it to his honour that I believe he tells a falsehood?

BARON He is mistaken merely.

AMELIA Indeed, my lord, in one respect I am sure he speaks truth. For our old butler told my waiting-maid of a poor young creature   15 who has been deceived, undone; and she, and her whole family, involved in shame and sorrow by his perfidy.

BARON Are you sure the butler said this?

AMELIA See him, and ask him. He knows the whole story, indeed he does; the names of the persons, and every circumstance.   20

BARON Desire he may be sent to me.

AMELIA (*goes to the door and calls*) Order old Verdun to come to the Baron directly.

BARON I know tale-bearers are apt to be erroneous. I'll hear from himself, the account you speak of.   25

AMELIA I believe it is in verse.

BARON (*angry*) In verse!

AMELIA But, then, indeed it's true.°

    Enter Verdun

AMELIA Verdun, pray have not you some true poetry?

VERDUN All my poetry is true—and so far, better than some people's   30 prose.

BARON But I want prose on this occasion, and command you to give me nothing else.

    Verdun bows

Have you heard of an engagement which Count Cassel is under to any other woman than my daughter?   35

VERDUN I am to tell your honour in prose?

BARON Certainly.

    Verdun appears uneasy and loath to speak

Amelia, he does not like to divulge what he knows in presence of a third person—leave the room.

    Exit Amelia

VERDUN No, no—that did not cause my reluctance to speak.   40

BARON What then?

VERDUN Your not allowing me to speak in verse—(*holding up a paper*) for here is the poetic poem.

BARON How dare you presume to contend with my will? Tell in plain language all you know on the subject I have named.   45

BUTLER Well then, my lord, if you must have the account in quiet prose, thus it was—Phoebus, one morning, rose in the East, and having handed in the long-expected day, he called up his brother Hymen—°

BARON Have done with your rhapsody.   50

BUTLER Aye; I knew you'd like it best in verse—

> There lived a lady in this land,
>   Whose charms made the heart tingle;
> At church she had not given her hand,
>   And therefore still was single.   55

BARON Keep to prose.

BUTLER I will, my lord; but I have repeated it so often in verse, I scarce know how.—Count Cassel, influenced by the designs of Cupid in his very worst humour,

> Count Cassel wooed this maid so rare,   60
>   And in her eye found grace;°
> And if his purpose was not fair,

BARON No verse.

VERDUN   -   It probably was base.

I beg your pardon, my lord; but the verse will intrude in spite of my   65
efforts to forget it. 'Tis as difficult for me at times to forget, as 'tis
for other men at times to remember. But in plain truth, my lord, the
Count was treacherous, cruel, forsworn.

BARON I am astonished!

VERDUN And would be more so if you would listen to the whole   70
poem. (*Most earnestly*) Pray, my lord, listen to it.

BARON You know the family? All the parties?

VERDUN I will bring the father of the damsel to prove the veracity of
my muse. His name is Baden—poor old man!

> The sire consents to bless the pair,   75
>   And names the nuptial day,
> When lo! the bridegroom was not there,
>   Because he was away.

BARON But tell me—Had the father his daughter's innocence to
deplore?   80

BUTLER Ah! my lord, ah! and you *must* hear that part in rhyme. Loss
of innocence never sounds well except in verse.

For ah! the very night before,
    No prudent guard upon her,
The Count he gave her oaths a score,   85
    And took in charge her honour.

MORAL

Then you, who now lead single lives,
    From this sad tale beware;
And do not act as you were wives,°   90
    Before you really are.

Enter Count

BARON (*to Verdun*) Leave the room instantly.

COUNT Yes, good Mr Family Poet, leave the room, and take your doggerels with you.

VERDUN Don't affront my poem, your honour; for I am indebted to   95
you for the plot.

'*The Count he gave her oaths a score*
And took in charge her honour.'

Exit Verdun

BARON Count, you see me agitated.

COUNT What can be the cause?   100

BARON I'll not keep you in doubt a moment. You are accused, young man, of being engaged to another woman while you offer marriage to my child.

COUNT To only *one* other woman?

BARON What do you mean?   105

COUNT My meaning is, that when a man is young and rich, has travelled, and is no personal object of disapprobation, to have made vows but to one woman, is an absolute slight upon the rest of the sex.

BARON Without evasion, sir, do you know the name of Baden? Was   110
there ever a promise of marriage made by you to his daughter? Answer me plainly: or must I take a journey to enquire of the father?

COUNT No—he can tell you no more than, I dare say, you already know; and which I shall not contradict.   115

BARON Amazing insensibility! And can you hold your head erect while you acknowledge perfidy?

COUNT My dear Baron—if every man, who deserves to have a charge

such as this brought against him, was not permitted to look up—it
is a doubt whom we might not meet crawling on all fours.   120

The Count accidentally taps the Baron's shoulder

BARON (*starts—recollects himself—then in a faltering voice*) Yet—
nevertheless—the act is so atrocious—

COUNT But nothing new.

BARON (*faintly*) Yes—I hope—I hope it is new.

COUNT What, did you never meet with such a thing before?   125

BARON (*agitated*) If I have—I pronounced the man who so
offended—a villain.

COUNT You are singularly scrupulous. I question if the man thought
himself so.

BARON Yes he did.   130

COUNT How do you know?

BARON (*hesitating*) I have heard him say so.

COUNT But he ate, drank, and slept, I suppose?

BARON (*confused*) Perhaps he did.

COUNT And was merry with his friends; and his friends as fond of   135
him as ever?

BARON Perhaps (*confused*)—perhaps they were.

COUNT And perhaps he now and then took upon him to lecture young
men for their gallantries?°

BARON Perhaps he did.   140

COUNT Why, then, after all, Baron, your villain is a mighty good,
prudent, honest fellow; and I have no objection to your giving me
that name.

BARON But do you not think of some atonement to the unfortunate
girl?   145

COUNT Did *your* villain atone?

BARON No: when his reason was matured, he wished to make some
recompense; but his endeavours were too late.

COUNT I will follow his example, and wait till my reason is matured,
before I think myself competent to determine what to do.   150

BARON And till that time I defer your marriage with my daughter.

COUNT Would you delay her happiness so long? Why, my dear Baron,
considering the fashionable life I lead, it may be these ten years
before my judgment arrives to its necessary standard.

BARON I have the headache, Count—These tidings have dis-   155
composed, disordered me—I beg your absence for a few minutes.

COUNT I obey—And let me assure you, my lord, that, although, from
the extreme delicacy of your honour, you have ever through life

shuddered at seduction; yet, there are constitutions, and there are
circumstances, in which it can be palliated.   160

BARON (*violently*) Never.

COUNT Not in a grave, serious, reflecting man such as *you*, I grant.
But in a gay, lively, inconsiderate, flimsy, frivolous coxcomb, such as
myself, it is excusable: for me to keep my word to a woman, would
be deceit: 'tis not expected of me. It is in my character to break   165
oaths in love; as it is in your nature, my lord, never to have spoken
anything but wisdom and truth.
    Exit [Count]

BARON Could I have thought a creature so insignificant as that, had
power to excite sensations such as I feel at present! I am, indeed,
worse than he is, as much as the crimes of a man exceed those of an   170
idiot.
    Enter Amelia

AMELIA I heard the Count leave you, my lord, and so I am come to
enquire—

BARON (*sitting down, and trying to compose himself*) You are not to
marry Count Cassel—And now, mention his name to me no more.

AMELIA I won't—indeed I won't—for I hate his name.—But thank   175
you, my dear father, for this good news.
    [*Amelia*] *draws a chair, and sits on the opposite side of the table*
    on which he leans.—After a pause—
And who am I to marry?

BARON (*his head on his hand*) I can't tell.
    Amelia appears to have something on her mind which she wishes
    to disclose

AMELIA I never liked the Count.

BARON No more did I.   180

AMELIA (*after a pause*) I think love comes just as it pleases, without
being asked.

BARON (*in deep thought*) It does so.

AMELIA (*after another pause*) And there are instances where, perhaps,
the object of love makes the passion meritorious.   185

BARON To be sure there are.

AMELIA For example; my affection for Mr Anhalt as my tutor.

BARON Right.

AMELIA (*after another pause*) I should like to marry. (*Sighing*)

BARON So you shall. (*A pause*) It is proper for everybody to marry.   190

AMELIA Why, then, does not Mr Anhalt marry?

BARON You must ask him that question yourself.

227

AMELIA I have.

BARON And what did he say?

AMELIA Will you give me leave to tell you what he said?   195

BARON Certainly.

AMELIA And what I said to him?

BARON Certainly.

AMELIA And won't you be angry?

BARON Undoubtedly not.   200

AMELIA Why, then—you know you commanded me never to disguise or conceal the truth.

BARON I did so.

AMELIA Why, then he said—

BARON What did he say?   205

AMELIA He said—he would not marry me without your consent for the world.

BARON (*starting from his chair*) And pray, how came this the subject of your conversation?

AMELIA (*rising*) *I* brought it up.   210

BARON And what did you say?

AMELIA I said that birth and fortune were such old-fashioned things to me, I cared nothing about either: and that I had once heard my father declare, he should consult my happiness in marrying me, beyond any other consideration.   215

BARON I will once more repeat to you my sentiments. It is the custom in this country for the children of nobility to marry only with their equals; but as my daughter's content° is more dear to me than an ancient custom, I would bestow you on the first man I thought calculated to make you happy: by this I do not mean to say that I   220 should not be severely nice° in the character of the man to whom I gave you; and Mr Anhalt, from his obligations to me, and his high sense of honour, thinks too nobly—

AMELIA Would it not be noble to make the daughter of his benefactor happy?   225

BARON But when that daughter is a child, and thinks like a child—

AMELIA No, indeed, papa, I begin to think very like a woman. Ask *him* if I don't.

BARON Ask him! You feel gratitude for the instructions you have received from him, and you fancy it love.   230

AMELIA Are there two gratitudes?

BARON What do you mean?

AMELIA Because I feel gratitude to you; but that is very unlike the gratitude I feel towards him.

BARON Indeed!   235

AMELIA Yes; and then he feels another gratitude towards me. What's that?

BARON Has he told you so?

AMELIA Yes.

BARON That was not right of him.   240

AMELIA Oh! if you did but know how I surprised him!

BARON Surprised him?

AMELIA He came to me by your command, to examine my heart respecting Count Cassel. I told him that I would never marry the Count.   245

BARON But him?

AMELIA Yes, him.

BARON Very fine indeed! And what was his answer?

AMELIA He talked of my rank in life; of my aunts and cousins; of my grandfather, and great-grandfather; of his duty to you; and 250 endeavoured to persuade me to think no more of him.

BARON He acted honestly.

AMELIA But not politely.

BARON No matter.

AMELIA Dear father! I shall never be able to love another—Never be 255 happy with any one else. (*Throwing herself on her knees*)

BARON Rise, I command you.
        As Amelia rises, enter Anhalt

ANHALT My lord, forgive me! I have ventured, on the privilege of my office, as a minister of holy charity, to bring the poor soldier, whom your justice has arrested, into the adjoining room; and I presume to 260 entreat you will admit him to your presence, and hear his apology, or his supplication.

BARON Anhalt, you have done wrong. I pity the unhappy boy; but you know I cannot, must not forgive him.

ANHALT I beseech you then, my lord, to tell him so yourself. From 265 your lips he may receive his doom with resignation.

AMELIA Oh father! See him and take pity on him; his sorrows have made him frantic.

BARON Leave the room, Amelia. (*On Amelia's attempting to speak, Baron raises his voice*) Instantly.—   270
        Exit Amelia

ANHALT He asked a private audience: perhaps he has some confession to make that may relieve his mind, and may be requisite for you to hear.

BARON Well, bring him in, and do you wait in the adjoining room, till our conference is over. I must then, sir, have a conference with you.   275

ANHALT I shall obey your commands.

Anhalt goes to the door, and re-enters with Frederick. Anhalt then retires at the same door

BARON (*haughtily to Frederick*) I know, young man, you plead your mother's wants in excuse for an act of desperation: but powerful as this plea might be in palliation of a fault, it cannot extenuate a crime like yours.   280

FREDERICK I have a plea for my conduct even more powerful than a mother's wants.

BARON What's that?

FREDERICK My father's cruelty.

BARON You have a father then?   285

FREDERICK I have, and a rich one—Nay, one that's reputed virtuous, and honourable. A great man, possessing estates and patronage in abundance; much esteemed at court, and beloved by his tenants; kind, benevolent, honest, generous—

BARON And with all those great qualities, abandons you?   290

FREDERICK He does, with all the qualities I mention.

BARON Your father may do right; a dissipated, desperate youth, whom kindness cannot draw from vicious habits, severity may.

FREDERICK You are mistaken—My father does not discard me for my vices—He does not know me—has never seen me—He abandoned   295 me, even before I was born.

BARON What do you say?

FREDERICK The tears of my mother are all that I inherit from my father. Never has he protected or supported me—never protected her.   300

BARON Why don't you apply to his relations?

FREDERICK They disown me, too—I am, they say, related to no one—All the world disclaim me, except my mother—and there again, I have to thank my father.

BARON How so?   305

FREDERICK Because I am an illegitimate son.—My seduced mother has brought me up in patient misery. Industry enabled her to give me an education; but the days of my youth commenced with hardship, sorrow, and danger.—My companions lived happily around

me, and had a pleasing prospect in their view, while bread and   310
water only were my food, and no hopes joined to sweeten it. But my
father felt not that!

BARON (*to himself*) He touches my heart.

FREDERICK After five years' absence from my mother, I returned this
very day, and found her dying in the streets for want—Not even a   315
hut to shelter her, or a pallet of straw—But my father, he feels not
that! He lives in a palace, sleeps on the softest down, enjoys all the
luxuries of the great; and when he dies, a funeral sermon will praise
his great benevolence, his Christian charities.

BARON (*greatly agitated*) What is your father's name?   320

FREDERICK —He took advantage of an innocent young woman,
gained her affection by flattery and false promises; gave life to an
unfortunate being, who was on the point of murdering his father.

BARON (*shuddering*) Who is he?

FREDERICK Baron Wildenhaim.   325

   The Baron's emotion° expresses the sense of amazement,
   guilt, shame, and horror

FREDERICK In this house did you rob my mother of her honour; and
in this house I am a sacrifice for the crime. I am your prisoner—I
will not be free—I am a robber—I give myself up.—You *shall*
deliver me into the hands of justice—You shall accompany me to
the spot of public execution. You shall hear in vain the chaplain's   330
consolation and injunctions. You shall find how I, in despair, will,
to the last moment, call for retribution on my father.

BARON Stop! Be pacified—

FREDERICK —And when you turn your head from my extended
corpse, you will behold my weeping mother—Need I paint how her   335
eyes will greet you?

BARON Desist—barbarian, savage, stop!

   Enter Anhalt, alarmed

ANHALT What do I hear? What is this? Young man, I hope you have
not made a second attempt.

FREDERICK Yes; I have done what it was your place to do. I have made   340
a sinner tremble.

   [*Frederick*] *points to the Baron, and exit*

ANHALT What can this mean?—I do not comprehend—

BARON He is my son!—He is my son!—Go, Anhalt—advise me—
help me—Go to the poor woman, his mother—He can show you
the way—make haste—speed to protect her—   345

ANHALT But what am I to—

BARON Go.—Your heart will tell you how to act.
        Exit Anhalt
        (*Distractedly*) Who am I? What am I? Mad—raving—no—I have a
        son—A son! The bravest—I will—I must—oh! (*With tenderness*)
        Why have I not embraced him yet? (*increasing his voice*) why not   350
        pressed him to my heart? Ah! see—(*looking after him* [*through a.
        window*])—He flies from the castle—Who's there? Where are my
        attendants?
        Enter two Servants
        Follow him—bring the prisoner back.—But observe my com-
        mand—treat him with respect—treat him as my son—and your   355
        master.
        Exeunt

5.1

Inside of the cottage (as in 2.1)

Agatha, Cottager, and his Wife discovered

AGATHA Pray look and see if he is coming.

COTTAGER It is of no use. I have been in the road; have looked up and down; but neither see nor hear anything of him.

WIFE Have a little patience.

AGATHA I wish you would step out once more—I think he cannot be   5
far off.

COTTAGER I will; I will go.
     Exit [Cottager]

WIFE If your son knew what heaven had sent you, he would be here very soon.

AGATHA I feel so anxious—   10

WIFE But why? I should think a purse of gold, such as you have received, would make anybody easy.

AGATHA Where can he be so long? He has been gone four hours. Some ill must have befallen him.

WIFE It is still broad daylight—don't think of any danger.—This   15
evening we must all be merry. I'll prepare the supper. What a good gentleman our Baron must be! I am sorry I ever spoke a word against him.

AGATHA How did he know I was here?

WIFE Heaven only can tell. The servant that brought the money was   20
very secret.

AGATHA (*to herself*) I am astonished! I wonder! Oh! surely he has been informed—Why else should he have sent so much money?
     Enter Cottager

AGATHA Well!—not yet!

COTTAGER I might look till I am blind for him—but I saw our new   25
rector coming along the road; he calls in sometimes. Maybe he will this evening.

WIFE He is a very good gentleman; pays great attention to his parishioners; and where he can assist the poor, he is always ready.   30
     Enter Anhalt

ANHALT Good evening, friends.

COTTAGER and WIFE Thank you, reverend sir.

    Cottager and Wife run to fetch Anhalt a chair

ANHALT I thank you, good people—I see you have a stranger here.

COTTAGER Yes, your reverence;° it is a poor sick woman, whom I took
in doors.   35

ANHALT You will be rewarded for it. (*To Agatha*) May I beg leave to
ask your name?

AGATHA Ah! If we were alone—

ANHALT Good neighbours, will you leave us alone for a few minutes?
I have something to say to this poor woman.   40

COTTAGER Wife, do you hear? Come along with me.

    Exeunt Cottager and his Wife

ANHALT Now—

AGATHA Before I tell you who I am, what I am, and what I was—I
must beg to ask—Are you of this country?

ANHALT No—I was born in Alsace.   45

AGATHA Did you know the late rector personally, whom you have
succeeded?

ANHALT No.

AGATHA Then you are not acquainted with my narrative?

ANHALT Should I find you to be the person whom I have long been in   50
search of, your history is not altogether unknown to me.

AGATHA 'That you have been in search of'! Who gave you such a
commission?

ANHALT A man, who, if it so prove, is much concerned with your
misfortunes.   55

AGATHA How? Oh, sir! tell me quickly—Whom do you think to find
in me?

ANHALT Agatha Friburg.

AGATHA Yes, I am that unfortunate woman; and the man who pre-
tends to take concern in my misfortunes is—Baron Wildenhaim—   60
he who betrayed me, abandoned me and my child, and killed my
parents.—He would now repair our sufferings with this purse of
gold. (*Takes out the purse*) Whatever may be your errand, sir,
whether to humble, or to protect me, it is alike indifferent. I therefore request you to take this money to him who sent it. Tell him,   65
my honour has never been saleable. Tell him, destitute as I am, even
indigence will not tempt me to accept charity from my seducer. He
despised my heart—I despise his gold.—He has trampled on me—
I trample on his representative.

    [*Agatha*] *throws the purse on the ground*

234

ANHALT Be patient—I give you my word, that when the Baron sent   70
  this present to an unfortunate woman, for whom her son had sup-
  plicated, he did not know that woman was Agatha.
AGATHA My son? what of my son?
ANHALT Do not be alarmed—The Baron met with an affectionate
  son, who begged for his sick mother, and it affected him.   75
AGATHA Begged of the Baron! of his father!
ANHALT Yes; but they did not know each other; and the mother
  received the present on the son's account.
AGATHA Did not know each other? Where is my son?
ANHALT At the castle.   80
AGATHA And still unknown?
ANHALT Now he is known—an explanation has taken place;—and I
  am sent here by the Baron, not to a stranger, but to Agatha
  Friburg—not with gold! his commission was—'do what your heart
  directs you'.   85
AGATHA How is my Frederick? How did the Baron receive him?
ANHALT I left him just in the moment the discovery was made. By
  this time your son is, perhaps, in the arms of his father.
AGATHA Oh! is it possible that a man, who has been twenty years deaf
  to the voice of nature, should change so suddenly?   90
ANHALT I do not mean to justify the Baron, but—he has loved you—
  and fear of his noble kindred alone caused his breach of faith to
  you.
AGATHA But to desert me wholly and wed another—
ANHALT War called him away—Wounded in the field, he was taken to   95
  the adjacent seat of a nobleman, whose only daughter, by anxious
  attention to his recovery, won his gratitude; and, influenced by the
  will of his worldly friends, he married. But no sooner was I received
  into the family, and admitted to his confidence, than he related to
  me your story; and at times would exclaim in anguish—'The proud   100
  imperious Baroness avenges the wrongs of my deserted Agatha.'
  Again, when he presented me this living, and I left France to take
  possession of it, his last words before we parted, were—'The
  moment you arrive at Wildenhaim, make all enquiries to find out
  my poor Agatha.' Every letter I afterwards received from him con-   105
  tained 'Still, still, no tidings of my Agatha.' And fate ordained it
  should be so, till this fortunate day.
AGATHA What you have said has made my heart overflow—where will
  this end?
ANHALT I know not yet the Baron's intentions: but your sufferings   110

demand immediate remedy: and one way only is left—Come with me to the castle. Do not start—you shall be concealed in my apartments till you are called for.

AGATHA I go to the Baron's?—No.

ANHALT Go for the sake of your son—reflect, that his fortunes may depend upon your presence. 115

AGATHA And he is the only branch on which my hope still blossoms: the rest are withered.—I will forget my wrongs as a woman, if the Baron will atone to the mother—he shall have the woman's pardon, if he will merit the mother's thanks—(*After a struggle*)—I *will* go to 120 the castle—for the sake of my Frederick, go even to his father. But where are my good host and hostess, that I may take leave, and thank them for their kindness?

ANHALT (*taking up the purse which Agatha had thrown down*) Here, good friend! Good woman! 125
    Enter Cottager and his Wife

WIFE Yes, yes, here am I.

ANHALT Good people, I will take your guest with me. You have acted an honest part, and therefore receive this reward for your trouble.
    Anhalt offers the purse to Cottager, who puts it by,° and turns away

ANHALT (*to the Wife*) Do *you* take it.

WIFE (*taking it*) I always obey my pastor. 130

AGATHA Goodbye. (*Shaking hands with Cottager and Wife*) For your hospitality to me, may ye enjoy continued happiness.

COTTAGER Fare you well—fare you well.

WIFE If you find friends and get health, we won't trouble you to call on us again: but if you should fall sick or be in poverty, we shall take 135 it very unkind if we don't see you.
    Exeunt Agatha and Anhalt on one side, Cottager and his Wife on the other

5.2

A room in the castle

Baron sitting upon a sofa.—Frederick standing near him, with one hand pressed between his—the Baron rises

BARON Been in battle too!—I am glad to hear it. You have known hard services, but now they are over, and joy and happiness will succeed.—The reproach of your birth shall be removed, for I will acknowledge you my son, and heir to my estate.

FREDERICK And my mother—   5

BARON She shall live in peace and affluence. Do you think I would leave your mother unprovided, unprotected? No! About a mile from this castle I have an estate called Weldendorf—there she shall live, and call her own whatever it produces. There she shall reign, and be sole mistress of the little paradise. There her past sufferings   10
shall be changed to peace and tranquillity. On a summer's morning, we, my son, will ride to visit her; pass a day, a week with her; and in this social intercourse time will glide pleasantly.

FREDERICK And, pray, my lord—under what name is my mother to live then?   15

BARON (*confused*) How?

FREDERICK In what capacity?—As your domestic°—or as—

BARON That we will settle afterwards.

FREDERICK Will you allow me, sir, to leave the room a little while, that you may have leisure to consider *now*?   20

BARON I do not know how to explain myself in respect to your mother more than I have done already.

FREDERICK My fate, whatever it may be, shall never part me from her. This is my firm resolution, upon which I call heaven to witness! My lord, it must be Frederick of Wildenhaim, and Agatha of   25
Wildenhaim—or Agatha Friburg, and Frederick Friburg.

        Exit [*Frederick*]

BARON (*calling after Frederick*) Young man! Frederick!—Hasty indeed! would make conditions with his father. No, no, that must not be. I just now thought how well I had arranged my plans—had relieved my heart of every burden, when, a second time, he throws   30
a mountain upon it. Stop, friend conscience, why do you take his part?—For twenty years thus you have used me, and been my torture.

        Enter Anhalt

Ah! Anhalt, I am glad you are come. My conscience and myself are at variance.   35

ANHALT Your conscience is in the right.

BARON You don't know yet what the quarrel is.

ANHALT Conscience is always right—because it never speaks unless it *is* so.

BARON Aye, a man of your order can more easily attend to its whispers,   40

237

than an old warrior. The sound of cannon has made him hard of hearing.—I have found my son again, Mr Anhalt, a fine, brave young man—I mean to make him my heir—Am I in the right?

ANHALT Perfectly.

BARON And his mother shall live in happiness—My estate, Welden-   45
dorf, shall be hers—I'll give it to her, and she shall make it her residence. Don't I do right?

ANHALT No.

BARON (*surprised*) No? And what else should I do?

ANHALT (*forcibly*) Marry her.   50

BARON (*starting*) I marry her!

ANHALT Baron Wildenhaim is a man who will not act inconsistently.—As this is my opinion, I expect your reasons, if you do not.

BARON Would you have me marry a beggar?   55

ANHALT (*after a pause*)° Is that your only objection?

BARON (*confused*) I have more—many more.

ANHALT May I beg to know them likewise?

BARON My birth!   60

ANHALT Go on.

BARON My relations would despise me.

ANHALT Go on.

BARON (*in anger*) 'Sdeath! are not these reasons enough?—I know no other.

ANHALT Now, then, it is my turn to state mine for the advice I have   65
given you. But first, I presume to ask a few questions.—Did Agatha, through artful insinuation, gain your affection? or did she give you cause to suppose her inconstant?

BARON Neither—but for me, she was always virtuous and good.

ANHALT Did it cost you trouble and earnest entreaty to make her   70
otherwise?

BARON (*angrily*) Yes.

ANHALT You pledged your honour?

BARON (*confused*) Yes.

ANHALT Called God to witness?   75

BARON (*more confused*) Yes.

ANHALT The witness you called at that time was the Being who sees you now. What you gave in pledge was your honour, which you must redeem. Therefore thank heaven that it is in your *power* to redeem it. By marrying Agatha the ransom's made: and she brings   80
a dower greater than any princess can bestow—peace to your con-

science. If you then esteem the value of this portion, you will not hesitate a moment to exclaim, 'Friends, wish me joy, I will marry Agatha'.

> *Baron, in great agitation, walks backwards and forwards, then takes Anhalt by the hand*

BARON 'Friend, wish me joy—I will *marry* Agatha'.   85

ANHALT I do wish you joy.

BARON Where is she?

ANHALT In the castle—in my apartments here—I conducted her through the garden, to avoid curiosity.

BARON Well, then, this is the wedding-day. This very evening you   90
shall give us your blessing.

ANHALT Not so soon, not so private. The whole village was witness of Agatha's shame—the whole village must be witness of Agatha's re-established honour. Do you consent to this?

BARON I do.   95

ANHALT Now the quarrel is decided. Now is your conscience quiet?

BARON As quiet as an infant's. I only wish the first interview was over.

ANHALT Compose yourself. Agatha's heart is to be your judge.

> *Enter Amelia*

BARON Amelia, you have a brother.

AMELIA I have just heard so, my lord; and rejoice to find the news   100
confirmed by you.

BARON I know, my dear Amelia, I can repay you for the loss of Count Cassel; but what return can I make to you for the loss of half your fortune?

AMELIA My brother's love will be ample recompense.   105

BARON I will reward you better. Mr Anhalt, the battle I have just fought, I owe to myself: the victory I gained, I owe to you. A man of your principles, at once a teacher and an example of virtue, exalts his rank in life to a level with the noblest family—and I shall be proud to receive you as my son.   110

ANHALT (*falling on his knees, and taking the Baron's hand*) My lord, you overwhelm me with confusion, as well as with joy.

BARON My obligations to you are infinite—Amelia shall pay the debt.

> *[Baron] gives Amelia to Anhalt*

AMELIA Oh, my dear father! (*embracing the Baron*) what blessings have you bestowed on me in one day. (*To Anhalt*) I will be your   115
scholar still, and use more diligence than ever to please my *master*.

ANHALT His present happiness admits of no addition.

BARON Nor does mine—And yet there is another task to perform that

will require more fortitude, more courage, than this has done! A
trial that!—(*Bursts into tears*)—I cannot prevent them—Let me—   120
let me—A few minutes will bring me to myself—Where is Agatha?

ANHALT I will go, and fetch her.

> *Exit Anhalt at an upper entrance*°

BARON Stop! Let me first recover a little.

> *Baron walks up and down, sighing bitterly—looks at the door*
> *through which Anhalt left the room*

That door she will come from—That was once the dressing-room
of my mother—From that door I have seen her come many times—   125
have been delighted with her lovely smiles—How shall I now
behold her altered looks! Frederick must be my mediator.—Where
is he? Where is my son?—Now I am ready—my heart is prepared
to receive her—Haste! haste! Bring her in.

> *Baron looks steadfastly at the door—Anhalt leads on Agatha—*
> *The Baron runs and clasps Agatha in his arms—Supported by*
> *him, she sinks on a chair which Amelia places in the middle of the*
> *stage—The Baron kneels by Agatha's side, holding her hand*

BARON Agatha, Agatha, do you know this voice?   130

AGATHA Wildenhaim.

BARON Can you forgive me?

AGATHA (*embracing him*) I forgive you.

> [*Enter Frederick*]

FREDERICK (*as he enters*) I hear the voice of my mother!—Ha! mother!
father!   135

> *Frederick throws himself on his knees by the other side of*
> *Agatha—She clasps Frederick in her arms.—Amelia is placed on*
> *the side of the Baron attentively viewing Agatha—Anhalt*
> *stands on the side of Frederick with his hands gratefully raised to*
> *heaven. The curtain slowly drops*°

Epilogue°

Written by Thomas Palmer, Esq. of the Temple°
Spoken by Mr Munden°

Our drama now ended, I'll take up your time
Just a moment or two, in defence of my *rhyme*—
'Though I hope that among you are *some* who *admired*
'What I've hitherto said, dare I hope none are tired?
'But whether ye have, or have not heard enough,   5
'Or whether nice critics will think it all stuff;°
'To myself *rhyme* has ever appeared, I must own,
'In its nature a sort of *philosopher's stone*.°
'And if Chymists would use it, they'd not make a pother,°
'And puzzle their brains to find out any other.'   10
Indeed 'tis most strange and surprising to me
That all folks in *rhyming* their int'rest can't see;
For I'm sure if its use were quite common with men,
The world would roll on just as pleasant again.
''Tis said, that while Orpheus was striking his lyre,°   15
'Trees and brutes danced along to the sound of the wire;
'That Amphion to walls soon converted the glebes,
'And they rose, as he sung, to a city called Thebes;°
'I suppose *they* were *butlers* (like me) of that time,
'And the tale shows our sires knew the wonders of *rhyme*.'   20
From time immemorial, your lovers, we find,
When their mistresses' hearts have been proud and unkind,
Have resorted to *rhyme*; and indeed it appears
That a *rhyme* would do more than a bucket of tears.
Of love, from experience, I speak—odds my life!°   25
I shall never forget how I courted my wife:
She had offers in plenty; but always stood neuter,
Till I, with my pen, started forth as a suitor;
Yet I made no mean present of *ribbon* or *bonnet*,
My present was caught from the stars—'twas a *sonnet*.   30
'And now you know this, sure 'tis needless to say,
'That prose was neglected, and *rhyme* won the day—
'But its potent effects you as well may discover
'In the *husband* and *wife*, as in *mistress* and *lover*;

'There are some of ye here, who, like me, I conjecture,   35
'Have been lulled into sleep by a good *curtain lecture*.°
'But that's a mere trifle; you'll ne'er come to blows,
'If you'll only avoid that dull enemy, *prose*.
'Adopt, then, my plan, and the very next time,
'That in words you fall out, let them fall into *rhyme*;   40
'Thus your sharpest disputes will conclude very soon,
'And from jangling to jingling you'll chime into *tune*.
'If my wife were to call me a *drunken old sot*,
'I should merely just ask her, what butler is not?
'And bid her take care that she don't go to pot.   45
'So our squabbles continue a very short season,
'If she yields to my *rhyme*—I allow she has reason.'
Independent of this I conceive *rhyme* has weight
In the higher employments of church and of state,
And would in my mind such advantages draw,   50
'Tis a pity that *rhyme* is not sanctioned by law;
'For 'twould *really* be serving us all to impose
'A capital fine on the man who spoke prose.'
Mark the pleader who clacks, in his client's behalf,°
His technical stuff for three hours and a half;   55
Or the fellow who tells you a long stupid story,
And over and over the same lays before ye;
Or the member who raves till the whole house are dozing.°
What d'ye say of such men? Why, you say they are prosing.°
So, of course, then, if *prose* is so tedious a *crime*,   60
It of consequence follows, there's *virtue* in *rhyme*.
The best piece of prose that I've heard a long while,
Is what gallant Nelson has sent from the Nile.°
And had he but told us the story in *rhyme*,
What a thing 'twould be; but, perhaps, he'd no time.   65
So, I'll do it myself—Oh! 'tis glorious news!
Nine *sail* of the line! Just a ship for each Muse.
As I live, there's an end of the French and their navy—
Sir John Warren has sent the Brest fleet to Old Davy.°
'Tis in the *Gazette*, and that, everyone knows,°   70
Is sure to be truth, though 'tis written in prose.

THE TWO FOSCARI

AN HISTORICAL TRAGEDY

by
LORD BYRON

The *father* softens, but the *governor*'s resolved.
CRITIC°

THE CHARACTERS OF THE PLAY

MEN

Francis Foscari, *Doge of Venice*
Jacopo Foscari, *son of the Doge*
James Loredano, *a patrician*
Marco Memmo,° *a chief of the Forty*
Barbarigo,° *a senator*
Other senators, the Council of Ten, guards, attendants [, a doctor (or
'leech'), familiars of the Ten, the six members of the Signory]°

WOMAN°

Marina,° *wife of young Foscari*
[Marina's woman]

SCENE: THE DUCAL PALACE, VENICE

244

1.1

A hall in the ducal palace

Enter Loredano and Barbarigo, meeting

LOREDANO Where is the prisoner?

BARBARIGO   Reposing from
The Question.

LOREDANO   The hour's past—fixed yesterday°
For the resumption of his trial.—Let us
Rejoin our colleagues in the council, and
Urge his recall.

BARBARIGO   Nay, let him profit by   5
A few brief minutes for his tortured limbs;
He was o'erwrought by the Question yesterday,
And may die under it if now repeated.

LOREDANO Well?

BARBARIGO   I yield not to you in love of justice,
Or hate of the ambitious Foscari,   10
Father and son, and all their noxious race;
But the poor wretch has suffered beyond nature's
Most stoical endurance.

LOREDANO   Without owning
His crime.

BARBARIGO Perhaps without committing any.
But he avowed the letter to the Duke   15
Of Milan, and his sufferings half atone for°
Such weakness.

LOREDANO   We shall see.

BARBARIGO   You, Loredano,
Pursue hereditary hate too far.

LOREDANO How far?

BARBARIGO   To extermination.

LOREDANO   When they are
Extinct, you may say this.—Let's in to council.   20

BARBARIGO Yet pause—the number of our colleagues is not
Complete yet; two are wanting ere we can
Proceed.

LOREDANO And the chief judge, the Doge?

BARBARIGO   No—he
    With more than Roman fortitude is ever
    First at the board in this unhappy process°   25
    Against his last and only son.
LOREDANO   True—true—
    His *last*.
BARBARIGO Will nothing move you?
LOREDANO   *Feels he*, think you?
BARBARIGO He shows it not.
LOREDANO   I have marked *that*—the wretch!
BARBARIGO But yesterday, I hear, on his return
    To the ducal chambers, as he passed the threshold   30
    The old man fainted.
LOREDANO   It begins to work, then.
BARBARIGO The work is half your own.
LOREDANO   And should be *all* mine—
    My father and my uncle are no more.
BARBARIGO I have read their epitaph, which says they died
    By poison.
LOREDANO   When the Doge declared that he   35
    Should never deem himself a sovereign till
    The death of Peter Loredano, both
    The brothers sickened shortly:—he *is* sovereign.°
BARBARIGO A wretched one.
LOREDANO   What should they be who make
    Orphans?
BARBARIGO But *did* the Doge make you so?
LOREDANO   Yes.   40
BARBARIGO What solid proofs?
LOREDANO   When princes set themselves
    To work in secret, proofs and process are
    Alike made difficult; but I have such
    Of the first, as shall make the second needless.
BARBARIGO But you will move by law?
LOREDANO   By all the laws   45
    Which he would leave us.
BARBARIGO   They are such in this
    Our state as render retribution easier
    Than 'mongst remoter nations. Is it true
    That you have written in your books of commerce,°
    (The wealthy practice of our highest nobles)   50

246

'Doge Foscari, my debtor for the deaths
Of Marco and Pietro Loredano,
My sire and uncle'?

LOREDANO   It is written thus.

BARBARIGO And will you leave it unerased?

LOREDANO   Till balanced.

BARBARIGO And how?

> *Two senators pass over the stage, as in their way to the Hall of*
> *the Council of Ten*°

LOREDANO   You see the number is complete.   55
Follow me.

> *Exit Loredano*

BARBARIGO (*alone*) Follow *thee*! I have followed long°
Thy path of desolation, as the wave
Sweeps after that before it, alike whelming
The wreck that creaks to the wild winds, and wretch
Who shrieks within its riven ribs, as gush   60
The waters through them; but this son and sire
Might move the elements to pause, and yet
Must I on hardily like them—Oh! would
I could as blindly and remorselessly!—
Lo, where he comes!—Be still, my heart! They are   65
Thy foes, must be thy victims: wilt thou beat
For those who almost broke thee?

> *Enter Guards, with young Foscari as prisoner, etc.*°

GUARD   Let him rest.
Signor, take time.

JACOPO FOSCARI   I thank thee, friend, I'm feeble;
But thou may'st stand reproved.

GUARD   I'll stand the hazard.°

JACOPO FOSCARI That's kind:—I meet some pity, but no mercy;   70
This is the first.

GUARD   And might be last, did they
Who rule behold us.

BARBARIGO (*advancing to the Guard*) There is one who does:
Yet fear not; I will neither be thy judge
Nor thy accuser; though the hour is past,
Wait their last summons—I am of the Ten,   75
And waiting for that summons sanction you
Even by my presence: when the last call sounds,
We'll in together.—Look well to the prisoner!

JACOPO FOSCARI What voice is that?—'Tis Barbarigo's! Ah!
  Our house's foe, and one of my few judges.   80
BARBARIGO To balance such a foe, if such there be,
  Thy father sits amongst thy judges.
JACOPO FOSCARI   True,
  He judges.
BARBARIGO Then deem not the laws too harsh
  Which yield so much indulgence to a sire
  As to allow his voice in such high matter   85
  As the state's safety——
JACOPO FOSCARI   And his son's. I'm faint;
  Let me approach, I pray you, for a breath
  Of air, yon window which o'erlooks the waters.
    Enter an Officer, who whispers to Barbarigo
BARBARIGO (*to the Guard*) Let him approach. I must not speak with him
  Further than thus; I have transgressed my duty   90
  In this brief parley, and must now redeem it
  Within the Council Chamber.
    Exit Barbarigo [with Officer]. Guard conducts Jacopo Foscari to
    the window
GUARD   There, sir, 'tis
  Open—How feel you?
JACOPO FOSCARI   Like a boy—Oh Venice!
GUARD And your limbs?
JACOPO FOSCARI   Limbs! how often have they borne me
  Bounding o'er yon blue tide, as I have skimmed   95
  The gondola along in childish race,
  And, masqued as a young gondolier, amidst
  My gay competitors, noble as I,
  Raced for our pleasure in the pride of strength,
  While the fair populace of crowding beauties,   100
  Plebeian as patrician, cheered us on
  With dazzling smiles, and wishes audible,
  And waving kerchiefs, and applauding hands,
  Even to the goal!—How many a time have I°
  Cloven with arm still lustier, breast more daring,   105
  The wave all roughened; with a swimmer's stroke
  Flinging the billows back from my drenched hair,
  And laughing from my lip the audacious brine,
  Which kissed it like a wine-cup, rising o'er
  The waves as they arose, and prouder still   110

The loftier they uplifted me; and oft,
In wantonness of spirit, plunging down
Into their green and glassy gulfs, and making
My way to shells and sea-weed, all unseen
By those above, till they waxed fearful; then   115
Returning with my grasp full of such tokens
As showed that I had searched the deep: exulting,
With a far-dashing stroke, and drawing deep
The long-suspended breath, again I spurned
The foam which broke around me, and pursued   120
My track like a sea-bird.—I was a boy then.

GUARD Be a man now: there never was more need
Of manhood's strength.

JACOPO FOSCARI (*looking from the lattice*)
                              My beautiful, my own,
My only Venice—*this is breath!* Thy breeze,
Thine Adrian sea-breeze, how it fans my face!°   125
Thy very winds feel native to my veins,
And cool them into calmness! How unlike
The hot gales of the horrid Cyclades,°
Which howled about my Candiote dungeon, and°
Made my heart sick.

GUARD   I see the colour comes   130
Back to your cheek: heaven send you strength to bear
What more may be imposed!—I dread to think on't.

JACOPO FOSCARI They will not banish me again?—No—no,
Let them wring on; I am strong yet.

GUARD   Confess,°
And the rack will be spared you.

JACOPO FOSCARI   I confessed   135
Once—twice before: both times they exiled me.

GUARD And the third time will slay you.

JACOPO FOSCARI   Let them do so,
So I be buried in my birthplace; better
Be ashes here than aught that lives elsewhere.

GUARD And can you so much love the soil which hates you?   140

JACOPO FOSCARI The soil!—Oh no, it is the seed of the soil
Which persecutes me; but my native earth
Will take me as a mother to her arms.
I ask no more than a Venetian grave,
A dungeon, what they will, so it be here.   145

Enter an Officer

OFFICER Bring in the prisoner!

GUARD   Signor, you hear the order.

JACOPO FOSCARI Aye, I am used to such a summons; 'tis
   The third time they have tortured me:—(*to the Guard*) then lend me
   Thine arm.

OFFICER   Take mine, sir; 'tis my duty to
   Be nearest to your person.

JACOPO FOSCARI   You!—you are he   150
   Who yesterday presided o'er my pangs—
   Away!—I'll walk alone.

OFFICER   As you please, signor;
   The sentence was not of my signing, but
   I dared not disobey the Council when
   They——

JACOPO FOSCARI Bade thee stretch me on their horrid engine.   155
   I pray thee touch me not—that is, just now;
   The time will come they will renew that order,
   But keep off from me till 'tis issued. As
   I look upon thy hands my curdling limbs
   Quiver with the anticipated wrenching,   160
   And the cold drops strain through my brow, as if——
   But onward—I have borne it—I can bear it.—
   How looks my father?

OFFICER   With his wonted aspect.

JACOPO FOSCARI So does the earth, and sky, the blue of ocean,
   The brightness of our city, and her domes,   165
   The mirth of her Piazza, even now°
   Its merry hum of nations pierces here,
   Even here, into these chambers of the unknown
   Who govern, and the unknown and the unnumbered
   Judged and destroyed in silence—all things wear   170
   The self-same aspect, to my very sire!
   Nothing can sympathize with Foscari,
   Not even a Foscari.—Sir, I attend you.

     Exeunt Jacopo Foscari, Officer, [and Guard]. Enter Memmo
     and another Senator

MEMMO He's gone—we are too late:—think you the Ten
   Will sit for any length of time today?   175

SENATOR They say the prisoner is most obdurate,
   Persisting in his first avowal; but

More I know not.

MEMMO   And that is much; the secrets
Of yon terrific chamber are as hidden
From us, the premier nobles of the state,   180
As from the people.

SENATOR   Save the wonted rumours,
Which (like the tales of spectres that are rife
Near ruincd buildings) never have been proved,
Nor wholly disbelieved: men know as little
Of the state's real acts as of the grave's   185
Unfathomed mysteries.

MEMMO   But with length of time
We gain a step in knowledge, and I look
Forward to be one day of the decemvirs.°

SENATOR Or Doge?

MEMMO   Why, no, not if I can avoid it.

SENATOR 'Tis the first station of the state, and may   190
Be lawfully desired, and lawfully
Attained by noble aspirants.

MEMMO   To such
I leave it; though born noble, my ambition
Is limited: I'd rather be an unit
Of an united and imperial Ten,   195
Than shine a lonely, though a gilded cipher.—
Whom have we here? The wife of Foscari?

        Enter Marina, with a female Attendant

MARINA What, no one?—I am wrong, there still are two;
But they are senators.

MEMMO   Most noble lady,
Command us.

MARINA   *I command!*—Alas! my life   200
Has been one long entreaty, and a vain one.

MEMMO I understand thee, but I must not answer.

MARINA (*fiercely*) True—none dare answer here save on the rack,
Or question save those——

MEMMO (*interrupting her*)   High-born dame! bethink thee
Whcre thou now art.

MARINA   Where I now am!—It was   205
My husband's father's palace.

MEMMO   The Duke's palace.

MARINA And his son's prison;—true, I have not forgot it;

251

And if there were no other nearer, bitterer
Remembrances, would thank the illustrious Memmo
For pointing out the pleasures of the place.   210
MEMMO Be calm!
MARINA (*looking up towards heaven*) I am; but oh, thou eternal God!
     Canst *thou* continue so, with such a world?
MEMMO Thy husband yet may be absolved.
MARINA   He is,
     In heaven. I pray you, signor senator,
     Speak not of that; you are a man of office,   215
     So is the Doge; he has a son at stake,
     Now, at this moment, and I have a husband,
     Or had; they are there within, or were at least
     An hour since, face to face, as judge and culprit:
     Will *he* condemn *him*?
MEMMO   I trust not.
MARINA   But if   220
     He does not, there are those will sentence both.
MEMMO They can.
MARINA   And with them power and will are one
     In wickedness:—my husband's lost!
MEMMO   Not so;
     Justice is judge in Venice.
MARINA   If it were so
     There now would be no Venice. But let it   225
     Live on, so the good die not, till the hour
     Of nature's summons; but the Ten's is quicker,
     And we must wait on't. Ah! a voice of wail!
          A faint cry offstage°
SENATOR Hark!
MEMMO   'Twas a cry of—
MARINA   No, no; not my husband's—
     Not Foscari's.
MEMMO   The voice was—
MARINA   *Not his*: no.   230
     He shriek! No; that should be his father's part,
     Not his—not his—he'll die in silence.
          A faint groan again offstage
MEMMO   What!
     Again?
MARINA *His* voice! it seemed so: I will not

Believe it. Should he shrink, I cannot cease
To love; but—no—no—no—it must have been   235
A fearful pang which wrung a groan from him.

SENATOR And, feeling for thy husband's wrongs, wouldst thou
Have him bear more than mortal pain, in silence?

MARINA We all must bear our tortures. I have not
Left barren the great house of Foscari,   240
Though they sweep both the Doge and son from life;
I have endured as much in giving life
To those who will succeed them, as they can
In leaving it: but mine were joyful pangs;
And yet they wrung me till I *could* have shrieked,   245
But did not, for my hope was to bring forth
Heroes, and would not welcome them with tears.

MEMMO All's silent now.

MARINA   Perhaps all's over; but
I will not deem it: he hath nerved himself,
And now defies them.

          Enter an Officer hastily

MEMMO   How now, friend, what seek you?   250

OFFICER A leech. The prisoner has fainted.

          Exit Officer

MEMMO   Lady,°
'Twere better to retire.

SENATOR (*offering to assist her*) I pray thee do so.

MARINA Off! *I* will tend him.

MEMMO   You! Remember, lady!
Ingress is given to none within those chambers,
Except the Ten, and their familiars.

MARINA   Well,°   255
I know that none who enter there return
As they have entered—many never; but
They shall not balk my entrance.

MEMMO   Alas! this
Is but to expose yourself to harsh repulse,
And worse suspense.

MARINA   Who shall oppose me?

MEMMO   They   260
Whose duty 'tis to do so.

MARINA   'Tis *their* duty
To trample on all human feelings, all

Ties which bind man to man, to emulate
The fiends, who will one day requite them in
Variety of torturing! Yet I'll pass.   265
MEMMO It is impossible.
MARINA   That shall be tried.
Despair defies even despotism: there is
That in my heart would make its way through hosts°
With levelled spears; and think you a few jailors
Shall put me from my path? Give me, then, way;   270
This is the Doge's palace; I am wife
Of the Duke's son, the *innocent* Duke's son,
And they shall hear this!
MEMMO   It will only serve
More to exasperate his judges.
MARINA   What
Are *judges* who give way to anger? They   275
Who do so are assassins. Give me way.
        Exit Marina [with her Attendant]
SENATOR Poor lady!
MEMMO   'Tis mere desperation; she
Will not be admitted o'er the threshold.
SENATOR   And
Even if she be so, cannot save her husband.
But, see, the officer returns.
        The Officer passes over the stage with another person°
MEMMO   I hardly   280
Thought that the Ten had even this touch of pity,
Or would permit assistance to this sufferer.
SENATOR Pity! Is't pity to recall to feeling
The wretch too happy to escape to death
By the compassionate trance, poor nature's last   285
Resource against the tyranny of pain?
MEMMO I marvel they condemn him not at once.
SENATOR That's not their policy: they'd have him live,
Because he fears not death; and banish him,
Because all earth, except his native land,   290
To him is one wide prison, and each breath
Of foreign air he draws seems a slow poison,
Consuming but not killing.
MEMMO   Circumstance°
Confirms his crimes, but he avows them not.

SENATOR None, save the letter, which he says was written,   295
    Addressed to Milan's duke, in the full knowledge
    That it would fall into the senate's hands,
    And thus he should be re-conveyed to Venice.°
MEMMO But as a culprit.
SENATOR   Yes, but to his country;
    And that was all he sought, so he avouches.   300
MEMMO The accusation of the bribes was proved.
SENATOR Not clearly, and the charge of homicide
    Has been annulled by the death-bed confession
    Of Nicolas Erizzo, who slew the late°
    Chief of the Ten.
MEMMO   Then why not clear him?
SENATOR   That   305
    They ought to answer; for it is well known
    That Almoro Donato, as I said,
    Was slain by Erizzo for private vengeance.
MEMMO There must be more in this strange process than
    The apparent crimes of the accused disclose—   310
    But there come two of the Ten; let us retire.
    Exeunt Memmo and Senator. Enter Loredano and Barbarigo
BARBARIGO (*addressing Loredano*) That were too much: believe me,
     'twas not meet
    The trial should go further at this moment.
LOREDANO And so the Council must break up, and justice
    Pause in her full career, because a woman°   315
    Breaks in on our deliberations?
BARBARIGO   No,
    That's not the cause; you saw the prisoner's state.
LOREDANO And had he not recovered?
BARBARIGO   To relapse
    Upon the least renewal.
LOREDANO   'Twas not tried.
BARBARIGO 'Tis vain to murmur; the majority   320
    In council were against you.
LOREDANO   Thanks to you, sir,
    And the old ducal dotard, who combined
    The worthy voices which o'erruled my own.
BARBARIGO I am a judge; but must confess that part
    Of our stern duty, which prescribes the Question,   325
    And bids us sit and see its sharp infliction,

Makes me wish——
LOREDANO   What?
BARBARIGO   That *you* would *sometimes* feel,
  As I do always.
LOREDANO   Go to, you're a child,°
  Infirm of feeling as of purpose, blown°
  About by every breath, shook by a sigh,   330
  And melted by a tear—a precious judge
  For Venice! and a worthy statesman to
  Be partner in my policy!
BARBARIGO   He shed
  No tears.
LOREDANO He cried out twice.
BARBARIGO   A saint had done so,
  Even with the crown of glory in his eye,   335
  At such inhuman artifice of pain
  As was forced on him; but he did not cry
  For pity; not a word nor groan escaped him,
  And those two shrieks were not in supplication,
  But wrung from pangs, and followed by no prayers.   340
LOREDANO He muttered many times between his teeth,
  But inarticulately.
BARBARIGO   That I heard not;
  You stood more near him.
LOREDANO   I did so.
BARBARIGO   Methought,
  To my surprise too, you were touched with mercy,
  And were the first to call out for assistance   345
  When he was failing.
LOREDANO   I believed that swoon
  His last.
BARBARIGO And have I not oft heard thee name
  His and his father's death your nearest wish?
LOREDANO If he dies innocent, that is to say,
  With his guilt unavowed, he'll be lamented.   350
BARBARIGO What, wouldst thou slay his memory?
LOREDANO   Wouldst thou have
  His state descend to his children, as it must,°
  If he die unattainted?
BARBARIGO   War with *them* too?
LOREDANO With all their house, till theirs or mine are nothing.

BARBARIGO And the deep agony of his pale wife,   355
    And the repressed convulsion of the high
    And princely brow of his old father, which
    Broke forth in a slight shuddering, though rarely,
    Or in some clammy drops, soon wiped away
    In stern serenity; these moved you not?   360
        Exit Loredano
    He's silent in his hate, as Foscari
    Was in his suffering; and the poor wretch moved me
    More by his silence than a thousand outcries
    Could have effected. 'Twas a dreadful sight
    When his distracted wife broke through into   365
    The hall of our tribunal, and beheld
    What we could scarcely look upon, long used
    To such sights. I must think no more of this,
    Lest I forget in this compassion for
    Our foes their former injuries, and lose   370
    The hold of vengeance Loredano plans°
    For him and me; but mine would be content
    With lesser retribution than he thirsts for,
    And I would mitigate his deeper hatred
    To milder thoughts; but for the present, Foscari   375
    Has a short hourly respite, granted at°
    The instance of the elders of the Council,
    Moved doubtless by his wife's appearance in
    The hall, and his own sufferings.—Lo! they come:
    How feeble and forlorn! I cannot bear   380
    To look on them again in this extremity:
    I'll hence, and try to soften Loredano.
        Exit

2.1

A hall in the Doge's palace

The Doge and a Senator

SENATOR Is it your pleasure to sign the report
  Now, or postpone it till tomorrow?

DOGE   Now;
  I overlooked it yesterday: it wants°
  Merely the signature. Give me the pen—
      *The Doge sits down and puts his pen to the paper, [without making
      a mark°]*
  There, signor.

SENATOR (*looking at the paper*) You have forgot; it is not signed.   5

DOGE Not signed? Ah, I perceive my eyes begin
  To wax more weak with age. I did not see
  That I had dipped the pen without effect.

SENATOR (*dipping the pen into the ink, and placing the paper before the
      Doge*) Your hand, too, shakes, my lord: allow me, thus—

DOGE 'Tis done, I thank you.

SENATOR   Thus the act confirmed   10
  By you and by the Ten, gives peace to Venice.

DOGE 'Tis long since she enjoyed it: may it be
  As long ere she resume her arms!

SENATOR   'Tis almost
  Thirty-four years of nearly ceaseless warfare
  With the Turk, or the powers of Italy;°   15
  The state had need of some repose.

DOGE   No doubt:
  I found her queen of ocean, and I leave her
  Lady of Lombardy; it is a comfort
  That I have added to her diadem
  The gems of Brescia and Ravenna; Crema   20
  And Bergamo no less are hers; her realm°
  By land has grown by thus much in my reign,
  While her sea-sway has not shrunk.

SENATOR   'Tis most true,°
  And merits all our country's gratitude.

DOGE Perhaps so.

SENATOR   Which should be made manifest.   25
DOGE I have not complained, sir.
SENATOR   My good lord, forgive me.
DOGE For what?
SENATOR   My heart bleeds for you.
DOGE   For me, signor?
SENATOR And for your——
DOGE   Stop!
SENATOR   It must have way, my lord:
  I have too many duties towards you
  And all your house, for past and present kindness,   30
  Not to feel deeply for your son.
DOGE   Was this
  In your commission?
SENATOR   What, my lord?
DOGE   This prattle
  Of things you know not: but the treaty's signed;
  Return with it to them who sent you.
SENATOR   I
  Obey. I had in charge, too, from the Council   35
  That you would fix an hour for their re-union.
DOGE Say, when they will—now, even at this moment,
  If it so please them: I am the state's servant.
SENATOR They would accord some time for your repose.
DOGE I have no repose, that is, none which shall cause   40
  The loss of an hour's time unto the state.
  Let them meet when they will, I shall be found
  Where I should be, and *what* I have been ever.
          Exit Senator. The Doge remains in silence. Enter an Attendant
ATTENDANT Prince!
DOGE   Say on.
ATTENDANT   The illustrious lady Foscari
  Requests an audience.
DOGE   Bid her enter. Poor   45
  Marina!
          Exit Attendant. The Doge remains in silence as before. Enter
          Marina.
MARINA I have ventured, father, on
  Your privacy.
DOGE   I have none from you, my child.
  Command my time, when not commanded by

259

The state.
MARINA   I wished to speak to you of *him*.
DOGE Your husband?
MARINA   And your son.
DOGE   Proceed, my daughter!   50
MARINA I had obtained permission from the Ten
    To attend my husband for a limited number
    Of hours.
DOGE   You had so.
MARINA   'Tis revoked.
DOGE   By whom?
MARINA The Ten.—When we had reached 'the Bridge of Sighs',°
    Which I prepared to pass with Foscari,   55
    The gloomy guardian of that passage first
    Demurred: a messenger was sent back to
    The Ten; but as the court no longer sat,°
    And no permission had been given in writing,
    I was thrust back, with the assurance that   60
    Until that high tribunal re-assembled
    The dungeon walls must still divide us.
DOGE   True,
    The form has been omitted in the haste
    With which the court adjourned, and till it meets
    'Tis dubious.
MARINA   Till it meets! and when it meets,   65
    They'll torture him again; and he and I
    Must purchase by renewal of the rack
    The interview of husband and of wife,
    The holiest tie beneath the heavens?—Oh God!
    Dost thou see this?
DOGE   Child—child——
MARINA (*abruptly*)   Call *me* not 'child'!   70
    You soon will have no children—you deserve none—
    You, who can talk thus calmly of a son
    In circumstances which would call forth tears
    Of blood from Spartans! Though these did not weep°
    Their boys who died in battle, is it written   75
    That they beheld them perish piecemeal, nor
    Stretched forth a hand to save them?
DOGE   You behold me:
    I cannot weep—I would I could; but if

Each white hair on this head were a young life,
This ducal cap the diadem of earth,   80
This ducal ring with which I wed the waves°
A talisman to still them—I'd give all
For him.
MARINA   With less he surely might be saved.
DOGE That answer only shows you know not Venice.
Alas! how should you? She knows not herself,   85
In all her mystery. Hear me—they who aim
At Foscari, aim no less at his father;
The sire's destruction would not save the son;
They work by different means to the same end,
And that is——but they have not conquered yet.   90
MARINA But they have crushed.
DOGE   Nor crushed as yet—I live.
MARINA And your son,—how long will he live?
DOGE   I trust,
For all that yet is past, as many years
And happier than his father. The rash boy,
With womanish impatience to return,   95
Hath ruined all by that detected letter;
A high crime, which I neither can deny
Nor palliate, as parent or as duke:
Had he but borne a little, little longer
His Candiote exile, I had hopes——he has quenched them—   100
He must return.
MARINA   To exile?
DOGE   I have said it.
MARINA And can I not go with him?
DOGE   You well know
This prayer of yours was twice denied before
By the assembled Ten, and hardly now
Will be accorded to a third request,   105
Since aggravated errors on the part
Of your lord renders them still more austere.
MARINA Austere? Atrocious! The old human fiends,
With one foot in the grave, with dim eyes, strange°
To tears save drops of dotage, with long white   110
And scanty hairs, and shaking hands, and heads
As palsied as their hearts are hard, they council,
Cabal, and put men's lives out, as if life

Were no more than the feelings long extinguished
In their accursèd bosoms.
DOGE   You know not——   115
MARINA I do—I do—and so should you, methinks—
That these are demons: could it be else that
Men, who have been of women born and suckled—
Who have loved, or talked at least of love—have given
Their hands in sacred vows—have danced their babes   120
Upon their knees, perhaps have mourned above them
In pain, in peril, or in death—who are,
Or were at least in seeming human, could°
Do as they have done by yours, and you yourself,
You, who abet them?
DOGE   I forgive this, for   125
You know not what you say.
MARINA   *You* know it well,°
And feel it nothing.
DOGE   I have borne so much,
That words have ceased to shake me.
MARINA   Oh, no doubt!
You have seen your son's blood flow, and your flesh shook not;
And, after that, what are a woman's words?   130
No more than woman's tears, that they should shake you.
DOGE Woman, this clamorous grief of thine, I tell thee,
Is no more in the balance weighed with that
Which——but I pity thee, my poor Marina!
MARINA Pity my husband, or I cast it from me;   135
Pity thy son! *Thou* pity!—'tis a word
Strange to thy heart—how came it on thy lips?
DOGE I must bear these reproaches, though they wrong me.
Couldst thou but read——
MARINA   'Tis not upon thy brow,
Nor in thine eyes, nor in thine acts—where then   140
Should I behold this sympathy? or shall?
DOGE (*pointing downwards*) There!
MARINA   In the earth?
DOGE   To which I am tending: when
It lies upon this heart, far lightlier, though
Loaded with marble, than the thoughts which press it
Now, you will know me better.
MARINA   Are you, then,   145

Indeed, thus to be pitied?
DOGE   Pitied! None
Shall ever use that base word, with which men
Cloke their soul's hoarded triumph, as a fit one°
To mingle with my name; that name shall be,
As far as *I* have borne it, what it was   150
When I received it.
MARINA   But for the poor children
Of him thou canst not, or thou wilt not save:
You were the last to bear it.
DOGE   Would it were so!
Better for him he never had been born,
Better for me.—I have seen our house dishonoured.   155
MARINA   That's false! A truer, nobler, trustier heart,
More loving, or more loyal, never beat
Within a human breast. I would not change
My exiled, persecuted, mangled husband,
Oppressed but not disgraced, crushed, overwhelmed,   160
Alive, or dead, for prince or paladin°
In story or in fable, with a world
To back his suit. Dishonoured!—*he* dishonoured!
I tell thee, Doge, 'tis Venice is dishonoured;
His name shall be her foulest, worst reproach,   165
For what he suffers, not for what he did.
'Tis ye who are all traitors, tyrant!—ye!
Did you but love your country like this victim
Who totters back in chains to tortures, and
Submits to all things rather than to exile,   170
You'd fling yourselves before him, and implore
His grace for your enormous guilt.
DOGE   He was
Indeed all you have said. I better bore
The deaths of the two sons heaven took from me°
Than Jacopo's disgrace.
MARINA   That word again?   175
DOGE Has he not been condemned?
MARINA   Is none but guilt so?°
DOGE Time may restore his memory—I would hope so.
He was my pride, my——but 'tis useless now—
I am not given to tears, but wept for joy
When he was born: those drops were ominous.   180

MARINA I say he's innocent! And were he not so,
    Is our own blood and kin to shrink from us
    In fatal moments?
DOGE   I shrank not from him:
    But I have other duties than a father's;
    The state would not dispense me from those duties;   185
    Twice I demanded it, but was refused,
    They must then be fulfilled.
            Enter an Attendant
ATTENDANT   A message from
    The Ten.
DOGE   Who bears it?
ATTENDANT   Noble Loredano.
DOGE He!—but admit him.
            Exit Attendant.
MARINA   Must I then retire?
DOGE Perhaps it is not requisite, if this   190
    Concerns your husband, and if not——
            Enter Loredano°
                                        Well, signor,
    Your pleasure!
LOREDANO   I bear that of the Ten.
DOGE   They
    Have chosen well their envoy.
LOREDANO   'Tis *their* choice
    Which leads me here.
DOGE   It does their wisdom honour,
    And no less to their courtesy.—Proceed.   195
LOREDANO We have decided.
DOGE   We?
LOREDANO   The Ten in Council.
DOGE What! have they met again, and met without
    Apprizing me?
LOREDANO   They wished to spare your feelings,
    No less than age.
DOGE   That's new—when spared they either?
    I thank them, notwithstanding.
LOREDANO   You know well   200
    That they have power to act at their discretion,
    With or without the presence of the Doge.
DOGE 'Tis some years since I learned this, long before

I became Doge, or dreamed of such advancement.
You need not school me, signor: I sat in   205
That Council when you were a young patrician.
LOREDANO True, in my father's time; I have heard him and
The admiral, his brother, say as much.
Your highness may remember them; they both
Died suddenly.
DOGE   And if they did so, better   210
So die than live on lingeringly in pain.
LOREDANO No doubt; yet most men like to live their days out.
DOGE And did not they?
LOREDANO   The grave knows best: they died,
As I said, suddenly.
DOGE   Is that so strange
That you repeat the word emphatically?   215
LOREDANO So far from strange, that never was there death
In my mind half so natural as theirs.
Think *you* not so?
DOGE   What should I think of mortals?
LOREDANO That they have mortal foes.
DOGE   I understand you;
Your sires were mine, and you are heir in all things.   220
LOREDANO You best know if I should be so.
DOGE   I do.
Your fathers were my foes, and I have heard
Foul rumours were abroad; I have also read°
Their epitaph, attributing their deaths
To poison. 'Tis perhaps as true as most   225
Inscriptions upon tombs, and yet no less
A fable.
LOREDANO Who dares say so?
DOGE   I!—'Tis true
Your fathers were mine enemies, as bitter
As their son e'er can be, and I no less
Was theirs; but I was *openly* their foe: 230
I never worked by plot in Council, nor
Cabal in commonwealth, nor secret means
Of practice against life by steel or drug.
The proof is, your existence.
LOREDANO   I fear not.
DOGE You have no cause, being what I am; but were I   235

That you would have me thought, you long ere now
Were past the sense of fear. Hate on; I care not.
LOREDANO I never yet knew that a noble's life
    In Venice had to dread a Doge's frown,
    That is, by open means.
DOGE   But I, good signor,   240
    Am, or at least *was*, more than a mere duke,
    In blood, in mind, in means; and that they know
    Who dreaded to elect me, and have since
    Striven all they dare to weigh me down: be sure,
    Before or since that period, had I held you   245
    At so much price as to require your absence,
    A word of mine had set such spirits to work
    As would have made you nothing. But in all things
    I have observed the strictest reverence;
    Not for the laws alone, for those *you* have strained   250
    (I do not speak of *you* but as a single
    Voice of the many) somewhat beyond what
    I could enforce for my authority
    Were I disposed to brawl; but, as I said,
    I have observed with veneration, like   255
    A priest's for the high altar, even unto
    The sacrifice of my own blood and quiet,
    Safety, and all save honour, the decrees,
    The health, the pride, and welfare of the state.
    And now, sir, to your business.
LOREDANO   'Tis decreed,   260
    That, without farther repetition of
    The Question, or continuance of the trial,
    Which only tends to show how stubborn guilt is,
    (The Ten, dispensing with the stricter law
    Which still prescribes the Question till a full   265
    Confession, and the prisoner partly having
    Avowed his crime in not denying that
    The letter to the Duke of Milan's his),
    James Foscari return to banishment,°
    And sail in the same galley which conveyed him.   270
MARINA Thank God! At least they will not drag him more
    Before that horrible tribunal. Would he
    But think so, to my mind the happiest doom,
    Not he alone, but all who dwell here, could

Desire, were to escape from such a land.   275
DOGE That is not a Venetian thought, my daughter.
MARINA No, 'twas too human. May I share his exile?
LOREDANO Of this the Ten said nothing.
MARINA   So I thought:
  That were too human, also. But it was not
  Inhibited?
LOREDANO It was not named.
MARINA (*to the Doge*)   Then, father,°   280
  Surely you can obtain or grant me thus much:
  (*To Loredano*) And you, sir, not oppose my prayer to be
  Permitted to accompany my husband.
DOGE I will endeavour.
MARINA   And you, signor?
LOREDANO   Lady!
  'Tis not for me to anticipate the pleasure   285
  Of the tribunal.
MARINA   Pleasure! what a word
  To use for the decrees of——
DOGE   Daughter, know you
  In what a presence you pronounce these things?
MARINA A prince's and his subject's.
LOREDANO   Subject!
MARINA   Oh!
  It galls you:—well, you are his equal, as   290
  You think; but that you are not, nor would be,
  Were he a peasant:—well, then, you're a prince,
  A princely noble; and what then am I?
LOREDANO The offspring of a noble house.
MARINA   And wedded°
  To one as noble. What or whose, then, is   295
  The presence that should silence my free thoughts?
LOREDANO The presence of your husband's judges.
DOGE   And
  The deference due even to the lightest word
  That falls from those who rule in Venice.
MARINA   Keep
  Those maxims for your mass of scared mechanics,   300
  Your merchants, your Dalmatian and Greek slaves,
  Your tributaries, your dumb citizens,°
  And masked nobility, your sbirri, and°

Your spies, your galley and your other slaves,
To whom your midnight carryings off and drownings, 305
Your dungeons next the palace roofs, or under
The water's level; your mysterious meetings,
And unknown dooms, and sudden executions,
Your 'Bridge of Sighs', your strangling chamber, and
Your torturing instruments, have made ye seem 310
The beings of another and worse world!
Keep such for them: I fear ye not. I know ye;
Have known and proved your worst, in the infernal°
Process of my poor husband! Treat me as°
Ye treated him:—you did so, in so dealing 315
With him. Then what have I to fear *from* you,
Even if I were of fearful nature, which
I trust I am not?
DOGE   You hear, she speaks wildly.
MARINA Not wisely, yet not wildly.
LOREDANO   Lady! words
Uttered within these walls, I bear no further 320
Than to the threshold, saving such as pass
Between the Duke and me on the state's service.
Doge! have you aught in answer?
DOGE   Something from
The Doge; it may be also from a parent.
LOREDANO My mission *here* is to the *Doge*.
DOGE   Then say 325
The Doge will choose his own ambassador,
Or state in person what is meet; and for
The father——
LOREDANO   I remember *mine*.—Farewell!
I kiss the hands of the illustrious lady,
And bow me to the Duke.
          Exit Loredano
MARINA   Are you content? 330
DOGE I am what you behold.
MARINA   And that's a mystery.
DOGE All things are so to mortals; who can read them
Save he who made? or, if they can, the few
And gifted spirits, who have studied long
That loathsome volume—man, and pored upon 335
Those black and bloody leaves, his heart and brain,

But learn a magic which recoils upon
The adept who pursues it: all the sins
We find in others, nature made our own;
All our advantages are those of fortune;   340
Birth, wealth, health, beauty, are her accidents,
And when we cry out against Fate, 'twere well
We should remember Fortune can take nought
Save what she *gave*—the rest was nakedness,
And lusts, and appetites, and vanities,   345
The universal heritage, to battle
With as we may, and least in humblest stations,
Where hunger swallows all in one low want,
And the original ordinance, that man°
Must sweat for his poor pittance, keeps all passions   350
Aloof, save fear of famine! All is low,
And false, and hollow—clay from first to last,
The prince's urn no less than potter's vessel.°
Our fame is in men's breath, our lives upon
Less than their breath; our durance upon days,   355
Our days on seasons; our whole being on
Something which is not *us!*—So, we are slaves,
The greatest as the meanest—nothing rests
Upon our will; the will itself no less
Depends upon a straw than on a storm;   360
And when we think we lead, we are most led,
And still towards death, a thing which comes as much
Without our act or choice, as birth, so that
Methinks we must have sinned in some old world,
And *this* is hell: the best is, that it is not   365
Eternal.
MARINA   These are things we cannot judge
   On earth.
DOGE   And how then shall we judge each other,
Who are all earth, and I, who am called upon
To judge my son? I have administered
My country faithfully—victoriously—   370
I dare them to the proof, the *chart* of what°
She was and is: my reign has doubled realms;
And, in reward, the gratitude of Venice
Has left, or is about to leave, *me* single.
MARINA And Foscari? I do not think of such things,   375

269

So I be left with him.

DOGE   You shall be so;
Thus much they cannot well deny.

MARINA   And if
They should, I will fly with him.

DOGE   That can ne'er be.
And whither would you fly?

MARINA   I know not, reck not—
To Syria, Egypt, to the Ottoman—°   380
Anywhere, where we might respire unfettered,
And live nor girt by spies, nor liable
To edicts of inquisitors of state.

DOGE What, wouldst thou have a renegade for husband,
And turn him into traitor?

MARINA   He is none!   385
The country is the traitress, which thrusts forth
Her best and bravest from her. Tyranny
Is far the worst of treasons. Dost thou deem
None rebels except subjects? The prince who
Neglects or violates his trust is more   390
A brigand than the robber-chief.

DOGE   I cannot
Charge me with such a breach of faith.

MARINA   No; thou
Observ'st, obey'st, such laws as make old Draco's°
A code of mercy by comparison.

DOGE I found the law; I did not make it. Were I   395
A subject, still I might find parts and portions
Fit for amendment; but as prince, I never
Would change, for the sake of my house, the charter
Left by our fathers.

MARINA   Did they make it for
The ruin of their children?

DOGE   Under such laws, Venice   400
Has risen to what she is—a state to rival
In deeds, and days, and sway, and, let me add,
In glory, (for we have had Roman spirits
Amongst us), all that history has bequeathed
Of Rome and Carthage in their best times, when   405
The people swayed by senates.

MARINA   Rather say,°

Groaned under the stern oligarchs.
DOGE   Perhaps so;°
But yet subdued the world: in such a state
An individual, be he richest of
Such rank as is permitted, or the meanest,   410
Without a name, is alike nothing, when°
The policy, irrevocably tending
To one great end, must be maintained in vigour.
MARINA This means that you are more a Doge than father.
DOGE It means, I am more a citizen than either.   415
If we had not for many centuries
Had thousands of such citizens, and shall,
I trust, have still such, Venice were no city.
MARINA Accursèd be the city where the laws
Would stifle nature's!
DOGE   Had I as many sons   420
As I have years, I would have given them all,°
Not without feeling, but I would have given them
To the state's service, to fulfil her wishes
On the flood, in the field, or, if it must be,°
As it, alas! has been, to ostracism,°   425
Exile, or chains, or whatsoever worse
She might decree.
MARINA   And is this patriotism?
To me it seems the worst barbarity.
Let me seek out my husband: the sage Ten,
With all its jealousy, will hardly war   430
So far with a weak woman as deny me
A moment's access to his dungeon.
DOGE   I'll
So far take on myself, as order that
You may be admitted.
MARINA   And what shall I say
To Foscari from his father?
DOGE   That he obey   435
The laws.
MARINA   And nothing more? Will you not see him
Ere he depart? It may be the last time.
DOGE The last!—my boy!—the last time I shall see
My last of children! Tell him I will come.
        Exeunt

3.1

The prison of Jacopo Foscari

Jacopo Foscari alone

JACOPO FOSCARI No light, save yon faint gleam, which shows me walls
    Which never echoed but to sorrow's sounds,
    The sigh of long imprisonment, the step
    Of feet on which the iron clanked, the groan
    Of death, the imprecation of despair!   5
    And yet for this I have returned to Venice,
    With some faint hope, 'tis true, that time, which wears
    The marble down, had worn away the hate
    Of men's hearts; but I knew them not, and here
    Must I consume my own, which never beat   10
    For Venice but with such a yearning as
    The dove has for her distant nest, when wheeling
    High in the air on her return to greet
    Her callow brood. What letters are these (*approaching the wall*) which
    Are scrawled along the inexorable wall?   15
    Will the gleam let me trace them? Ah! the names
    Of my sad predecessors in this place,
    The dates of their despair, the brief words of
    A grief too great for many. This stone page
    Holds like an epitaph their history,   20
    And the poor captive's tale is graven on
    His dungeon barrier, like the lover's record
    Upon the bark of some tall tree, which bears
    His own and his beloved's name. Alas!
    I recognize some names familiar to me,   25
    And blighted like to mine, which I will add,
    Fittest for such a chronicle as this,
    Which only can be read, as writ, by wretches.
        He engraves his name. Enter a familiar of the Ten [with a
        torch and food and water]°
FAMILIAR I bring you food.
JACOPO FOSCARI   I pray you set it down;

I am past hunger: but my lips are parched—   30
The water!
FAMILIAR   There.
JACOPO FOSCARI (*after drinking*) I thank you: I am better.
FAMILIAR I am commanded to inform you that
Your further trial is postponed.
JACOPO FOSCARI   Till when?
FAMILIAR I know not.—It is also in my orders
That your illustrious lady be admitted.   35
JACOPO FOSCARI Ah! they relent, then—I had ceased to hope it:
'Twas time.
        Enter Marina
MARINA   My best belovèd!
JACOPO FOSCARI (*embracing her*) My true wife,
And only friend! What happiness!
MARINA   We'll part
No more.
JACOPO FOSCARI How! wouldst thou share a dungeon?
MARINA   Aye,
The rack, the grave, all—anything with thee,   40
But the tomb last of all, for there we shall
Be ignorant of each other, yet I will
Share that—all things except new separation;
It is too much to have survived the first.
How dost thou? How are those worn limbs? Alas!   45
Why do I ask? Thy paleness——
JACOPO FOSCARI   'Tis the joy
Of seeing thee again so soon, and so
Without expectancy has sent the blood
Back to my heart, and left my cheeks like thine,
For thou art pale too, my Marina!
MARINA   'Tis   50
The gloom of this eternal cell, which never
Knew sunbeam, and the sallow sullen glare
Of the familiar's torch, which seems akin
To darkness more than light, by lending to
The dungeon vapours its bituminous smoke,°   55
Which cloud whate'er we gaze on, even thine eyes—
No, not thine eyes—they sparkle—how they sparkle!
JACOPO FOSCARI And thine!—but I am blinded by the torch.
MARINA As I had been without it. Couldst thou see here?

JACOPO FOSCARI Nothing at first; but use and time had taught me   60
    Familiarity with what was darkness;
    And the gray twilight of such glimmerings as
    Glide through the crevices made by the winds
    Was kinder to mine eyes than the full sun,
    When gorgeously o'ergilding any towers   65
    Save those of Venice; but a moment ere
    Thou camest hither I was busy writing.
MARINA What?
JACOPO FOSCARI My name: look, 'tis there—recorded next
    The name of him who here preceded me,
    If dungeon dates say true.
MARINA   And what of him?   70
JACOPO FOSCARI These walls are silent of men's ends; they only
    Seem to hint shrewdly of them. Such stern walls
    Were never piled on high save o'er the dead,
    Or those who soon must be so—*What of him?*
    Thou askest.—What of me? may soon be asked,   75
    With the like answer—doubt and dreadful surmise—
    Unless thou tell'st my tale.
MARINA   *I speak* of thee!
JACOPO FOSCARI And wherefore not? All then shall speak of me:
    The tyranny of silence is not lasting,
    And, though events be hidden, just men's groans   80
    Will burst all cerement, even a living grave's!
    I do not *doubt* my memory, but my life;
    And neither do I fear.
MARINA   Thy life is safe.
JACOPO FOSCARI And liberty?
MARINA   The mind should make its own.
JACOPO FOSCARI That has a noble sound; but 'tis a sound,   85
    A music most impressive, but too transient:
    The mind is much, but is not all. The mind
    Hath nerved me to endure the risk of death,
    And torture positive, far worse than death
    (If death be a deep sleep), without a groan,   90
    Or with a cry which rather shamed my judges
    Than me; but 'tis not all, for there are things
    More woeful—such as this small dungeon, where
    I may breathe many years.
MARINA   Alas! and this

Small dungeon is all that belongs to thee   95
    Of this wide realm, of which thy sire is prince.

JACOPO FOSCARI That thought would scarcely aid me to endure it.
    My doom is common, many are in dungeons,
    But none like mine, so near their father's palace;
    But then my heart is sometimes high, and hope   100
    Will stream along those moted rays of light
    Peopled with dusty atoms, which afford
    Our only day; for, save the gaoler's torch,
    And a strange firefly, which was quickly caught
    Last night in yon enormous spider's net,   105
    I ne'er saw aught here like a ray. Alas!
    I know if mind may bear us up, or no,
    For I have such, and shown it before men;
    It sinks in solitude: my soul is social.

MARINA I will be with thee.

JACOPO FOSCARI   Ah! if it were so!   110
    But *that* they never granted—nor will grant,
    And I shall be alone: no men—no books—
    Those lying likenesses of lying men.
    I asked for even those outlines of their kind,
    Which they term annals, history, what you will,   115
    Which men bequeath as portraits, and they were
    Refused me, so these walls have been my study,
    More faithful pictures of Venetian story,
    With all their blank, or dismal stains, than is
    The hall not far from hence, which bears on high   120
    Hundreds of doges, and their deeds and dates.

MARINA I come to tell thee the result of their
    Last council on thy doom.

JACOPO FOSCARI   I know it—look!

    He points to his limbs, as referring to the tortures which he had
      undergone

MARINA No—no—no more of that: even they relent
    From that atrocity.

JACOPO FOSCARI   What then?

MARINA   That you   125
    Return to Candia.

JACOPO FOSCARI   Then my last hope's gone.
    I could endure my dungeon, for 'twas Venice;
    I could support the torture, there was something

In my native air that buoyed my spirits up
Like a ship on the ocean tossed by storms,   130
But proudly still bestriding the high waves,
And holding on its course; but *there*, afar,
In that accursèd isle of slaves, and captives,
And unbelievers, like a stranded wreck,°
My very soul seemed mouldering in my bosom,   135
And piecemeal I shall perish, if remanded.°

MARINA And *here*?

JACOPO FOSCARI At once—by better means, as briefer.
What! would they even deny me my sires' sepulchre,
As well as home and heritage?

MARINA   My husband!
I have sued to accompany thee hence,   140
And not so hopelessly. This love of thine
For an ungrateful and tyrannic soil
Is passion, and not patriotism; for me,
So I could see thee with a quiet aspect,
And the sweet freedom of the earth and air,   145
I would not cavil about climes or regions.
This crowd of palaces and prisons is not
A paradise; its first inhabitants
Were wretched exiles.

JACOPO FOSCARI   Well I know *how* wretched!°

MARINA And yet you see how from their banishment   150
Before the Tartar into these salt isles,°
Their antique energy of mind, all that
Remained of Rome for their inheritance,
Created by degrees an ocean-Rome;°
And shall an evil, which so often leads   155
To good, depress thee thus?

JACOPO FOSCARI   Had I gone forth
From my own land, like the old patriarchs, seeking
Another region, with their flocks and herds;
Had I been cast out like the Jews from Zion,°
Or like our fathers, driven by Attila°   160
From fertile Italy to barren islets,
I would have given some tears to my late country,
And many thoughts; but afterwards addressed
Myself, with those about me, to create
A new home and fresh state: perhaps I could   165

Have borne this—though I know not.
MARINA   Wherefore not?
　It was the lot of millions, and must be
　The fate of myriads more.
JACOPO FOSCARI   Aye—we but hear
　Of the survivors' toil in their new lands,
　Their numbers and success; but who can number   170
　The hearts which broke in silence of that parting,
　Or after their departure; of that malady°
　Which calls up green and native fields to view
　From the rough deep, with such identity
　To the poor exile's fevered eye, that he   175
　Can scarcely be restrained from treading them?
　That melody, which out of tones and tunes°
　Collects such pasture for the longing sorrow
　Of the sad mountaineer, when far away
　From his snow canopy of cliffs and clouds,   180
　That he feeds on the sweet, but poisonous thought,
　And dies. You call this *weakness*! It is strength,
　I say—the parent of all honest feeling.
　He who loves not his country, can love nothing.
MARINA Obey her, then; 'tis she that puts thee forth.   185
JACOPO FOSCARI Aye, there it is: 'tis like a mother's curse
　Upon my soul—the mark is set upon me.°
　The exiles you speak of went forth by nations,
　Their hands upheld each other by the way,
　Their tents were pitched together—I'm alone.   190
MARINA You shall be so no more—I will go with thee.
JACOPO FOSCARI My best Marina!—and our children?
MARINA   They,
　I fear, by the prevention of the state's
　Abhorrent policy (which holds all ties
　As threads, which may be broken at her pleasure),   195
　Will not be suffered to proceed with us.
JACOPO FOSCARI And canst thou leave them?
MARINA   Yes. With many a pang.
　But—I *can* leave them, children as they are,
　To teach you to be less a child. From this
　Learn you to sway your feelings, when exacted   200
　By duties paramount; and 'tis our first
　On earth to bear.

277

JACOPO FOSCARI   Have I not borne?
MARINA   Too much°
   From tyrannous injustice, and enough
   To teach you not to shrink now from a lot,
   Which, as compared with what you have undergone   205
   Of late, is mercy.
JACOPO FOSCARI   Ah! you never yet
   Were far away from Venice, never saw
   Her beautiful towers in the receding distance,
   While every furrow of the vessel's track
   Seemed ploughing deep into your heart; you never   210
   Saw day go down upon your native spires
   So calmly with its gold and crimson glory,
   And after dreaming a disturbèd vision
   Of them and theirs, awoke and found them not.
MARINA   I will divide this with you. Let us think   215
   Of our departure from this much-loved city
   (Since you must *love* it, as it seems), and this
   Chamber of state her gratitude allots you.
   Our children will be cared for by the Doge,
   And by my uncles: we must sail ere night.   220
JACOPO FOSCARI   That's sudden. Shall I not behold my father?°
MARINA   You will.
JACOPO FOSCARI   Where?
MARINA   Here or in the ducal chamber—
   He said not which. I would that you could bear
   Your exile as he bears it.
JACOPO FOSCARI   Blame him not.
   I sometimes murmur for a moment; but   225
   He could not now act otherwise. A show
   Of feeling or compassion on his part
   Would have but drawn upon his aged head
   Suspicion from the Ten, and upon mine
   Accumulated ills.
MARINA   Accumulated!   230
   What pangs are those they have spared you?
JACOPO FOSCARI   That of leaving
   Venice without beholding him or you,
   Which might have been forbidden now, as 'twas
   Upon my former exile.
MARINA   That is true,

278

And thus far I am also the state's debtor,   235
And shall be more so when I see us both
Floating on the free waves—away—away—
Be it to the earth's end, from this abhorred,
Unjust, and——

JACOPO FOSCARI   Curse it not. If I am silent,
Who dares accuse my country?

MARINA   Men and angels!   240
The blood of myriads reeking up to heaven,
The groans of slaves in chains, and men in dungeons,
Mothers, and wives, and sons, and sires, and subjects,
Held in the bondage of ten bald-heads; and
Though last, not least, *thy silence. Couldst thou* say   245
Aught in its favour, who would praise like *thee*?

JACOPO FOSCARI Let us address us then, since so it must be,
To our departure. Who comes here?

          Enter Loredano, attended by [two] familiars

LOREDANO (*to the [three] familiars*)   Retire,
But leave the torch.

          *Exeunt Loredano's two familiars. [The third, who had entered
          earlier in the scene, leaves his torch, and retires, to be just
          within earshot]*°

JACOPO FOSCARI   Most welcome, noble signor.
I did not deem this poor place could have drawn   250
Such presence hither.

LOREDANO   'Tis not the first time
I have visited these places.

MARINA   Nor would be
The last, were all men's merits well rewarded.
Came you here to insult us, or remain
As spy upon us, or as hostage for us?   255

LOREDANO Neither are of my office, noble lady!
I am sent hither to your husband, to
Announce the Ten's decree.

MARINA   That tenderness
Has been anticipated: it is known.

LOREDANO As how?

MARINA   I have informed him, not so gently,   260
Doubtless, as your nice feelings would prescribe,
The indulgence of your colleagues; but he knew it.
If you come for our thanks, take them, and hence!

The dungeon gloom is deep enough without you,
And full of reptiles, not less loathsome, though   265
Their sting is honester.

JACOPO FOSCARI   I pray you, calm you:
What can avail such words?

MARINA   To let him know
That he is known.

LOREDANO   Let the fair dame preserve
Her sex's privilege.

MARINA   I have some sons, sir,°
Will one day thank you better.

LOREDANO   You do well   270
To nurse them wisely. Foscari—you know
Your sentence, then?

JACOPO FOSCARI   Return to Candia?

LOREDANO   True—
For life.

JACOPO FOSCARI Not long.

LOREDANO   I said—for *life*.

JACOPO FOSCARI   And I
Repeat—not long.

LOREDANO   A year's imprisonment
In Canea—afterwards the freedom of°   275
The whole isle.

JACOPO FOSCARI Both the same to me: the after
Freedom as is the first imprisonment.
Is't true my wife accompanies me?

LOREDANO   Yes,
If she so wills it.

MARINA   Who obtained that justice?

LOREDANO One who wars not with women.

MARINA   But oppresses   280
Men: howsoever, let him have *my* thanks
For the only boon I would have asked or taken
From him or such as he is.

LOREDANO   He receives them
As they are offered.

MARINA   May they thrive with him
So much!—no more.

JACOPO FOSCARI   Is this, sir, your whole mission?   285
Because we have brief time for preparation,

And you perceive your presence doth disquiet
This lady, of a house noble as yours.
MARINA Nobler!
LOREDANO   How nobler?
MARINA   As more generous!°
We say the 'generous steed' to express the purity   290
Of his high blood. Thus much I've learnt, although
Venetian (who see few steeds save of bronze),°
From those Venetians who have skimmed the coasts
Of Egypt, and her neighbour Araby:°
And why not say as soon 'the *generous man*'?   295
If race be aught, it is in qualities
More than in years; and mine, which is as old
As yours, is better in its product, nay—
Look not so stern—but get you back, and pore
Upon your genealogic tree's most green   300
Of leaves and most mature of fruits, and there
Blush to find ancestors, who would have blushed
For such a son—thou cold inveterate hater!
JACOPO FOSCARI Again, Marina!
MARINA   Again! *still*, Marina.
See you not, he comes here to glut his hate   305
With a last look upon our misery?
Let him partake it!
JACOPO FOSCARI   That were difficult.
MARINA Nothing more easy. He partakes it now—
Aye, he may veil beneath a marble brow
And sneering lip the pang, but he partakes it.   310
A few brief words of truth shame the devil's servants
No less than master; I have probed his soul°
A moment, as the eternal fire, ere long,
Will reach it always. See how he shrinks from me!
With death, and chains, and exile in his hand   315
To scatter o'er his kind as he thinks fit:°
They are his weapons, not his armour, for
I have pierced him to the core of his cold heart.
I care not for his frowns! We can but die,
And he but live, for him the very worst   320
Of destinies: each day secures him more
His tempter's.
JACOPO FOSCARI This is mere insanity.

MARINA It may be so; and *who* hath made us *mad*?
LOREDANO Let her go on; it irks not me.
MARINA   That's false!
  You came here to enjoy a heartless triumph   325
  Of cold looks upon manifold griefs! You came
  To be sued to in vain—to mark our tears,
  And hoard our groans—to gaze upon the wreck
  Which you have made a prince's son—my husband;°
  In short, to trample on the fallen—an office   330
  The hangman shrinks from, as all men from him!
  How have you sped? We are wretched, signor, as°
  Your plots could make, and vengeance could desire us,
  And how *feel you*?
LOREDANO   As rocks.
MARINA   By thunder blasted:
  They feel not, but no less are shivered. Come,   335
  Foscari; now let us go, and leave this felon,
  The sole fit habitant of such a cell,
  Which he has peopled often, but ne'er fitly
  Till he himself shall brood in it alone.
      Enter the Doge
JACOPO FOSCARI My father!
DOGE (*embracing him*)   Jacopo! my son—my son!   340
JACOPO FOSCARI My father still! How long it is since I
  Have heard thee name my name—*our* name!
DOGE   My boy!
  Couldst thou but know——
JACOPO FOSCARI   I rarely, sir, have murmured.
DOGE I feel too much thou hast not.
MARINA   Doge, look there!
      She points to Loredano
DOGE I see the man—what mean'st thou?
MARINA   Caution!
LOREDANO   Being   345
  The virtue which this noble lady most
  May practise, she doth well to recommend it.
MARINA Wretch! 'tis no virtue, but the policy
  Of those who fain must deal perforce with vice:
  As such I recommend it, as I would   350
  To one whose foot was on an adder's path.
DOGE Daughter, it is superfluous; I have long

Known Loredano.

LOREDANO   You may know him better.

MARINA Yes; *worse* he could not.

JACOPO FOSCARI   Father, let not these
Our parting hours be lost in listening to   355
Reproaches, which boot nothing. Is it—is it,
Indeed, our last of meetings?

DOGE   You behold
These white hairs!

JACOPO FOSCARI   And I feel, besides, that mine
Will never be so white. Embrace me, father!
I loved you ever—never more than now.   360
Look to my children—to your last child's children:
Let them be all to you which he was once,
And never be to you what I am now.
May I not see *them* also?

MARINA   No—not *here*.

JACOPO FOSCARI They might behold their parent anywhere.   365

MARINA I would that they beheld their father in
A place which would not mingle fear with love,
To freeze their young blood in its natural current.
They have fed well, slept soft, and knew not that
Their sire was a mere hunted outlaw. Well,   370
I know his fate may one day be their heritage,
But let it only be their *heritage*,
And not their present fee. Their senses, though°
Alive to love, are yet awake to terror;
And these vile damps, too, and yon *thick green* wave°   375
Which floats above the place where we now stand—
A cell so far below the water's level,
Sending its pestilence through every crevice,
Might strike them: *this is not their* atmosphere,
However you—and you—and, most of all,   380
As worthiest—*you*, sir, noble Loredano!
May breathe it without prejudice.

JACOPO FOSCARI   I had not
Reflected upon this, but acquiesce.
I shall depart, then, without meeting them?

DOGE Not so: they shall await you in my chamber.   385

JACOPO FOSCARI And must I leave them *all*?

LOREDANO   You must.

JACOPO FOSCARI   Not one?
LOREDANO They are the state's.
MARINA   I thought they had been mine.
LOREDANO They are, in all maternal things.
MARINA   That is,
   In all things painful. If they're sick, they will
   Be left to me to tend them; should they die,   390
   To me to bury and to mourn; but if
   They live, they'll make you soldiers, senators,
   Slaves, exiles—what *you* will; or if they are
   Females with portions, brides and *bribes* for nobles!
   Behold the state's care for its sons and mothers!   395
LOREDANO The hour approaches, and the wind is fair.
JACOPO FOSCARI How know you that here, where the genial wind°
   Ne'er blows in all its blustering freedom?
LOREDANO   'Twas so
   When I came here. The galley floats within
   A bow-shot of the Riva di Schiavoni.°   400
JACOPO FOSCARI Father! I pray you to precede me, and
   Prepare my children to behold their father.
DOGE Be firm, my son!
JACOPO FOSCARI   I will do my endeavour.
MARINA Farewell! at least to this detested dungeon,
   And him to whose good offices you owe   405
   In part your past imprisonment.
LOREDANO   And present
   Liberation.
DOGE   He speaks truth.
JACOPO FOSCARI   No doubt: but 'tis
   Exchange of chains for heavier chains I owe him.
   He knows this, or he had not sought to change them.
   But I reproach not.
LOREDANO   The time narrows, signor.   410
JACOPO FOSCARI Alas! I little thought so lingeringly
   To leave abodes like this: but when I feel
   That every step I take, even from this cell,
   Is one away from Venice, I look back
   Even on these dull damp walls, and——
DOGE   Boy! no tears.   415
MARINA Let them flow on: he wept not on the rack
   To shame him, and they cannot shame him now.

They will relieve his heart—that too kind heart—
And I will find an hour to wipe away
Those tears, or add my own. I could weep now,   420
But would not gratify yon wretch so far.
Let us proceed. Doge, lead the way.

LOREDANO (*to the familiar*)   The torch, there!

MARINA Yes, light us on, as to a funeral pyre,
With Loredano mourning like an heir.

DOGE My son, you are feeble; take this hand.

JACOPO FOSCARI   Alas!   425
Must youth support itself on age, and I
Who ought to be the prop of yours?

LOREDANO   Take mine.

MARINA Touch it not, Foscari; 'twill sting you. Signor,
Stand off! Be sure, that if a grasp of yours
Would raise us from the gulf wherein we are plunged,   430
No hand of ours would stretch itself to meet it.
Come, Foscari, take the hand the altar gave you;
It could not save, but will support you ever.

        Exeunt

4.1

A hall in the ducal palace

Enter Loredano and Barbarigo

BARBARIGO And have you confidence in such a project?

LOREDANO I have.

BARBARIGO   'Tis hard upon his years.

LOREDANO   Say rather
  Kind to relieve him from the cares of state.

BARBARIGO 'Twill break his heart.

LOREDANO   Age has no heart to break.
  He has seen his son's half broken, and, except   5
  A start of feeling in his dungeon, never
  Swerved.

BARBARIGO In his countenance, I grant you, never;
  But I have seen him sometimes in a calm
  So desolate, that the most clamorous grief
  Had nought to envy him within. Where is he?   10

LOREDANO In his own portion of the palace, with
  His son, and the whole race of Foscaris.

BARBARIGO Bidding farewell.

LOREDANO   A last. As soon he shall
  Bid to his dukedom.

BARBARIGO   When embarks the son?

LOREDANO Forthwith—when this long leave is taken. 'Tis   15
  Time to admonish them again.

BARBARIGO   Forbear;
  Retrench not from their moments.

LOREDANO   Not I, now°
  We have higher business for our own. This day
  Shall be the last of the old Doge's reign,
  As the first of his son's last banishment,   20
  And that is vengeance.

BARBARIGO   In my mind, too deep.

LOREDANO 'Tis moderate—not even life for life, the rule
  Denounced of retribution from all time;°
  They owe me still my father's and my uncle's.

BARBARIGO Did not the Doge deny this strongly?

LOREDANO   Doubtless.   25
BARBARIGO And did not this shake your suspicion?
LOREDANO   No.
BARBARIGO But if this deposition should take place
    By our united influence in the council,
    It must be done with all the deference
    Due to his years, his station, and his deeds.   30
LOREDANO As much of ceremony as you will,
    So that the thing be done. You may, for aught
    I care, depute the Council on their knees,
    (Like Barbarossa to the Pope), to beg him°
    To have the courtesy to abdicate.   35
BARBARIGO What, if he will not?
LOREDANO   We'll elect another,
    And make him null.
BARBARIGO   But will the laws uphold us?
LOREDANO What laws?—The Ten are laws; and if they were not,
    I will be legislator in this business.
BARBARIGO At your own peril?
LOREDANO   There is none, I tell you,   40
    Our powers are such.
BARBARIGO   But he has twice already
    Solicited permission to retire,
    And twice it was refused.
LOREDANO   The better reason
    To grant it the third time.
BARBARIGO   Unasked?
LOREDANO   It shows
    The impression of his former instances: 45
    If they were from his heart, he may be thankful;
    If not, 'twill punish his hypocrisy.
    Come, they are met by this time; let us join them,
    And be *thou* fixed in purpose for this once.
    I have prepared such arguments as will not   50
    Fail to move them, and to remove him: since
    Their thoughts, their objects, have been sounded, do not°
    You, with your wonted scruples, teach us pause,
    And all will prosper.
BARBARIGO   Could I but be certain
    This is no prelude to such persecution   55
    Of the sire as has fallen upon the son,

I would support you.
LOREDANO   He is safe, I tell you;
His fourscore years and five may linger on
As long as he can drag them: 'tis his throne
Alone is aimed at.
BARBARIGO   But discarded princes   60
Are seldom long of life.
LOREDANO   And men of eighty
More seldom still.
BARBARIGO   And why not wait these few years?
LOREDANO Because we have waited long enough, and he
Lived longer than enough. Hence! In to council!
    Exeunt Loredano and Barbarigo. Enter Memmo and a Senator
SENATOR A summons to the Ten! Why so?
MEMMO   The Ten   65
Alone can answer: they are rarely wont
To let their thoughts anticipate their purpose
By previous proclamation. We are summoned—
That is enough.
SENATOR   For them, but not for us;
I would know why.
MEMMO   You will know why anon,   70
If you obey, and, if not, you no less
Will know why you should have obeyed.
SENATOR   I mean not
To oppose them, *but*——
MEMMO   In Venice *But*'s a traitor.
But me no '*buts*', unless you would pass o'er
The Bridge which few repass.
SENATOR   I am silent.
MEMMO   Why   75
Thus hesitate? The Ten have called in aid
Of their deliberation five and twenty
Patricians of the senate—you are one,
And I another; and it seems to me
Both honoured by the choice or chance which leads us   80
To mingle with a body so august.
SENATOR Most true. I say no more.
MEMMO   As we hope, signor,
And all may honestly (that is, all those
Of noble blood may) one day hope to be

Decemvir, it is surely for the senate's   85
Chosen delegates, a school of wisdom, to
Be thus admitted, though as novices,
To view the mysteries.
SENATOR   Let us view them: they,
No doubt, are worth it.
MEMMO   Being worth our lives
If we divulge them, doubtless they are worth   90
Something, at least to you or me.
SENATOR   I sought not
A place within the sanctuary; but being
Chosen, however reluctantly so chosen,
I shall fulfil my office.
MEMMO   Let us not
Be latest in obeying the Ten's summons.   95
SENATOR All are not met, but I am of your thought
So far—let's in.
MEMMO   The earliest are most welcome
In earnest councils—we will not be least so.

     Exeunt [Memmo and Senator]. Enter the Doge, Jacopo Foscari,
     and Marina

JACOPO FOSCARI Ah, father! though I must and will depart,
Yet—yet—I pray you to obtain for me   100
That I once more return unto my home,
Howe'er remote the period. Let there be
A point of time as beacon to my heart,
With any penalty annexed they please,
But let me still return.
DOGE   Son Jacopo,   105
Go and obey our country's will: 'tis not
For us to look beyond.
JACOPO FOSCARI   But still I must
Look back. I pray you think of me.
DOGE   Alas!
You ever were my dearest offspring, when
They were more numerous, nor can be less so   110
Now you are last; but did the state demand
The exile of the disinterrèd ashes
Of your three goodly brothers, now in earth,
And their desponding shades came flitting round°
To impede the act, I must no less obey   115

A duty, paramount to every duty.

MARINA My husband! let us on: this but prolongs
    Our sorrow.

JACOPO FOSCARI   But we are not summoned yet;
    The galley's sails are not unfurled:—who knows?
    The wind may change.

MARINA   And if it do, it will not   120
    Change *their* hearts, or your lot: the galley's oars
    Will quickly clear the harbour.

JACOPO FOSCARI   Oh, ye elements!
    Where are your storms?

MARINA   In human breasts. Alas!
    Will nothing calm you?

JACOPO FOSCARI   Never yet did mariner
    Put up to patron saint such prayers for prosperous   125
    And pleasant breezes, as I call upon you,
    Ye tutelar saints of my own city! which
    Ye love not with more holy love than I,
    To lash up from the deep the Adrian waves,
    And waken Auster, sovereign of the tempest!°   130
    Till the sea dash me back upon my own shore
    A broken corpse upon the barren Lido,°
    Where I may mingle with the sands which skirt
    The land I love, and never shall see more!

MARINA And wish you this with *me* beside you?

JACOPO FOSCARI   No—   135
    No—not for thee, too good, too kind! May'st thou
    Live long to be a mother to those children
    Thy fond fidelity for a time deprives
    Of such support! But for myself alone,
    May all the winds of heaven howl down the Gulf,°   140
    And tear the vessel, till the mariners,
    Appalled, turn their despairing eyes on me,
    As the Phoenicians did on Jonah, then°
    Cast me out from amongst them, as an offering
    To appease the waves. The billow which destroys me   145
    Will be more merciful than man, and bear me,
    Dead, but *still bear* me to a native grave,
    From fisher's hands upon the desolate strand,
    Which, of its thousand wrecks, hath ne'er received
    One lacerated like the heart which then   150

Will be——But wherefore breaks it not? why live I?
MARINA To man thyself, I trust, with time, to master
  Such useless passion. Until now thou wert
  A sufferer, but not a loud one: why,
  What is this to the things thou hast borne in silence—   155
  Imprisonment and actual torture?
JACOPO FOSCARI   Double,
  Triple, and tenfold torture! But you are right,
  It must be borne. Father, your blessing.
DOGE   Would
  It could avail thee! But no less thou hast it.
JACOPO FOSCARI Forgive——
DOGE   What?
JACOPO FOSCARI   My poor mother for my birth,   160
  And me for having lived, and you yourself
  (As I forgive you) for the gift of life,
  Which you bestowed upon me as my sire.
MARINA What hast thou done?
JACOPO FOSCARI   Nothing. I cannot charge
  My memory with much save sorrow: but   165
  I have been so beyond the common lot
  Chastened and visited, I needs must think
  That I was wicked. If it be so, may
  What I have undergone here keep me from
  A like hereafter.
MARINA   Fear not: *that's* reserved   170
  For your oppressors.
JACOPO FOSCARI   Let me hope not.
MARINA   Hope not?
JACOPO FOSCARI I cannot wish them *all* they have inflicted.
MARINA *All!* the consummate fiends! A thousandfold
  May the worm which ne'er dieth feed upon them!°
JACOPO FOSCARI They may repent.
MARINA   And if they do, heaven will not   175
  Accept the tardy penitence of demons.
      Enter an Officer and Guards
OFFICER Signor! the boat is at the shore—the wind
  Is rising—we are ready to attend you.
JACOPO FOSCARI And I to be attended. Once more, father,
  Your hand!
DOGE   Take it. Alas! how thine own trembles!   180

JACOPO FOSCARI No—you mistake; 'tis yours that shakes, my
    father.
    Farewell!
DOGE   Farewell! Is there aught else?
JACOPO FOSCARI   No—nothing.
    (*To the Officer*) Lend me your arm, good signor.
OFFICER   You turn pale—
    Let me support you—paler—ho! some aid there!
    Some water!
MARINA   Ah, he is dying!
JACOPO FOSCARI   Now, I'm ready—   185
    My eyes swim strangely—where's the door?
MARINA   Away!
    Let me support him—my best love! Oh, God!
    How faintly beats this heart—this pulse!
JACOPO FOSCARI   The light!
    Is it the light?—I am faint.
        Officer presents him with water
OFFICER   He will be better,
    Perhaps, in the air.
JACOPO FOSCARI   I doubt not. Father—wife—   190
    Your hands!
MARINA There's death in that damp clammy grasp.
    Oh God!—My Foscari, how fare you?
JACOPO FOSCARI   Well!
        Jacopo Foscari dies
OFFICER He's gone!
DOGE   He's free.
MARINA   No—no, he is not dead;
    There must be life yet in that heart—he could not   195
    Thus leave me.
DOGE   Daughter!
MARINA   Hold thy peace, old man!
    I am no daughter now—thou hast no son.
    Oh, Foscari!
OFFICER   We must remove the body.
MARINA Touch it not, dungeon miscreants! your base office
    Ends with his life, and goes not beyond murder,   200
    Even by your murderous laws. Leave his remains
    To those who know to honour them.
OFFICER   I must

Inform the signory, and learn their pleasure.°
DOGE Inform the signory from *me*, the Doge,
    They have no further power upon those ashes: 205
    While he lived, he was theirs, as fits a subject—
    Now he is *mine*—my broken-hearted boy!
        Exit Officer
MARINA And I must live!
DOGE   Your children live, Marina.
MARINA My children! true—they live, and I must live
    To bring them up to serve the state, and die   210
    As died their father. Oh! what best of blessings
    Were barrenness in Venice! Would my mother
    Had been so!
DOGE   My unhappy children!
MARINA   What!
    You feel it then at last—*you!*—Where is now
    The stoic of the state?
DOGE (*throwing himself down by the body*)
        Here!
MARINA   Aye, weep on!°   215
    I thought you had no tears—you hoarded them
    Until they are useless; but weep on! he never
    Shall weep more—never, never more.
        Enter Loredano and Barbarigo
LOREDANO   What's here?°
MARINA Ah! the devil come to insult the dead! Avaunt!
    Incarnate Lucifer! 'tis holy ground.   220
    A martyr's ashes now lie there, which make it
    A shrine. Get thee back to thy place of torment!
BARBARIGO Lady, we knew not of this sad event,
    But passed here merely on our path from council.
MARINA Pass on.
LOREDANO   We sought the Doge.
MARINA (*pointing to the Doge, who is still on the ground by his son's
    body*)
                    He's busy, look,   225
    About the business *you* provided for him.
    Are ye content?
BARBARIGO   We will not interrupt
    A parent's sorrows.
MARINA   No, ye only make them,

Then leave them.
DOGE (*rising*)   Sirs, I am ready.
BARBARIGO   No—not now.
LOREDANO Yet 'twas important.
DOGE   If 'twas so, I can   230
Only repeat—I am ready.
BARBARIGO   It shall not be
Just now, though Venice tottered o'er the deep
Like a frail vessel. I respect your griefs.
DOGE I thank you. If the tidings which you bring
Are evil, you may say them; nothing further   235
Can touch me more than him thou look'st on there:
If they be good, say on; you need not *fear*
That they can *comfort* me.
BARBARIGO   I would they could!
DOGE I spoke not to *you*, but to Loredano.
He understands me.
MARINA   Ah! I thought it would be so.   240
DOGE What mean you?
MARINA   Lo! there is the blood beginning
To flow through the dead lips of Foscari—
The body bleeds in presence of the assassin.°
(*To Loredano*) Thou cowardly murderer by law, behold
How death itself bears witness to thy deeds!   245
DOGE My child! this is a fantasy of grief.°
(*To the Guards*) Bear hence the body. [*To Barbarigo and Loredano*]
    Signors, if it please you,°
Within an hour I'll hear you.
            Exeunt Doge, Marina, and Guards with the body
BARBARIGO   He must not
Be troubled now.
LOREDANO   He said himself that nought
Could give him trouble farther.
BARBARIGO   These are words;   250
But grief is lonely, and the breaking in
Upon it barbarous.
LOREDANO   Sorrow preys upon
Its solitude, and nothing more diverts it
From its sad visions of the other world
Than calling it at moments back to this.   255
The busy have no time for tears.

BARBARIGO   And therefore
  You would deprive this old man of all business?
LOREDANO The thing's decreed. The Giunta and the Ten°
  Have made it law—who shall oppose that law?
BARBARIGO Humanity!
LOREDANO   Because his son is dead?   260
BARBARIGO And yet unburied.
LOREDANO   Had we known this when
  The act was passing, it might have suspended
  Its passage, but impedes it not—once passed.
BARBARIGO I'll not consent.
LOREDANO   You have consented to
  All that's essential—leave the rest to me.°   265
BARBARIGO Why press his abdication now?
LOREDANO   The feelings
  Of private passion may not interrupt
  The public benefit; and what the state
  Decides today must not give way before
  Tomorrow for a natural accident.   270
BARBARIGO You have a son.
LOREDANO   I *have*—and *had* a father.
BARBARIGO Still so inexorable?
LOREDANO   Still.
BARBARIGO   But let him
  Inter his son before we press upon him
  This edict.
LOREDANO   Let him call up into life
  My sire and uncle—I consent. Men may,   275
  Even aged men, be, or appear to be,
  Sires of a hundred sons, but cannot kindle
  An atom of their ancestors from earth.
  The victims are not equal: he has seen
  His sons expire by natural deaths, and I   280
  My sires by violent and mysterious maladies.
  I used no poison, bribed no subtle master
  Of the destructive art of healing, to
  Shorten the path to the eternal cure.°
  His sons, and he had four, are dead, without   285
  My dabbling in vile drugs.
BARBARIGO   And art thou sure
  He dealt in such?

LOREDANO   Most sure.
BARBARIGO   And yet he seems
  All openness.
LOREDANO   And so he seemed not long
  Ago to Carmagnuola.
BARBARIGO   The attainted°
  And foreign traitor?
LOREDANO   Even so: when *he*,   290
  After the very night in which the Ten
  (Joined with the Doge), decided his destruction,
  Met the great Duke at daybreak with a jest,
  Demanding whether he should augur him
  'The good day or good night', his Doge-ship answered,   295
  That he in truth had passed a night of vigil,
  'In which' (he added with a gracious smile),
  'There often has been question about you'.°
  'Twas true; the question was the death resolved
  Of Carmagnuola, eight months ere he died;   300
  And the old Doge, who knew him doomed, smiled on him
  With deadly cozenage, eight long months beforehand—
  Eight months of such hypocrisy as is
  Learnt but in eighty years. Brave Carmagnuola
  Is dead; so are young Foscari and his brethren—   305
  I never *smiled* on *them*.
BARBARIGO   Was Carmagnuola
  Your friend?
LOREDANO   He was the safeguard of the city.
  In early life its foe, but, in its manhood,
  Its saviour first, then victim.
BARBARIGO   Ah! that seems
  The penalty of saving cities. He   310
  Whom we now act against not only saved
  Our own, but added others to her sway.
LOREDANO The Romans (and we ape them) gave a crown
  To him who took a city; and they gave
  A crown to him who saved a citizen   315
  In battle: the rewards are equal. Now,°
  If we should measure forth the cities taken
  By the Doge Foscari, with citizens
  Destroyed by him, or *through* him, the account
  Were fearfully against him, although narrowed   320

To private havoc, such as between him°
And my dead father.

BARBARIGO   Are you then thus fixed?

LOREDANO   Why, what should change me?

BARBARIGO   That which changes me:
But you, I know, are marble to retain
A feud. But when all is accomplished, when   325
The old man is deposed, his name degraded,
His sons all dead, his family depressed,°
And you and yours triumphant, shall you sleep?

LOREDANO   More soundly.

BARBARIGO   That's an error, and you'll find it
Ere you sleep with your fathers.

LOREDANO   They sleep not   330
In their accelerated graves, nor will°
Till Foscari fills his. Each night I see them
Stalk frowning round my couch, and, pointing towards
The ducal palace, marshal me to vengeance.

BARBARIGO   Fancy's distemperature! There is no passion   335
More spectral or fantastical than hate;
Not even its opposite, love, so peoples air
With phantoms, as this madness of the heart.

    Enter an Officer

LOREDANO   Where go you, sirrah?

OFFICER   By the ducal order
To forward the preparatory rites   340
For the late Foscari's interment.

BARBARIGO   Their
Vault has been often opened of late years.

LOREDANO   'Twill be full soon, and may be closed for ever.

OFFICER   May I pass on?

LOREDANO   You may.

BARBARIGO   How bears the Doge
This last calamity?

OFFICER   With desperate firmness.   345
In presence of another he says little,
But I perceive his lips move now and then;
And once or twice I heard him, from the adjoining
Apartment, mutter forth the words—'My son!'
Scarce audibly. I must proceed.

    Exit Officer

BARBARIGO   This stroke   350
  Will move all Venice in his favour.
LOREDANO   Right!
  We must be speedy: let us call together
  The delegates appointed to convey
  The Council's resolution.
BARBARIGO   I protest
  Against it at this moment.
LOREDANO   As you please—   355
  I'll take their voices on it ne'ertheless,
  And see whose most may sway them, yours or mine.
     Exeunt

5.1

The Doge's apartment

The Doge and Attendants

ATTENDANT My lord, the deputation is in waiting;
　　But add, that if another hour would better
　　Accord with your will, they will make it theirs.

DOGE To me all hours are like. Let them approach.
　　　　Exit Attendant

AN OFFICER Prince! I have done your bidding.

DOGE　　　　　　　　　　　　　　　What command?°　　5

OFFICER A melancholy one—to call the attendance
　　Of——

DOGE　　　True—true—true: I crave your pardon. I
　　Begin to fail in apprehension, and°
　　Wax very old—old almost as my years.
　　Till now I fought them off, but they begin　　　10
　　To overtake me.
　　　　Enter the deputation, consisting of six of the Signory and the
　　　　Chief of the Ten.
　　　　　　　　Noble men, your pleasure!

CHIEF OF THE TEN In the first place, the Council doth condole
　　With the Doge on his late and private grief.

DOGE No more—no more of that.

CHIEF OF THE TEN　　　　　　　　Will not the Duke
　　Accept the homage of respect?

DOGE　　　　　　　　　　　　I do　　　15
　　Accept it as 'tis given—proceed.

CHIEF OF THE TEN　　　　　　　　　The Ten,
　　With a selected Giunta from the senate
　　Of twenty-five of the best born patricians,
　　Having deliberated on the state
　　Of the republic, and the o'erwhelming cares　　20
　　Which, at this moment, doubly must oppress
　　Your years, so long devoted to your country,
　　Have judged it fitting, with all reverence,
　　Now to solicit from your wisdom (which
　　Upon reflection must accord in this),　　　25
　　The resignation of the ducal ring,

Which you have worn so long and venerably;
And to prove that they are not ungrateful nor
Cold to your years and services, they add
An apanage of twenty hundred golden°   30
Ducats, to make retirement not less splendid
Than should become a sovereign's retreat.

DOGE Did I hear rightly?

CHIEF OF THE TEN   Need I say again?

DOGE No.—Have you done?

CHIEF OF THE TEN   I have spoken. Twenty-four
Hours are accorded you to give an answer.   35

DOGE I shall not need so many seconds.

CHIEF OF THE TEN   We
Will now retire.

DOGE   Stay! Four and twenty hours
Will alter nothing which I have to say.

CHIEF OF THE TEN Speak!

DOGE   When I twice before reiterated
My wish to abdicate, it was refused me;   40
And not alone refused, but ye exacted
An oath from me that I would never more
Renew this instance. I have sworn to die°
In full exertion of the functions, which
My country called me here to exercise,   45
According to my honour and my conscience—
I cannot break *my* oath.

CHIEF OF THE TEN   Reduce us not
To the alternative of a decree,
Instead of your compliance.

DOGE   Providence
Prolongs my days to prove and chasten me;   50
But ye have no right to reproach my length
Of days, since every hour has been the country's.
I am ready to lay down my life for her,
As I have laid down dearer things than life:
But for my dignity—I hold it of   55
The *whole* republic; when the *general* will
Is manifest, then you shall all be answered.

CHIEF OF THE TEN We grieve for such an answer; but it cannot
Avail you aught.

DOGE   I can submit to all things,

But nothing will advance; no, not a moment.   60
What you decree—decree.
CHIEF OF THE TEN   With this, then, must we
Return to those who sent us?
DOGE   You have heard me.
CHIEF OF THE TEN With all due reverence we retire.
        Exeunt the [Chief of the Ten and the] deputation. Enter an
        Attendant
ATTENDANT   My lord,
The noble dame Marina craves an audience.
DOGE My time is hers.
        Enter Marina[. The Attendants and Officer retire]
MARINA   My lord, if I intrude—   65
Perhaps you fain would be alone?
DOGE   Alone!
Alone, come all the world around me, I
Am now and evermore. But we will bear it.
MARINA We will; and for the sake of those who are,
Endeavour——Oh my husband!
DOGE   Give it way;   70
I cannot comfort thee.
MARINA   He might have lived,
So formed for gentle privacy of life,
So loving, so beloved; the native of
Another land, and who so blessed and blessing
As my poor Foscari? Nothing was wanting   75
Unto his happiness and mine save not
To be Venetian.
DOGE   Or a prince's son.
MARINA Yes; all things which conduce to other men's
Imperfect happiness or high ambition,
By some strange destiny, to him proved deadly.   80
The country and the people whom he loved,
The prince of whom he was the elder born,
And——
DOGE   Soon may be a prince no longer.
MARINA   How?
DOGE They have taken my son from me, and now aim
At my too long worn diadem and ring.   85
Let them resume the gewgaws!
MARINA   Oh the tyrants!

In such an hour too!
DOGE   'Tis the fittest time:
An hour ago I should have felt it.
MARINA   And
Will you not now resent it?—Oh for vengeance!
But he, who, had he been enough protected,   90
Might have repaid protection in this moment,
Cannot assist his father.
DOGE   Nor should do so
Against his country, had he a thousand lives
Instead of that——
MARINA   They tortured from him. This
May be pure patriotism. I am a woman: 95
To me my husband and my children were
Country and home. I loved *him*—how I loved him!
I have seen him pass through such an ordeal as
The old martyrs would have shrunk from: he is gone,
And I, who would have given my blood for him,   100
Have nought to give but tears! But could I compass
The retribution of his wrongs!—Well, well;
I have sons, who shall be men.
DOGE   Your grief distracts you.°
MARINA I thought I could have borne it, when I saw him
Bowed down by such oppression; yes, I thought   105
That I would rather look upon his corpse
Than his prolonged captivity:—I am punished
For that thought now. Would I were in his grave!
DOGE I must look on him once more.
MARINA   Come with me!
DOGE Is he——
MARINA   Our bridal bed is now his bier.   110
DOGE And is he in his shroud?
MARINA   Come, come, old man!
       Exeunt the Doge and Marina. Enter Barbarigo and Loredano
BARBARIGO (*to an Attendant*) Where is the Doge?
ATTENDANT   This instant retired hence
With the illustrious lady his son's widow.
LOREDANO Where?
ATTENDANT   To the chamber where the body lies.
BARBARIGO Let us return, then.
LOREDANO   You forget, you cannot.   115

We have the implicit order of the Giunta
To await their coming here, and join them in
Their office: they'll be here soon after us.

BARBARIGO And will they press their answer on the Doge?

LOREDANO 'Twas his own wish that all should be done
    promptly.   120
He answered quickly, and must so be answered;
His dignity is looked to, his estate
Cared for—what would he more?

BARBARIGO   Die in his robes.
He could not have lived long; but I have done
My best to save his honours, and opposed   125
This proposition to the last, though vainly.
Why would the general vote compel me hither?

LOREDANO 'Twas fit that someone of such different thoughts
From ours should be a witness, lest false tongues
Should whisper that a harsh majority   130
Dreaded to have its acts beheld by others.

BARBARIGO And not less, I must needs think, for the sake
Of humbling me for my vain opposition.
You are ingenious, Loredano, in
Your modes of vengeance, nay, poetical,   135
A very Ovid in the art of *hating*; °
'Tis thus (although a secondary object,°
Yet hate has microscopic eyes), to you
I owe, by way of foil to the more zealous,°
This undesired association in   140
Your Giunta's duties.

LOREDANO   How!—*my* Giunta!

BARBARIGO   *Yours!*
They speak your language, watch your nod, approve
Your plans, and do your work. Are they not *yours*?

LOREDANO You talk unwarily. 'Twere best they hear not
This from you.

BARBARIGO   Oh! they'll hear as much one day   145
From louder tongues than mine; they have gone beyond
Even their exorbitance of power: and when°
This happens in the most contemned and abject
States, stung humanity will rise to check it.

LOREDANO You talk but idly.

BARBARIGO   That remains for proof.   150

Here come our colleagues.
          Enter [the Chief of the Ten and] the deputation as before
CHIEF OF THE TEN   Is the Duke aware
     We seek his presence?
ATTENDANT   He shall be informed.
          Exit Attendant
BARBARIGO The Duke is with his son.
CHIEF OF THE TEN   If it be so,
     We will remit him till the rites are over.
     Let us return. 'Tis time enough tomorrow.   155
LOREDANO (*aside to Barbarigo*) Now the rich man's hell-fire upon
          your tongue,°
     Unquenched, unquenchable! I'll have it torn
     From its vile babbling roots, till you shall utter
     Nothing but sobs through blood, for this! (*Aloud to the others*)
          Sage signors,
     I pray ye be not hasty.
BARBARIGO   But be human!   160
LOREDANO See, the Duke comes!
          Enter the Doge
DOGE   I have obeyed your summons.
CHIEF OF THE TEN We come once more to urge our past request.
DOGE And I to answer.
CHIEF OF THE TEN   What?
DOGE   My only answer.
     You have heard it.
CHIEF OF THE TEN Hear *you* then the last decree,
     Definitive and absolute!
DOGE   To the point—   165
     To the point! I know of old the forms of office,
     And gentle preludes to strong acts—go on!
CHIEF OF THE TEN You are no longer Doge; you are released
     From your imperial oath as sovereign;
     Your ducal robes must be put off; but for   170
     Your services, the state allots the apanage
     Already mentioned in our former congress.
     Three days are left you to remove from hence,
     Under the penalty to see confiscated
     All your own private fortune.
DOGE   That last clause,   175
     I am proud to say, would not enrich the treasury.

CHIEF OF THE TEN Your answer, Duke!

LOREDANO   Your answer, Francis Foscari!

DOGE If I could have foreseen that my old age
    Was prejudicial to the state, the chief
    Of the republic never would have shown   180
    Himself so far ungrateful, as to place
    His own high dignity before his country;
    But this *life* having been so many years
    Not useless to that country, I would fain
    Have consecrated my last moments to her.   185
    But the decree being rendered, I obey.

CHIEF OF THE TEN If you would have the three days named
    extended,
    We willingly will lengthen them to eight,
    As sign of our esteem.

DOGE   Not eight hours, signor,
    Nor even eight minutes.—There's the ducal ring,   190
        (*Taking off his ring and cap*)
    And there the ducal diadem. And so
    The Adriatic's free to wed another.°

CHIEF OF THE TEN Yet go not forth so quickly.

DOGE   I am old, sir,
    And even to move but slowly must begin
    To move betimes. Methinks I see amongst you°   195
    A face I know not—Senator! your name,
    You, by your garb, Chief of the Forty!

MEMMO   Signor,°
    I am the son of Marco Memmo.

DOGE   Ah!
    Your father was my friend.—But *sons* and *fathers*!
    What, ho! my servants there!

ATTENDANT   My prince!

DOGE   No prince—   200
        (*Pointing to the Ten's deputation*)
    There are the princes of the prince!—Prepare
    To part from hence upon the instant.

CHIEF OF THE TEN   Why
    So rashly? 'twill give scandal.

DOGE (*to the Ten*)   Answer that;
    It is your province.—(*To the servants*) Sirs, bestir yourselves:
    There is one burden which I beg you bear°   205

305

With care, although 'tis past all further harm—
But I will look to that myself.

BARBARIGO   He means
The body of his son.

DOGE   And call Marina,
My daughter!

    Enter Marina

DOGE   Get thee ready, we must mourn
Elsewhere.

MARINA   And everywhere.

DOGE   True; but in freedom,   210
Without these jealous spies upon the great.
Signors, you may depart: what would you more?
We are going: do you fear that we shall bear
The palace with us? Its *old* walls, ten times
As *old* as I am, and I'm very old,   215
Have served you, so have I, and I and they
Could tell a tale; but I invoke them not
To fall upon you! Else they would, as erst
The pillars of stone Dagon's temple on
The Israelite and his Philistine foes.°   220
Such power I do believe there might exist
In such a curse as mine, provoked by such
As you; but I curse not. Adieu, good signors!
May the next duke be better than the present!

LOREDANO The *present* duke is Paschal Malipiero.°   225

DOGE Not till I pass the threshold of these doors.

LOREDANO Saint Mark's great bell is soon about to toll
For his inauguration.

DOGE   Earth and heaven!
Ye will reverberate this peal; and I
Live to hear this!—the first doge who e'er heard   230
Such sound for his successor! Happier he,
My attainted predecessor, stern Faliero—°
This insult at the least was spared him.

LOREDANO   What!
Do you regret a traitor?

DOGE   No—I merely
Envy the dead.

CHIEF OF THE TEN My lord, if you indeed   235
Are bent upon this rash abandonment

Of the state's palace, at the least retire
By the private staircase, which conducts you towards
The landing-place of the canal.

DOGE   No. I
Will now descend the stairs by which I mounted   240
To sovereignty—the Giant's Stairs, on whose°
Broad eminence I was invested duke.
My services have called me up those steps,
The malice of my foes will drive me down them.
There five and thirty years ago was I   245
Installed, and traversed these same halls from which
I never thought to be divorced except
A corpse—a corpse, it might be, fighting for them—
But not pushed hence by fellow citizens.
But, come; my son and I will go together—   250
He to his grave, and I to pray for mine.

CHIEF OF THE TEN What thus in public?

DOGE   I was publicly
Elected, and so will I be deposed.
Marina! art thou willing?

MARINA   Here's my arm!

DOGE And here my *staff*: thus propped will I go forth.   255

CHIEF OF THE TEN It must not be—the people will perceive it.

DOGE The people!—There's no people, you well know it,
Else you dare not deal thus by them or me.
There is a *populace*, perhaps, whose looks
May shame you; but they dare not groan nor curse you,   260
Save with their hearts and eyes.

CHIEF OF THE TEN   You speak in passion,
Else——

DOGE   You have reason. I have spoken much°
More than my wont: it is a foible which
Was not of mine, but more excuses you,
In as much as it shows that I approach   265
A dotage which may justify this deed
Of yours, although the law does not, nor will.
Farewell, sirs!

BARBARIGO   You shall not depart without
An escort fitting past and present rank.
We will accompany, with due respect,   270
The Doge unto his private palace. Say!

My brethren, will we not?
DIFFERENT VOICES   Aye!—Aye!
DOGE   You shall not
  Stir—in my train, at least. I entered here
  As sovereign—I go out as citizen
  By the same portals, but as citizen.°   275
  All these vain ceremonies are base insults,
  Which only ulcerate the heart the more,
  Applying poisons there as antidotes.
  Pomp is for princes—I am *none*!—That's false,
  I *am*, but only to these gates.—Ah!
LOREDANO   Hark!   280
        The great bell of St Mark's tolls
BARBARIGO The bell!
CHIEF OF THE TEN   St Mark's, which tolls for the election
  Of Malipiero.
DOGE   Well I recognize
  The sound! I heard it once, but once before,
  And that is five and thirty years ago;
  Even *then* I *was not young*.
BARBARIGO   Sit down, my lord!   285
  You tremble.
DOGE   'Tis the knell of my poor boy!
  My heart aches bitterly.
BARBARIGO   I pray you sit.
DOGE No; my seat here has been a throne till now.
  Marina! let us go.
MARINA   Most readily.
        The Doge walks a few steps, then stops
DOGE I feel athirst—will no one bring me here   290
  A cup of water?
BARBARIGO   I——
MARINA   And I——
LOREDANO   And I——
        The Doge takes a goblet from the hand of Loredano
DOGE I take *yours*, Loredano, from the hand
  Most fit for such an hour as this.
LOREDANO   Why so?
DOGE 'Tis said that our Venetian crystal has
  Such pure antipathy to poisons as   295
  To burst, if aught of venom touches it.

You bore this goblet, and it is not broken.
LOREDANO Well, sir!
DOGE   Then it is false, or you are true.
  For my own part, I credit neither; 'tis
  An idle legend.
MARINA   You talk wildly, and   300
  Had better now be seated, nor as yet
  Depart. Ah! now you look as looked my husband!
BARBARIGO He sinks!—support him!—quick—a chair—support him!
DOGE The bell tolls on!—Let's hence—my brain's on fire!°
BARBARIGO I do beseech you, lean upon us!
DOGE   No!   305
  A sovereign should die standing. My poor boy!
  Off with your arms!—*That bell!*
     The Doge drops down and dies
MARINA   My God! My God!
BARBARIGO (*to Loredano*) Behold! Your work's completed!
CHIEF OF THE TEN   Is there then
  No aid? Call in assistance!
ATTENDANT   'Tis all over.
CHIEF OF THE TEN   If it be so, at least his obsequies   310
  Shall be such as befits his name and nation,
  His rank and his devotion to the duties
  Of the realm, while his age permitted him
  To do himself and them full justice. Brethren,
  Say, shall it not be so?
BARBARIGO   He has not had   315
  The misery to die a subject where
  He reigned: then let his funeral rites be princely.
CHIEF OF THE TEN We are agreed then?
ALL (*except Loredano*)   Yes.
CHIEF OF THE TEN   Heaven's peace be with him!
MARINA Signors, your pardon: this is mockery.
  Juggle no more with that poor remnant, which,   320
  A moment since, while yet it had a soul,
  (A soul by whom you have increased your empire,
  And made your power as proud as was his glory),
  You banished from his palace, and tore down
  From his high place, with such relentless coldness;   325
  And now, when he can neither know these honours,
  Nor would accept them if he could, you, signors,

Purpose, with idle and superfluous pomp,
To make a pageant over what you trampled.
A princely funeral will be your reproach,   330
And not his honour.
CHIEF OF THE TEN   Lady, we revoke not
Our purposes so readily.
MARINA   I know it,
As far as touches torturing the living.
I thought the dead had been beyond even *you*,
Though (some, no doubt) consigned to powers which may   335
Resemble that you exercise on earth.
Leave him to me; you would have done so for
His dregs of life, which you have kindly shortened:
It is my last of duties, and may prove
A dreary comfort in my desolation.   340
Grief is fantastical, and loves the dead,
And the apparel of the grave.
CHIEF OF THE TEN   Do you
Pretend still to this office?
MARINA   I do, signor.°
Though his possessions have been all consumed
In the state's service, I have still my dowry,   345
Which shall be consecrated to his rites,
And those of——
          She stops with agitation
CHIEF OF THE TEN Best retain it for your children.
MARINA Aye, they are fatherless, I thank you.
CHIEF OF THE TEN   We
Cannot comply with your request. His relics°
Shall be exposed with wonted pomp, and followed°   350
Unto their home by the new Doge, not clad
As *Doge*, but simply as a senator.
MARINA I have heard of murderers, who have interred
Their victims; but ne'er heard, until this hour,
Of so much splendour in hypocrisy   355
O'er those they slew. I've heard of widow's tears—
Alas! I have shed some—always thanks to you!
I've heard of *heirs* in sables—you have left none°
To the deceased, so you would act the part
Of such. Well, sirs, your will be done! as one day,   360
I trust heaven's will be done too!

CHIEF OF THE TEN   Know you, lady,
   To whom ye speak, and perils of such speech?
MARINA I know the former better than yourselves;
   The latter—like yourselves; and can face both.
   Wish you more funerals?
BARBARIGO   Heed not her rash words;   365
   Her circumstances must excuse her bearing.
CHIEF OF THE TEN We will not note them down.
BARBARIGO (*turning to Loredano, who is writing upon his tablets*)
                                  What art thou writing,
   With such an earnest brow, upon thy tablets?°
LOREDANO (*pointing to the Doge's body*) That *he* has paid me!
CHIEF OF THE TEN   What debt did he owe you?°
LOREDANO A long and just one; Nature's debt and *mine*.   370
    Curtain falls

EXPLANATORY NOTES

The following abbreviations are used in the notes:

1821	Lord Byron, *Sardanapalus, A Tragedy. The Two Foscari, A Tragedy. Cain, A Mystery* (1821).
Correspondence	*The Yale Edition of Horace Walpole's Correspondence*, ed. W. S. Lewis *et al.* (New Haven, London, and Oxford, 1937–83), 48 vols., cited by volume and page number.
Letters	*Byron's Letters and Journals*, ed. Leslie A. Marchand (London, 1973–82), 12 vols.
LS	*The London Stage 1660–1800*, ed. William Van Lennep *et al.* (Carbondale, Ill., 1965–8), 11 vols., *Part 5: 1776–1800*, ed. Charles Beecher Hogan (1968) [vol. iii].
OED	*The Oxford English Dictionary* (2nd edn.: Oxford, 1989), 20 vols.
SJ	Samuel Johnson, *A Dictionary of the English Language* (London, 1755), 2 vols.; reference is always to the entry for the word or phrase under discussion.
Summers	*Constable's Edition of The Castle of Otranto and The Mysterious Mother*, ed. Montague Summers (London, 1924).

Biblical references are given by book, chapter, and verse to *The Holy Bible Containing the Old and New Testaments Translated out of the Original Tongues*, the so-called 'Authorized' or 'King James' Bible (1611). The works of John Milton are cited by book and line number, or line number only, from John Milton, *Poems*, ed. B. A. Wright (London, 1976). The works of William Shakespeare are cited by act, scene, and line number from William Shakespeare, *The Complete Works*, ed. Stanley Wells and Gary Taylor (compact edn.: Oxford, 1988). The works of John Webster are cited by act, scene, and line number from John Webster, *The Duchess of Malfi and Other Plays*, ed. René Weis (Oxford, 1996). Citations of classical authors are by chapter or by book and line number as established in the Oxford Classical Texts series; translations are our own. Editions for less commonly cited works are given at appropriate points in the notes.

The Mysterious Mother

Epigraph *Sit . . . loqui! [Virgil]*: Virgil, *Aeneid*, vi. 266: literally, 'may it be lawful for me to speak the things I have heard'.

Preface to the 1781 edition This untitled preface was written for the edition printed for J. Dodsley, 1781. It was first published in an edition printed at Dublin, 1791.

5 *disgusting*: in the less forceful sense, common in the period, of 'distasteful'.

8 *a few copies . . . given away*: Walpole printed fifty copies on his private press at Strawberry Hill; by no means all of these were circulated.

10 *different editions . . . present publication*: Walpole feared a piracy of the work in 1781 and had an edition printed to forestall it; in the event no piracy appeared and the 1781 edition was not formally published.

The Characters of the Play 1 *Narbonne*: a city in southern France, 5 miles from the Mediterranean; of strategic importance even in pre-Roman times. Several members of the Narbonne–Pelet aristocracy are mentioned in Walpole's correspondence.

Adeliza: Walpole found this name in George Vertue's manuscript *Tour into Sussex* (1747) (BL Add. MS 23,089, fo.17), on which he made some notes; Adeliza appears there as the second wife of Henry I (1068–1135); she is more usually known as Adelaide. 'In all my tragedy, Adeliza contents me the least', Walpole admitted later; *Correspondence*, xli. 297.

Prologue Not present in any edition before *The Works of Horatio Walpole, Earl of Orford. In Five Volumes* (1798), iv. 396–7, where it was printed amongst Walpole's verse, not with the play. The 1798 text is used here. The Epilogue was clearly written in 1768 and it may be assumed that the Prologue was too.

1 *no French model*: Walpole argues both here and in the postscript to the play that English theatre was crippled by its reliance on French theatrical practice, with its statuesque, declamatory style and insistence on dramatic decorum. However, two French plays which might have provided some inspiration for story are Voltaire's *Sémiramis*, which Walpole saw and enjoyed in Paris in 1766 (*Correspondence*, vii. 312), and Racine's *Phèdre*.

2 *horrid*: in the stronger eighteenth-century sense, 'Hideous; dreadful; shocking' (SJ).

7 *Hamlet's spectre . . . midnight round?*: in the opening scene of Shakespeare's *Hamlet* (1.1.47–122) the ghost of Hamlet's father (also called Hamlet) appears after midnight.

8 *Banquo's issue . . . crowned?*: in Shakespeare's *Macbeth* (4.1.84–140) the descendants of the murdered Banquo appear to Macbeth as future kings, in a vision produced by witches.

9 *scene!*: 'The stage; the theatre of dramatick poetry' (SJ).

13 *censor*: corrector of public morality.

16 *pit*: ground floor of theatre auditorium, meaning here the spectators seated there.

24 *veiled . . . mote*: an allusion to Christ's words in the Sermon on the Mount (Matt. 7: 3–4): 'why beholdest thou the mote that is in thy brother's eye, but considerest not the beam that is in thine own eye?'

27 *Electra*: in Greek mythology Electra encouraged her brother Orestes to avenge the murder of their father. The story was dramatized by Aeschylus, Sophocles, and Euripides, the three major Athenian tragedians from whom the classical tradition of drama derives.

28–9 *parricide . . . nuptial bands*: 'the Theban' is Oedipus, who in Greek mythology unwittingly killed his father and married his mother. The story was most famously treated by Sophocles, but Walpole knew several more recent stage versions, for example the gore-laden one by John Dryden and Nathaniel Lee (1679). Voltaire also wrote an *Œdipe* (1718). Walpole connects the Electra and Oedipus stories, which went on to become foundational myths for Freudian psychoanalysis, by writing a rare triplet of rhyming lines.

31 *tremendous*: fearful; terrifying.

1.1.1 *awful*: 'that which strikes with awe, or fills with reverence' (SJ).

1–7 *What awful . . . Is circumstance!*: Ann Radcliffe used a relineated version of the first seven lines of this speech as a scene-setting epigraph to Chapter II of *The Romance of the Forest* (1791).

16 *rude*: rough; inelegant.

17 *aspect*: 'look; air; appearance' (SJ).

16–17 *like the tenant . . . worn to habitude*: Ann Radcliffe used a version of this description as epigraph to *The Italian* (1797), Volume I, Chapter IX.

28 *twentieth of September*: possibly an allusion to the feast day of St Eustace, who was converted while out hunting by the apparition of a stag, and which thus has a faint connection with the story of the play. 20 September was also the birthday of Walpole's cousin George Townshend, which has led some critics to speculate that Walpole (whose own birthday was 24 September) was using a coded or surrogate version of himself in an Oedipal fantasy; see Martin Kallich, *Horace Walpole* (New York, 1971), 105–17.

47 *bewildered*: lost or strayed from the path.

55 *must*: which must.

67 *cry you mercy*: ask your pardon.

73 *moping melancholies*: compare Milton, *Paradise Lost*, xi. 485: 'Daemoniack Phrenzie, moping Melancholie . . . '.

77 *mainly*: 'greatly; powerfully' (SJ).

83 *messenger*: a figure of portent seen on the hearth. William Cowper alludes to this superstition in *The Task*, iv. 291–5 (*Poetical Works*, ed. H. S. Milford (4th edn.: Oxford, 1967), 189); and S. T. Coleridge mentions it

in *Frost at Midnight*, l. 26, where the figure is called a 'stranger' (*Poems*, ed. John Beer (London, 1978), 138).

93 *leagues*: a league is an archaic measure of distance, approximately 3 miles.

94 *hearty*: 'vigorous; strong' (SJ).

100 *ruthless*: devoid of pity.

108 *wist*: knew (with a faint sexual connotation, as with 'knew' in the previous line).

I warrant him: I guarantee it of him; no doubt.

122 S.D. *The Countess in weeds*: i.e., 'widow's weeds', 'the mourning dress of a widow' (SJ).

126–7 *minist'ring . . . means*: giving help to those who need medicine or money.

130 *impending*: overhanging.

138 *confessor*: here, as often in the plays in this volume, accented on the first syllable.

142 *Mass!*: an oath, a shortened form of 'by the Mass'.

144 *lose . . . prating*: lose my means of subsistence by talking too much.

145 *wo't*: for 'wouldst thou', would you (a Shakespearean usage: see *Hamlet*, 5.1.272–3).

149 S.D. *severally*: in different directions; by different stage exits.

153 *council*: i.e., a church council, meeting of church authorities.

155 *amuse*: delude; deceive; engage attention.

161–2 *What is . . . penance cleanse?*: used by Ann Radcliffe as epigraph to *The Italian* (1797), Volume I, Chapter I.

165 *death's artificer*: contriver of his death; the suggestion of artifice then carries on into Martin's notion of the Countess's possibly counterfeit grief.

166 *affect*: pretend.

174 *incontinence*: sexual transgression.

187 *owned*: confessed; admitted.

194 *conscious sense*: self-aware or strongly felt good sense.

195–6 *I would pawn . . . veracity*: an unconscious irony, since Benedict's order has little claim to credit in this dramatization.

202 *scoffs*: scoffs at; mocks.

206 *adamant*: 'a stone, imagined by writers, of impenetrable hardness' (SJ).

206–8 *Though . . . stream*: though her reason is firm, charity can wear it down (as a stream wears down a rock), and we (as monks) are familiar with the dispensation of charity.

210 *mystic*: mysterious.

212 *Or soon, or late*: sooner or later. The use of 'Or . . . or' instead of 'Either . . . or' is common in these plays.

213 *spoil*: plunder; reward for victory.

215–16 *form her tenants . . . report them*: induce or instruct her tenants to imagine visions and phantoms, and report them to her.

217 *fond*: foolish; deluded.

224–6 *nor remember . . . Give o'er my purpose*: nor remember that I tried to take advantage of her fears, and having been foiled, now give up my original intention. Though 'Gave' seems more logical after 'remember', Walpole retained the present tense in all editions; Benedict is perhaps indicating the present, recurrent state of affairs, with 'Give' in sequence with 'relate' and 'think'.

233 *creeds myself would laugh at*: 'Alluding to Sixtus Quintus' [Walpole's note, in editions from 1770 onwards]. Sixtus Quintus (Felice Peretti, 1521–90) was Pope from 1585 to 1590. Walpole owned a copy of Gregorio Leti's *Vita di Sisto V* (Amsterdam, 1693), and often joked about his outward austerity and inner hypocrisy (see *Correspondence*, xxi. 395; xxiii. 157; xxiv. 14, 24–5). In a standard vein of anti-Catholic satire, Walpole suggests that priests foist absurd beliefs on the credulous without giving any credence to them themselves.

237–8 *Deluded . . . doubt*: the deluded think that boldness (in others) comes from a conscious strength, and so are decived by their own lack of scepticism.

240 *A crimson bonnet . . . toils*: you may be made a cardinal as a reward for your labours.

247 *exhibition*: 'allowance; salary; pension' (SJ).

250 *Usurped from her own wants*: wrongfully seized from her own needs.

251 *portion*: fortune which comes to the husband from the wife at marriage.

253 *veiled*: become a nun.

261 *cowls and scapularies*: the hoods and short cloaks worn by some orders of monks (the 'scapular' was originally prescribed in the rule of St Benedict).

265 *mental*: spiritual.

hov'ring: in a state of suspense; about to land or fix on a choice.

273 *moment of projection*: moment when all our aspirations will be realized; 'In chemistry, an operation; crisis of an operation; moment of transmutation' (SJ).

294 *snap the thread*: like the third of the Fates, in Greek mythology, responsible for the length of human lives. The sense is that the Countess resists the idea of suicide.

297 *ministry*: ministration; charitable help.

301 *widow's mite*: by allusion to the New Testament story about charity: Mark 12: 42–4.

302 *prevents occasion*: anticipates moment of need. The Countess offers charity before it is asked.

307–8 *suspect . . . dissembling*: possibly a deliberate irony from the Countess, but she seems to be in two minds about Benedict's motives until 3.1; for the rest of 1.1 she veers between suspicion and apology in her dealings with him. In 5.1 she still appears to believe that Benedict may have some genuinely holy powers.

311–12 *Will flattery . . . hollow jaws?*: a reminiscence of the graveyard scene in Shakespeare, *Hamlet*, 5.1.180–90.

313 *solemn audit*: day of judgement.

316 *Pagan virtues*: virtues derived from reason unassisted by Christianity. The Countess then takes the word 'Pagan' to indicate something barbaric and outside the pale of Christianity.

323 *blasted*: horrified; damned by the judgement of heaven.

328 *I have it not*: the 'it' refers to the 'faith' about which Benedict is beginning to speak.

331–2 *Death . . . retrospect*: the idea is something like Hamlet's in the 'To be, or not to be' speech, Shakespeare, *Hamlet*, 3.1.58–90.

339 *Friday's dreams*: proverbial: 'a Friday night's dream on the Saturday told, is sure to come true be it never so old'; *Oxford Dictionary of Proverbs*, rev. F. P. Wilson (3rd edn.: Oxford, 1970). As a priest Benedict perhaps also claims special status for the dreams which occur after a day of fasting.

347 *destined*: doomed.

356 *still small voice*: 'and after the fire a still small voice', 1 Kgs. 19: 12. The 'still small voice', originally heard by the prophet Elijah after a colossal storm, was a widely used metaphor for the promptings of conscience. In the contrast with 'This poetry of fond enthusiasm', however, Walpole may be remembering the use of the phrase by his friend John Chute, to describe the appropriate role of poetry; see Thomas Gray to Walpole, *c*. January 1748, *Correspondence*, xiv. 36.

358 *my son's birth, not his mortality*: 'On the death of the comte de Vermand-ois, his mother, the duchess de la Valière said, Must I weep for his death before I have done weeping for his birth?' [Walpole's note, in editions from 1770 onwards]. The comte de Vermandois (Louis de Bourbon) was the illegitimate son of Louis XIV by the Duchess de la Vallière, born in 1666, and died in 1682. Summers ascribes the original report to Madame de Caylus (Summers, 297–8).

361 *Illy . . . deem*: you think badly of me.

367 *character*: profession; reputation.

368 *monitor*: 'one who warns of faults, or informs of duty' (SJ).

377 *sacred casuistry*: application of religious rules to special cases of conscience. In his postscript Walpole cites a case similar to that of the Countess being brought to the archbishop of Canterbury, and several analogues for the story he cites are to be found in the works of Protestant theologians (e.g. Martin Luther, *Colloquia Mensalia*, trans. Henry Bell, 1652, 257). None the less, 'casuistry' carries with it to one of Walpole's persuasion the sense of corrupt or specious reasoning.

379–80 *Unfold . . . discord*: used by Ann Radcliffe as epigraph to *The Italian* (1797), Volume I, Chapter IV.

382 *What should I inquire?*: 'Imitated from Cato's speech in Lucan, beginning, Quid quaeri, Labiene, jubes?' [Walpole's note in all editions]. See Lucan, *Pharsalia*, ix. 566–84: Cato is rejecting the opportunity to enquire of an oracle concerning the outcome of the war; literally, 'What do you command, Labienus, to be asked?' Cato eventually loses.

398–400 *No codicil . . . casual custody*: no instruction additional to the original rules of duty was placed here or there in some random saint's keeping.

402 *jugglers*: deceivers; tricksters.

402–5 *Me . . . torment*: neither oracles nor prophets can prove to me—only Death can—whether, after justice's full dues have been demanded and paid, any drop of mercy shall be granted to assuage my pain.

2.1 s.d. *[A platform before the castle]*: the copy-text reads *The scene continues*, i.e., the location remains the same as in 1.1.

12–13 *For that . . . joy*: because my emerging passion's swelling fervour stimulated irresistible and mutually enjoyed sexual satisfaction.

49 *collateral*: connected; concurrent.

50 *Sable*: black, the traditional colour of mourning garments and coverings in houses of mourning. The word itself is a poetical or heraldic one, according to SJ; it is used here for its association with ritualized psychological gloom.

52–4 *a specious theatre . . . inward tribute*: a plausible external display to which the mind can direct its attention and with apparent decency forget the real subject of its mourning.

55 *shade*: spirit; soul; ghost.

59 *lordships*: domains; estates.

75 *approved*: proven.

76 *quarrels . . . nor my own?*: quarrels which are neither my country's nor my own.

78 *At Buda 'gainst the Turk*: Buda, one half of what has been since 1872 Budapest, was from 1541 to 1686 the seat of a Turkish pasha; Pest, the other half, was sacked by the Turks in 1526. It is probably this period which Walpole has in mind.

82 *crescent . . . cross*: emblems respectively of Islamic and Christian states and armies.

91–2 *Thibalt, Raoul, | Or Clodomir*: probably fictitious names, but Count Thibaut IV of Champagne and Brie (1201–53) was king of Navarre, and *Raoul de Cambrai*, an Old French *chanson de geste*, tells the story of ruinous baronial wars.

101 *arrayed*: set in readiness for battle.

118 *Magdalen*: Mary Magdalen, one of Christ's followers, often pictured as a harlot saved by repentance and faith.

126 *marked*: showed, indicated.

134–7 *Self-denial . . . machine*: self-denial, whose strong difference from nature's kindest laws gains (by being contradictory) a victory over our perverseness, is gross fanaticism's favourite device.

142 *Teresa*: Teresa de Cepeda, 1515–82, visionary and reformer, canonized 12 May 1622. Walpole called the Countess of Huntingdon 'the Saint Theresa of the Methodists—Judge how violent bigotry must be in such mad blood!' (letter to Horace Mann, 7 May 1760, *Correspondence*, xxi. 398).

144 *riot*: 'wild and loose festivity' (SJ).

146 *desolation*: the act of rendering waste or devastating.

151 *pensioner*: one whose position is paid for by another; Adeliza is a 'pensioner' or paying resident of the convent, placed there for protection and education at the Countess's expense. She is not a nun or probationer.

156 *beauty's type*: beauty's original model or template.

156–9 *Like blooming Eve . . . to charm*: mingled general reminiscences of descriptions of Eve in Milton, *Paradise Lost* (for example, iv. 304–11, and viii. 471–90); and of Miranda in Shakespeare, *The Tempest*, especially 5.1.185–7.

160 *kind*: sexually willing.

166 *match her nobly*: find her a noble husband.

168 *convenient*: 'fit; suitable; proper' (SJ).

171 *office of devotion*: act of religious worship.

175 S.D. *stage-door*: perhaps the door opposite the one from which the procession has entered; doors would be situated in front of the proscenium arch in the theatre which Walpole knew. Or the procession might enter from or head towards a door in a painted castle at the back.

185 *palm*: token of victory.

189 *conductor*: leader; guide.

192 *In whose behoof*: on whose behalf.

201 *lusty life's full 'vantage*: in the prime of life; at the peak of his powers.

202 *no account ... absolution!*: the Count died suddenly, before he had the chance to go to confession and receive absolution for his sins. Compare Hamlet's father: 'No reck'ning made, but sent to my account | With all my imperfections on my head'; Shakespeare, *Hamlet*, 1.5.78–9.

203 *scant*: scarcely.

206 *year's mind*: annual commemoration by requiem of saint or departed soul.

212 *breathings*: utterances. *Pious Breathings* was the title of a popular compilation of the works of Augustine of Hippo (e.g. 5th edn.: London, 1720); see note to 4.1.55 below.

213–14 *whose occupation ... tomb*: whose profession rarely looks closely at the (short) distance between pleasure and death.

223 *clotted*: covered with clots of blood.

burning stars: comets; stars of ill omen.

226 *straight*: straight away.

235 *Kneels to Omnipotence*: shows obedience or submissiveness to the divine power.

259–64 *What if ... ruby grape?*: this speech is marked with quotation marks in all editions, apparently for no other reason than to point it out as a particular 'beauty' in a fashion not uncommon in eighteenth-century printing.

282–90 *The seasons ... crimes we know not!*: portents such as these accompany symbolic parricide in Shakespeare's *Julius Caesar* and *Macbeth*, and Walpole is also thinking of the opening scene of Sophocles' *Oedipus Tyrannus*, where the plague is caused by Oedipus' concealed crimes.

291 *To edge suspended vengeance*: to urge on or give incisive force to the vengeance which is currently hanging over us.

295 *Revere*: (and I) revere.

299 *haunt*: dwelling.

300 *St Bridget's nunnery*: Walpole may be thinking of St Bridget (Birgitta) of Sweden (1303–73, canonized 1391), a visionary who founded the Brigettine order after three years of penitence following her husband's death. Her writings are much concerned with the punishment of sin.

306–10 *'Tis delicate Felicity ... security*: a reminiscence of Lear's assaults on his daughters' finery and the 'poor naked wretches' in the storm; Shakespeare, *King Lear*, 3.4.28.

316 *sure*: surely.

331 *'clipse fell out*: eclipse came to pass.

339 *say him nay*: deny him; refute his argument.

384 *the vulgar*: the common people.

384–5 *how old . . . Narbonne?*: how long have you been staying in Narbonne?

386 *Brabant*: a region in what is now Belgium.

387 *St Orme*: no such place has been traced, but Walpole might be thinking of St. Omer in north-east France, which is often mentioned in his letters.

388 *letters of exchange*: letters of credit or bills of exchange by which Florian can get funds until the legacy is his.

389 *succession*: inheritance; legacy.

406 *saucy*: 'pert; petulant; . . . insolent; impudent; impertinent' (SJ).

408 *enthusiasm*: 'a vain belief of private revelation; a vain confidence of divine favour or communication' (SJ). The word is used pejoratively in the period to indicate a fanatical or extreme belief in one's individual closeness to God.

412–13 *train | That waits on*: retinue (group of followers) that attends.

3.1.4–5 *as fractious children . . . by proxy*: as cross children are disciplined by scolding some other figure as example.

8 *doom*: 'judicial sentence; judgment' (SJ).

17 *inquisitors*: officers of the church with jurisdiction over the detection and punishment of heresy, most notoriously by public burning.

20 *faggots*: bundles of sticks used to burn those condemned by the Inquisition.

21 *torch*: waxed stick or cloth used to light fires.

57 *How happy . . . innocence*: 'Dr. Young relates that Mr. Addison, on his death-bed, spoke in this manner to his pupil Lord Warwick' [Walpole's note, in editions from 1770 onwards]. See Edward Young, *Conjectures on Original Composition* (1759), 101–2.

83 *conscious*: guilty; aware of guilt.

85 *vent*: give vent to; pour out.

110 *Pent*: shut up; confined.

157 *task*: interrogate; tax.

163 *views . . . heav'n*: earthly rather than heavenly purposes.

164 *ghostly*: spiritual; religious.

183 *Heaven's law . . . follow*: once Heaven's law has been proclaimed, it remains that obedience should follow it.

184–7 *And when . . . grant them*: and when heaven, in its supremacy, puts that obedience to the test, not by asking for some unachievable level of perfection, but by offering its profusion of blessings in return for simple belief in its power to grant them.

189 *'We will . . . deserve it?'*: 'We will do more, Sempronius, we'll deserve it. Portius in CATO.' [Walpole's note in editions from 1770 onwards.] See Joseph Addison, *Cato* (1713), 1.2.45 (originally, 'But we'll do more, *Sempronius*; we'll Deserve it').

207 *bolt*: thunderbolt; metaphorically, divine vengeance.

229 *what boots*: what profits; what matters.

234 *brook*: tolerate.

235 *warrant*: evidence; guarantee; authorization.

236 *assure*: certify; prove.

263 *apprehension*: understanding.

272 *winged from other orbs*: sped from other spheres or realms (e.g. celestial).

279 *touch me not*: the words of Christ to Mary Magdalene after his resurrection (John 21: 17).

297 *sapped*: perhaps here with the military sense of 'undermined'.

303 *sleeveless*: 'wanting reasonableness; wanting propriety; wanting solidity' (SJ).

312–13 *Though frail . . . thy race*: perhaps recalling Elizabeth I's famous speech to the troops at Tilbury, 1588: 'I have the body of a weak and feeble woman, but I have the heart and stomach of a king.'

316–17 *'Tis not ripe | As yet my purpose*: my purpose is not yet ready to be fulfilled.

4.1 S.D. *[The garden]*: copy-text reads *The scene continues*, that is, the location is as described at the start of 3.1.

2 *mask of art*: disguised expression or behaviour.

6 *I want . . . faith*: I do not lack trust in you; I am sure of your trustworthiness.

11 *casuist! and apply*: a casuist is 'one that studies and settles cases of conscience' (SJ); compare note on 'casuistry' in 1.1.377 above. The syntax is: 'a casuist, who goes on to apply . . . '.

26 *forgot I am a man*: renounced my claim to marriage or sexual fulfilment. As a monk Benedict has vowed to live celibate.

47–9 *E'en stern philosophy . . . worse than ours*: in 1791 Walpole copied out these lines with the comment: 'Lines in the Mysterious Mother that have proved to be a Prophecy of what has happened in France since the Revolution of 1789'; *Horace Walpole's Miscellany 1786–1795*, ed. Lars E. Troide (New Haven and London, 1978), 127.

54 *thence comes sects*: from this problem emerges (the phenomenon of) religious divisions.

55 *Zeno . . . Ignatius*: 'Zeno' is either the Athenian Stoic philosopher (*c.*340–265 BC), or Zeno of Elea, a disciple of Parmenides (*c.*450 BC). St Ignatius

Loyola (1491–1556) was founder of the Jesuit order and opponent of the Reformation. In the 1770 edition Walpole substituted 'Augustine' for 'Ignatius', probably meaning the great church father St Augustine (354–430), bishop of Hippo and author of *The City of God* and *Confessions*, rather than St Augustine the first archbishop of Canterbury (d.604).

57 *interest*: self-interest.

59 *singing saints . . . vale*: Walpole visited the mountains of Savoy in 1739, comparing them with the brooding landscapes of Salvator Rosa (*Correspondence*, xiii, 181). He was later interested in the contemporary politics of the region. The 'singing saints' may be the Vaudois or Waldensians, mentioned in 5.1.141, though the sarcastic mention of psalm-singing and a claim to stricter holiness indicate Protestantism generally.

81 *if we fail*: perhaps a reminiscence of Lady Macbeth's 'We fail' speech, Shakespeare, *Macbeth*, 1.7.59–61.

86 *ANTHEM*: Sir Edward Walpole, a fine musician whose forte was 'pathetic melancholy' offered to produce music for this anthem and the orphans' song in 2.1; Walpole probably conceived of the 'chant' as more like modern singing. See *Correspondence*, xxxvi. 53.

103 *art thou then to learn*: have you not yet learnt.

108 *pale*: protected or restricted space.

116 *Tobit's guardian spirit*: 'Alluding to a picture of Salvator Rosa, in which the story is thus told' [Walpole's note in editions from 1770 onwards]. In common with many Italian artists, Rosa (1615–73) painted the subject more than once, but Walpole probably alludes to 'Landscape with Tobias and the Angel', dated 1660–73, now in the National Gallery in London. It was owned by the Hon. James Ansell, and was sold in April 1773. The story, in the apocryphal Book of Tobit, 5 and 6, relates how the angel Raphael protected Tobias on his journey to recover his father's fortune and preserved him from the evil spirits which beset his wife. See also *The Book of the Words of Tobit*, with introductory essay by E. H. Short (London, 1927).

142 *desolate!*: alone and friendless.

144 *spoilers*: a spoiler is 'a robber; a plunderer; a pillager' (SJ).

154 *how . . . offended?*: compare the words of Cariola and Bosola in John Webster, *The Duchess of Malfi*, 4.2.238 and 249.

160 *furies*: deities of vengeance in Greek mythology, present in tragic treatments of the Orestes story such as Aeschylus' *Eumenides*.

177 *ruder*: rougher; harsher.

182 *luxury*: luxuriousness or voluptuousness (though the modern sense is perhaps also in play).

189 *siren*: in Greek mythology, 'a goddess who enticed men by singing, and

devoured them'; figuratively, 'any mischievous enticer' (SJ). Here used adjectivally to mean 'alluring, irresistibly tempting'.

192 *virgin veil*: nun's veil.

204 *festival*: feast-day.

219 *think him over*: consider him.

261 *Recall*: playing on the two senses, 'summon' and 'remember'.

264 *little imp of darkness!*: little devil or servant of Satan.

265 *to gird*: 'to reproach; to gibe' (SJ).

267 *medley*: mixture of unlike elements.

269 *charm*: magic spell.

273–4 *Consummate . . . coolness*: bring to completion the ceremonial display of horror with dreadful self-control.

290 *transport*: 'rapture; ecstasy' (SJ).

coinage: fraudulent invention.

311 *errant*: straying from the truth; perhaps also with an echo of 'arrant': downright or notorious.

337 *Forbear*: possibly an unconscious pun, since although Adeliza means 'refrain', Edmund is her 'forebear' or father.

341 *first*: best; finest.

350 *her charities circumscribe her wishes*: her charitable donations prevent her from doing all that she wishes (for Adeliza).

364–5 *Better | Profit of that behest*: you would do better to take advantage of that instruction.

5.1 S.D. *[The garden]*: copy-text reads *The scene continues*, that is, it is as in 3.1.

6 *th'impure suggestion*: insinuation or hint of an evil idea.

13–14 *envenomed robe . . . revenged*: alluding to the story in Greek mythology of Medea's destruction of Jason's new wife Glauce through a magic cloak which burned her; a similar story is told of Deianeira and Heracles and treated in Sophocles' *Trachiniae*.

17 *frock*: long loose-sleeved gown worn by monks.

18 *lillied*: 'embellished with lillies' (SJ, citing John Milton's *Arcades*); here alluding to the fleur-de-lis, heraldic emblem of French royalty.

19 *poor friar's knife*: 'Alluding to the assassinations of Henry III. and IV.' [Walpole's note in editions from 1770 onwards]. Henry III (1551–89) was assassinated by the Dominican Jacques Clement on 1 August 1589; Henry IV (1553–1610) was assassinated by François Ravaillac, a religious fanatic who had been refused entry to several orders, on 14 May 1610. These references are appropriately placed in the future tense in Benedict's speech, so that his prediction can be seen to have been fulfilled.

21 *scant*: stint; limit.

25 *naughty*: evil. The sense is stronger in the eighteenth century, even if already slightly comic. By 'naughty bev'rage' the porter probably means a drug or potion rather than alcohol.

27 *but now*: even now; just now.

30–1 *holy wit . . . waves of the ocean*: a mingled reminiscence of the soldier Marcellus prompting the scholar Horatio to speak to the ghost of Hamlet's father (Shakespeare, *Hamlet*, 1.1.43) and the popular superstition that ghosts could be laid in the Red Sea, to which Walpole alludes in later letters (*Correspondence*, xxxi. 319; xi. 230). It is also mentioned by Joseph Addison and Samuel Johnson; see Johnson's *A Journey to the Western Islands of Scotland* (1775), ed. J. D. Fleeman (Oxford, 1985), 15 and 162, note. Its origin lies in the biblical story of the destruction of Pharaoh and his army (Exod. 14), perhaps mediated through liturgical rites of exorcism (Summers, 301).

38–9 *those are paid | For being saints*: some people who are paid to behave in a supposedly saintly fashion. The sarcasm is an insult to Benedict.

41 *Judgments*: divine vengeance.

44 *clerks*: clerics; clergymen.

50 *worship*: honour; respect.

41–61 *Judgments already . . . gossiping morality?*: these speeches are enclosed in quotation marks in all editions, presumably for the reason cited in the note to 2.1.264 above.

73 *moping air*: melancholy atmosphere. Walpole may be remembering Milton, *Paradise Lost*, xi. 485: 'Daemoniack Phrenzie, moping Melancholie | And Moon-struck madness'. The phrase also recalls Peter's words to Florian at 1.1.73.

80 *suit*: courtship; petition (to consummate the marriage).

86 *chaplet*: 'a string of beads used in the Romish church for keeping an account of the number rehearsed of pater nosters and ave marias' (SJ).

89–90 *cricket . . . ominously*: the chirping of the cricket was supposed to be a bad omen, though as with the cry of the owl in *De Monfort*, 4.1.32, it can also be considered quite neutrally; here Florian is mocking the porter's superstitions, as he did in 1.1.85. See also Lady Macbeth in Shakespeare, *Macbeth*, 2.2.15: 'I heard the owl scream and the crickets cry', and Delio in Webster, *Duchess of Malfi*, 2.2.74–7: 'The throwing down salt . . . Or singing of a cricket, are of power | To daunt the whole man in us.'

94 *sixteen years*: sixteen years ago.

104 *favour*: look; expression.

108 *Delphic god*: Apollo, presiding deity of the oracle at Delphi near Mount Parnassus; prophecies and answers to questions were traditionally delivered in ambiguous and obscure terms.

115 *pity thee!*: inspire you with pity.

119 *mintage*: production of coins, here with the sense of 'fraudulent invention' underlying 'coin' in the next line.

129 *interludes*: short dramatic representations between acts of a play; Florian accuses the church, once again, of imposing on the credulous by well-rehearsed but empty display.

131 *Th'enlightened age*: Florian uses this phrase to indicate the emerging Reformation, the religious movement which sought to end what it perceived as superstitious practices and abuses of power in the Roman Catholic Church. The phrase also has a distinct resonance for Walpole's period: the Enlightenment was a contemporary philosophical movement, active particularly in France and Scotland, which stressed the 'light' of reason and the empirical sciences of nature against what it saw as the superstitious dogma and metaphyscial fictions of the church. Walpole implicitly links the Reformation with the Enlightenment.

137–8 *Pagan chivalry . . . rising glories*: Benedict responds by casting the argument back to the days of the early church, when 'the Pagan chivalry' or Roman armies persecuted the first Christians.

141 *illumined*: enlightened (ironically, to Benedict's mind).

Vaudois: modern name for the Waldensians, a reformist Christian sect originally founded by Peter Waldo of Lyon, southern France, in 1170. They were much persecuted, and on supporting the Reformation were massacred in Provence in 1545. A second massacre prompted a sonnet by John Milton. Walpole refers to the persecution in a letter to Lady Ossory, 10 September 1792; *Correspondence*, xxxiv. 161.

146 *conscientious*: 'regulated by conscience' (SJ); willing to suffer martyrdom for firmly held beliefs.

150 *tent*: 'To search as with a medical tent' (SJ, who further defines 'tent' as 'A roll of lint put into a sore'. Johnson cites Hamlet's 'I'll tent him to the quick', Shakespeare, *Hamlet*, 2.2.599).

162 *shoot the gulf*: the phrase means 'cross the abyss' but is often figurative; 'gulf' in Shakespeare always appears as a threatening chasm, and for the Countess it probably has connotations of hell.

176 *anticipate*: arrive before (my appointment).

178 *distract*: disturbed; deranged.

202 *too much for art*: too intense to be feigned.

208 *distraction*: 'madness; frantickness; loss of the wits' (SJ).

220 *distracted*: deranged; mad.

221 *Tremendous innuendoes!*: dreadful implications or inferences.

225 *Sometimes an angel*: Sometimes, like an angel . . . .

226 *whirl the orbs*: fly round the planets.

227 *array*: dress. The sense is, 'I am clothed with'.

228 *suggest*: hint at; place in mind as a possible action.

233 *bias*: the weight which controls the course of a bowl.

S.D. *[which he obeys]*: quite how far Peter 'retires' is open to question, since it does not appear to imply a formal exit (in 1.1 and subsequently characters 'withdraw' but do not leave the stage). He is not later called for specifically, though he might come forward at the entrance of Florian, Benedict, and the Attendants later in the scene. He presumably does not overhear the Countess's revelations.

241 *thy profession*: what you profess loyalty to.

252 *Gownmen*: civilians, as opposed to soldiers. A gownman is 'A man devoted to the acts of peace; one whose proper habit is a gown' (SJ).

272 *casket*: perhaps an awkward prop for the Countess suddenly to discover that she has about her, given the state in which she enters; but she can hardly get it from anywhere else on stage. It might be of use to indicate the desperateness with which she clings to her plan in the midst of derangement.

305 *Distinctions horrible*: degrees of blood-relationship kept separate by the taboo of incest.

318 *Incest! good heavens!*: a stronger imprecation then than now. Compare Tom Jones's outburst when he is told (inaccurately) that he has slept with his mother: Henry Fielding, *Tom Jones* (1749), ed. R. C. P. Mutter (Harmondsworth, 1981), 815: 'O good Heavens! Incest—with a mother!'

319 *devoted victim!*: predestined or chosen victim for sacrifice. The sense of 'emotionally entwined' may still be in play in 'devoted'.

334 *starts*: makes a sudden movement of surprise or horror.

351 S.D. *[After a pause]*: Walpole indicates this by indenting the Countess's speech at this point, and a more controlled tone is required for the final confession.

luxurious: 'Voluptuous: enslaved to pleasure' (SJ).

381 *distempered*: diseased; mixed from improper mixture.

385 *dare not succour either*: (I) dare not help either (Adeliza or the Countess). Edmund feels that touching either woman is now forbidden.

386 *frame some legend*: invent some fiction.

387 S.D. *[Some . . .] bear off Adeliza*: Not all the attendants can leave here, since someone must be left for Edmund to command to 'Bear away | That hateful monk' at 5.1.400–1.

390 *Who . . . Myself*: the exchange is reminiscent of Shakespeare, *Othello*, 5.2.124–5.

391 *gulf*: see note to 5.1.162.

395 *'tis accomplished!*: it is fulfilled or completed. The Countess perhaps echoes Christ's dying words on the cross: 'It is finished' (John 20: 30).

398 *I have no wife*: an echo of Shakespeare, *Othello*, 5.2.106: 'What wife? I ha' no wife'.

402 *Remember me!*: the exit-line also of Hamlet's father's ghost in Shakespeare, *Hamlet*, 1.5.91.

S.D. *[Exit . . . Attendants]*: alternatively, Peter, if still on stage, might be an appropriate guard. Clearly no one must be left on stage except Edmund, Florian, and the dead Countess.

404 *burn*: passionately desire.

420 S.D. *[Curtain falls]*: Walpole marks no exeunt, supplying only 'FINIS' ('The End') after Edmund's final speech. Edmund's words seem to imply that he and Florian leave the stage, which would leave the 'mysterious mother' in final possession of the stage and the spectator's viewpoint; but in the absence of a definite S.D. we have preferred to imagine a final tableau on which the curtain falls, in line with the common theatrical practice which most of the other plays in this volume also follow.

Epilogue Written in 1768, as it appears from the letter cited in the next note. Not printed in any edition of the play before it was included, with the Prologue, amongst other verses in *The Works of Horatio Walpole*, 5 vols. (1798), iv. 397–8, from which it is printed here.

Mrs Clive: Catherine ('Kitty') Clive (1711–85) was a popular singer and actress, especially in broad comic roles, and was well known as a performer of prologues and epilogues. She retired in 1769 after forty years on the stage, mostly at Drury Lane; Walpole, who was a close friend, wrote a somewhat more sober epilogue for her to speak on that occasion, also included in his 1798 *Works* (iv. 399–400). Walpole gave her the use of a small house near his own at Strawberry Hill. The Epilogue takes account of her notorious powerful temper as well as her good humour. 'I have written an epilogue *in character* for the Clive, which she would speak admirably—but I am not so sure that she would like to speak it' (letter to George Montagu, 15 April 1768; *Correspondence*, x. 260). Tragedies, however dismal, were often followed by epilogues in a much lighter vein, even to the extent of appearing to mock tragic pieties, as in this case. The most famous (or notorious) example of this practice in the eighteenth century was Eustace Budgell's surprisingly skittish epilogue to Ambrose Philips's *The Distrest Mother* (1712), which Walpole saw in 1735 and disliked (*Correspondence*, xiii. 75). In the brief moment when Walpole considered actual stage performance of his play, his favoured actress for the title role was not Clive but Hannah Pritchard (1711–68), like Clive a comic actress, but also known for her portrayal of strong female roles in tragedy, including Lady Macbeth, Hamlet's mother, and the title character in Samuel Johnson's exotic tragedy *Irene* (1749).

1 *Gothic fancies*: Walpole's pioneering Gothic novel *The Castle of Otranto* (1764) had been a huge success. As with his tragedy, it was an attempt to render an established form more interesting by creating an imagined past where extreme crimes and sexual passions were played out in ruinous buildings against a dark, foreboding landscape.

5–6 *though mine . . . the epilogue*: Mrs Clive is made to claim that the comic style of epilogue, of which she was a noted performer, is the most fashionable and therefore better than a recital of pieties by the author's 'nun' (Adeliza).

10 *green-room*: room behind or to the side of the stage to accommodate performers before and after a performance.

11 *Heroes . . . half-laced*: actors and actresses half-dressed in costumes representing mythological or legendary figures.

24 *Parnassus . . . Strawb'rry hill*: Mount Parnassus, the conventional home of the Muses; Strawberry Hill, Walpole's Gothicized house in Twickenham, where *The Mysterious Mother* was finished and printed.

25 *hum*: applaud. 'Approbation was commonly expressed in publick assemblies by a hum, about a century ago' (SJ).

29 *I'll be kissed*: modelled on the formula 'I'll be damned' but rendered more apt to Mrs Clive's stage persona.

30 *methodist*: follower of evangelistic movement begun by John and Charles Wesley and George Whitfield; along with many other observers, Walpole characterized their claims to strictness of life and special piety as a form of religious extremism, if not hypocrisy.

31–42 *Saints . . . throne*: the second half of the Epilogue (originally marked by an extra space before 'Saints') is different in tone, and offers a more serious assault on forms of religious sectarianism. Walpole argues that only in lawless or vicious times is there any profit in pretending to special piety or virtue, and he imagines several categories on both Catholic and Dissenting wings of the Christian religion: 'Saints' (those claiming, like seventeenth-century Puritans, an especial holiness of life); 'sectaries' (members of religious sects, especially Puritan ones during the English Civil War); 'canting confessor' (a priest who receives a penitent's confession and may determine penance or grant absolution—for Walpole always a byword for hypocritical and corrupt power); 'flaming bigot' (religious zealot); 'grim enthusiasts' (humourless fanatics). The compliment to George III in the final line indicates that such false and

329

self-interested extremes of religious fervour cannot flourish under a benign and virtuous monarch.

37 *flights*: hasty escapes.

deplore: lament, bewail.

Postscript 5 *terror and pity*: the two principal attributes of tragedy according to Aristotle's *Poetics* (ch. xiv). The *Poetics* was the foundational theoretical statement which underlay all critical writing to the mid-eighteenth century.

6 *scene*: see note to Prologue, 9.

9 *revolution*: complete or violent change.

19 *Oedipus*: see note to Prologue, ll. 28–9.

22 *Orestes*: see note to Prologue, l. 27.

26 *catastrophe*: in dramatic theory, 'the change or revolution which produces the conclusion or final event of a dramatick piece' (SJ).

31 *Archbishop Tillotson*: John Tillotson (1630–94), archibishop of Canterbury (from 1691) and a popular preacher.

50 *queen of Navarre*: Marguerite de Navarre (1492–1549), a free-thinking and voluminous writer; Walpole correctly cites the 'Trentiesme Nouvelle' from the unfinished cycle of tales, *L'Heptaméron* (first printed 1558); the friend who pointed out the source was John Chute (*Correspondence*, xxxix. 102).

54 *King William*: William III (1650–1702), king of England 1689–1702.

55 *the Reformation*: see note to 5.1.131.

56 *Louis XII*: Louis XII (1462–1515), king of France 1499–1515.

57 *Languedoc*: mountainous area of southern France, a little north of Narbonne.

59 *canvas*: picture; scenario.

71–2 *effectuating . . . stage*: securing her acceptance as a fit subject for representation on the stage.

76 *interesting*: capable of arousing compassionate interest

80 *imagination*: mental image or idea

85 *enthusiasm*: see note to 2.1.408

100 *criminal*: guilty; sinful. By the phrase as a whole Walpole indicates the female part of the audience.

106 *'Lutes . . . amber'*; Belvidera utters this line in Thomas Otway's *Venice Preserv'd, or, A Plot Discover'd*, 5.2.243 (Malcolm Kelsall, ed. 1969).

100 *distempers*: deranged mental states.

127 *three unities*: the unities of time, place, and action, loosely derived from Aristotle's *Poetics* and much elaborated in the dramatic theory of

seventeenth-century French writers such as Nicholas Boileau (*Art Poétique*, 1674). These 'rules' were designed to make the action of plays conform to the events they represented: the time of performance should correspond to the length of time represented by the events of the play; place should not vary; and there should be only one, main action. Walpole argues that his play conforms to these rules, but at the same time he wishes to minimize their importance and stress his freedom from crippling French conventions.

147 *manners*: social behaviour.

153–5 *I have chalked out . . . . more genius than I possess*: for this future history see Bertrand Evans, *Gothic Drama from Walpole to Shelley* (Berkeley and Los Angeles, 1947) and Jeffrey N. Cox, *In the Shadows of Romance: Romantic Tragic Drama in Germany, England, and France* (Athens, Oh., 1989).

165 *Hottentot*: belonging to a South African race, a byword in the eighteenth century for savagery and lack of culture.

166 *tragicomedies*: dramas of mixed tragic and comic elements, disliked by many critics for their lack of clear generic focus, but popular in the late seventeenth-century theatre. One such tragicomedy, however, probably provided Walpole with inspiration: John Dryden's *The Spanish Fryar* (1681) contains a monstrously hypocritical and corrupt friar, Father Dominic, whose canting machinations may have fed into Walpole's Benedict.

169 *Dryden . . . Fenton*: in this paragraph Walpole sketches a kind of tradition of high tragedy leading up to his own work, emphasizing boldness, pathos, and strong female roles. John Dryden (1631–1700) wrote several rhymed heroic plays in a vein of high, passionate utterance; Walpole particularly admired his *All for Love* (1677), a neo-classical reworking of Shakespeare's *Antony and Cleopatra*, and *Don Sebastian* (1689), which deals with incest. Dryden was also an eminent critic and his discussion of the relative merits of French and English drama in *Of Dramatick Poesie* (1668) was widely influential. Thomas Otway (1652–85) was the author of three highly respected tragedies, from one of which, *Venice Preserv'd*, Walpole quotes earlier in the Postscript; he may also have derived material from *Don Carlos* (1676), which deals with incest, and *The Orphan* (1680), which has a prominent female role. Nicholas Rowe (1674–1718) was best known for what he called 'She-Tragedies', exploring the passions of penitent women; *The Fair Penitent* (1703) and *Jane Shore* (1714) were still being acted at the end of the eighteenth century, each providing prominent roles for Sarah Siddons (Joanna Baillie's Jane De Monfort). Walpole admired both plays hugely, rating *Jane Shore* the best English play after Shakespeare. Joseph Addison (1672–1719) produced one hugely successful tragedy (*Cato*, 1713), described by Samuel Johnson as 'rather a poem in dialogue than a drama' because of its stately

discussion of philosophical and political positions; it adhered to the unities fairly strictly and Walpole referred to it elsewhere as 'a dull tragedy' (*Correspondence*, xxxiv. 386). Thomas Southerne (1649–1746) had two outstanding successes with the tragedies *The Fatal Marriage* (1694) and *Oroonoko* (1695); the former, which was revived by the actor-manager David Garrick in 1757, was in keeping with Walpole's liking for pathetic female roles (Sarah Siddons again played the female lead in later productions). William Congreve (1670–1729) was best known for witty comedies of manners, but his one tragedy, *The Mourning Bride* (1697) was a popular success; Kitty Clive took one of her few tragic roles in this play. Nathaniel Lee (1653?-92) collaborated with Dryden on a version of *Oedipus* (1679) and on his own account wrote several tragedies of an extravagant and passionate nature before his sanity gave way. Edward Young (1683–1765) was better known as a poet, but his tragedy *The Revenge* (1721) was moderately successful. John Hughes (1677–1720) may have collaborated with Addison on *Cato*; his exotic tragedy *The Siege of Damascus* (1720) continued to be produced through the century, and Walpole thought it 'very pure' (*Correspondence*, xli. 296). Elijah Fenton (1683–1730) produced one tragedy, *Mariamne* (1723), apparently with some help from Southerne. It was initially immensely successful, though Johnson later commented on Fenton's over-regular metre, and it did not hold the stage despite a revival in 1758. The other plays listed here were nearly all standard repertory pieces until the late eighteenth century, with the works by Otway, Rowe, Southerne, and Congreve especially popular; the three least revived were the 'incest' plays, *Oedipus*, *Don Sebastian*, and *Don Carlos*, a fact which Walpole may have noted. Critical biographies of Dryden, Otway, Rowe, Addison, Congreve, Young, Hughes, and Fenton were included in Johnson's *Lives of the English Poets* (1779–81); his comments on their dramas offer an alternative view of their standing in the latter half of the eighteenth century. Walpole's own later thoughts on these dramatists are set forth in three letters of February 1775 to the dramatist Robert Jephson, who in 1781 produced a stage version of Walpole's novel *The Castle of Otranto* under the title *The Count of Narbonne*—presumably in homage to Walpole's own play; *Correspondence*, xli. 286–98.

Wat Tyler

The main source of historical information for these notes is R. B. Dobson's commentary and anthology of sources, *The Peasants' Revolt of 1381* (2nd edn.: Basingstoke, 1983).

Wat Tyler: in *1837*, subtitled 'A Drama', in *1817* 'A Dramatic Poem'.

Preface From *The Poetical Works of Robert Southey Collected by Himself in Ten Volumes, Vol. II* (1837).

3 *letter*: Southey's *A Letter to William Smith, Esq. M. P.* (1817).

7 *Beza*: Theodore de Beze, a sixteenth-century French Calvinist poet, dramatist, and biblical commentator, one of whose most influential works was a set of meditations on the penitential psalms (1581). The reference here is to his conversion from Catholicism, in 1548.

10 *St Augustine*: 354–430. Converted to Christianity in 386, after a life he represents in his *Confessions* as dissolute, he became the bishop of Hippo, in North Africa. The main reference here is to his earlier espousal, and later vehement denunciation, of the doctrine of the Manichees, a belief in the essential and irreconcilable separateness of good and evil.

21–3 *Quicunque . . . legerit*: 'St Augustine' (Southey's note). This is from Augustine's *Retractions* (*Retractationum libri duo*, prologue, 3), a systematic review and correction of 'errors' in his work, written at the end of his life, though later presented, by Erasmus among others, as a preface to his writings. 'Let those, therefore, who are going to read this book not imitate me when I err, but rather when I progress toward the better. For, perhaps, one who reads my work in the order in which they were written will find out how I progressed while writing.' (Trans. Sr. Mary Inez Bogan, *The Fathers of the Church*, vol. 60, Washington, 1968.)

28 *not . . . any kind*: this is not entirely true. Changes between the two texts—except for changes in punctuation which do not affect meaning—are marked in the following notes. The punctuation of our text is largely that of *1837*, except in the case of modernization consistent with the rest of the volume, and some instances where the punctuation of *1817* clarifies the sense.

The Characters of the Play Compiled for this edition, not provided in the 1837 edition. Cast lists of the period, like those of most of the other plays in this volume, were organized hierarchically, and with men and women listed separately, women second (as in Hone's 1817 printing). But the more modern convention of a list 'in order of speaking' seems to suit the concerns of this play better.

Wat Tyler, a blacksmith: the historical Wat Tyler is a mysterious figure, whom even contemporary accounts tend to confuse with Jack Straw (see below). He emerged as the spokesman for the rebels, and it was his eloquence which drew him the attention both of chroniclers of the story and of his killers. Southey makes him a blacksmith, rather than the 'tiler' his name suggests (and which Paine, the immediate source of the play, confirms); this links him to a kind of work of growing importance in early industrial England but still given a sentimental sheen by its rural roots. It also allows him access to theatrically spectacular weaponry.

333

Hob Carter: an invented character. Like the equally fictitious Tom Miller, and the real Wat Tyler, his second name is an indication of his profession— the driver of a cart transporting goods to and from market—and so helps to place the character as representing the range of artisanal (not strictly speaking peasant) occupations involved in the rebellion. Hob is a country diminutive of Robert or Robin, and as such can be used as a derogatory term for 'rustic', or even (as in 'hobgoblin') as a synonym for Robin Goodfellow, or Puck, as a mischievous earth-spirit. But the character here is too vestigially sketched to take on these connotations.

Jack Straw: contemporary accounts (which call him 'Rackstraw') link and confuse Straw and Tyler as rebel leaders. Straw has been immortalized in several London place-names, and early ballad and dramatic versions of the story assign the (fictitious) assault on the daughter to him. But Southey chooses to categorize Straw as the extremist, as opposed to Tyler, the honest family man driven beyond endurance.

John Ball: a priest and preacher, possibly originally based at York, whose egalitarian sermons gained him widespead notoriety from the 1360s onwards. He had been excommunicated by the Pope and imprisoned by the time the rebels rescued him in 1381.

King Richard, the second, of England: king of England from 1377, when he was 10 years of age, until 1399, when he was deposed by the future Henry IV and murdered. Twentieth-century scholars have often presented his reign as a high point of English literary and aesthetic culture, but dramatists, among them Shakespeare in *Richard II*, have tended to focus on the crises of his reign and their implications for the idea of kingship with which he is identified.

Walworth, Lord Mayor of London: the mayor of the 'city', the commercial enclave in London 1380–1 (the post had a one-year tenure). Walworth, a fishmonger by trade, was a powerful and unpopular figure, who was also reputed to run brothels, which the rebels attacked, on the Southwark side of the river.

Sir John Tresilian, Chief Justice of the King's Bench: newly appointed at the time the play is set, he became notorious for his ferocity in punishing those involved in the rebellion, and was himself executed by Bolingbroke and his supporters in 1387.

1.1   S.D. *may-pole*: a high pole crowned with flowers and with ribbons hanging from it, which were held by dancers and interwoven as they moved round the pole. This has become synonymous with 'Merrie Englande' in the context of its banning, with other May Day celebrations, by mid-seventeenth-century Puritans, but May Day is also associated with popular uprising and rebellion, and the maypole may well have some connection here to the Jacobin 'Tree of Liberty' which, adopted from French revolutionary symbolism, figured in demonstrations of the time.

s.d. *[Enter] Alice and Piers[, with other young people and Hob Carter. The young people sing]*: This s.d. is an expansion of Southey's *ALICE, PIERS, etc.* Neither *1817* nor *1837* gives entrances and exits at the beginning and end of scenes; the effect is of a series of tableaux, of stage pictures revealed or concealed by an opening or closing of the curtain.

4 *primrose lifts*: altered in *1837* from *1817*'s 'primrose rears'.

16 s.d. *the door*: in *1817* his door.

20 *morris dance*: a folk-dance, traditionally performed only by men, which takes different forms according to area. It seems to have medieval origins; the name derives from *moresco* or moorish, which suggests a distorted version of Arabic or North African music and dance.

22 *the heyday of the blood*: a reminiscence of Shakespeare, *Hamlet* (3.4.68).

30 *barley-brake*: a traditional game, played in couples; this and its boisterous nature make it, in earlier literature, often the source of a sexual reference, but Southey seems unaware of this.

34 *Up with the lark*: at day-break (when larks wake from their nests in the fields, and fly upward towards the sun).

50 *groats*: a unit of currency common to various European countries, in England at this time equivalent to about 4*d.*, roughly the daily wage of an unskilled labourer.

63 *Richard or a Charles*: the English or French king (Charles VI).

84 *Privileged ruffians!*: ruffians given licence by royal authority to work to their own laws, unaccountable to others. 'Ruffians' is 'r——s' in *1817*.

89 *queen*: Alice has been chosen as the 'May Queen', and crowned with flowers as the presiding figure of the festivities, with power to give rewards and determine the course of games and contests. This marks her as a virtuous, just incipiently sexual figure, 'not yet fifteen' (1.1.137). The collector's attempted investigation as to whether she is 'under age' (1.1.194) and Tyler's sanctioning of her relationship with Piers may seem contradictory in this context, but it is Southey's aim to create an edenic, self-regulating world, where Alice's passage to 'womanhood' is safely pastoral, until the collector disrupts it. Then she is queen of May Day in a different sense, as the unwitting instigator of the kind of proletarian and peasant uprising associated with the date in the nineteenth and twentieth century.

91 *simple*: in the non-pejorative sense of modest, artless.

196 s.d. *Alice and her mother enter the shop*: Southey envisages Alice and her mother, who seems to have stayed inside during the beginning of the scene, entering into the back of Tyler's shop, as from the living space behind it, while the main action happens outside, at the front of the stage.

234 *our shepherd*: an echo of Christ as 'the good shepherd' (John 10: 12). *OED* gives its date of first use for a mundane 'spiritual guardian' as 1300.

240 *lewd hand*: 'lewd' here combines the earlier meaning of ignorant or uncouth with the modern sense of 'lecherous'. Southey is tactfully vague as to what the tax collector was actually attempting to do, but accounts contemporary with events, which passed into oral tradition, mention a collector who threatened to examine for himself whether a girl was a virgin or not, and so terrorized families into handing over the tax without question.

245 *contumelies*: expressions of scorn. The word is best known from the 'To be, or not to be' speech in Shakespeare's *Hamlet* (3.1.73), where the context is again a call to action and vengeance—though Hamlet is of course a lot less decisive than Tyler.

256 *Liberty! . . . Justice!*: exclamation marks from *1817*; not in *1837*.

2.1 S.D. *Blackheath*: a large open space on the south side of the River Thames, facing the city of London but outside its jurisdiction.

S.D. *Jack Straw, Tom Miller and their supporters. They sing*: an addition to Southey's S.D., replacing his '*etc.*'.

1–2 *'When Adam . . . gentleman?'*: a proverbial rhyme that predates the action of the play; Southey's quotation marks instate it as a quoted aphorism. It refers to the state of mankind after the fall, when physical labour became a necessity, and many visual depictions of Adam and Eve working exist from the period in which the play is set. John Ball used the rhyme in his sermons; apologists for feudalism claimed that class difference existed as a consequence of the second great transgression in the history of human-kind, when Cain, who laboured on the land, killed his brother Abel. Peasants were descended from Cain, aristocrats from their surviving brother Seth.

30 *called lords*: 'call'd lord' in *1817*.

48 *preach*: 'teach' in *1817*.

52 *mealy-mouthed*: evasive, not speaking directly; a sixteenth-century meta-phor from 'meal', a soft bland mixture based on flour or root vegetables.

57 *career*: 'headlong rush', often used of uncontrolled horses.

65–7 *Woe unto ye . . . poor*: a version of Matt. 19: 21, though the rhetoric is that of Luke 6: 24, and Jesus's attack on the Pharisees in Matt. 23: 13–36.

72 *arraigned the lot*: 'accused the destiny'.

80–1 *argued . . . murmured*: *1817* has rather differently inflected punctu-ation: 'argued thus! | The voice of truth has murmur'd;—Came ye not | As helpless to the world?'

86 *Saw and pronounced that it was very good*: Gen. 1: 31.

88 *sweet breeze*: 'soft breeze' (*1817*).

98 *This is something like a sermon*: this is what a sermon should be.

106 *blood-purpled*: from *1817*; *1837* has 'blood purpled'. Purple is a traditional colour for royalty to wear, deriving from the Roman emperors. Southey's earlier punctuation makes the link between status and violence more forcefully.

112 *Blush . . . humanity*: the phrase seems to be Southey's own, but in both *1817* and *1837* he sets it in inverted commas for emphasis, and to give it (like the 'When Adam delved . . . ' couplet) the feeling of a proverb.

118 *spared*: from *1817*; *1837* has 'spare'.

125 *Be bold—be resolute—be merciful*: an echo of the advice 'Be bloody, bold, and resolute' given by an 'apparition' to the protagonist of Shakespeare's *Macbeth* (4.1.95). The adaptation of the phrase to a more Christian sentiment is significant, and probably designed to be spotted by an audience.

2.2.4 *grant them*: 'yield them' (*1817*).

15 *requires*: comma supplied from *1817*.

18 *divinity about your person*: see Shakespeare's *Hamlet*, 4.5.122. The idea that the king's office was given him by God—and so that it was to God, and not to his subjects, that he was ultimately answerable, and was to that extent divinely protected—is recurrent from the Middle Ages through to the execution of Charles I. Shakespeare explores its implications in his play on the later career and death of Richard II.

2.3 S.D. *Smithfield*: until comparatively recently the main market in the city of London for livestock and meat. The rebels are now at the centre of the city, though the space they occupy could be seen as ominous.

14 *Berwick-upon-Tweed*: Berwick-on-Tweed was in the Middle Ages a much-disputed town on the border between England and Scotland, and as such had an anomalous status. Shortly after the events of this play it was captured by the Scots, but reverted to the English soon after. Southey's pedantry here has an unintentionally comic effect, but the town's transnational and therefore nominally independent position has apparently continued to create problems into the twentieth century. In response to the question 'Is it true that Berwick-upon-Tweed is still at war with the Russians', in the *Guardian* newspaper's 'Notes and Queries' section (27 Aug. 1997), a Mr Tom Seldon of Liverpool answered:

> Berwick was listed as a separate entity on declarations of war and peace treaties. At the outbreak of the Crimean war, Berwick duly appeared as one of the belligerents taking on the Russian Empire, but in the Treaty of Paris, 1856, ending the war, Berwick was left out, hence the continuing state of hostilities. In 1968, however, Berwick decided to end this crippling conflict and signed a peace treaty with the Soviet Union (who gamely went along with the exercise). At the accompanying civic event the mayor of Berwick is reputed to have assured the Soviet ambassador that 'from now on, the Russians can sleep safely in their beds'.

23 S.D. *and their supporters*: an addition, where Southey only has '*etc.*'

31 *the Lord's anointed*: the king, as the recipient of a sanctioned power, was anointed with blessed oils at his coronation. See Macduff's description, in *Macbeth*, of Duncan as 'The Lord's anointed temple'(2.3.67). There is perhaps a more direct Shakespearean reference in *Richard III*, when the title-character uses the phrase of himself (4.4.151).

35–8 *The throne . . . demand justice*: this exchange is metrically awkward, in a way that may have dramatic point; the king's line can only be spoken metrically if 'listen' is elided as 'list'n', and 'petitions' pronounced as three syllables. Tyler's challenge is outside the metrical scheme. *1817* presents the exchange differently, with 'King . . . weak' presented as one line, with a comma after England, and, for emphasis, italicizes the phrases *petitioning for pity* and *demand justice*.

43 *His . . . grievous*: a parodic reversal of Jesus's characterization of himself at Matt. 11: 30.

67 *good*: 'food' in *1817*; probably a misprint, if a natural one given the context.

73–6 *Do you not call . . . offers*: laws to restrict the right of killing animals and birds for food to the owners of the land (the feudal and ecclesiastical lords, originally) were passed in 1389, and not revoked in England until 1831. They were a major spur to revolt and protest both in the time the play is set and at the time of its writing. Indeed, by Southey's time they had been made more punitive, and were more strictly enforced; the punishments included transportation to Australia.

84 *grant you all*: *1837*; *1817* has 'grant all you'.

89 *Your vassalage abolished*: the state of vassalage, the situation by which a peasant's rights were limited by the lord who could command him, was the larger political grievance of the peasants' revolt, and did not long outlast it.

96 S.D. *Curtain falls*: Southey does not supply an 'exeunt' at this point. Given the pictorial tableau-like style of the play the convention used here seems apposite, as elsewhere in this volume.

3.1 S.D. *and others*: another replacement for '*etc.*'. But it is not clear what Southey means here; for example, are Tom and Hob on stage at this point? Perhaps they enter later with the mob, but there are some unspecified supporters on stage, not taking part in the discussion, but there to suggest that Ball's and Piers's debate is not simply a private matter.

1 *to John Ball*: *1817* has 'meeting JOHN BALL'.

12–13 *A true high priest! | Preaching . . . on!*: as *1817*. *1837* has 'priest, . . . on;'.

22 *sable*: black fur, with connotations both of luxury and of sinister darkness.

38 *mangled*: lacerated.

42 *cool deliberate*: from *1817*; *1837* has 'calm deliberate', but the presence of 'calmer' in the next line suggests that this is a mistranscription rather than a revision.

53 *not*: from *1817*. *1837* has 'nor', probably a pedantic correction of the grammar of the sentence, rather than a misprint, but more awkward for a modern reader.

66 *palace of the Gaunt*: John of Gaunt, Duke of Lancaster, was the king's uncle, one of the richest and most powerful men in England and a focus of popular hatred. His palace and estate, the Savoy, occupied most of the land on the northern bank of the Thames, where the Strand now is.

73 *control*: from *1817*; *1837* has 'controul', an archaic spelling.

82 *these presents*: a legal phrase, 'used in a document to denote the document itself', according to *OED*, which gives 1389 as its first usage.

96 *Embodied*: together 'as a body'; a military term.

101 S.D. *Exit Herald*: followed by Southey by an '*etc.*'. Perhaps he imagines some of the mob to disperse at this point, perhaps (though less likely, as nothing of the kind was mentioned earlier) the herald is attended, or perhaps this unhelpful formula has by this stage become automatic to him.

106 *aguish*: literally, suffering from a severe cold; metaphorically, feverish with a sense of sin (perhaps short-lived, as the lines suggest that the first might have given rise to the second). A choice of word with archaic overtones.

111 *ennobled into MAN*: in inverted commas in *1817*; an allusion (though not as direct quotation) to Thomas Paine's *Rights of Man*, the seminal egalitarian text which provided Southey's source and inspiration, and whose publication led to Paine's being outlawed and fleeing to France. Initially welcomed there as a hero, he was then imprisoned by the French for opposing the execution of the king.

135 *weak leech*: incompetent doctor (another archaism, though in Southey's time leeches, bloodsucking aquatic creatures, were still used to drain 'infected' blood from the sick).

146 *And . . . 'scaped*: *1817* has, in place of these lines, 'Fain would I die in peace to hope thee safe. | I shall soon join thee, Tyler!'

148 *word*: 'vows' in *1817*.

151 S.D. *seizes John Ball*: supplied from *1817*.

155 *bell-wether*: the sheep that tends to lead a flock, around whose neck shepherds used to place a bell.

156 *easily*: 'easy' (*1817*).

156 S.D. *leading ... Mob*: *1817* has *They lead off* JOHN BALL—*the tumult increases.*

3.2 S.D. *Westminster Hall*: the change of scene marks the king and his court's return to the palace of Westminster, the chief royal residence and centre of goverment, after their earlier retreat to the more securely fortified Tower of London.

28–32 *That kings ... oppressive*: a passage that shows evidence of Paine's influence, and of the 'pantisocratic' ideas of community that Coleridge and Southey were evolving in 1794, when *Wat Tyler* was written. The reference to 'sacred rights of property' is of course sarcastic.

29 *rank*: *1817* has 'ranks'.

66 *electric*: not a word available to the historical John Ball, as it only came into currency through experiments with magnetics in the early seventeenth century. But in Southey's century, through the interest of men like Benjamin Franklin, electricity became an emblem of progress, of a new awakening in a psychological and physical sense. Southey had experimented with the effect of electric shocks on himself, and considered trying to persuade his rather placid wife Edith to follow his example, in order to liven herself up.

79 *aught*: Southey has 'ought', an archaic expression for 'at all', 'in anything'.

94–9 *you ... gates*: this, the long-established punishment for treason, was still on the statute books in Southey's time. The Treason Trials of 1794 held it as a threat over twelve radicals charged, without foundation, with a conspiracy to assassinate George III.

103 *divulged*: publicized.

104 *torments*: *1817* has 'torment'.

111 *Moloch*: an idol of the Canaanites, to which, according to the Bible, they sacrificed children (Lev. 18: 21).

Appendix

4 *checking*: restraining.

31 *creatures of the court*: those whose fortunes were made by court patronage, and who acted automatically on its behalf.

40 *John ... Runnymede*: the Barons made a series of demands to limit the power of the crown to levy taxes and establish the rule of law for all freemen; the resulting treaty was Magna Carta, signed by King John at Runnymede in 1215.

De Monfort

From Baillie's . . . Plays (1798). The 'Introductory Discourse' occupies the first seventy-two pages of the first volume of *A Series of Plays: In Which it is Attempted to Delineate the Stronger Passions of the Mind* (1798), the edition which is the copy-text for the play itself. The passages reproduced here are taken from pp. 41–3, 58–61, 64–5, and 71.

14 *enlarged*: heightened; intensified.

22 *low degree*: low social rank or class.

94 *limitation of dramatic time*: see note to *The Mysterious Mother*, Postscript, l. 127.

The Characters of the Play The play was first staged in an adapted, cut form at Drury Lane, London, on Tuesday 29 April 1800, with the following cast: De Monfort, John Philip Kemble; Rezenvelt, Montague Talbot; Freberg, William Barrymore; Manuel, John Powell; Jerome, William Dowton; Grimbald, Thomas Caulfield; Jane, Mrs Sarah Siddons; Countess Freberg, Miss Elizabeth Heard; Theresa, Miss Charlotte Tidswell; Abbess, Mrs Anna Maria Crouch. Miss Maria Theresia De Camp and Miss Stephens, '&c' are listed as nuns, and the following are also listed in contemporary sources without assignment to parts: Thomas Cory, John Hayman Packer, Charles Holland, Alexander Archer, Walter Maddocks, John Woodruffe Clarke, Hugh Sparks, Mr Trueman, Mr Surmount, Joshua Bridges Fisher, William Chippendale, and Corbet Ryder. See *LS*, 2267.

De Monfort: Baillie possibly chose the name for its baronial connotations via the Montfort family of French barons. In particular, Simon de Montfort, Earl of Leicester (d. 1265), is often described as harsh, masterful, ambitious, and impatient.

Jerome, De Monfort's old landlord: the landlord with whom he lodged for some time on a previous stay.

Grimbald: in the 1802 edition of *A Series of Plays*, Baillie changed the name to 'Conrad'.

Jacques: simply identified as a 'Servant' in the stage directions to 3.3, but he identifies himself by this name; it may be assumed that the 'Servant' who enters twice in 1.2 is the same character, and the name has been given throughout.

Lay Sister: in the 1802 edition of *A Series of Plays*, Baillie changed the designation of this character in stage directions to 'a young pensioner'. Like Adeliza in *The Mysterious Mother*, she is not a nun or probationer but is placed in the convent for education or safety.

SCENE: a Town in Germany: later identified in the text as Amberg, in Bavaria; it was the site of a battle between the French and the Austrians in 1796.

1.1.17 *inmate*: occupant; guest.

19 *Lib'ral he will*: he will be liberal (generous).

21 *faith*: 'in faith', an oath.

53 *churl*: man of humble birth; rude or niggardly person.

79 *sullenly repels*: the 1799 edition has 'suddenly repels' for the 'sullenly repells' of the copy-text.

80 *not love*: a reminiscence of Shakespeare, *Hamlet*, 3.1.165: 'Love? His affections do not that way tend . . .'.

95 S.D. *behind backs*: behind De Monfort, and unseen by him.

143 *mask*: 'a festive entertainment, in which the company is masked' (SJ).

181–2 *gloom . . . waste*: this passage might have prompted Wordsworth's more famous formulation, 'There are in our existence spots of time. . .', *The Prelude: A Parallel Text*, ed. J. C. Maxwell (Harmondsworth, 1978), 478 (1805–6 text, xi. 258–68).

191 *Franconia*: one of the stem-duchies of medieval Germany, situated along the valley of the Main from the Rhine to Bohemia; bounded on the north by Saxony and Thuringia, and on the south by Swabia and Bavaria.

217 *book-formed*: deriving character or knowledge only from books.

1.2.68 *fulsome*: 'nauseous; offensive' (SJ).

95 *foppery*: folly.

150 *Count Waterlan . . . so named*: there is a discrepancy between Freberg's ignorance of Waterlan and his later knowledge of him in 3.1.124, which Baillie never corrected.

151 *Bâle*: Basel, a town in Switzerland near the French and German borders.

161 *postman's speed*: the speed of a courier sent with an urgent message.

174 *ev'ning glass*: i.e., of alcohol.

181 S.D. *pulls the bell*: i.e., the bell to summon a servant.

199 *conscious*: knowing.

202 *Hate shalt thou have!*: compare Milton's Satan, *Paradise Lost*, i. 107: 'And study of revenge, immortal hate . . .'.

208 *men*: 'men' is the reading of the editions of 1800 and 1802, replacing '——' in the texts of 1798 and 1799.

2.1.36–7 *usual weeds . . . habitual state*: the usual garments of one accustomed to her noble rank.

60 *temper*: temperament; disposition.

79 *guise*: 'external appearance; dress' (SJ).

97 *train*: company.

103 *prove*: test.

115 *May Day queen*: girl crowned for duration of rural May Day festivities (compare note to *Wat Tyler*, 1.1. S.D.).

129–30 *though whimsical . . . fancy owned*: be it as whimsical and strange as was ever admitted by anyone's imagination.

133 *brown*: dark-skinned.

148 *native*: natural.

180 *idle*: frivolous; trifling.

189 *envious shroud*: grudging or malicious covering.

198 *or pain or pleasure*: either pain or pleasure.

208–9 *even to a proverb . . . lovers' faith*: see Morris Palmer Tilley, *A Dictionary of the Proverbs in England in the Sixteenth and Seventeenth Centuries* (Ann Arbor, 1950), L570: 'Lovers' vows are not to be trusted'. The idea is of course a standard one in Shakespearean comedy, in particular *Twelfth Night*, *As You Like It*, and *Love's Labour's Lost*.

209 *I had borne such slight*: I would have quietly endured such an insult.

225 *poised*: weighed.

239 *Roman matron*: married woman responsible for running of household and family matters, of particular prominence in Roman period; Shakespeare's Volumnia, in *Coriolanus*, is the most familiar dramatic exploration of the kind of character De Monfort has in mind.

253 S.D. *the scene closes*: i.e., by the fall of the curtain.

2.2.3 *participation*: sharing.

15 *piteous*: 'compassionate; tender' (SJ).

19 *I had disclosed*: I would have revealed.

25 *rising grove*: growing group of trees, here signifying the younger siblings.

65 *kindred living ties*: the living bonds of family or blood.

67 *conjure*: 'enjoin with the highest solemnity' (SJ). Accented here as often in these plays on the second syllable.

90 *kindred peace*: peaceful life with my family.

100 *Some sprite . . . mates*: some accursed spirit has become an intimate part of you.

110 *reverse*: opposite.

111 *Each 'gainst . . . ready pledge*: each against the other readily issued a challenge (to fight).

168 *light*: alight; fall.

176 S.D. *side scene*: the scenery at the side of the stage space.

198 *heav'n-enduèd*: supplied or equipped by heaven.

209 *closet*: 'small room of privacy and retirement' (SJ).

2.3 In the 1802 edition of *A Series of Plays* Baillie supplied a new version of this scene (renumbered 3.1); it is reproduced as an appendix in the present edition in order to indicate the kind of revisions Baillie made to her play.

1 S.D. *packets*: i.e., of letters.

13 *my cards unwritten*: my visiting or invitation cards have not been prepared.

50 *character*: reputation.

3.1 S.D. *[De Monfort's apartments]*: the scene location is editorial, repeated from 2.2; De Monfort is there seen to exit for Jane's 'closet', which is another possible location for this scene.

16 *love thine enemy*: a fundamental Christian principle, established in the Sermon on the Mount; see Matt. 5: 44 and Luke 6: 27.

19 *'Hold! hold! have mercy'*: a reminiscence of Macbeth's final speech, Shakespeare, *Macbeth*, 5.9.34.

20 *the man . . . my nature*: De Monfort's refusal of reconcilement echoes Satan's, in Milton's *Paradise Lost*, iv. 93–9.

39 *the plant . . . do shrink*: the so-called 'sensitive plant', various species of the genus Mimosa, most commonly Mimosa Pudica. Shelley's poem 'The Sensitive Plant' was written in 1820. De Monfort's physiognomical contortions here echo those of Satan in Milton's *Paradise Lost*, iv. 114–19.

98 *garnish*: embellish, decorate.

109 *short while dead*: recently dead.

126 *spreads the board*: sets the table for a feast.

139 *by times*: betimes; early.

169 *clown . . . mercury*: 'clown' is here 'a country fellow' (SJ); 'Mercury' is in classical mythology the messenger of the Gods, whose speed is enhanced by wings on his helmet and heels; figuratively, any speedy messenger.

210 S.D. *(Carelessly)*: light-heartedly or jokingly; perhaps with a sense that Rezenvelt is deliberately trying to goad De Monfort (which he does).

217 *By the good light*: by the light of heaven (an oath).

3.2 In the 1802 edition of *A Series of Plays* Baillie cut the first portion of this scene, showing only the guests leaving the banquet and beginning with Freberg's 'Alas! my Rezenvelt' speech. It was also renumbered 4.1.

GLEE: piece of music for three or more voices, unaccompanied. 'It anciently signified musick played at feasts' (SJ). No musicians are called for and the glee is presumably sung by some of the guests; over thirty singers are listed as performing in the original production, which had music by Thomas Shaw in this act, and by Michael Kelly in the second and fourth acts (see *LS*, 2267).

4 *glancing*: shining; glinting.

54 *had caressed*: would have treated affectionately.

83 *vain-assuming wealth*: the empty presumptions of the wealthy.

3.3.4 *dainty*: delicious.

6–7 *hemlock . . . deadly night-shade . . . hellebore*: poisonous plants.

8 *mess*: feed.

27 *heaven alone should hear?*: in the 'Introductory Discourse' to *A Series of Plays* (1798, 31), Baillie writes: 'For who hath followed the great man into his secret closet, or stood by the side of his nightly couch, and heard those exclamations of the soul which heaven alone may hear, that the historian should be able to inform us?'; see also Introduction, p. xx.

29 *hold*: keep my peace any longer.

104 *deportment*: behaviour or conduct.

116–17 *proof clear . . . foul charge as this*: drawing on Othello's demand for 'ocular proof' of Desdemona's infidelity; Shakespeare, *Othello*, 3.3.364–446.

127 *short-beechen walk*: pathway with a clipped beech hedge.

150 S.D. *against the scene*: against the scenery representing the wall or door of the interior.

193 *all forms are over*: all social politeness is done with.

217 *crosses it alone*: an ominous reminiscence of Banquo's final journey in Shakespeare, *Macbeth*, 3.3.

231 *Save you*: i.e., God save you.

4.1.1 *How hollow . . . tread*: reminiscences of Macbeth's fears before the murder of Duncan: Shakespeare, *Macbeth*, 2.1.49–60; also Lady Macbeth's wish for suitable darkness, 1.5.49–53. The contrast between De Monfort's fears and Rezenvelt's confidence also matches the contrast between Macbeth's guilty imagination and Duncan's and Banquo's appreciation of the natural scenery around Macbeth's castle (1.6.1–9).

13 *screech-owl's cry*: another ominous reminiscence of Shakespeare, *Macbeth*, 2.2.15: 'I heard the owl scream and the crickets cry'.

15 *instinctive*: instinctively.

35–9 *Oft when a boy . . . converse held*: Rezenvelt's nostalgia appears very similar to the famous 'Boy of Winander' passage from Wordsworth and Coleridge's *Lyrical Ballads* (vol. II, 1800): 'There was a Boy. . .'. Baillie's passage was definitely written before Wordsworth's.

46 *Pegasus*: winged horse in Greek mythology, beloved by the Muses of Mount Helicon.

4.2.23 *dwell!*: 'dwell?' in 1798 edition; 'dwell!' in 1799 edition and subsequently.

51 S.D. *knocking . . . offstage*: another reminiscence of *Macbeth*, after the murder of Duncan: Shakespeare, *Macbeth*, 2.2.55–72 and 2.3.1–19.

87–8 *If . . . I've seen it*: the syntax is awkward but expressive.

4.3.88 *look me*: look at me.

91 S.D. *dashing his head . . . falls upon the floor*: in Christopher Marlowe's *Tamburlaine the Great, Part I*, 5.1.304, Bajazeth 'brains himself' against his cage, as does his wife Zabina (5.1.318); Marlowe, *Doctor Faustus and Other Plays*, ed. David Bevington and Eric Rasmussen (Oxford, 1995), 62–3.

5.1.23 *fact*: deed; crime.

5.2.1–22 *Oh that I had ne'er known . . . Oh would I could*: this speech contains several reminiscences of Claudio's fears of death in Shakespeare, *Measure for Measure*, 3.1.118–32, but unlike Claudio, De Monfort does not lament death.

44 S.D. *accents*: tones of voice.

65 *stay*: support.

lowers: to lower is to 'appear dark, stormy, and gloomy; to be clouded' (SJ).

84–91 *Death's stroke . . . the soul recoils*: further reminiscences of Claudio's fear of death, Shakespeare, *Measure for Measure*, 3.1.118–32; and also of Hamlet's, Shakespeare, *Hamlet*, 3.1.58–90. Now De Monfort does fear death, in the shape of separation from Jane.

109 S.D. *to herself*: inaudibly.

133 *do not offer*: copy-text reads 'do not after', but this was changed in the 1799 edition and subsequent editions to 'do not offer', which is clearly right. 'Offer' here means 'try to effect'.

5.3 In the 1802 edition of *A Series of Plays*, Baillie replaced this with a new scene (numbered 5.5) in which the nuns are replaced by monks; Thomas and Bernard share in the narration of De Monfort's illness and death.

27 *ruddy-tide*: blood (De Monfort is haemorrhaging).

5.4.30 *move*: i.e., move as, in motion as, alive as.

57 *grizzly*: Baillie writes 'grisly' (horrible) which suits the atmosphere, but the context demands 'grizzly' (grey). When the words are spoken, both senses can be in play.

66 S.D. *[covering the bodies]*: someone must cover the bodies again, because they are covered when Jane examines them in the next S.D. Though Bernard's 'draw back' is an indication to the others to move away from the bodies, he might also suitably cover them while speaking these words.

80 *mean*: humble; low-born (not here derogatory).

91 *'The wretched have no friends'!*: the words are Antony's, in John Dryden, *All for Love* (1692), 3.1.83; in *John Dryden: Four Tragedies*, ed. L. A. Beaurline and Fredson Bowers (Chicago, 1967), 237.

92 *sensible*: sympathetic, sensitive.

113 *how died he?*: copy-text reads 'how died?' which leaves the line metrically complete; but the 1799 edition of *A Series of Plays* has 'how died he?' which is the reading of all later editions and seems preferable for sense.

113 S.D. *repressing*: restraining.

141 *pedestal*: in the edition of 1800, Baillie inserted the following note: '*Note.*—The last three lines of the last speech are not intended to give the reader a true character of *De Monfort*, whom I have endeavoured to represent throughout the play as, notwithstanding his other good qualities, proud, suspicious and susceptible of envy, but only to express the partial sentiments of an affectionate sister, naturally more inclined to praise him from the misfortune into which he had fallen.' A further note was added at the very end of the play: '☞ *Since this edition was given to the press, the Tragedy of* DE MONFORT *has been brought out at Drury-Lane theatre, adapted to the stage by Mr.* Kemble. *I am infinitely obliged to that Gentleman for the excellent powers he has exerted, assisted by the incomparable talents of his sister, Mrs.* Siddons, *in endeavouring to obtain for it that publick favour, which I sincerely wish it had been found more worthy of receiving.*'

Lovers' Vows

Preface 4 *Kotzebue's Child of Love*: August Friedrich Ferdinand von Kotzebue, 1761–1819 (the ennobling 'von' was added in 1785). The German play was called *Das Kind der Liebe* (1790). Kotzebue's sentimental melodramas, of which he wrote an enormous number, were very popular with the audiences of revolutionary Europe; eight plays based on his work were performed in the London season of 1798–9 alone. *Menschenhass und Reue* (1789), adapted by Benjamin Thompson as *The Stranger*, opened at Drury Lane on 24 March 1798, providing Sarah Siddons with one of her best roles (she was once again cast opposite her brother John Philip Kemble in the Drury Lane production of 1798: see *LS*, 2053). The play held the stage for much of the nineteenth century.

25 *manager of Covent Garden Theatre*: Thomas Harris, with whom Inchbald had many not altogether amicable dealings; see Cecil Price, 'Thomas Harris and the Covent Garden Theatre', in *The Eighteenth-Century Stage*, ed. Kenneth Richards and Peter Thomson (London, 1972), 105–22.

37 *catastrophe*: see note to *The Mysterious Mother*, Postscript, l. 26.

39 *sanction*: recommendation.

43 *1791*: it had been performed in 1790.

55 *Dramatis Personae*: 'persons of the drama', the list of characters normally given at the start of a printed text.

Prologue *John Taylor, Esq.*: miscellaneous writer, theatre critic, and journalist, 1757–1832; supplied Inchbald with a number of other prologues and epilogues.

Spoken by Mr Murray: Charles Murray, who played Baron Wildenhaim in the original production.

12 *starts a ghost*: the vogue for Gothic plays replete with spectres was just beginning: Matthew Lewis's *The Castle Spectre* (1797) was a recent runaway success at Drury Lane (see further Jeffrey N. Cox (ed.), *Seven Gothic Dramas 1789–1825* (Athens, Oh., 1992)).

16 *rosin*: solid derived from turpentine, used in the theatre for ghostly lighting effects.

19 *Muse*: one of nine goddesses of the arts in Greek mythology; here, figuratively, standing for poetry.

28 *STRANGER*: 'Hamlet' [original note]. See Shakespeare, *Hamlet*, 1.5.165.

The Characters of the Play: The play was first performed at Covent Garden, London, on Thursday 11 October 1798, with the following cast: Baron Wildenhaim, Charles Murray; Count Cassel, Thomas Knight; Anhalt, Henry Erskine Johnston; Frederick, Alexander Pope; Verdun, Joseph Shepherd Munden; Landlord, James Thompson; Cottager, Sparks Powel; Farmer, Thomas David Rees; Countryman, Mr Curties; Agatha, Mrs Elizabeth Johnson; Amelia, Mrs Nanette Johnston; Cottager's Wife, Mrs Mary Ann Davenport; Country Girl, Miss Anna Maria Leserve. See *LS*, 2116. A print of Mrs Johnston as Amelia was published by Vernor and Hood in 1805; it is reproduced in R. W. Chapman's edition of Jane Austen's *Mansfield Park* (3rd edn.: Oxford, 1943), opposite p. 481.

1.1.140–1 *master . . . profession*: Frederick offered himself as an apprentice to a master in an unspecified guild of craftsmen in return for tuition in that craft.

155 *natural*: illegitimate.

239 *Alsace*: region which is now French territory, much disputed between France and Germany over the centuries.

268 *pent-house*: 'A shed hanging out aslope from the main wall' (SJ).

2.1.38 *living*: clergyman's post in a particular parish.

56 S.D. *(addressing . . . Agatha)*: rather than giving the neutral indication '*to*

Agatha' here, Inchbald seems to wish to indicate a stronger level of private speech—perhaps a kind of gossiping which the Cottager is not meant to overhear.

2.2 s.d. *Gentleman in Waiting*: a servant with the duty of personal attendance on the Baron.

5 *ape*: fop; fashion addict.

30 *ask for the ring*: i.e., in the process of conducting the marriage ceremony between the Count and Amelia.

35 *capered*: danced ludicrously.

94 *Colonel*: the precise rankings of baron and count are not easy to establish in this context, but by referring to the Baron as 'Colonel' the Count seems to intend an assertion of his own rank against the Baron's.

97 *Hebe . . . Venus*: Hebe, the handmaiden to the Greek gods, associated with perpetual youth; Venus, Roman goddess of beauty and love.

112 *the whole system is exploded*: the processes of love are treated with contempt. 'System' indicates a kind of artificiality in the Count's notion of love wholly foreign to Amelia's conception of it.

115 *Intrigue*: secret liaison or illicit sexual affair, of a kind often found in the world of restoration comedy—from which the Count seems an old-fashioned refugee in this company.

126 *Alexander*: Alexander III, the Great, king of Macedonia and conqueror of much of the known world, 356–323 BC.

157 *one German woman . . . mother?*: a topical compliment to the then queen of England, Charlotte-Sophia of Mecklenburg-Strelitz.

184 *sensibility*: delicacy of feeling.

190 *interest you in favour of*: make you look favourably on.

3.1.8 s.d. *Halloo*: 'a word of encouragement when dogs are let loose on their game' (SJ), though Frederick uses it in his first speech in 1.1.64.

13 s.d. *Exit Baron looking after the dogs*: i.e., watching them as he goes.

18 *What police is here!*: the Count complains that the forces of law and order have failed to protect him. 'Police' means 'the regulation and government of a city or country, so far as regards the inhabitants' (SJ).

31 *dollar*: 'a Dutch and German coin of different value, from about two shillings and sixpence to four and sixpence' (SJ).

3.2.4 *auriculas*: i.e., Primula Auricula or 'Bear's Ear', an alpine plant naturalized in European gardens from the seventeenth century and a favourite show and breeding plant.

46 *tear them from the root*: uproot those thorns.

83 *dull*: stupid.

93 *resolving a problem*: solving a set mathematical question.

153 *lyre*: stringed instrument of the harp family, associated with classical Greek poets (or 'lyrists').

180 *forkèd mount*: Mount Parnassus, home of the Muses, has two peaks.

187 *gadzooks*: a mild expletive, corrupted from 'God's Hooks' or possibly 'gadso' (penis); here comically archaic.

190 *for why, because*: comically archaic and redundant formulation to introduce the reason for the Baron's return home.

223 *dying speech*: it was the custom (in England) for condemned prisoners to make a speech at the scaffold; printed versions (or fabrications) of such 'Last Dying Speeches' were often hawked at the execution.

302 *comfortable*: sustaining.

4.1.15 *cordial*: 'a medicine that increases the force of the heart, or quickens the circulation' (SJ).

4.2.9 *a hundred female hearts will at least be broken*: the force of 'at least' is probably with 'a hundred' rather than 'broken'.

27–8 *verse . . . true*: playing on the connection between poetry and truth often disputed for comic effect in Shakespeare: see for example *As You Like It*, 3.2.86–390, and *The Winter's Tale*, 4.4.257–82.

49 *Phoebus . . . Hymen*: Phoebus, an epithet of the Greek god Apollo, especially in his role as sun-god; Hymen, Greek god of marriage, more often seen as a son of Apollo by a Muse.

61 *found grace*: found favour (of a sexual kind).

90 *act as*: behave as if.

139 *gallantries*: seductions; love affairs.

218 *content*: happiness; contentment (accented on second syllable).

221 *nice*: 'accurate in judgement to minute exactness; superfluously exact. It is often used to express a culpable delicacy' (SJ).

326 S.D. *The Baron's emotion*: the phrase appears tautologous, but may indicate a specifically theatrical sense of 'emotion', i.e., the 'acting of emotion' through facial expression, gesture, and so on. See George Taylor, '"The Just Delineation of the Passions": Theories of Acting in the Age of Garrick', in *The Eighteenth-Century Stage*, ed. Kenneth Richards and Peter Thomson (London, 1972), 51–72.

5.1.34 *reverence*: 'title of the clergy' (SJ).

128 S.D. *puts it by*: refuses to accept it.

5.2.17 *domestic*: household servant.

56 S.D. *after a pause*: while, presumably, Anhalt considers his own situation as a 'beggar' seeking to marry the noble Amelia.

122 S.D. *upper entrance*: one of the doors in front of the proscenium arch.

135 S.D. *curtain slowly drops*: the reprint of the play in the series *The British Theatre* (xxiii, 1808), which was supervised by Inchbald, has a frontispiece illustrating this scene just before the final 'tableau'; it is reproduced in R. W. Chapman's edition of Jane Austen's *Mansfield Park* (3rd edn.: Oxford, 1943), opposite p. 475.

Epilogue 'The lines between inverted commas are not spoken' (original note); i.e., in performance the Epilogue was cut.

Thomas Palmer, Esq. of the Temple: Thomas Palmer is possibly the son of John Palmer of Bath, a man with theatrical interests in Bath and Bristol; the son entered Trinity College Cambridge in 1793 and went on to train as a lawyer at Lincoln's Inn in 1794; he is not otherwise known to have written anything. The Inner Temple and Middle Temple were Inns of Court, where lawyers trained.

Spoken by Mr Munden: i.e., Joseph Shepherd Munden (1758–1832), in his character as the rhyming butler, Verdun. Munden excelled at broad comic roles, though he was sometimes criticized for caricature. Charles Lamb praised his inventiveness highly; see his 'On the Acting of Munden', in *Lamb as Critic*, ed. Roy Park (London, 1980), 72–4.

6 *stuff*: worthless nonsense.

8 *philosopher's stone*: 'stone dreamed of by alchemists, which, by its touch, converts base metals into gold' (SJ).

9 *Chymists*: alchemists.

15 *Orpheus*: legendary pre-Homeric poet, credited with the power to charm beasts and move trees and rocks by the music of his lyre.

17–18 *Amphion . . . Thebes*: in Greek mythology, Amphion built with his brother Zethus the city of Thebes, using lyre music to charm the stones into place. 'Glebe' land is sometimes technically land belonging to a clergyman but is here used as a poetic term for 'field'.

25 *odds my life!*: mild expletive, corrupted from 'God's my life!'.

36 *curtain lecture*: 'a reproof given by a wife to her husband in bed' (SJ).

54 *pleader*: lawyer pleading a cause in court.

58 *member*: member of parliament (the 'house' of the same line).

59 *prosing*: talking tediously.

63 *Nelson . . . Nile*: Viscount Horatio Nelson (1758–1805); the victory over Napoleon's fleet on the Nile occurred on 1 August 1798 and made Nelson a national hero. The 'piece of prose' is presumably the dispatch which brought news of the victory, though it was also of course much described in the newspapers.

69 *Sir John Warren . . . Brest fleet . . . Old Davy*: Admiral Sir John Borlase Warren, 1753–1822, defeated a French fleet of 5000 men on their way to Ireland in October 1798. Brest was a fortified seaport in north-west

France. 'Old Davy' is a nickname for the Devil, but also has connections with 'Davy Jones's Locker', the ocean floor.

70 *Gazette*: the *London Gazette* was the official government newspaper for the publication of proclamations and announcement of promotions and appointments.

The Two Foscari

Byron appended to the edition of 1821 extracts from *L'Histoire de la République de Venise par P. Daru de L'Académie Française. Tom. II* and from *L'Histoire des Républiques Italiennes du Moyen Age. Par J. C. L. Simonde de Sismondi. Tom. X.* Rather than reprinting these in full, I refer to them in these notes as the major sources of the play, in my own (EB's) translation. Page references in the notes to Daru and Simonde de Sismondi are to this appendix of 1821.

John Julius Norwich's *A History of Venice* (Harmondsworth, 1982) has been used as a source of historical information, and Hugh Honour's *The Companion Guide to Venice* (Collins, 1965) for topographical and architectural facts.

CRITIC: a slightly misquoted line from the burlesque play *The Critic* (1781), by Byron's late friend Richard Brinsley Sheridan (1751–1816). Sheridan's is 'The *father* softens—but the *governor* | Is fix'd!' (*The School for Scandal, and Other Plays*, ed. Michael Cordner (Oxford, 1998), 2.1. 399–400).

The Characters of the Play *Memmo*: this role is expanded from a passing mention in the sources; 'Le doge ayant remarqué parmi les conseillers qui lui portèrent cet ordre, un chef de la quarantie qu'il ne connoissait pas, demanda son nom: "Je suis le fils de Marco Memmo," lui dit le conseiller.—"Ah! ton père était mon ami," lui dit le vieux doge, en soupirant' (Simonde de Sismondi, 323). (The doge having noticed, among the councillors who conveyed that order to him, a chief of the Forty whom he did not recognize, asked his name: "I am the son of Marco Memmo," the councillor told him.—"Ah!—Your father was my friend," the old man replied, sighing. EB.) Byron, in the two scenes he adds, makes the character conformist and careerist. The council, or court, of the Forty (*Quarantia*) dated from the late twelfth century (predating the Ten); it later became solely a judicial body. Francesco Foscari had been President of the Forty himself.

Barbarigo: in the sources a state inquisitor; 'A l'instigation de Loredano, Jérome Barbarigo, inquisiteur d'état, proposa au conseil de dix, au mois d'Octobre 1457, de sommettre Foscari à une nouvelle humiliation . . . Barbarigo demanda qu'on nommât un autre doge' (Simonde de Sismondi, 322). (At the instigation of Loredano, Jerome Barbarigo, a state inquisitor, proposed to the Council of Ten, in October 1457, that Foscari be submitted to a new humiliation . . . Barbarigo asked that another doge be nominated. EB.) Byron develops the (unhistorical) idea of Barbarigo as Loredano's accomplice throughout the play, without making clear the source of Loredano's power over him.

a doctor . . . Signory.: in his own *Dramatis Personae* Byron gives up after *Attendants*, and simply adds *&c. &c.*, a favourite formula of his. Here, the effect of aristocratic insouciance is compounded in the text by a vagueness about the comings and goings of the silent characters. See also notes on those figures as they appear.

WOMAN: like '*MEN*', this is Byron's unconventional label for the convention of gender-classified cast lists. It emphasizes both Marina's sex and her isolation, especially as the non-speaking male roles are listed under 'men' rather than after her name; the inclusion of her silent attendant under modern conventions somewhat occludes Byron's intent.

Marina: Jacopo's wife historically was Lucrezia Contarini; Marina was the name of Francesco's wife, the *Dogaressa*. She is nowhere mentioned in the play, but the historical *Dogaressa* accused the council of mockery in their granting Foscari a state funeral in terms transferred in the final moments of the play to Byron's Marina. The change of name, reversed in Verdi's operatic adaptation *I due Foscari*, may well be prompted by Byron's wish to suggest the sea in connection with the character (in Italian *mare*, and in Latin the name means 'woman of the sea'—for further thoughts on this see Introduction, p. xxix); 'sa veuve, qui de son nom était Marine Nani, déclara qu'elle ne le souffrirait point; qu'on ne devait pas traiter en prince après sa mort celui que vivant on avait dépouillé de la couronne' (Daru, 316). (His widow, whose own name was Marina Nani, said that she would in no way allow it; that he was not to be treated as a prince after his death who, before it, had been stripped of his crown. EB.)

1.1.2 *The Question*: much of the emphasis on torture in accounts of Venetian history derives from propaganda disseminated by Bonaparte to justify the French destruction of the republic in 1797. Daru, Simonde de Sismondi, and Byron continue this emphasis. Historically, Jacopo and the servants found carrying his letters were spared torture at the first trial, though it was inflicted—without any success in forcing a confession—at the second, on the most tenuous of the accusations, the attack on Ermalao Dona, whom Byron, following Daru, calls 'Almoro Donato' (see note at 1.1.304 on Nicolas Erizzo, the man to whom Byron and his sources assign guilt for this crime). This is conflated by Byron into the third and final trial, at which again, historically, no torture was used.

The 'question' was the use of the *strappado*, 'in which' according to the *OED*, 'the victim's hands were tied across his back and secured to a pulley; he was then hoisted from the ground and let down half way with a jerk'. 'Foscari fut remis à la torture, et on lui donna trente tours d'estrapade, pour voir s'il confirmerait ensuite ses dépositions. Quand on le détacha de la corde, on le trouva déchiré par ces horribles secousses' (Simonde de Sismondi, 321). (Foscari was put to the torture, and was given thirty times to the *strappado*, to see if he would finally confirm his depositions. When the rope was taken off, he was found to be torn into horrible blisters. EB.)

15–16 *the letter to the Duke | Of Milan*: 'Jacques Foscari fut accusé, en 1445, d'avoir reçu des présents de quelques princes ou seigneurs étrangers, notamment, disait-on, du duc de Milan, Phillipe Visconti. C'était nonseulement une bassesse, mais une infraction des lois positives de la république . . . Enfin le conseil des dix lui permit de se retirer à Trévise, en lui imposant l'obligation d'y rester sous peine de mort, et de se présenter tous les jours devant le gouverner . . . il fit une lettre pour le nouveau duc de Milan, par laquelle, au nom des bons offices que Sforce avait reçus du chef de la république, il implorait son intervention en faveur d'un innocent . . . Ce fut un nouveau délit dont on eut à punir Jacques Foscari. Réclamer la protection d'un prince étranger était un crime, dans un sujet de la république' (Daru, [305]–307). (Jacopo Foscari was accused, in 1445, of having received presents from certain foreign princes or lords, notably, it was said, the duke of Milan, Phillipo Visconti. This was not simply dishonourable, but against the explicit laws of the republic . . . finally, the council of Ten allowed him to withdraw to Treviso, while imposing on him the obligation of presenting himself every day to the governor . . . He sent a letter to the new duke of Milan, in which, in the name of the good service which Sforza had received from the chief of the republic, he begged for his intervention in favour of an innocent man . . . This was another misdemeanour, for which Jacopo Foscari was to be punished. To seek the protection of a foreign prince was a crime, in a subject of the republic. EB.)

25 *process*: trial, legal process.

38 *The brothers sickened shortly: —he is sovereign*: 'Dans tous ses conseils, dans toutes les affaires, le doge trouvait toujours les Loredans prêts à combattre ses propositions ou ses intérêts. Il lui échappa un jour de dire qu'il ne se croirait réellement prince, que lorsque Pierre Loredan aurait cessé de vivre. Cet amiral mourut quelque temps après d'une incommodité assez prompte qu'on ne put expliquer. Il n'en fallut pas davantage aux malveillants pour insinuer que François Foscari, ayant désiré cette mort, pouvait bien l'avoir hâtée. . . . Ces bruits s'accréditèrent encore lorsqu'on vit aussi périr subitement Marc Loredan, frère de Pierre . . . On écrivait sur la tombe de l'amiral qu'il avait été elevé à la patrie par le poison. . . . Cependant, Jacques Loredan, fils de Pierre, croyait ou feignait de croire avoir à venger les pertes de sa famille' (Daru, 310–11). (In all his counsels, in all his business, the Doge continually found the Loredanos

ready to fight against his recommendations or his interests. One day he let slip that he would never believe himself really the prince, until Piero Loredano no longer lived. The admiral died sometime after, from a rather sudden infirmity that could not be explained. It could not be but that his enemies would insinuate that Francisco Foscari, having desired the death, could well have hastened it. These rumours gained further credit when Marco Loredano, Piero's brother, was seen to perish just as suddenly . . . It was written on his tomb that the admiral had been taken from his country by poison. EB.)

49 *your books of commerce*: 'Dans ses livres de comptes (car il faisait le commerce, comme à cette époque presque tous les patriciens,) il avait inscrit de sa propre main le doge au nombre de ses débiteurs, pour la mort, y était-il dit, de mon père et de mon oncle. De l'autre côté du registre, il avait laissé une page en blanc, pour y faire mention du recouvrement de cette dette' (Daru, 311). (In his account-books—for he was engaged in business, as at that time were almost all the patricians—he had written down, in his own hand, the Doge as one of his debtors, for the death, as he said there, 'of my father and my uncle'. The facing page of the register he had left blank, so that he could record there the repayment of that debt. EB.)

54 S.D. *the Hall of the Council of Ten*: the Council of Ten was established in 1310, ostensibly to protect the Republic from abuses of personal power. Members were elected by the Great Council of Venetian citizens, which could number as many as 2,000, and held office for six months only. Its three chiefs took office in rotation for a month at a time, and had to stay in the palace for that period. They met as a group with the Doge and his six advisers (the Signory), and had equal power with the Senate, an elected group of 120 plus *ex officio* members; but where the Senate dealt with day-to-day business, the Ten dealt on a freer basis with special affairs, and acquired a sinister reputation as a result. The *Sala del Consiglio dei Dieci* (council room of the Ten) is on the third floor of the Doge's palace, the Doge's apartments on the second. One of the rooms on either side of it, the *Sala della Bussola*, from which a door leads directly into the *Sala del Cosiglio*, or (possibly, though less likely) the *Sala della Quattro Porte*, a larger and more general meeting place, is the setting for the first act of the play (see p. xxxvii).

56 S.D. *alone*: here and elsewhere Byron uses the Latin *solus*; we have translated in line with the policy of this series.

67 S.D. *etc.*: what Byron means here in his use of a typical rhetorical tic is by no means clear. No more characters are required on the stage at this point. The phrase seems to belong with *as prisoner*, and so it could mean 'with all that that implies'.

69 *stand reproved*: be blamed.

104 *Even to the goal*: right to the finishing-line.

125 *Thine Adrian sea-breeze*: a sea-breeze from the Adriatic.

128 *Cyclades*: a group of small scattered islands in the Eastern Mediterranean. Venice acquired them as a colony towards the end of the fourteenth century. Jacopo refers to the dry winds blowing across them from the plains of Turkey.

129 *Candiote*: i.e., in Candia, the chief city of Crete, another Mediterranean island over which Venice had ruled since the thirteenth century; it was lost to the Turks in 1669. Candia was formerly a Saracen fortress.

134 *Wring on*: impose more torture (in wringing his limbs).

166 *Piazza*: the Piazza San Marco, the centre of social life in Venice.

188 *decemvirs*: a Latin term, from the words for 'ten' and 'men', originally applied to the group who, in 451 and 450 BC, formulated a code of laws for Rome, adopted here for the Ten of the Venetian republic.

228 S.D. *offstage*: an emendation in line with the editorial policy of this series; Byron, here and four lines later, has *within*, which emphasizes the sense of secrecy, of hidden rooms, which the play creates in its presentation of the architecture of the Doge's palace. See note on *the Hall of the Council of Ten*, 1.1.54.

251 *A leech*: an archaism for doctor, as in *Wat Tyler*, 3.1.135.

255 *familiars*: confidential servants, with a sinister overtone in English usage, through association with witchcraft. The term is biblical; Saul asks the Witch of Endor, 'I pray thee, divine unto me by the familiar spirit . . .' 1 Sam. 28: 8.

268 *hosts*: armies.

279 S.D. *person*: the doctor (or 'leech').

293 *Circumstance*: circumstantial evidence.

298 *thus*: as a consequence.

304 *Nicolas Erizzo*: 'Nicolas Erizzo, homme déjà noté pour un précédent crime, confessa, en mourant, que c'était lui qui avait tué Almoro Donato' (Sismondi, 320). (Niccolo Erizzo, a man already noted for an earlier crime, confessed, on his death-bed, that it was he who had killed Almoro Donato. EB.)

315 *her full career*: a metaphor from horse-riding, where it means a short gallop at full speed.

328 *Go to*: 'leave this'—an archaic and slightly contemptuous phrase.

329 *Infirm of feeling as of purpose*: an echo of Lady Macbeth: 'Infirm of purpose! | Give me the daggers' (Shakespeare, *Macbeth*, 2.2.50–1).

352 *his state*: his rank; though in the more general sense of wealth and social status, as the post of doge was not hereditary.

371 *hold*: grip, but also possibly shelter (as in 'stronghold').

376 *hourly*: lasting an hour.

2.1.3 *overlooked*: 'looked over', rather than 'disregarded', the more usual modern sense of the word.

   4 S.D. *puts his pen to the paper without making a mark*: after *and* Byron's stage direction has *signs the paper*; this has been emended here to clarify the action. The Doge has not dipped his pen deeply enough into the ink well to allow it to make a mark, but as he has not felt able to look at the paper he does not realize this until the senator points it out to him in the next line.

15 *The Turk*: the Sultan Mehmet had taken Constantinople in 1453, thirty years into Foscari's reign. Venice had been seen as a defender of Christendom against the Turk, but in this instance her fleet arrived too late, and it is perfectly possible that the strength of the Turks made it seem wiser to Foscari and his advisers to leave the outcome open for future diplomatic strategy. The historical Jacopo's third and final trial was triggered by his attempt to interest Mehmet in rescuing him from Crete, a fact omitted by Daru and Byron in the interest of weighting sympathy towards him, though Marina later makes a glancing reference to this possibility: see note on *the Ottoman*, 2.1.380.

20–1 *Brescia ... Bergamo*: 'Depuis trente ans, la république n'avait pas déposé les armes. Elle avait acquis les provinces de Brescia, de Bergame, de Crême, et la principauté de Ravenne' (Daru, [305]). (For thirty years, the republic had not put down her arms. She had acquired the provinces of Brescia, of Bergamo, of Crema, and the principality of Ravenna. EB.)

23 *While her sea-sway has not shrunk*: i.e., Venice's control over shipping on the Adriatic has not been adversely affected by Foscari's concentration on land warfare.

54 *'The Bridge of Sighs'*: a secure passage across the canal linking the palace to the prisons, to enable prisoners to be brought secretly to the Council of Ten. Byron had begun canto iv of *Childe Harold's Pilgrimage* (1818) with 'I stood in Venice, on the Bridge of Sighs; | A palace and a prison on each hand', but the presence of the bridge in this play is wildly anachronistic; it wasn't completed until 1614.

58 *sat*: Byron has 'sate', one of his rare archaisms. He uses it again later in this scene, line 205.

74 *Spartans*: the kingdom of Sparta, or Lacedaemon, was famed in ancient Greece for its intense military culture and scorn of individual suffering.
   weep: weep for.

81 *This ducal ring with which I wed the waves*: in Venetian tradition, on Ascension Day (the feast of Christ's rising into heaven, forty days after his resurrection, and so celebrated forty days after Easter), the Doge was rowed out to sea and threw a ring into the Adriatic. It was claimed that

this was a marriage, originally witnessed by Pope Alexander III in 1177, but this seems to be a retrospective fiction to reinterpret an act of propitiation dating from 1000.

109 *With one foot in the grave*: a proverbial phrase for extreme old age, first recorded in *OED* in 1632.

123 *Or were at least in seeming human*: 'or were human at least in appearance'.

126 *You know not what you say*: in the Gospel according to Luke, Jesus says of his persecutors, 'Father, forgive them; for they know not what they do' (Luke 23: 34). Francis can be seen, like God the Father, to sacrifice his only son.

148 *cloke*: a Scots dialect word meaning something between 'claw' and 'clutch', according to *OED*, which gives a first recorded usage in 1785. This gives better sense than 'cloak', which would be a possible reading if one took Byron's 'cloke' to be an archaic spelling.

161 *paladin*: a term from Renaissance chivalric romance for a warrior of Islamic or Asiatic origin.

174 *The deaths of the two sons heaven took from me*: 'si son ambition avait eu pour but l'aggrandissement de sa famille, elle fut cruellement trompée: trois de ses fils moururent dans les huit années qui suivirent son élection' (Sismondi, 318). (If his ambition had had as its aim the aggrandisement of his family, he was cruelly thwarted: three of his sons died in the eight years which followed his election. EB.) Sismondi goes on to call Jacopo 'le quatrième', which suggests that Byron has misread his source at this point.

176 *Is none but guilt so?*: 'are none but the guilty condemned?'

191 S.D. *Enter Loredano: 1821* has '[*To* Loredano, *entering.*]', after 'pleasure!'

223 *were abroad*: were in circulation.

269 *James*: the English equivalent of Jacopo, itself archaic in relation to the current Italian 'Giacomo'.

280 *Inhibited*: prohibited.

294 *The offspring of a noble house*: the historical 'Marina' (actually Lucrezia) was a Contarini, one of the oldest and most important families in Venice, and her marriage to Jacopo was a spectacular public event.

302 *tributaries*: those who play tribute (a payment made in token of subjection).

303 *masked*: the Venetian nobility of Byron's time often wore masks in public, to maintain their anonymity. The custom (which, like many of Marina's references, dates from some time after the setting of the play) has links to the Venetian tradition of carnival, but is cited by her in the context of sinister secrecy.

sbirri: an Italian police officer; a word current in Byron's own time, but anachronistic to the Venice of the play. *OED* records its first usage in an English context as 1668.

313 *proved*: endured.

314 *process*: trial., as in 1.1.25.

349 *original ordinance*: the Doge refers to Gen. 3: 19, 'In the sweat of thy face shalt thou eat bread . . . '.

353 *potter's vessel*: the making and breaking of pots provides a recurrent image in the Bible for the vulnerability of mankind in relation to God. See, for example, Isa. 41: 25, 64: 8, and 30: 14; Ps. 2: 9.

371 *the chart*: the map of Venice's possessions (now and in the past).

380 *the Ottoman*: the Turks, or Mehmet, the Ottoman emperor. See note on *the Turk*, 1.1.15.

393 *Draco's*: Draco was an Athenian law-giver, famous for the strictness of the code he introduced in 621 BC; hence 'draconian', meaning absolutely severe.

405–6 *when | The people swayed by senates*: Foscari argues that the period of republican rule in Carthage and Rome was their 'best', using imperial expansion as his criterion.

407 *oligarchs*: rulers by virtue of their membership of a small group (from the Greek words for 'few' and 'rule').

411 *Without a name*: without a public reputation or status (though the line might, hyperbolically, include the modern implication of complete loss of identity).

420–1 *Had I as many sons | As I have years, I would have given them all*: perhaps an echo of Shakespeare's Volumnia: 'had I a dozen sons, each in my love alike . . . I had rather had eleven die nobly for their country than one voluptuously surfeit out of action' (*Coriolanus*, 1.3.21–5).

424 *On the flood*: at sea.

425 *ostracism*: a ballot, established in ancient Athenian law, whereby citizens could vote on whether an individual who seemed too powerful or dangerous should be sentenced to a short period of banishment.

3.1.28 S.D. *[with a torch and food and water]*: this phrase has been added to Byron's stage direction, on the assumption that the familiar holds the torch referred to later in the dialogue, and then commandeered by Loredano when he dismisses this character along with the two other familiars who arrive with him. Marina could bring a torch with her; but as Jacopo is disturbed by the light and smell this would be less apt. Neither Marina nor Loredano seem to have predicted quite how dark the prison would be.

55 *bituminous*: with the qualities of asphalt, or pitch, thick inflammable strong-smelling substances, and so used to give a long-lasting if limited

light. Milton, whom Byron is probably remembering here, associates it with 'the mouth of Hell' (*Paradise Lost*, xii. 41).

134 *unbelievers*: non-Christians.

136 *remanded*: returned there.

149 *wretched exiles*: Venice's origins lie in the settlement of refugees from the mainland of northern Italy, fleeing the Huns, invaders from central Asia. Such settlements were initially temporary, but the town grew, and a clash between the Pope and the Byzantine emperor, then nominally at least the ruler of the area, led to communities declaring themselves independent, and in Venice's case appointing a commander who set the foundations for the institution of the doge-ship.

151 *Tartar*: a native of central Asia. Byron uses the term as equivalent to 'Hun', though it was more normally used of a later wave of Asian invaders of Europe, those led by Genghis Khan in the thirteenth century.

salt isles: emphasizes the barrenness and infertility of the original home of those who became 'Venetians'.

154 *ocean-Rome*: 'In Lady Morgan's fearless and excellent work on "Italy", I perceive the expression of "Rome of Ocean" applied to Venice. The same phrase occurs in the "Two Foscari". My publisher can vouch for me that the tragedy was written and sent to England some time before I had seen Lady Morgan's work, which I only received on the 16th of August. I hasten, however, to notice the coincidence, and to yield the originality of the phrase to her who first placed it before the public. I am the more anxious to do this as I am informed (for I have seen but few of the specimens, and those accidentally) that there have been lately brought against me charges of plagiarism' (Byron, *1821*, appendix, 325). Byron then goes on, by way of a defence of himself, to align himself with Shelley and to respond to Southey's attack on them, as part of the so-called 'Satanic School'.

159 *like the Jews from Zion*: Byron is thinking of Ps. 137, the Hebrew hymn of lament for the historical exile in Babylon.

160 *Attila*: the leader of the invasion of Huns into Italy, in the fifth century.

172 *that malady*: 'The calenture' (Byron's footnote.) The calenture was the name given, from the late sixteenth century onwards, to a psychological malady in which a seagoer in the tropics, gazing into the sea, took it to be grassland and leapt into it.

177 *That melody*: 'Alluding to the Swiss air and its effects' (Byron's footnote.) In a journal-style letter written 18–28 September 1816, significantly to Augusta Leigh, the half-sister whose relationship with him was one of the major causes of his exile, Byron reflects on the clear acoustic and nostalgic potential of the Alpine landscape: 'The music of the Cows' bells . . . in the pastures . . . and the Shepherds' shouting to us from crag to

crag & playing on their reeds . . .' (*Letters*, v. 99). Byron used the experiences he described in the letter in *Manfred*, a closet drama with an incestuous relationship at its heart, written at about the same time (1.2.47–56). There the sounds, unlike here, where 'melody' chimes ominously with the earlier 'malady', are at least potentially restorative.

186–7 *'tis like a mother's curse | Upon my soul—the mark is set upon me*: in Byron's *Cain*, first published in the same volume as this play and *Sardanapalus*, Cain is cursed after murdering his brother Abel by his mother Eve; an angel sets a 'mark' on him to prevent anyone killing him, and so to condemn him both to exile and to indefinite life. The second incident has its source in Gen. 4: 15; the first does not.

201–2 *our first | On earth to bear*: 'first' could refer to 'duties', and so 'our' refers to the whole of postlapsarian humanity, for whom the necessity of suffering ('to bear') was the first and defining fact of passage from Eden into the world. If this is Byron's meaning, the expression is uncomfortably compressed. It is less likely, but still possible, that Marina means simply herself and her husband, whose life until these incidents has been privileged, so that this suffering is their 'first'.

221 *That's sudden*: an echo of Shakespeare, *Measure for Measure*: 'He must die tomorrow. | Tomorrow? O, that's sudden!' (2.2.84–5).

248 S.D. *(The third . . . earshot)*: an addition to Byron's S.D. The familiar is needed later in the scene, when Loredano summons him to carry the torch out before them. Here, either he fixes the torch on the wall, or Loredano takes it and holds it himself. He does not want them to overhear the conversation (Marina is too impulsive to bother about this), but he does want them to be within earshot, in case he needs them. Hence 'retire', to just outside the cell, where he may be still visible to the audience.

269 *Her sex's privilege*: to speak her mind; though, condescendingly, at the price of not really being listened to.

275 *Canea*: a name for Crete.

289 *generous*: in addition to the more common modern meaning of 'kindly' or 'charitable', Byron draws on the sense of 'of noble blood', already archaic in his time, though still (then) as Marina goes on to point out, applied to pedigree animals.

292 *few steeds save of bronze*: this is anachronistic; the rich citizens of medieval Venice, then with much more open space and less dependent on canals than it was to become, were famous for their stables and their importation and breeding of horses from the East. But this allows Byron to focus on the bronze horses, of unknown but probably Greek origin, that had stood outside San Marco; they had been impounded by Bonaparte's army in 1798, and taken to Paris, so this line is prophetic of the decline and final defeat that seem to have prompted Byron's interest in Venetian history.

294 *Araby*: Arabia, the source of the most expensive pedigree breeds of horse.

311–12 *A few brief words of truth shame the devil's servants | No less than master*: 'tell the truth and shame the devil' is a British proverbial phrase.

316 *o'er his kind*: over his fellow human beings.

328–9 *to gaze upon the wreck | Which you have made a prince's son*: possibly an echo of Shakespeare, *The Tempest*; 'Weeping again the King my father's wreck' (1.2.393).

332 *sped*: succeeded.

373 *fee*: reward, in a general sense, not just financial.

375 *damps*: gases, usually smelly and/or poisonous.

397 *genial*: 'conducive to growth' (*OED*), but carrying over some sense of conveying a 'genius', a special spirit that Jacopo shares with his native Venice.

400 *Riva di Schiavoni*: the street on which the Doge's palace stands; it runs alongside the water.

4.1.17 *retrench not*: take nothing away from.

22–3 *life for life, the rule | Denounced of retribution from all time*: as in the Old Testament (Lev. 24: 17, Deut. 19: 21); but in the New Testament (Matt. 5: 38–40) Jesus revokes this in the name of forgiveness. Loredano belongs to an earlier dispensation than that which is figured, if impotently, in the Catholic triad of the Foscari and Marina.

34 *Like Barbarossa to the Pope*: in 1177 Pope Alexander III met the Emperor Frederick Barbarossa in Venice, in order to heal the schism in which Barbarossa denied the Pope's legitimacy and sought control of the Lombard states of northern Italy. The result, in which Barbarossa knelt publicly to Alexander, was a triumph for both Venice and the Pope.

52 *sounded*: tested, as in the modern 'sounded out'.

114 *desponding shades*: mournful ghosts.

130 *Auster*: the south wind.

132 *corpse*: Byron has the archaism 'corse'.

Lido: the Lido, now a summer resort, is a long strip of land across the lagoon from Venice, with the Adriatic sea on the other side.

140 *the Gulf*: Byron gives the word a capital letter, most probably to point up that, unlike other, metaphorical, uses of the word in the text, this is literal, a geographical reference to the Adriatic beyond the Lido.

143 *As the Phoenicians did on Jonah*: a storm was sent by God to threaten the merchant ship on which the prophet Jonah was travelling, because he had disobeyed God's command to go to preach in Nineveh. He identifies himself to the sailors, is thrown overboard, swallowed by a large fish, and

eventually cast up unharmed. He goes to Nineveh. Jonah 1:10–2: 10. The biblical source does not identify the sailors by race (they are of many religions) but modern scholars have assumed the officers were Phoenician on the grounds that the Phoenicians controlled many of the Mediterranean shipping routes in biblical times (see W. K. Lowther, *Concise Biblical Commentary* (1952), 604). The Venetians occupied a similarly commanding position.

174 *the worm which ne'er dieth*: from the Gospels, Mark 9: 48, where it is part of a description of hell.

203 *the signory*: the group of six assigned to advise the doge, and, in effect, to supervise him; he could make no effective decisions without them.

215 *stoic*: one of a group of Greek philosophers, of the third century BC, who believed in the value of patient suffering and the denial of pain.

218 *never, never more*: an echo of Lear: 'Thou'lt come no more. | Never, never, never, never, never.' (Shakespeare, *King Lear*, 5.3.283–4).

243 *The body bleeds in presence of the assassin*: a common superstition; see Shakespeare, *Richard III* (1.2.55–9).

246 *fantasy*: Byron had the archaic 'phantasy'.

247 S.D. *Guards*: here, and in the subsequent S.D., *1821* has the less specific '*Attendants*'.

258 *Giunta*: a term, derived from Venetian politics (in Venetian dialect *zonta*), for a specially formed group with extraordinary executive power. Here, a group specially co-opted from the Senate to strengthen the Ten.

265 *leave the rest to me*: another reminiscence of Lady Macbeth: 'Leave all the rest to me' (Shakespeare, *Macbeth*, 1.5.72).

284 *the eternal cure*: death, which settles things for ever.

289 *Carmagnuola*: formerly in the service of the Visconti of Milan, Francesco Bussone Carmagnola was a *condottiere* or highly paid professional soldier, reputedly the best of his time. He switched allegiance to Genoa, and then to Venice, to lead the land wars in Italy which marked Foscari's reign. But when he failed to deliver he was summoned back to Venice by the Ten for an interview with Foscari. Foscari was unavailable, and Carmagnola was diverted on his way out of the palace into the dungeons where he was tortured on suspicion of being still in the pay of the Visconti. Foscari voted against the death penalty, but Carmagnola was still executed.

298 *'There often has been question about you'*: 'An historical fact' (Byron's footnote). But Byron gives no source, either here or in his appendix.

313–16 *The Romans . . . rewards are equal*: the 'mural crown', awarded to the first soldier to scale the wall of an enemy town, was golden; the 'civic crown', awarded for saving a citizen in battle, was of oak leaves.

321 *havoc*: destruction.

327 *depressed*: degraded, excluded from office.

331 *accelerated*: premature.

5.1 S.D. *Attendants*: the plural is Byron's, but only one of these figures is marked in the text as speaking. He seems to have meant that from now on the Doge is never really alone, and becoming more dependent on others. The stage directions indicate this with a vagueness that it would, per- haps, be unrewarding to clarify further.

5 *AN OFFICER ... command?*: the Doge is losing track of events, and has forgotten that he has already sent the officer out to bring the deputation in. This figure is one of the attendants already on stage when the scene starts, and he tries tactfully to explain the situation.

8 *fail in apprehension*: lose (through age) the ability to understand.

30 *apanage*: a French term (Byron has the less usual Anglicized 'appanage') dating from the period of the play's setting, for a province granted to the maintenance of a dependent prince, normally a child. By Byron's time the word could simply mean a financial grant, but possibly the sense of child-like dependence, even the idea of the dependence of the Venice of Byron's time *on* France, marks the choice of word as insulting to the Doge.

43 *instance*: urgent entreaty, insistence.

65 *The Attendants and Officer retire*: an addition to Byron's S.D. As in 3.1, the central characters are never completely alone, however intimate their situation, and 'attendants' have to hover on the margin, in order to be in summons when required.

103 *distracts*: maddens.

136 *A very Ovid in the art of hating*: Publius Ovidius Naso (43 BC–AD 17), a poet of the Rome of Augustus, was infamous in post-classical European culture for his *Ars Amatoria* (The Art of Love), which, together with the rumour of an affair with the emperor's daughter Julia, was, according to legend, the cause of his banishment to Scythia.

137 *although a secondary object*: Barbarigo is saying that he fears he is himself a 'secondary object' of Loredano's plotting, someone less important than the Foscaris (the first 'object'), but still prey to a 'microscopic' project of revenge in being drawn into the plot to be eventually dishonoured.

139 *by way of foil*: as a contrast.

147 *exorbitance of power*: gross excessiveness of the power they have assumed.

156 *the rich man's hell-fire upon your tongue*: in Christ's parable of the rich man (called Dives in the Vulgate Bible) and the poor man, Lazarus, the posi- tions of the two men are reversed after their death, and Dives prays to

Lazarus for water to cool the fires of hell that are on his tongue (Luke 16: 23).

192 *The Adriatic's free to wed another*: Foscari mockingly uses the idea of the Doge's wedding to the sea (see note on *this ducal ring*, 2.1.81) to undercut the idea of succession by characterizing the Adriatic as a suddenly widowed or divorced wife, making her own choices.

194–5 *even to move but slowly must begin | To move betimes*: perhaps a Shakespeare echo; certainly 'betimes' is a favourite Shakespearean word. See *Twelfth Night*, 2.3.2.

197 *garb, Chief of the Forty!*: see note on Memmo under The Characters of the Play.

205 *burden*: *1821* has the archaic 'burthen'.

219–20 *The pillars of stone Dagon's temple on | The Israelite and his Philistine foes*: for the story of Samson's destruction of the Philistine temple see Judg. 16: 23–30.

225 *Malipiero*: doge from 1457 to 1462. 'Les électeurs entrèrent au conclave et nommèrent au dogat Paschal Malipier le 30 Octobre, 1457. La cloche de Saint-Marc, qui annonçait à Vénise son nouveau prince, vint frapper l'oreille de François Foscari; cette fois sa fermeté l'abandonna, il éprouva un tel saisissement, qu'il mourut le lendemain' (Daru, 316). (The electorate went into conclave and nominated Pasquale Malipiero to the dogeship on the 30 October 1457. The bell of San Marco, which used to announce to Venice its new prince, happened to strike the ear of Francisco Foscari; at that point his strength left him, he underwent a seizure such that he was to die the next day. EB.)

232 *Faliero*: Marin Falier (1354–5). The elderly Faliero, the subject of Byron's first tragedy, *Marino Faliero*, engaged in a conspiracy against the state of Venice when the council refused to exact punishment he deemed adequate for a libel a young patrician had issued concerning his marriage to a younger wife. Faliero and the other conspirators were caught and executed, and Faliero's memory solemnly expunged from the list of doges.

241 *the Giant's Stairs*: a monumental flight of stairs in the courtyard of the doge's palace, at the apex of which he was crowned, after a ceremony in St Mark's.

262 *You have reason*: you are right.

275 *but as citizen*: 'but' could bear the force of 'only', or (contradictorily, and I think less likely) take the more modern sense of 'but', and so suggest that leaving 'as citizen' has a value of its own, to counterbalance the loss of sovereignty.

304 *my brain's on fire*: perhaps an echo of Bracchiano's death in Webster's *The White Devil*, 5.3.4.

343 *pretend*: lay claim.

349 *relics*: remains (his body).

350 *wonted pomp*: usual ceremony; not necessarily derogatory.

358 *heirs in sables*: i.e., those who have inherited flaunting their success by wearing the black furs of the animal of that name, as imported at great expense from Siberia.

368 *tablets*: pocket-book. A reminiscence of a less successful revenger, Hamlet, in his case at the beginning of his mission (Shakespeare, *Hamlet*, 1.5.107–8).

369 *has paid me*: ' "*L'ha pagata*." An historical fact. See the History of Venice, by P. Daru, page 411, vol. 2d.' (Byron's footnote, *1821*); 'et en effet, après la perte du doge, il écrivit sur son régistre: il me l'a payée, l'ha pagata' (Daru, 311). (And as a consequence, after the fall of the doge, he wrote in his register 'he has paid it to me'—*l'ha pagata*. EB.)

GLOSSARY

Note: definitions ascribed to '(SJ)' are derived from Samuel Johnson, *A Dictionary of the English Language* (1755), 2 vols.

accoutrements trappings

adamant 'a stone, imagined by writers, of impenetrable hardness' (SJ)

address demeanour; bearing; manner

adieu a final goodbye (French, literally 'to God')

affect pretend

ague fever

alike equally

almoner official who distributes charity

alms charitable donations or gifts

an if

an please if it pleases

anon at once

apprize inform

aspect 'look; air; appearance' (SJ)

aspen quivering

athirst thirsty

attainted convicted

aught anything

augur predict from signs

avaunt begone; 'a word of abhorrence by which any one is driven away' (SJ)

Ave-Mary Ave Maria, a prayer to the Virgin Mary

avouch confess

avow confess

balk block

balm comforting substance

banditti brigands; robbers

bating except; apart from

beadsman 'a man employed in praying, generally for another' (SJ)

beauty-blazing of conspicuous or dazzling beauty or beauties (beautiful women)

beholden indebted; obliged

behoof behalf

behoves befits; suits

belike 'probably; likely; perhaps' (SJ)

beseems suits; befits

beshrew curse

bespeak speak out; address; engage with apology

bestir wake up; exert; rouse

bethink remind; consider

betimes early

bier stretcher, usually for carrying corpse

billet letter; note

blast (n.) windy storm

blast (vb.) horrify; destroy; blight; damn

blasted horrified; destroyed; damned

boon favour; gift

boor peasant; ill-bred person

bootless unprofitable; pointless

boots benefits; profits

burgher citizen

but except; only; just

but now even now; just now

by the light exclamation of surprise or emphasis

cabal (n.) secret committee

cabal (vb.) to conspire by means of such a committee

caitiff villainous

cantoned protected in small area of power or jurisdiction

caress treat fondly; coax with affection

carl man; fellow

cerement waxed shroud for the dead

chafe irritate; make angry; be angry

chaff (n.) discarded exterior of grain; worthless stuff

chaff (vb.) rail at; perhaps a form of 'chafe'

changeling idiot; fool

chaplet wreath of flowers worn as ornament; string of beads used in counting prayers

character reputation; profession

cherubim celestial beings

chidden scolded

churl low-born man

clack chatter loudly or lengthily

clime country

closet 'small room of privacy and retirement' (SJ)

cockatrice mythical reptile supposedly hatched from cock's egg, with ability to kill with its eye

comely attractive

compassing encircling

compassionate (vb.) pity

congress meeting

conjure earnestly or solemnly entreat; beseech

conscious self-aware; guilty; strongly-felt; confident; knowing

contemn treat with disdain

contumacious scornful

contumely insolence

coquette lightly flirtatious woman

cot cottage

countenance facial expression; air; poise

coxcomb a fop; a superficial pretender to knowledge or accomplishments

cozenage deceit; betrayal of trust

cur dog

curdling stiffening with horror

dame lady; wife

darkling in the dark

dastard coward

decemvir one of the group of rulers known in Venice as the Ten

deck decorate; clothe

deem believe; think

demigod semi-divine being

demur object; obstruct

deportment behaviour

destine appoint; allot

destined doomed

diadem crown; 'mark of royalty worn on the head' (SJ)

dirge funeral music or song

discovered made visible by the raising of curtain or parting of scenery

disgusting distasteful

distain sully; dishonour

distemper disease; disorder; improperly balanced mixture

distemperature excess; imbalance

distent distended

distract (adj.) deranged

distracted deranged

doff take off (clothes)

doom fate; sentence

dotard 'a man whose age has impaired his intellects' (SJ)

dower woman's fortune given to husband at marriage

dowered endowed with dowry or fortune

dowry woman's fortune given to husband at marriage

ducat 'coin valued at about nine shillings and sixpence (gold) or four shillings and sixpence (silver)' (SJ)

ductile easily led; malleable

duetto Italian form of duet; musical composition for two parts

dull slow; stupid

durance survival; ability to last

ebon dark

ebriety drunkenness

e'en even

e'er ever

effulgence radiance; clarity

eke also

elixir potion with magical effect

ell 'taken proverbially for a long measure' (SJ); about 45 in.

emoving affecting with emotion

encomium speech of praise

endued supplied, equipped

ensanguined bloody

enthusiasm belief in private favour from or communication with God

envenomed poisoned

epitome condensed summary

equipage furniture; requisites; necessary materials

ere before

errant wandering; sinning

erst formerly

espouse marry

eve evening

ev'n even

execrable accursed; detestable

exorbitance gross excess

expectancy expectation

fain gladly; by desire

faith, in faith, i'faith, 'faith in truth (a mild oath)

falchion 'a short crooked sword' (SJ)

fell (feller, fellest) cruel; savage; bloody

flasket small flask

fond mistaken; foolish; injudicious; deluded

fondling much fondled or caressed

forsooth in truth (a mild oath)

forthwith immediately

frolic high-spirited; sportive

frowardness 'peevishness; perverseness' (SJ)

fulsome gross; nauseating (by excess)

furlough 'a licence given to a soldier to be absent' (SJ)

gadzooks archaic or comic oath, corruption of 'God's hooks'

gait manner of walking

Gallia France

Gallic French

gay sprightly; cheerful

gazette newspaper

genealogic genealogical; pertaining to family history

gewgaw worthless jewel

gibing mocking

girt encircled

Giunta a group of Venetian aristocrats who advised the Ten

glebe ground; field

glee song for two or three voices, usually unaccompanied

goodly handsome

goodman form of polite address, 'generally ironical' (SJ)

go to exclamation of impatience or remonstrance

grange farmhouse

greybeard old man

gripe painful clutch

gulf abyss

gyvèd fettered; shackled

habitude customary state

hair-cloths 'stuff made of hair, very rough and prickly, worn sometimes in mortification' (SJ)

halloo 'a word of encouragement when dogs are let loose on their game' (SJ)

hapless unfortunate

harbinger herald; messenger

hauteur proud or haughty manner

heresy religious opinion contrary to doctrine of the church

heretic one who holds religious opinion contrary to doctrine of the church

hie go

hind peasant

hireling hired man; mercenary

Hock type of wine

Holy See papacy or papal court

horrid 'hideous; dreadful; shocking' (SJ)

host army

how expression of surprise or indignation

humour, out of in a bad mood

huzza utter cries of triumph

hymeneal pertaining to marriage

importune plead urgently

imposture fraudulent deception

imprecation curse

indemnified compensated

ingress entrance

inmate lodger; guest; intimate companion

inquisition church court to detect heresy

inquisitor officer of inquisition; interrogator

irremissible unpardonable

juggle (n.) deceit; trick

juggle (vb.) trick; play

juggler trickster; deceiver

kerchief small scarf

league archaic measure of distance, about 3 miles

leathern made of leather

leech doctor

light alight; fall

liveried dressed in uniform as servant of particular lord

livery distinctive guise; servant's uniform

lo look; see (an interjection calling attention to some new visible object or person)

madding frenzied

mailèd wearing chain-mail armour
mainly strongly
mangled lacerated
mantling frothing; bubbling
marry mild exclamation signifying surprise, indignation, or sarcastic agreement
mass-priest priest ordained for sole purpose of saying mass for the dead in private chapels
massy weighty
matron motherly figure; woman with responsibility for domestic management
maugre in spite of
mayhap perhaps
mead meadow
mechanic worker
meet suitable
methinks it seems to me
mien demeanour; bearing
minion favourite; servant; 'a word of contempt, or of slight and familiar kindness' (SJ)
mintage coined or counterfeited product
miscreant heretic; vile wretch
monitor 'one who warns of faults, or informs of duty' (SJ)
moppet 'fondling name for a girl' (SJ)
motley of various (incongruous) colours
mummery ridiculous ceremony
mummings mumblings; deceitful masquerades
murmur 'utter secret and sullen discontent' (SJ)
myriad ten thousand
native by nature; from birth
nice fastidious; particular; hard to please
nurseling infant
obsequies funeral rites
o'ergilding (overgilding) covering over (as with gold leaf)
o'erstrained (overstrained) exaggerated
o'erwrought overwrought
orison prayer
own confess; admit
pale restricted or protected enclosure
paly pale

parley formal pause in hostilities, to allow negotiation; conversation
patrimony inherited property or endowment
pensioner one whose lodging is paid for by another
pent confined
perfidy treachery
plaint lament
plighted solemnly promised
poltroon coward; scoundrel
portion dowry; woman's fortune given to husband at marriage; share; inheritance
pose puzzle
pother 'bustle; tumult; flutter' (SJ)
practice trick; plot
prate chatter; talk too much.
pray please
prelate high-ranking church official such as archbishop
prevent anticipate
prithee (I) pray thee; please
privity 'private concurrence' (SJ)
progenitor forefather
prognostic prediction; prophecy
project (vb.) scheme; intend; plan.
proscription exile; sentence of death
proxy substitute; stand-in
psha exclamation indicating impatience or contempt
puling whining; whimpering
purlieus outskirts
quondam former
quoth said
raiment clothing
rankling festering; irritating
rankly virulently; grossly
rapine plundering
reck care
recreant cowardly; apostate
Reformation sixteenth-century religious movement culminating in establishment of Protestant churches
relict widow; 'a wife desolate by the death of her husband' (SJ)
relume rekindle; light once more
remit spare
rencounter casual meeting; coincidence
reprobate person hardened in sin

requiem hymn or mass sung on behalf of the dead
respire breathe
Rhenish type of wine
rhino money
rioting luxuriating
riven split
rood cross; **by the rood,** a mild oath
rubric rule of a religious order; 'directions printed in books of law and in prayer books' (SJ)
ruth 'mercy; pity; tenderness' (SJ)
sable black
saint one who claims special holiness of life (perhaps hypocritically)
saucy disrespectful
save except
savour add flavour to
scaffold place of execution
scan view
scant neglect; skimp
scape escape
scathe harm; damage
scene 'the stage; the theatre of dramatick poetry' (SJ)
scoff mock
'sdeath an oath, corrupted from 'God's teeth' or 'God's death'
sectary member of religious sect
seemly decorous
semblance likeness; appearance
sensibility delicacy of feeling
sepulture burial
sequestered remote; isolated
seraph celestial being
severally in different directions; by different stage exits
shade spirit of dead person
shrilly shrill
Signor lord
Signory governing body of Venice
sire father
sirrah form of 'sir', usually used contemptuously and/or of a social inferior
sod turf
sojourn stay; reside
somewhat something
sooth truth
sot drunkard; fool

spectatress female spectator
spray twig
sprite ghost; spirit
start (n.) sudden movement of surprise
start (vb.) make sudden movement in surprise
stilly still
stipend wage; salary
stoic classical philosopher espousing indifference to pleasure and pain
straight straight away
strumpet prostitute
succour assist; relieve
suggest hint at idea for (evil) action
suit petition; request
suitor petitioner
sup dine
supereminent eminent above all
suppliant petitioner
sure surely
sycophant flatterer; servile politician
temper mood; temperament
thrid 'slide through a narrow passage' (SJ)
throstle song thrush
'tis it is
toper drinker; drunkard
torch waxed stick for lighting fires or lamps
touchstone stone for testing gold; criterion of authenticity
trammels nets; impediments
transport 'rapture; ecstasy' (SJ)
trappings ornamental accessories
tremendous terrifying
trope rhetorical figure
tuft ornamental tassel
twain two
'twas it was
unattainted unconvicted
uncumbered unencumbered; without burden
unhallowed unholy
unmeet unfit
unsunned innocent; sheltered
untoward vexatious; intractable
upbraiding reproach
urchin mischievous child

vassal servant; dependant
vent give vent or voice to
verdure greenery
verily in truth
vernal of the spring
viands foods
visage face
vulgar, the vulgar common people; mob
warrant guarantee
waxed grew
weal 'happiness; prosperity' (SJ)
weeds clothes
ween think; suppose; reckon
whelming overturning and covering

whelp offspring of dog or other beast; young man
whelped given birth to (usually used of dogs)
wherefore why
whipper-in hunt official responsible for management of hounds
whizzen windpipe (corruption of 'weasand')
wist knew
without outside; offstage
witling pretender to wit and humour
wont used; accustomed
wonted usual; customary
wot knows
yon yonder; over there

	Oriental Tales
WILLIAM BECKFORD	Vathek
JAMES BOSWELL	Boswell's Life of Johnson
FRANCES BURNEY	Camilla
	Cecilia
	Evelina
	The Wanderer
LORD CHESTERFIELD	Lord Chesterfield's Letters
JOHN CLELAND	Memoirs of a Woman of Pleasure
DANIEL DEFOE	Captain Singleton
	A Journal of the Plague Year
	Memoirs of a Cavalier
	Moll Flanders
	Robinson Crusoe
	Roxana
HENRY FIELDING	Joseph Andrews and Shamela
	A Journey from This World to the Next and The Journal of a Voyage to Lisbon
	Tom Jones
	The Adventures of David Simple
WILLIAM GODWIN	Caleb Williams
	St Leon
OLIVER GOLDSMITH	The Vicar of Wakefield
MARY HAYS	Memoirs of Emma Courtney
ELIZABETH HAYWOOD	The History of Miss Betsy Thoughtless
ELIZABETH INCHBALD	A Simple Story
SAMUEL JOHNSON	The History of Rasselas
CHARLOTTE LENNOX	The Female Quixote
MATTHEW LEWIS	The Monk

WASHINGTON IRVING	The Sketch-Book of Geoffrey Crayon, Gent.
HENRY JAMES	The Ambassadors
	The Aspern Papers and Other Stories
	The Awkward Age
	The Bostonians
	Daisy Miller and Other Stories
	The Europeans
	The Golden Bowl
	The Portrait of a Lady
	Roderick Hudson
	The Spoils of Poynton
	The Turn of the Screw and Other Stories
	Washington Square
	What Maisie Knew
	The Wings of the Dove
SARAH ORNE JEWETT	The Country of the Pointed Firs and Other Fiction
JACK LONDON	The Call of the Wild
	White Fang and Other Stories
	John Barleycorn
	The Sea-Wolf
	The Son of the Wolf
HERMAN MELVILLE	Billy Budd, Sailor and Selected Tales
	The Confidence-Man
	Moby-Dick
	Typee
	White-Jacket
FRANK NORRIS	McTeague
FRANCIS PARKMAN	The Oregon Trail
EDGAR ALLAN POE	The Narrative of Arthur Gordon Pym of Nantucket and Related Tales
	Selected Tales
HARRIET BEECHER STOWE	Uncle Tom's Cabin

The Oxford World's Classics Website

www.worldsclassics.co.uk

- Information about new titles
- Explore the full range of Oxford World's Classics
- Links to other literary sites and the main OUP webpage
- Imaginative competitions, with bookish prizes
- Peruse *Compass*, the Oxford World's Classics magazine
- Articles by editors
- Extracts from Introductions
- A forum for discussion and feedback on the series
- Special information for teachers and lecturers

www.worldsclassics.co.uk

American Literature

British and Irish Literature

Children's Literature

Classics and Ancient Literature

Colonial Literature

Eastern Literature

European Literature

History

Medieval Literature

Oxford English Drama

Poetry

Philosophy

Politics

Religion

The Oxford Shakespeare

A complete list of Oxford Paperbacks, including Oxford World's Classics, OPUS, Past Masters, Oxford Authors, Oxford Shakespeare, Oxford Drama, and Oxford Paperback Reference, is available in the UK from the Academic Division Publicity Department, Oxford University Press, Great Clarendon Street, Oxford OX2 6DP.

In the USA, complete lists are available from the Paperbacks Marketing Manager, Oxford University Press, 198 Madison Avenue, New York, NY 10016.

Oxford Paperbacks are available from all good bookshops. In case of difficulty, customers in the UK can order direct from Oxford University Press Bookshop, Freepost, 116 High Street, Oxford OX1 4BR, enclosing full payment. Please add 10 per cent of published price for postage and packing.